The Eighteenth-Century Commonwealthman

Caroline Robbins

The Eighteenth-Century Commonwealthman

Studies in the Transmission,
Development, and Circumstance
of English Liberal Thought from the
Restoration of Charles II until the
War with the Thirteen Colonies

Caroline Robbins

Liberty Fund

Amagi books are published by Liberty Fund, Inc.,
a foundation established to encourage study of the
ideal of a society of free and responsible individuals.

The cuneiform inscription that appears in the logo and serves
as a design element in all Liberty Fund books is the earliest-known
written appearance of the word "freedom" (*amagi*), or "liberty."
It is taken from a clay document written about 2300 B.C.
in the Sumerian city-state of Lagash.

Back cover photo courtesy of Bryn Mawr College Library. Photo: Karl Dimler.
Frontispiece courtesy of Bryn Mawr College Library.

23   24   25   26   27   P   6   5   4   3   2

Library of Congress Cataloging-in-Publication Data
Robbins, Caroline.
    The eighteenth-century commonwealthman: studies in the transmission,
    development, and circumstance of English liberal thought from the restoration of
    Charles II until the war with the thirteen colonies / Caroline Robbins.
        p.   cm.
    Originally published: Cambridge, Mass., Harvard University Press, 1959.
    Includes bibliographical references and index.
    ISBN 0-86597-427-6 (pbk.: alk. paper)
        1. Great Britain—Politics and government—18th century.   2. Liberalism—Great
    Britain—History—18th century.   3. Political science—Great Britain—History—18th
    century.   I. Title.

JN210.R6   2004
320.51′0941′09033—dc22   2003054617

LIBERTY FUND, INC.
11301 North Meridian Street
Carmel, Indiana 46032
libertyfund.org

For my brother,

whose constant affection and interest

have helped me throughout my life.

Contents

Foreword to the Atheneum Edition

A third reprinting, this time in paperback, affords an opportunity to amend some more textual errors, and to offer, nearly a decade after publication, a few reflections upon treatment of the subject matter of the book.

First let me offer some explanation of the restriction of the subject matter to British material. Originally some investigation of similar persons and theories in continental Europe was made, and was intended to form a part of the contents. In a study of the growth of religious liberty, the story, for example, of Salters's Hall and the debate about subscription must eventually be connected with arguments of like nature being put forward in the same century in the Low Countries and Geneva. Analyses of the best government, whether accompanied by nostalgia for republican Rome or for gothic Europe, were as frequent elsewhere as in Britain right up to the French Revolution. Writers on religious and civil liberty commonly appealed to the same authorities, though of course national pride in common law or frankish freedom dictated different proportions in illustrative material. Europeans read the Whig Canon and the Commonwealthmen who preserved it, as they also studied those scriptural, classical, and renaissance books which had influenced them. The narrow sea between islands and mainland often protected but never isolated. No one can read the Commonwealthmen without realizing how constantly they were aware of the common origins, institutions, and intellectual heritage of themselves and their neighbors. That in some way eighteenth-century Britain secured a greater measure of liberty and stability in no sense removes her development from the general stream of European history. But the difficulty of both tracing in one compassable volume the small though significant stream of republican ideas in the British Isles, and of placing these in the larger environment of European thought and event, seemed too great. Instead concentration on a few metropolitan figures has been avoided and persons and circumstances in Ireland, Scotland, and England discussed.

The decision to deal with persons and groups or coteries, rather than with categories of ideas, was also slowly reached. The various forms of contract, the matter of natural rights, the questions of party, of corruption, of the role and character of parliament, the character of ministerial responsibility, and the separation of powers, to list no more, demand explanation and historical treatment. Eventually consideration decided a concentration on transmission, and thus on those people who studied and wrote about commonwealth ideas. There have been excellent books written about, for example, natural rights and contractual theories. Since this book appeared two first-rate studies of the separation of powers have come out: W. B. Gwyn, *The Meaning of the Separation of Powers* (Tulane, 1965), and M. J. C. Vile, *Constitutionalism and the Separation of Powers* (Oxford, 1967), the first of which relates chiefly to the period of the *Commonwealthman*, the second concentrates on the theories' development from the seventeenth century until the present in England, France, and America. These admirable volumes confirm my belief that such more extended treatment does better justice to political theory, and that in history the person must still be studied in context of events.

In planning this book, I had expected to end with the accession of George III. The use by then of the Whig Canon was obvious, and the gap which had seemed to exist between the flowering of theory during the troubles with the Stuarts and the outbreak of the disputes with the American colonists seemed at least partially filled. But, in the event, it was impossible to stop without examining, however briefly, some of those in England after 1760 who so vigorously revived and even extended republicanism, shared colonial enthusiasm for the saints and martyrs of an earlier period, and supported protests against real or supposed infringement of rights. Even so, I deliberately omitted discussion of the always fascinating Thomas Paine as one who had thrown in his lot with the Americans, and I stopped short of any description of the ideas of the Commonwealthmen in America during the momentous period of revolution and constitution making, a subject demanding not a chapter but a book. Such a volume has now been produced most felicitously by Bernard Bailyn in *The Ideological Origins of the American Revolution* (Harvard, 1967), and all students of the period look forward to the promised continuation of this work.

Bailyn has already begun to examine that change in the climate of opinion, and of the character of political theory, which is so marked throughout the western world in the nineteenth century. In this revolution of thought and of approach to political problems America played a leading role. Thomas Pownall and other observers had noticed the evolution of a society very much less dominated by considerations of class and hierarchical distinctions even before the troubles with England began. During the French Revolution new slogans and different attitudes, even faintly toward property, appeared. Moral considerations and numerical criteria among the Benthamites and followers of Jefferson and readers of John Taylor began to supplant ancient definitions and political categories. None the less, anyone reading the debates in Philadelphia in 1787 or some of the radical literature of the nineteenth century will discover many an echo of the work of the Commonwealthmen. Transformation of earlier libertarian philosophies into the democratic beliefs was eventually to swamp considerations like the "balance," the virtues of mixed government, and the obligations of an elite, but it too demands a volume.

In selecting those who carried on republican ideas, it was difficult to eliminate peripheral characters, and to differentiate between the politics and tactics of opposition and the evolution of liberal ideas. The numbers involved anyhow created structural and stylistic problems never entirely solved. Yet in the long run a "case history" seemed the most useful service in tracing the relation of idea and prejudice to circumstance. I elected to deal with men who themselves consciously hoped and worked for commonwealth ideals, and with some few others who seemed aware of deficiencies in society and constitution and who suggested remedies for these. David Hume, it may be remembered, is passed over but the temptation to include good Bishop Berkeley proved too great to resist. Berkeley and Dr. Samuel Johnson were two of the few who in their time truly concerned themselves with the welfare of the poor. While the Doctor perforce was neglected, it seemed impossible to ignore the searching and revelatory questions in *The Querist.*

But about the omission of another eighteenth-century Tory who

certainly wrote in the "Old Whig" or commonwealth tradition, Henry
St. John, Viscount Bolingbroke, others than myself have raised forceful objections. Bolingbroke's attacks on the government of Walpole,
examination of party, reflections upon history, and denunciation of
corruption led him to utilize "Whig history" and whiggish political
writing. He was widely read on both sides of the Atlantic and might
thus be considered to have extended the canon and its influence. The
brilliant style so noticeably lacking in the philosophical work adorns
the polemical tracts and explains in part their currency. In part this
may also be attributed to an astute use of what might be called regular
opposition tactics. The cry of corruption, undue influence of minister, junto, or monarch, of placemen and courtier was always popular.
Andrew Marvell raised it against the Earl of Danby and Charles II,
Trenchard and Harley against the Whig ascendancy under William III.
Bonnie Prince Charlie is reported to have made notes on what he
would promise in the event of his staging another Jacobite rising, and
these include denunciation of standing armies, remarks about annual
parliaments, the purification of politics, and guarantees of civil and
religious liberty. In Parliament as well as in *Craftesman* and other opposition journals many an old commonwealth slogan may be found, but
by no means denotes in its proponent a reformer. The outs when seeking office seized on popular cries. In office that record was, or might
have been, different. Bolingbroke was out of office and extremely articulate in voicing all those grievances which might establish the rot-
ten character of the ministry in power. But, more important, there
was in Bolingbroke no interest in continuing reform of the constitution. He was no new modeller of the ship of state, had no program to
bound the executive or solve social ills. The importance surely of the
eighteenth-century Commonwealthmen was not only that they maintained a tradition but that they developed and extended it as the conceit of a "Patriot King" certainly did not. Even Bolingbroke's emphasis on virtue was but an echo of that renaissance note sounded by
Neville and Moyle when attempting to adapt the old constitution to
contemporary circumstance and avert the fate which befell republican
Rome.

There will be more and better studies of the Commonwealthmen and these will treat them differently and I hope profit by my mistakes and omissions. Now I can only add hearty thanks to all who helped me during the composition of the book, and those, as numerous, who have assisted me since with reviews, criticisms, and interesting information I should otherwise have missed.

The
Eighteenth-
Century
Commonwealthman

"A True *Whig* is not afraid of the name of a *Commonwealthsman*, because so many foolish People, who know not what it means, run it down."
—Robert Molesworth, Preface to *Franco-Gallia*, 1721

"If they mean by those lovers of Commonwealth *Principles*, men passionately devoted to the Public good, and to the common Service of their Country, who believe that kings were instituted for the good of the People, and Government ordained for the sake of those that are to be governed, and therefore complain or grieve when it is used to contrary ends, every Wise and Honest man will be proud to be ranked in that number. . . . To be fond therefore of such *Commonwealth Principles*, becomes every *Englishman*."
—John, Lord Somers, *Just and Modest Vindication*, 1681

"Thus friendly are the principles of the genuine *Whigs* to the office and dignity of kings and princes. But then, on the other hand, they consider all men as invested by God and nature with *certain inalienable* rights and privileges, which they can't without a crime sacrifice themselves, and of which they can't without the highest oppression and cruelty be deprived by others."
— *The Old Whig*, I, no. 2, 1739

"A *Whig out of Power*, ever since the *Revolution*, hath been a Kind of *State-Enthusiast;* his head is *turned* with dreaming of a *Rotation of Power*, from Harrington's *Oceana, Plato's Commonwealth*, Sir Thomas More's *Utopia* and other *visionary Schemes* of Government."
— *The London Journal*, in *Gentleman's Magazine*, 1734

I

Introduction

The Name of a Commonwealthman

"A True Whig is not afraid of the name of a Commonwealthsman, because so many foolish People who know not what it means, run it down."[1] This often-quoted definition proudly claimed for the Real Whigs—as they liked to call themselves—kinship with luminaries of republican thought like Milton, Harrington, Sidney, and others. In the eighteenth century the majority of the ruling oligarchy and the greater part of their fellow countrymen emphatically denied any continuity or connection between the innovators and Levellers of the Puritan Revolution (1641–1660), and the philosophers and Whiggish statesmen of the struggle (1679–1710) to exclude James Stuart and secure the Glorious Revolution. An eccentric antiquarian might hang a copy of Charles the First's execution writ in his closet and speak slightingly of kings and superstitions, but in general all talk of '41 alarmed Englishmen as much or more than the sight of Jacobite toasts "over the water." Any proposed tampering with the fabric of the church and state produced dismal recollections and dire predictions.

The Commonwealthmen were only a fraction of politically conscious Britons in the Augustan Age, and formed a small minority among the many Whigs. No achievements in England of any consequence can be credited to them. English development shows scarcely a trace of efforts to restore or amend the mixed or Gothic government they esteemed. Their continued existence and activity, albeit of a limited kind, served to maintain a revolutionary tradition and to link the histories of English struggles against tyranny in one century with those of American efforts for independence in another. The American constitution employs many of the devices which the Real Whigs vainly besought Englishmen to adopt and in it must be found their abiding memorial. An examination of the sources and development of the Commonwealthmen's politics over a period of several generations will not only clarify a part of Whig history; it will also increase understanding of the peculiarities and limitations of that protean century which produced Levellers, diggers, republicans, and Whigs, to say nothing of their opponents and opposites.

The neglect suffered by the seventeenth-century innovators and philosophers has been exaggerated, in part because of misunderstandings of the purpose of their work and the meaning of words and phrases employed in it; in part because of overemphasis on the extent to which they anticipated modern thought. The debates which took place among the men of Cromwell's army at Whitehall, Putney, and elsewhere were unknown before the publication of *The Clarke Papers* at the end of the nineteenth century, though of course the Agreement of the People was familiar to many. The debates have, I think, unduly influenced students of the political climate of the Interregnum. Civil war and the opportunity afforded by free speech and free press stimulated a vast variety of projects concerning government and society. These were studied by the Real Whigs to whose efforts is largely due the preservation of many of the tracts of 1640–1661. In the eighteenth century, the so-called Levellers—a missile word as accurately used then as Communist is today—found inspiration in works of a more varied character than their critics admitted.

The Commonwealthman laid less stress on the ephemera of tract and sermon than on the work of major political philosophers. Some last traces of wildly experimental projects may be discovered at the time of the conspiracies of 1683 and during Monmouth's ill-judged attempt in 1685. In 1689 Ludlow and other innovators received short shrift. Nevertheless the sacred canon revered by the Real Whigs of the next century retained enormous revolutionary potential. This canon included the works of Harrington, Nedham, and Milton who wrote when Cromwell ruled; of Sidney, Neville, and Locke who were active during the controversies of the reigns of Charles II and his brother. The writings of such divers thinkers as Cumberland and Newton were a part of it as also were the slimmer writings of Somers, whose genius found its chief fulfillment in a settlement which nearly all Englishmen accepted. The Commonwealthmen themselves produced, soon after 1689, accounts, arguments, essays, and histories, which might be dubbed the apocryphal books of the Whig Bible as it was to be read by reformers and revolutionaries all around the Atlantic world.

The natural rights doctrines of the Real Whigs formed an amalgam of theories drawn from several periods. Experience and history revealed the possibilities and the dangers of violent upheavals. The Commonwealthmen shared some of the conservatism of their contemporaries and much of the general misunderstanding of the nature and development of the ancient constitution. They had no difficulty in reconciling the rule of the Hanoverians with the precepts of classical republicans. They hoped to preserve and enlarge the merits of the "Gothic" system under which they thought they were living. They saw in the "rota" and separation of powers advocated by men like Harrington and Moyle useful and possible reforms which would secure liberty. Between them and other Englishmen differences were always more violently articulated than their extent would seem to demand. The Commonwealthmen could be regarded as the conservators of the older order; they must also be seen as the spiritual heirs and ancestors of revolutionaries everywhere.

Three generations of Commonwealthmen will be described in this book. The first appeared not long after the Revolution of 1689 and most of its members were dead by 1727; the second grew to manhood during the mid-eighteenth century and brought up the third generation of the age of the American Revolution. The party of movement, sometimes calling themselves the "Old Whigs," or the "Real Whigs," may be detected less than four years after the acceptance of the Dutch Deliverer. Agitation for reform which went further than that offered by the Bill of Rights and the Toleration Act may be said to have begun with the appearance of Robert Molesworth's *Account of Denmark* in December 1693 and to have ended with the last of *Cato's Letters* in 1723, and the appearance of three volumes of Walter Moyle's *Works* in 1726 and 1727.

These reformers were to be found in dissenters' meetings and in certain country houses, for example in Essex and at Swords near Dublin. They frequented the Grecian Tavern in Devereux Court off Essex Street in London, the resort until his death of old "Plato Neville." At the Grecian, so it was said in 1698 by the author of "A Brief Reply," a club of mistaken politicians set themselves up as champions of people's liberties and "Sidney's maxims." A part of their activity, the pamphleteer maintained, was the publication of heterodox works on religion and politics. The appearance of pieces by known habitués— Moyle, Andrew Fletcher, John Trenchard, John Toland, Matthew Tindal—as well as the publication of works by Sidney, Ludlow, Milton, Neville, and Harrington between 1697 and 1701, powerfully supports the description of concerted effort.[2]

Among the Real Whigs of this period Robert Molesworth was a leading figure. The third earl of Shaftesbury was a self-declared disciple of his; Toland, Molyneux, and Henry Maxwell were pensioner and friends respectively; Moyle, Trenchard, and Fletcher, acquaintances and associates. They worked for a federal system in the British Isles, an amendment of parliament, a diminution of ministerial prerogative, an increased toleration, and some modification of mercantilist regulations. Neither then nor at any time thereafter did they receive support or encouragement from Whigs in office. Perhaps only three ministers —Godolphin,[3] Stanhope, and later Chatham—besides a mere handful of members of parliament, really seriously attempted or wished for the implementation of any of their policies.

Such success as they could claim, the Treason Act, the repeal of Occasional Conformity and Schism Acts, cannot be attributed exclusively to their efforts. Their real achievement lay in the bringing up of a second generation of Commonwealthmen who were to continue the study not only of the seventeenth-century classics but of the "arguments" and "essays" of the post-Revolution period. They themselves produced works which maintained and developed Harringtonian principles, for example, at a time when constitutional practice was increasingly divorced from the systems they admired. These men are to be found amongst divines and teachers, such men as Hutcheson, Grove, Foster, Watts, and Edmund Law. Few of the reformers and pro-Americans of the age of George III did not spend some of their formative years under teachers at Glasgow, at certain Cambridge colleges, or at such dissenting academies as Warrington. Editors and printers—

Baron, Griffiths of the *Monthly Review,* Bruce and Smith in Dublin, even Foulis of Glasgow—preserved, reproduced, and reviewed the "canonical works." Fresh studies of Harrington may be found in Thomas Pownall's earliest essay, *Principles of Polity* (1752), and in Archdeacon Squire's rather conservative *English Constitution* (1745). The most radical speculation of this middle period may be found in the sermons of Robert Wallace and in his *Various Prospects* (1761), utopian in form but with a very real appreciation of contemporary circumstances.

The third and last generation are often called early radicals. Priestley, Price, the pro-Americans, the men of the Society for Constitutional Information and similar bodies endorsed most of the political theories of the Real Whigs and sought, still unsuccessfully, to influence parliamentary affairs.

It might seem simpler to call all three generations of Commonwealthmen radicals. But the word, Halévy tells us, comes late, after 1819, into common English usage.[4] Moreover, an examination of the ideas of the Real Whigs will show that they are more closely connected philosophically and politically with the Commonwealthmen of the seventeenth century than with radicals of the nineteenth, or even with those of their number who survived into the Napoleonic period.

Ideas

The association of the eighteenth-century Commonwealthmen with the Levellers and republicans embittered controversy by suggesting that such Whigs could not be good subjects. We may admit the ancestry of their ideas without endorsing the accusations recalled in sermons commemorating the execution of Charles I on every thirtieth of January. The Whigs cherished ideas about checks on government from within and without, about individual freedoms and about the ranks of society, as we must later discuss, but their inheritance of the revolutionary tradition was tempered by the admiration for the English Constitution which they shared with nearly all their contemporaries. All Whigs until the French Revolution maintained that in theory at least tyrants could be resisted, and by so doing, justified the events of 1689. This was their chief advantage over Tories like Bolingbroke and Hume who accepted the Revolution without a logical defense for it. But even amongst the greatest admirers of Sidney and Milton, few promoted reform through violent means. Resistance rights, in fact, were only exercised by the Jacobites or by an occasional rioter. The Civil War had taught Lilbourne and Neville as well as many generations thereafter that the introduction of "green wood" into the constitutional fabric was likely to cause more trouble than lasting reform. The Real Whig did not advocate the overthrowing of government by force after the failure of the Rye House Plot, although he continued to justify it and thus to confirm L'Estrange's theory (echoed by Burke's bitter attack on the Unitarians and reformers of 1792) that:

> A *Whig* is a Certain *Bold* kind of a Boysterous *Animal,* that will not *Brook* so much as the *Breath* of a *King,* or a *Bishop;* And where he cannot *Undermine* them by fair *Means,* he makes it his business to *Destroy* them by *Foul.*[5]

The Commonwealthmen saw in the development of Cabinet government a threat to the balance of the constitution. They believed in a separation of powers and hoped that each of the three parts of the government would balance or check the others. They fully recognized that ministerial predominance could be as dangerous as monarchical. They, therefore, wished to separate legislative and executive branches more completely, and roundly condemned placemen and party cliques and cabals.

Republicanism of this variety found expression in suggestions about devices which would safeguard the virtues of the mixed government. Frequent allusions to Sparta's Ephors and Aragon's Justiciars as guardians of the constitution, as well as to Ludlow's proposed Conservators, familiar at least to eighteenth-century readers of his often-reprinted *Memoirs,* represented one method. Even more familiar was a proposal for rotation in office as a preventive against the ascendancy of juntas of willful men. Harrington was followed by men like Walter Moyle, Francis Hutcheson, Joseph Priestley, and John Campbell, the supposed author of *Liberty and Right,* to name but a fraction of his disciples. Even Hume, in spite of his political prejudices, modeled his Ideal Commonwealth upon *Oceana.* In a rota and in the separation of powers, many offered preservatives against the evils of party which contrast greatly with the panaceas propounded by Lord Bolingbroke.

Reform of parliament by a wider franchise and some redistribution of seats removing anomalies like Old Sarum was urged throughout the century by Real Whigs. Molesworth suggested enfranchisement of leaseholders. Hutcheson and Campbell would have allowed all men of property to vote. By 1780 Brand Hollis and his associates were advocating manhood suffrage. Members would be brought in closer touch with public opinion. Commonwealthmen, however, favoured the selection as members of parliament of those rich enough to be independent of bribes. They were vociferous advocates of annual parliaments, this expedient securing one kind of rotation. Management of the Commons, always resented by all factions out of office, was particularly offensive to the Real Whigs who heaped abuse on Walpole and ignored the possibility that he understood the public temper at least as well as they.

The Real Whigs greatly extended the application of general statements of right so frequent in English constitutional pronouncements. Two such principles were vigorously expressed in the works of Molyneux, Molesworth, Fletcher, and Trenchard, which were entirely denied by most contemporary politicians. One of these insisted that an Englishman was entitled to be ruled by laws to which he had himself consented, wherever he was, at home or abroad, and the other extended this right to all mankind. The first claim would have meant considerable modification of mercantilist theory, an absolute denial of the rights of the English, or British, House of Lords to determine cases arising in Ireland, and, in general, extension of the powers of bodies like the Irish parliament, or, as time went on, colonial legislatures. Andrew Fletcher, closely associated with Moyle and Trenchard in their campaign against a standing army, was an early Scottish nationalist who opposed the Union. He instead supported a system for England, Ireland, Scotland, and Wales which would have attempted to equalize the distribution of power as well as abolish political and economic discrimination. In Scotland, after some early discomfort and a flood of criticism, the Union he bitterly opposed was not unsuccessful and received many kind words as the century wore on. In Ireland,

Anglo-Irishmen continued to talk and write in favour of a system like the one Fletcher had advocated, and in so doing vastly enlarged the application of the Whig theory of the rights of man.

Such interpretations needed scarcely any emendation to be relevant to the situation of the colonies. Trenchard (like Molesworth and Molyneux, a graduate of Trinity, Dublin), Hutcheson, and James Burgh put forward arguments Americans were to develop. Only a few writers or politicians sympathetic to colonial aspirations can be found outside the Whigs now under discussion; it was largely among this group that Franklin and later Adams were to find friends and to discuss politics. What is more, the period in which the Anglo-Irish were producing writings critical of mercantilism and dependency in their own country coincided with the great Protestant Irish migration to Pennsylvania, New Jersey, and Virginia. Some of the so-called pro-Americans (like Cartwright) of the age of George III proposed loose federations or unions on lines not dissimilar to those suggested long before by Fletcher and Molesworth in relation to the less privileged parts of the British Isles. There may be those today who will regret their lack of success.

The second principle extended the rights of Englishmen to all mankind. The right of conquest was no longer recognized. Conquest did not, according to these men, confer rights of long duration, nor did it deprive the conquered of their privileges as human beings. This lay at the base of all sorts of theories, productive of both good and bad results in our own day. The same process of thought began to modify old assumptions about slavery. These were not unaffected by the influence of the Quakers and the growth of humanitarianism. The role played by Hutcheson, James Foster, and Isaac Watts, in preaching the doctrines expressed so forcibly by Molyneux and Locke, and in influencing all sorts of people whom the other groups did not affect was important. In many ways the most enduring influence of the Commonwealthmen may be found in their emphasis, for many different reasons, upon the rights of the less privileged sections of society and of the British dominions. These "Whigs" did not forget Milton's admonition to remind Englishmen of their precedence of teaching nations how to live.

Another topic constantly discussed amongst the Real Whigs was freedom of thought. This was by no means confined to the agitation of the dissenters—still an oppressed, though prosperous and diminishing, minority—for fuller religious liberty and equal political status. The question of the Jews was raised. Discussion can be found amongst members of the Established Church who hoped for such changes in its discipline and dogma as would allow of greater freedom amongst its members and might induce a wider degree of conformity to it by those then outside it. Newtonianism was a powerful element in the theories of liberal churchmen and dissenters alike. These groups were unsuccessful in achieving their main objectives between 1718 and 1812. The papists did, it is true, obtain some amelioration in the reign of George III, but how far this was due to the growth of tolerance and how far to an attempt to secure and encourage a relatively stable group in the population by a government apprehensive of revolutionary activity, is too delicate a question to settle here.

Constant discussions of religious liberty were significant for at least two reasons: reiteration of a need for greater toleration and the development among Christians of a less ferocious dogmatism. The idea of a state in which no one was more privileged than another because of his religion nor in any way penalized for his lack of orthodoxy was kept before the people in tracts, sermons, treatises. The Real Whigs had very early advocated a tolerance which went far beyond the theories of Locke or Milton. Molesworth and Toland included in its scope Jews, Atheists, Unitarians, Mohammedans, and even well-behaved Catholics, though it was not until Priestley's time that many were convinced that papists were also to benefit in the right of freedom of religion. The Commonwealthman kept before the public the Whig tradition of toleration in spite of the fact that the ruling oligarchy—under Walpole in a position of greater power than any party had ever enjoyed—never conceded anything but a meagre financial dole to the demands of dissent, and was unsuccessful in relieving the Jews whom the Pelhams were not unwilling to help. In this last case popular prejudice brought about the repeal of the Jew Bill though perhaps less apathy on the part of Whigs in general might have prevented the setback. A few members like Nicholas Hardinge, a good Old Whig, were convinced that it was wrong to deny fundamental human rights to anyone domiciled in England. A general naturalization, though often limited to Protestants, was, like religious toleration, advocated as a means of increasing the population and the prosperity of the country. For this ancient Rome afforded ample precedent.

A second contribution made by these friends to religious liberty was in the liberalizing of the attitude of some churchmen and Puritans. During the Interregnum, the majority of the Puritans had hoped to establish their own church as the dominant body in the state. The Independents and Baptists, the minority, were always against a national establishment. After St. Bartholomew's Day in 1662 and after the failure to effect certain modifications in 1689 in the Liturgy and the Articles, none of the English sects supported an alliance of church and state. A small but significant majority at Salters Hall rejected a demand for subscription in 1719. They became much more tolerant of each other. Amongst the Anglicans, the Latitudinarians, and amongst Presbyterians, the New Lights, manifested an increasing respect for the rights of individuals to use their reason for themselves. The growth of rationalism and the spread of skepticism, of which undogmatical piety was a product, have often been blamed for many of the spiritual shortcomings of this period. Merits have been credited to the Christian faith revived by evangelicals and mystics. Individual freedom of thought and worship increased, however, chiefly through the efforts of the rational Christians.

Another part of the program concerned education in a free state. Education should be secularized and directed toward the training of citizens rather than of clergy, whatever their denomination. These ideas may be traced from Milton, through Molesworth and his famous *Preface*, Stanhope's university scheme supported by Toland, the many experiments of the mid-eighteenth century in institutions run by dissenters, to the plans put forward by John Jebb before he left Cambridge in the seventies. The discussion of method and subject matter in schools and colleges was conducted, of course, for the most part outside parliament. Even Stanhope's scheme, although circulating in draft before 1717, was largely theoretical and experimental. At Cambridge the tradition of Newtonian science and the teaching of Locke's philosophy, together with discussions of civil and religious liberty by such dons as Newcome, Law, and Jebb, stirred up two generations at least of men interested in public affairs, inclined to a radical point of view, and, although even at the height of their influence, merely a minority in the University, playing a very considerable part in the policies of the Commonwealth group. It is less easy to discover their Oxford contemporaries. In dissenting institutions at Exeter, Taunton, Newington, and Warrington, among many others, as well as in the grammar schools like Leeds, Hull, and Grantham at certain periods, and in the Scottish universities, efforts were made to put into practice educational reforms. These were accompanied by discussion and instruction in liberal ideas. Not all the students taught in such institutions turned to radical politics, but a sufficient number who studied in them carried into their active careers many of the political ideas of the textbooks which their teachers examined with them.[6]

Lively controversy in the realm of theology as well as reiterated demands for an untrammeled freedom of enquiry may well be admitted to have been an important contribution of this section of the Whigs. This admission does not, however, answer the question whether these Commonwealthmen were egalitarian or levelling in any real sense of the term. The answer must be sought in several directions. A great deal about attitudes toward social classes and inequality of privilege may be discovered in contemporary examination of the function of the charity schools. Closely connected with this, and very often to be found in the same sermons or tracts, were investigations into the ranks of society and their different duties in the state. With this last question was associated some consideration of wealth and its possible redistribution which, in turn, was closely linked with the fear of undue luxury. A shift in the balance of property and an excessive indulgence in the pleasures it could bring were matters of the deepest interest to many.

A great many people who were in no sense of the word egalitarian accepted ideas about human nature derived from Locke and Shaftesbury. Man's virtue or character was the product of education and environment. The third earl of Shaftesbury modified this theory by the belief that a moral sense within man would enable him—if not prevented by adverse circumstance or environment—to discover the laws of nature and to attain virtue. In the long run the influence of such theories was to lead Frenchmen to an emphasis on equality, but in England the chief influence of the philosophers was outside practical politics. Discussion about charity schools is illustrative of this.

The controversy is familiar. It is no less important than the questions raised by thoughtful men in Ireland over mercantilist restrictions. Would not, in the long run, the general welfare of the British Isles be raised by increasing the possibility of the acquisition of wealth in all the parts? Would allowing Irish manufacture of wool ruin England's economy? Was it to the advantage of the whole community to have all ranks of society educated? If all classes were educated would there not be none to perform the laborious tasks by which the wealth of society was produced, and would not all, therefore, become poorer? Such questions were endlessly debated. I will illustrate only from the work of two men whose ideas are those of the Commonwealthmen: Isaac Watts, the hymn writer who died in 1748, and Robert Wallace, an acquaintance of Hume, who died in 1771.

Both men believed the charity schools performed a useful function in training good Protestant citizens. In arguing for more than the minimum of education against those who distrusted the experiment, Watts put forward the notion that the poor but clever boy should not be denied the use of his talents even if by so doing he advanced his social position. Wallace was led further to a discussion as to whether it was necessary at all to condemn the majority of mankind to drudgery and whether some division of such labours could not be discovered. As the century went on there were not wanting radicals who suggested that education should be provided for all. Though agreeing with this, Priestley was to betray nervousness over possible government interference with individual freedom should the schools be state-endowed.

The manner of education raised questions about the inequalities of society which were solved more dogmatically in France by her revolutionary philosophers than in England. Equality was never a battle cry during the Civil War and Interregnum, although egalitarian speculations occasionally found written or spoken expression. That men might ideally share all in common as the apostles were once supposed to have done was the wish of small groups of men. These men on the whole, like Lilbourne and Winstanley, belong in that Christian tradition of which More's *Utopia* was still the most important English document. A very small section only believed such a community of property practicable. The eighteenth-century Levellers, as their critics called our Whigs, read tracts propounding these ideas. Some levelling tracts found their way into the *Harleian Miscellany*. Book sales reveal boxes or bundles of them being bought and sold. William Harris, the biographer of Hugh Peter, the celebrated Mrs. Macaulay, and William Godwin (of Puritan descent) used such material extensively in their work. The economic ideas of Harrington and Neville attracted considerable attention and were endlessly referred to. Property, its definition, and the position its owners enjoyed in the state were constantly examined. A few of the Commonwealthmen—Francis Hutcheson and Mrs. Macaulay for example—supported so-called "agrarian laws" for a moderate limitation of wealth.

The suggestion of an agrarian law in the eighteenth century did not spring from any drastic desire to distribute wealth more evenly in an endeavour to make the real condition of man more consonant with the ideal equality he enjoyed at birth. Support of the Agrarian stemmed from a belief that too great an accumulation of wealth in a few hands might disturb the balance of the state. Men like Edward Wortley Montagu (or the writer who used his name) in his *Rise and Fall of Antient Republicks,* and John Brown in his *Estimate,* as well as some Irish observers, found in the existence of luxury a danger to society, to morale, and to the survival of the nation. A few men at the end of the eighteenth century put forward ideas which appear socialist in character, but these seem to have had little connection either with the Commonwealthmen of their own day or with the literature of the Interregnum.

On the whole, the Real Whig was not egalitarian although he might emphasize to an embarrassing degree the equality of man before God, or in a state of nature. A ruling class and an uneducated and unrepresented majority were for a long time taken for granted. Most of these Whigs wanted to provide education, to increase religious liberty, and were willing to recognize the political rights of all those who, through the acquisition of property, should be qualified as citizens. By "people" most seventeenth-century Republicans had meant people of some state and consequence in the community. Cobblers, tinkers, or fishermen were not people but *scum* to Whigs like James Tyrrell—who used the term—to Locke, Withers, and Trenchard. Constant discussion of the greatest good of the greatest number, and an optimistic interpretation of the workings of an untrammeled moral sense eventually brought about an attitude of mind which made it impossible to justify deprivation of the means of exercising and developing human potentialities. I doubt whether many of the later Whigs of any kind in the eighteenth century expressed, much less endorsed, what might appear to be modern democratic ideas brought forward from time to time in the parliaments of a century before. References to "the poorest man" and his right to a voice could be cited from a speech by D'Ewes in 1640, inferred from notes by Coventry in 1677, and comments by Sawyer in 1689.[7]

Dissemination of the Ideas

Until the great parliamentary researches now proceeding are complete, it will be difficult to say how many of the self-styled Real Whigs found their way into parliament. There were probably very few, though their ideas may have found expression during election contests. Candidates may have made speeches full of antimonarchical and revolutionary sentiments—for the benefit not only of voters but of the crowds at large—which failed to influence their actions once they were elected to the House. Many contests passed with little local excitement, but even septennial parliamentary changes served to stir up political debates. A certain disgust with the revered institution of the House of Commons is noticeable. Men like Thomas Hollis refused even to vote. Christopher Wyvill worked for reform through extra-parliamentary association. Parliament afforded very little opportunity for the discussion of their ideas. Even if these ideas gained some public support, this by no means insured effective action in the divisions. Commonwealthmen relied therefore on other means of disseminating the principles they held—teachers and textbooks, clubs and coteries, correspondence, domestic and foreign, preachers and publications, both of the classical Republicans and of periodical and polemical treatises.

These methods may be very rapidly summarized here. The influence of the academies and of the liberal teachers at Cambridge, Glasgow, and elsewhere has always been acknowledged, if not very carefully analyzed or appraised. The continental tradition of Utrecht, Leyden, and other universities must here be ignored. The printed or manuscript lectures which remain to us from British institutions reveal methods of instruction as well as recommended reading which were likely to produce amongst some of the students at least a tendency toward radical ideas. Harrington, Neville, and Sidney and many lesser writers were constantly consulted. Politics and liberal philosophy, closely allied with political and economic thought, received an enormous amount of attention in the curriculum even of the divinity students and the method of instruction left room for argument and discussion. Over and over again we are informed that a teacher was unwilling to contradict his students or to appear to force his ideas upon them.

Teachers and students continued to write to each other and a great deal of instruction was carried on in an epistolary way. Persons quite unknown to their advisers wrote to admired contemporaries for guidance and were often answered with astonishing patience and frankness. Horace Walpole's well-known habit of engaging in a regular exchange of views and news, on special topics, was by no means peculiar to him. Many letters were exchanged between clergymen and their friends, writers and their admirers, men overseas with strangers in the British Isles. The letters of Lord Molesworth, Archdeacon Blackburne, Nathaniel Lardner, and Joseph Priestley, and the transatlantic as well as British correspondence of the Hollis connection throughout the country need only to be cited here as familiar examples.

Sermons kept both divine right and republican theories alive and sometimes extended them. Divines endlessly discussed the nature of obedience, obligation to subscription (Anglican or dissenting), the limits of freedom of thought. Hoadly stirred up the most famous, perhaps, but Stephens, Bradbury, Abernethy, Wishart, Mayhew, and Eliot, to name only a few amongst so many, contributed to the political discussions of the age. In their printed form such sermons must still be studied in order to understand the development of liberal and conservative philosophy alike.

The clubs of the period are familiar to students of literature. There were innumerable small groups which hardly count as formal organizations, who met together to exchange ideas and wrote or inspired the writing of pamphlets and occasional papers. Even informal groups met with some formality to argue predetermined problems. The Sunday-night suppers of Anthony Collins, the freethinker, Thomas Bradbury the Calvinist, and Lord Barrington the antisubscriber; the talks at the Grecian Tavern already mentioned; the meetings of the unorthodox

William Whiston and his friends; the later suppers of Franklin's honest Whigs near St. Paul's and the evenings in John Lee's chambers shared by Priestley and Lindsey—all suggest themselves as examples. The many written dialogues merely reflect a habit congenial to the age. Important treatises like Burgh's *Political Disquisitions* owed much to meetings in London taverns. Over and over again in memorials of preachers, writers, teachers, and statesmen, we learn that they loved "conversation." Enough evidence about a large number of such debating groups amongst the Commonwealthmen exists to show that they met and talked a great deal about their work.

Some reference should be made to the work of historians as they contribute to the dissemination of the ideas of the Commonwealthmen. Ancient and medieval or Gothic history, the history of parliamentary institutions and of revolutions in church and state, all afforded at various periods opportunity for political propaganda. Hobbes early noticed the unfortunate influence of Greek and Roman histories on the men responsible for the English Civil War. During the controversy over Exclusion or over the events of '88, treatises on the early constitution and powers of parliament flowed from the press, and men as prominent as Somers added to their number. Molesworth after the Revolution was to see in Danish history as well as in the literature of the French civil war lessons of the utmost relevance to his own age. Moyle turned from attacks on the standing armies to his studies of the Roman Republic and of the Lacedaemonians. Gordon left active journalism to write commentaries on Tacitus and Sallust which were to be admired by Jefferson, Franklin, and Adams. Middleton alarmed contemporaries with the libertarianism implicit in his studies of Cicero and Livy. The fortunes of ancient republics afforded to men like Edward Montagu gloomy parallels to the possible fate of the English Empire. As the Commonwealthmen extended their ideas of natural rights they turned increasingly to the studies of the Levellers of the Civil War period as well as of the classical republicans. Mrs. Macaulay and William Godwin, as already noticed, were well acquainted with the Agreement of the People and the tracts of Winstanley. The aristocratic republicanism of a Sidney began to be merged with the democratic ideas of a Lilbourne. The historians imposed a consistency on the character of seventeenth-century ideas which had only previously appeared in the careless criticisms of their opponents.

Lastly, but very important in the propaganda of the Real Whigs, it must be repeated, was the preservation of tracts and the publication of books. The flood of print in 1698, the production of Dublin and Glasgow presses, as well as the editorial work of Richard Baron and Thomas Hollis of Lincoln's Inn, the tracts of the Society for Constitutional Information, all were "paper shot." Every eighteenth-century edition of the seventeenth-century republicans can be associated with the Real Whigs. We cannot, unfortunately, guess how large was the public reached. A few marked and annotated copies remain to attest their study by an Onslow or a Lofft. A better indication is provided by references to these books in contemporary press and correspondence. That the books were generally known may be assumed, even though their ideas were not adopted by many Englishmen. The English-speaking world of the eighteenth century read the same books and pamphlets, whatever their politics. The significance attaching to books generally approved by the Commonwealthmen lies chiefly in the emphasis placed upon them and in the lessons constantly discussed and examined which seemed to relate to causes they wished to further.

Measure of Achievement

A gifted and active minority of the population of the British Isles continued to study government in the spirit of their seventeenth-century ancestors. They kept alive, during an age of extraordinary complacency and legislative inactivity, a demand for increased liberty of conscience, for an extension of the franchise, and for a reëxamination of the distribution of parliamentary seats. They discussed rotation in office, the separation of powers, and such expedients as the Ephors or Conservators recommended by Ludlow and Moyle, which would guard the balance of the different parts of the constitution and preserve it from corruption. They considered the relations of different parts of the old empire to each other. Men like Molesworth, Fletcher, Trenchard, and Pownall made suggestions which included equal or federal union between the different parts of the British Isles and a partnership or family compact between Britain and her distant colonies. They achieved no major success in the period. The radicals and liberals of the nineteenth century paid some lip service to their reputation and their efforts, but in fact their utilitarian assumptions did not emphasize the old natural rights doctrines and their political conceptions ignored the forms and theories of the mixed government earlier generations had esteemed. Where both Commonwealthman and liberal shared a distrust of too powerful a government, the one relied upon a due balance between its different component parts, the other sought a release of individuals from statutory restrictions and controls as preservatives against the Leviathan state.

In the constitutions of the several United States many of the ideas of the Real Whigs found practical expression. A supreme court, rotation in office, a separation of powers, and a complete independence from each other of church and state fulfilled many a so-called utopian dream. The endless opportunities of the New World brought about a considerable degree of social equality, if not an equality stabilized by an agrarian law. The democratical element in the state was much extended. Neither in the New nor the Old World was the widely held ideal of a partyless government achieved. In the new republic of the West nearly all the other aspirations of the classical republicans or Real Whigs found a measure of fulfillment which would have astounded and delighted them could they have lived to see this.

The Commonwealthmen discussed conditions in England which were changing, perhaps more rapidly than they realized, while they were alive and have long since entirely altered. Ideas about liberty have also changed. The Real Whigs would perhaps have found the philosophy as well as the machinery of modern politics inconsistent with freedom as they understood it. In their time they emphasized the necessity for the adaptation of English institutions to meet new dangers or secure old virtues. Reformation was desirable. Even the best of constitutions could be altered or amended. Tyranny could and should be resisted. The chief service of these asserters of liberty was that, as Priestley explained, they believed that "uniformity is the characteristic of brute creation."[8]

II

Some Seventeenth-Century Commonwealthmen

Links with the Interregnum

Seven important contributors to the canon of Real Whig doctrine —Harrington, Nedham, Milton, Ludlow, Sidney, Neville, and Marvell —were linked with the Interregnum. Even among these there were important differences, though all had been stimulated by the civil commotions and experiments of their times to think freely and deeply about politics. All were critical of defects in the body politic of England and wrote forcibly about remedies for these. All wanted freedom and resisted tyranny, though none saw inconsistency between the panegyrics of liberty and polemics against Catholics. But this was the bitter fruit of the age and the popular association of popery with the arbitrary government of Stuart and Bourbon. Not all of them were republicans in the technical sense of opposing all semblance of monarchy; nor were they all anxious to remodel entirely the English structure of society and constitution. Most of them knew each other personally and all worked and wrote at one time and another for the Good Old Cause. They were not members of the same party or connection.

These men were active in different ways and at different times. Harrington, Nedham, and Milton wrote their political works before the Restoration. Harrington was concerned with the problems of a changing society; Milton with the defense both of tyrannicide and of liberty of thought, as well as with the propounding of a stream of suggestions related to rapidly succeeding crises; Nedham was at least briefly concerned with the merits of a free state. Of the other four, Ludlow lived in exile after the return of Charles II. The posthumously pub-

lished *Memoirs* preserve the record of his uncompromising republicanism and bear some of the marks of the intellectual fossilization that
besets the frustrated refugee. Sidney, Neville, and Marvell wrote with
the problems of the Restoration government in mind.

During the Interregnum, Ludlow never approved the Protectorate
and Sidney sulked in the country at his father's house. Milton, Marvell, and probably Nedham, worked for Cromwell in Thurloe's office.
Milton praised Sidney in the *Second Defence,* but they pursued different courses. Marvell and Neville were friends of Harrington throughout this period and the next, were members of the Rota, but were associated with opposed connections under the Cromwells. Harrington
was at all times an observer, a talker, and a writer, but, like the more
active Milton, he suffered persecution at the Restoration. Both owed
much to the loyalty of Marvell and Neville.

After 1660 and until his death in 1678, Marvell continued to represent Hull in the Commons. Unlike all but Sidney, he was more active
politically in this period than earlier. He achieved considerable reputation both in parliament and through his pamphlets, becoming steadily more unsympathetic with the restored monarchy. Neville, though
occasionally under suspicion, escaped serious inconvenience during
the rest of his life, and divided his time between London and the country, as seemed expedient, and between *Machiavelli* and *Plato Redivivus.*
Neville had criticized the Protectorate, but was never actively antagonistic to monarchical institutions if kept within due bounds. These
limits were outlined in the *Plato* in relation to the exclusion controversy. Sidney, on a mission to Denmark when the king came back,
thought it wiser to stay abroad for some years until family influence
and royal clemency permitted his return. He then tried his fortunes in
successive elections for parliament and failed to establish his claims to
a seat. Involved in the deliberations of the Council of Six, mentioned
so often in the depositions of 1683 about the Rye House Plot and other
conspiracies connected with it, Sidney was brought to trial and executed, more for the sentiments of his unpublished *Discourses,* than for
any proven treasonable act.

The importance of much that took place after the return of
Charles II attracted less attention from contemporaries than did more
ephemeral topics. Yet it could be argued with considerable justifica-

tion that the Restoration represented a constitutional settlement at least as important as the Glorious Revolution. The acts of the Long Parliament, with the exception of the Triennial Bill, were kept on the statute books. The Irish Settlement, for better or worse, remained as dictated by Cromwell and its repressions were reinforced by economic restrictions. The Navigation Act was confirmed and enlarged. The Militia was settled, though in the course of time the arrangements proved less to royal advantage than might have been expected. Public revenue was established on a system that developed but did not fundamentally change its character for over a hundred years. Abolition of feudal dues and tenures, like the famous Alienation Act of Henry VII, proved enormously weakening to royal authority. The so-called Clarendon Code, though modified in 1689, was to persist until the beginning of the nineteenth century. The flight of James II and its sequelae radically changed the affairs only of Scotland, though it brought about definitions of rights and confirmation of customs dear to all Englishmen.

The Restoration marked an important stage, but cannot be blamed for the disappearance of that creative impulse which moved the saints and soldiers to enrich so greatly the literature of the age of the Great Rebellion. Republicanism had already died before Monk crossed the Tweed. Democratic and levelling ideas had, except in a few over-fertile areas, fallen on stony ground. Their progenitors did not always remain true to the precepts they had written. Parliament was unsympathetic with social radicalism before and after the proclamation of the Republic. The Saints, as Cromwell impatiently remarked, were more concerned with discussion than with the implementation of reform. The same indecisiveness marked the regimes of the Anarchy when nothing but a failure of leadership and a complete unwillingness to compromise, even with their own associates, stood between the Republicans and a new order. Cromwell's dictatorship overthrew the first republic and the rule of the Saints, but when death removed him and an ambitious junta pushed out his son, the Innovators achieved nothing.

The Thomason Tracts—the collection now in the British Museum, preserved from day to day over a period of twenty years (1640–1661) by an interested bookman—represents an extraordinary phenomenon in the history of ideas. The same age inspired them and stimulated the major philosophers to creative activity. Naturally enough it was the considered treatises rather than the ephemera of camp and pulpit which contributed most to a continuing tradition, and it was chiefly in the major works that would-be reformers and revolutionaries in England, America, and France found the guidance as well as the theoretical weapons they required. A few echoes from mid-century storms may be heard after 1660, but they must be listened for carefully to be heard at all above the noise of rejoicing Cavaliers and churchmen.

At the accession of Charles II political controversy momentarily died down. There were indications in the Convention and even in early sessions of the Cavalier Parliament that a few members retained some sympathy with the experiments and ideas of the Interregnum. A considerable body continued to hope for a comprehension of large numbers within the Established Church, though these were disappointed both by the Conference at the Savoy and by the easy passage of the so-called Clarendon Code. A concern for law reform persisted. Hale and Vaughan were able to make a few slight changes. Public finance perennially attracted the attention of both reformers and courtiers. But in view of the overwhelming desire of most Englishmen to return to their ancient constitution, it seemed to all but a few desperate men inappropriate and futile to pursue objectives in political and religious matters for which they had earlier fought. Venner's revolt, followed by a scattering of uprisings in the North and West, increased the determination of Cavaliers and churchmen to yield nothing, however moderate the demands of peaceful innovators might be. Such rare pamphlets as *Mene Tekel* (1663), an incitement to rebellion and a criticism of the choice of knights or lords for rulers when there were a hundred better qualified with the spirit of government for the service of the people, helped men like L'Estrange enforce censorship and emphasize the dangerous character of this small continuing leveller element.

The result, which was almost certainly unforeseen, was that during the first decade of the restored monarchy, the prerogative reached unparalleled heights. Both the Venetian observer in London and Andrew Marvell recorded this. Indeed, Burnet was later to suggest that Charles had the example of Denmark, where the parliament had voluntarily brought about a royal despotism in 1660, to inspire him.[1] The bishops were restored to office in church and state. A penal code against nonconformity of a peculiarly embarrassing nature was enacted. Royal power was enhanced by the repeal of the Triennial Act as well as by the establishment of a palace guard and by the arrangements about the militia.

In the seventies there was a sharp decline in the cordiality between Charles and his Long Parliament. This decline was due less to constitutional conflicts than to a deep distrust of the foreign policies of the monarch and to prejudice against the popish religion of his successor. Added to these two facts was the inevitable clash of interest between powerful magnates and the king in which the Lords used religious and political differences to further public or private ends. It is extraordinarily difficult to disentangle the disinterested from the grasping and even frivolous elements in the activities of men like Buckingham and Shaftesbury.

In any case the existence of prominent men ready to lead the opposition was an important factor at this time. Many lesser folk, silent or discreet since 1660, like Marvell, found an opportunity for putting forward suggestions. The dissenters received increased sympathy. Open distrust of the bishops once more found expression in the popular press. Furthermore the adroit manipulation and management of parliament men by such statesmen as Danby began to attract criticism of corruption in high places. Courtiers were dubbed "pensioners." The growing power of France, the economic policies of Colbert and the misfortunes which were developing for the French Huguenots, together with the deepening apprehension about the growth of despotism throughout Europe, fed less well-founded fears, ephemeral jealousies, and discontents. The outburst of pamphlets at the time of the so-called Popish Plot contributes singularly little to permanent political literature. In the seventies the *Letter from a Person of Quality,* Marvell's *Rehearsal Transprosed, The Growth of Popery,* and a couple of speeches in the House of Lords were almost the only significant tracts.

The modern historian can discover certain constitutional developments which profited by the free discussions of the period. Was the restored monarchy to have enhanced powers in spite, or perhaps because of, the bloody struggles of the Interregnum? Was parliament to retain the preëminence somewhat prematurely described by Lord Burghley's alleged statement that parliament could do anything but make a man a woman? What was its duration to be, annual, triennial, or longer? How were the ministers and the officials of the administrative machine to fit into the pattern of a constitutional monarchy? What would the relationship of church and state be if the monarch were a member of the Catholic Church? None of these problems was solved. This Long Parliament was at length dissolved and the new elections revealed greatly intensified political consciousness amongst those who played any part whatever in them. One great statute, the Habeas Corpus Act, was passed. Almost no evidence remains to show the role the demand for it played in the controversies, surprising though this may seem in view of its sacred character in Anglo-Saxon political history. The hysteria, the lies, the betrayals and injustices of the Popish Plot concern the historian of political ideas only in so far as they affect the reputation of some important party politicians. Shaftesbury's patronage of Oates and his support of Monmouth a little later did much to discredit with moderate men the ideas of the Country, or, as it now came to be called, Whig party.

Charles, when he chose to exert himself, was extraordinarily clever. The role he played during the plot period and during the Exclusion parliaments was that of a wise and skillful politician. He generally succeeded through the flexibility and acumen of his approach to the problems as they came up from day to day. As the controversy degenerated into conspiracy and plot, he was able to get rid of all the most influential of his opponents. Charles came nearer establishing despotism than any member of his family, or indeed any other English ruler.

The most interesting political literature of the post-Interregnum period appeared during, or resulted from, the Exclusion controversy of 1679–81. Marvell's *Growth of Popery* had appeared just before the Popish Plot, and achieved wider currency because of developments after its appearance. It had been one of Shaftesbury's opening shots against James Stuart. In 1679 parliament began to consider York's exclusion from the throne. The quality of Tory publications defending not only James, but monarchical power in general, was high. Dryden was enlisted in the royal cause and wrote both satires and plays to help it. Filmer's *Patriarcha*, written long before, was published in 1680. Antiquarians and historians like Brady were drawn into the fray; Sir George Mackenzie wrote *Jus Regium: Or, the Just and Solid Foundations of Monarchy* (1684) against Buchanan, *Naphthali*, Dolman and Milton.

On the Whig side, as it may now be called, James Tyrrell and Sidney both wrote to refute Filmer, though the latter had not printed his *Discourses* when he was executed. Neville wrote *Plato Redivivus,* like William Penn's *England's Great Interest,* designed to influence opinion in and out of parliament. John Somers, just beginning his career, wrote or had a hand in writing, *A Brief History of the Succession, The Security of Men's Lives,* and *A Just and Modest Vindication.* Recent scholarship assigns most of John Locke's *Two Treatises* to this period.[2] John Sadler's *Rights of the Kingdom: or Customs of Our Ancestors,* first published in 1649, was reprinted in 1682.

What at the time of the Revolution of 1688 can compare with this impressive body of work? Tyrrell again entered the lists; Locke printed the *Treatises* and his famous *Letters on Toleration.* For the most part significant literature must be sought in translations of tracts like the *Vindiciae;* works of Grotius and Buchanan; reprints of "Dying Speeches," of *A Brief History of the Succession,* and others.

When parliamentary attempts at settlement were ended by the dissolution of the Oxford Parliament in 1681, revolution of a violent kind once more seemed imminent. Earlier plots had revealed disaffection among old soldiers and fanatics of the Interregnum. Modern researches have discovered some indications of conversations in England and in Holland which may not excuse but do something to confirm the constant anxieties expressed by L'Estrange. A study of these as well as of some of the coteries in the Shaftesbury orbit produces little of interest compared with the programs reported in the depositions of persons apprehended in 1683 in connection with the many treasonable intrigues and cabals which are usually classified under the name of one of them, the Rye House Plot. This extraordinary complex of conspiracy, real and imaginary, provides us with a microcosm of the political ideas of all the more determined opponents of the government of Charles and his brother.

There were three groups or types of conspirators concerned in attempts which were timed for 1683. The so-called Council of Six consisted of an aristocratic group of which Sidney and Russell were a part. Both died on the block for their real or supposed connections with the violence admitted by some of the lesser men arrested at the same time but always denied by them. The Six had certainly discussed ways of combatting the kind of government they felt to have developed, and of preventing the popish and despotic regime which they foresaw in the near future. As Hampden, grandson of the hero of the Ship Money case, was later to suggest, their plans were no more, certainly no less, revolutionary than those of the "immortal seven" who invited William to England in 1688.

Further plans were being made amongst the Scottish Presbyterians, headed by Argyle. Robert Ferguson, the Plotter, provided the chief bond with the English malcontents. There is a good deal of evidence that the aspirations of the Scottish and of the English Council of Six were not identical.

The third element was provided by a rather miscellaneous collection of men from Wapping and from other areas. Some of these, like Rumbold, were old Cromwellians. A few were men of education who had cause for dissatisfaction, sometimes of a quite personal nature, with the government. A variety of motives impelled them. The group planned violent revolutions which would have brought about drastic changes in government and in society. Some who planned the capture of the royal person in the lane that formed a part of the royal route from Newmarket to London, did not intend to do more than force the king to carry out their wishes. Others expected to kill one or both of the Stuarts. The Rye House Plot proper concerns only the conspiracy to seize the king near the Maltster's property. Schemes had developed, for example, to raise soldiers of the Interregnum in different districts of London, and to make attempts on the royal family in the city rather than in the country. Many wild ideas were revealed once the investigation was under way in that spring.

In these we can find for almost the last time some echoes of the experimental spirit of the Commonwealth. The conspirators, even in this third category, were not entirely of one mind. Most of them planned to modify the royal power, some to abolish it completely. All hoped to reform the House of Lords. A few expected that nobles who had acted in a manner contrary to the interests of the people would be degraded. Taxation was to be adjusted; the expenses and the delays of legal proceedings were to be lessened. Zachary Bourn told his interrogators that the plotters wished the militia to be in the hands of the people, that sheriffs should be elected in each county, that all should enjoy liberty of conscience, that parliament should meet annually and be elected annually. He expected an attack on aristocratic privilege. Robert West, a lawyer who had a private grievance against the government, in his deposition emphasized only parliamentary independence; parliament was to meet annually, there were to be fixed times for elections which were no longer to depend on royal writs; meetings of the legislature should be for stated periods and ended only by its own consent; most or all of its acts, if passed through both Houses, should be enforced even without the consent of the prince.

These demands were radical. They revealed a continuation of some elements in Commonwealth political speculation of which few other traces remain. Perhaps the only part of the program of any of these three groups common to them all was a fear of the Stuarts and determination to control them. Even in this we can detect no unity of purpose as to possible substitutes for the family. Monmouth, Buckingham, the Prince of Orange as substitute kings, as well as a Commonwealth, represent four different schemes no one of which had a chance of success without a general uprising—at that time, a most unlikely event. In the Council of Six opinion was divided and the aspirations of Sidney and Russell were probably entirely different in character. Argyle, in Scotland, was a monarchist concerned with the problem of his Presbyterian compatriots. His interest in supporting a Monmouth, for example, was determined only by his estimate of what terms for the party could be extracted from him.

The depositions also represent some at least of the ideas among the Anabaptists and Independents of the west country who joined Monmouth's ill-fated attempt in 1685. The republicanism of Colonel Abraham Holmes and others on the scaffold show that the spirit of the more radical debaters at army councils persisted in a few men. The old army men and fanatics who joined Monmouth found themselves supporting a would-be king. What effect this might have had in the event of his victory cannot be known. The only certain result, as affairs turned out, was in the strengthened association of dissent with levelling republican ideas. Whether Jeffreys's revenge obliterated the last of these Commonwealthmen, or whether they abandoned hope of help from royal pretenders, there was little sign of interest among them when William landed at Torbay.[3]

After the Revolution, when James had fled the country, few programs show even as much of a levelling character as these of the Rye House. Perhaps the most interesting is the tract and its supplement reprinted in the Somers's collection, entitled *Now is the Time: a Scheme for a Commonwealth* (1689). It suggested a reform of Westminster Hall, comprehension and indulgence, a rotation in the council, salaried officers, annual parliaments, chosen triennially, balanced by the executive, part permanent, part biennial, and presided over by the prince. A continuing council of this kind might prevent the dangers of a standing army, whilst at the same time providing continuity amongst those responsible for naval and military forces. A land register was recommended, the iniquities of hearth money and the sale and purchase of offices were emphasized, but the tract is not of an extreme character. With the Rye plotters, a very small, almost inarticulate minority revealed by Monmouth's rebellion, and tracts like *Now is the Time,* the existence of this form of republican aspiration may be said to have ended. Few if any suggestions of this character are to be found in the pamphlet literature between 1692 and 1760, though in private discussions or even in an occasional dispute during parliamentary and local elections antimonarchical and radical sentiments may have found voice. That people continued to read and endorse many or all of the political ideas put forward by the more important writers of the so-called "Whig Canon," however, is easy enough to demonstrate.[4] Their contribution and their biographies must now be considered.

Neville and Harrington

Henry Neville (1620–1694) was a Berkshire gentleman educated at Oxford at about the same time that Marchamont Nedham studied there and Marvell was at Cambridge. He traveled widely in Italy and was, like so many others in the period, enormously influenced by what he found. The list of Commonwealthmen who went to Italy is impressive: John Hampden of Ship Money fame; Henry Marten, the first avowed republican; his friend, Thomas Chaloner, the Regicide; John Pym, leader of the Long Parliament; Andrew Fletcher, the Scotsman; as well as Sidney, Marvell, and Milton. Neville returned to an active role in Interregnum affairs. Later his popular translation of the works of Machiavelli (1675 and again 1680) attests the continued influence of his earlier reading and also contributes to the quite common idea that the father of modern politics was himself a Whig. He went into parliament as a "recruiter" representing Abingdon in 1649. He was elected to the Council of State in 1651, but in common with Marten, Scott, and Haselrig disliked the increasingly monarchical character of Cromwell's government. He tried to enter parliament in 1656. He was elected for Reading in Richard's Parliament where his activity with the Commonwealth group anxious to limit or abolish the protectoral power made him prominent and drew a wry comment from Marvell, then a Cromwellian "courtier." On the fall of Richard and the return of the Rump he continued attempts to set up a system on Harringtonian principles. He twice at least sat on councils of state during the Anarchy. He attended the Rota Club which met at the Sign of the Turk's Head in Palace Yard, Westminster, from September 1659 to the eve of the dissolution of the Long Parliament in March. He may have continued for a couple of years discussions of a similar character at Nonsuch House, Bow Street, Covent Garden, a tavern run by a subordinate of Major John Wildman.[5]

During the sixties Neville seems to have been in and out of London, sometimes in the aristocratic company his birth and education opened to him. He saw much of Cosmo III of Tuscany during his visit to England in 1669. He treasured a present from the Florentine until he died when he left it to a favourite nephew. He wrote the *Isle of Pines* (1668). He continued the offices of friendship for poor Harrington. Occasionally, as for example, Marvell reported rather cryptically in a letter to Hull in 1669, his appearance nearby alarmed nervous Parliament men. He must have been much occupied with his Machiavelli in the early seventies. In 1678 he traveled abroad with Buckingham and Wildman and may have wished to enter the Commons again on the dissolution of the second Long Parliament in 1678–79. But like Wildman he might not have voted for Exclusion had he been successful in winning a seat in any of the last three sessions of the reign. He wrote *Plato Redivivus* with the second of these in mind. In spite of the date 1681 on the title page of the first edition, this book appeared just as the session began in late October 1680 and went into an enlarged edition the next spring about the time of the ill-fated Oxford Parliament. Neville was carefully watched by the government during the plots of the next few years. Not even the vengeful spirit of the court could discover enough indiscretions to make an indictment feasible. He survived the Revolution and is reported by Walter Moyle—collaborator of John Trenchard in some famous tracts, and antiquarian and historian in his own right—to have talked to their group at the Grecian Tavern, where he was known as "Plato Neville" and where he continued those political debates which had occupied him so long before at the Turk's Head and Nonsuch taverns. He died in 1694. In his will the free-thinking Puritan directed that he should be buried with "no Jewish ceremonies." *England's Confusion,* a libel of 1659 against the men of "the good old cause," had listed them with various uncomplimentary epithets, and Neville as "religious Harry." He seems to have shared little of the enthusiasm of the fanatics of the Interregnum; his religion like his politics was one of "limitations" and moderation.[6]

In a prefatory note to *Plato Redivivus* its publisher, after explaining that he had received the volume in mid-October, assured his readers that on examination he had noticed its relevance to the immediate constitutional crisis, but had found that "it contained no harm" likely to get him into trouble. He decided to print it at once. He then went on to dispose of an expected criticism that Neville's book was merely a repetition of Harrington's *Oceana* in its emphasis on the connection of empire and property and on the importance of the study of history for the student of government. The publisher observed that anyone who read Thucydides, Polybius, Livy, and Plutarch was likely to find in them the same doctrine of dominion and wealth which Harrington and Neville professed. Harrington had attempted to prove that only democratic government was suitable to England, whereas the latter had applied the principles derived from history "to the redressing and supporting one of the best monarchies in the world which is that of England."[7]

Neville's authorship was soon known but even had anonymity been preserved, the connection between *Plato Redivivus* and *Oceana* was obvious. In 1737 Bruce and Smith, Dublin publishers, printed the works of Harrington and Neville's treatise in one volume. Both were constantly cited by writers of the eighteenth century, though Harrington's reputation was greater and has continued down to the present whereas his friend, Neville, has seldom attracted attention. Harrington's *Oceana*, unlike Neville's book, was utopian in form. Although its references to contemporary problems were but transparently disguised, like his other writings it was much more than a polemical tract and was intended as a thorough-going examination of the nature of the best government. His work stands out as the chief contribution of the Interregnum to the great succession of English political writings from Fortescue through Hooker to Locke and Hume.

Oceana may be summarily divided into two parts: the devices and form for preservation of the liberty which the state was created to preserve, and the explanation of the manner of achieving stability. Harrington derived these expedients from various sources. His greatest debt was to the Venetian system, often regarded as the most perfect example of the mixed or Gothic government favoured by European liberal thinkers. The individual was entitled to the security of a government based on consent, to the safeguards of a rule of laws, not men, and to the recognition of certain natural rights like the exercise of his own religion. The evils of factions in the state and of ambitious administrators were to be restrained by the ballot, the rotation in legislative body and in office alike, and by a division of power between different parts of the constitution. A balance must be maintained so that no one section of community or government could overpower the other. Public and private liberty would thus be equally preserved.

The smooth working of the system depended upon a measure of equality between a number of persons with a stake in the country. Property was more widely distributed than formerly, and political power must be adjusted to these conditions. In a free state wealth might be expected to increase and Harrington was concerned lest a constant flux should lead to political confusion. His suggested limitations upon property, his agrarian system or hierarchy, were designed for a rural, not an urban economy. He was not thinking of the "laborious poor" of his period nor foreseeing the industrial proletariat of a latter one. He was writing in an age of revolution when the adoption of a considered scheme for ensuring future stability in the relations of dominion and property, which he rightly blamed for much of contemporary chaos, seemed possible or at any rate worth working for. Neville, though also fully aware of the social changes which had taken place since the feudal age, and less nostalgic about its passing than Sidney and Fletcher, was convinced that limitations upon political power were more likely to preserve and extend freedom than Harrington's utopian schemes. Both saw that the balance of power had passed to the Commons—that is the gentry—and both saw the need for constitutional acknowledgment of the economic changes which had taken place. Both the *Oceana* and *Plato Redivivus* were to be studied by the Americans considering a constitution in the days of George III.

Neville's interest for the student of eighteenth-century ideas lies then partly in his reinterpretation of Harringtonian ideas. His work is also of very considerable significance in its own right. *Plato Redivivus* is not simply an adaptation of the *Oceana*. If Neville was jointly responsible for the earlier work, as Hobbes suggested, the latter shows development on his part and a sensitivity to contemporary problems. If Neville had no hand in Harrington's book, his discourses show a flexibility and an acumen which is not characteristic of his friend. Neville was the one republican of eminence—with the possible exception of Andrew Marvell, who died before the controversies of the eighties had reached the critical stage, and Sidney, whose intentions between his return in 1679 and his execution in 1683 are really unknown—who quite definitely accepted a part at least of the Restoration Settlement. This makes him extraordinarily significant in tracing the history of the transmission of the ideas of one period to another.

He is separated from Milton, Harrington, and even Ludlow as definitely as time and space separate from them their eighteenth-century admirers like Molesworth, Trenchard, Moyle, and Gordon, not to mention a still later generation, Lofft, Burgh, Price, and Priestley. Hammond, one of these eighteenth-century commentators, pointed out in writing to Moyle about his *Essay on the Lacedaemonian Government* that Neville might not be entirely original in his analysis of property but "we must," he continues, "do him the Right to declare that the late Happy Revolution has brought such a change in our Constitution in those several branches which he only wished and proposed to King Charles II."[8] The same writer went on to list such things as the condemnation of the dispensing power, the limitation of the right of making war and peace, the reform of the coinage, and the settling of the Civil List. The naming and choosing of great offices was still left to the discretion of the crown. With a monarch under a necessity of calling parliament annually and a parliament which wields the weapons of impeachment and attainder, there was surely no need to be apprehensive of such royal prerogatives as remain. Neville's immediate concern had been, as this analysis shows, to discuss not an ideal commonwealth but the English constitutional monarchy and he wished both to prevent the selection of some puppet ruler like Monmouth and to forestall any possible disposition on the part of James toward unparliamentary government. He suggested limitations on the monarchy which would have made impossible some of James's illegal acts and might, indeed, have made unnecessary the Revolution itself.[9]

Neville's book takes the form of three dialogues. Each of these takes place among three people—a visiting Venetian, who is identified only as in need of medical care, the physician who has been treating him (who has been variously identified with Harvey, though more commonly with a Doctor Lower), and an Englishman who must certainly represent Neville himself. Locke has been suggested as the prototype of the doctor but there seems to be no confirmation whatever for this. In the dialogues themselves the doctor was said never to have left England, whereas the philosopher's travels, even before he went into exile with Shaftesbury, were quite well known.

The first dialogue starts rather slowly though probably not according to seventeenth-century standards. It says very little and has probably deterred modern readers from prolonging their study of the book. Almost its only contribution lies in its rather contemptuous dismissal of violent remedies for public ills. This may be due to the fact that Neville was not as interested in revolutionary wars as the bellicose Sidney. In the second dialogue Neville attempted to answer the question why England, formerly so great, is now very little esteemed. He explained the anxiety of all to avoid strife. He suggested that it is a mistake to confuse cause and effect, that is to say, to blame evil counsellors, pensioned parliaments, unjust judges, flattering divines, or French advice. These had arisen from the evil situation of England but were not directly responsible for it. The "breach and ruin" of our government was at hand, the end of a process of decay which had gone on for over two hundred years. He refused to discuss the beginnings of government anywhere, although he declared his love of reading not the historians but the archives of any country. Government must start by necessity. Laws to maintain property must be made. Government for the good of the government could not exist merely for the exaltation of the government. Force or fraud might alter its character, property must "found and eternalize it."

The present confusions, Neville said, were caused by the break-up of large estates. A state of virtual anarchy prevailed. The people were not contented with their role in political society; that is to say, they had no acknowledged right to approve or disapprove legislation, alliances, declarations of war, and treaties of peace. They had no hand in the selection of officers nor were their juridical rights at all plain. Since they were discontented, they debated in the marketplaces, made their orators their leaders, and, he suggested, took to themselves senatorial powers not properly theirs. In this second dialogue Neville devoted some attention to such European governments as the German, Swiss, Dutch, Turkish, and Venetian, but returned in the discussion once more to his native country and commented on solecisms in Chancery and in the ordinary workings of the legal system. He noted that trial by jury had recently been "vindicated,"[10] and the reference is, of course, to Bushell's Case in which William Penn was concerned.

England's difficulties lay chiefly in the changing economic balance. The king had now become dependent on the people. The executive was therefore not in the position of proper independence. Neville contrasted with current customs the pre–Civil War parliamentary practice. After a reference to the land laws of the Gracchi he said:

> I will not trouble myself nor you, to search into the particular causes of this change, which has been made in the possessions here in *England;* but it is visible that the fortieth part of the Lands which were at the beginning in the hands of the Peers and Church, is not there now; besides that not only all Villanage is long since abolished, but the other Tenures are so altered and qualified, that they signify nothing towards making the Yeomanry depend upon the Lords. The consequence is, that the natural part of our Government which is Power, is by means of Property in the hands of the People, whilst the artificial part, or the Parchment, in which the

Form of Government is written, remains the same . . . This alone is the cause of all the disorder you have heard of, and now see in *England* . . . some impute all to the decay of Trade, others to the growth of Popery; which are both great Calamities, but they are Effects, and not Causes.

Neville illustrated his argument by an analogy. If by your own carelessness and the prudence of your servants a major part of your income passed to them, could you really believe that they would remain in your service?

It is just so with a whole Kingdom. In our Ancestors times, most of the Members of our House of Commons thought it an honour to retain to some great Lord, and to wear his blew Coat: And when they had made up their Lord's train, and waited upon him from his own House to the Lord's House, and made a Lane for him to enter, and departed to sit themselves in the Lower House of Parliament, as it was then (and very justly) called; can you think that anything could pass in such a Parliament that was not ordered by the Lords?[11]

Neville suggested how to prevent future troubles. If the government were broken, it would be because it was founded on property, and that foundation was now shaken. It followed that prosperity and peace could only be achieved when the political system had been adjusted to the distribution of wealth. This adjustment should be made since an attempt to restore the lands now in other hands to the Lords and to the king, Neville considered utterly impossible. An adjustment of the relation between the Commons and the king was necessary. A part of this should consist in a voluntary relinquishment of some of the regal power.

Neville considered the vexed question of Catholicism and of the popish successor to Charles II. In a long passage, published only in his second and later editions, he declared that Monmouth was utterly unsuited for the royal job and that the supporters of the Duke were completely mistaken. Not only was Monmouth a bastard but his claims to the throne could be secured only by a successful war. Neville also negated the pleas of the Republicans. People were already crying

'Forty-one, and were terrified of a repetition of the chaotic changes of the Civil War era. Only a fraction of the population wanted a republic. Neville proposed instead limitations on regal power not unlike those put forward by Halifax. The Venetian doctor, at this point in the dialogue sensibly inquired how the king could be persuaded to give up a part of his power. Neville's reply was that he must consent since if he did not, he might cease to be king.[12]

Were those prerogatives listed as dangerous abolished, and were proper provisions made for a rotation in the council, the threat of a popish monarchy would be almost negligible. He would take from the king the power of making war and peace, control of the militia, appointment to office, and the control of expenditure. Furthermore, guarantees about the writ of habeas corpus, the sanctity of charters, the rights of petitioning, the calling and dissolving of parliament, and the election of its members, should be given. Neville concluded with a reflection that civil strife merely opened the way for the triumph of France and thus for the overthrow of the English body politic. His stress on the rotation of officers might be accounted for by his republican and Venetian heritage. His analysis, however, was dictated by his appraisal of the situation in 1680. Fundamentally, what he was attempting to protect was the ancient English constitution adapted to the new domestic balance of power.

Neville and Harrington were English republicans. Unlike some of the Irish and Scottish amongst their later disciples or the sympathizers with colonial claims to self-government, they were imperialists. In *Plato Redivivus* the Venetian described his own republic in Italy and its dependencies. He asked the Englishman whether his maxim about political power and property should be applied to provincial government:

> No, Sir [replied his friend], so far from that, that it is just contrary; for as in National or Domestick Government, where a Nation is governed either by its own People or its own Prince, there can be no settled Government, except they have the Rule who possess the Country. So in Provincial Governments, if they be wisely ordered, no man must have any the least share in the managing Affairs of State, but strangers, or such as have no share or part in the pos-

sessions there, for else they will have a very good opportunity of shaking off their Yoak.

To which the third participant in the dialogue, the doctor, added the remark that England had been wise enough to forbid all native rule in Ireland. The evolution of the idea that even conquest could not take from men the right to govern themselves had not yet made any progress.[13]

The replies to Neville's tract attacked his republicanism and laughed at his endorsement of Venetian devices. They were not slow to connect his ideas in an uncomplimentary way with those of Machiavelli. By the time that Northleigh had printed *The Triumph of Our Monarchy* in 1685, Sidney had died on the scaffold having made a last speech which was a passionate defense of the "good old cause," and of the right of resisting tyranny. Neville, in his calm analysis, reflected little of the passion which pervaded Sidney's utterances. Nonetheless, pamphleteers of the period connected Sidney, Neville, the Whigs as a whole, all Venetian constitutional ideas, and the rebellions of all sorts during the century in one wild hodgepodge of what they disliked and feared.[14]

Neville had attacked the unrepresentative nature of contemporary parliaments. He had disclaimed any ability to describe the history of English institutions. He had, after early hesitations, endorsed the not very accurate work of Petyt and Atwood, whose chief object was to prove the continuity of representative government from before Alfred up to the present.[15] In this respect, Neville's book was a part of the renewed controversy about the antiquity and power of parliament. The prejudices and passions of the discussion of Whigs and Tories about parliamentary history have complicated and confused the researches of students ever since.

It is extraordinarily hard to estimate Neville's influence during the next hundred years while his book was still being reissued and read. The close association with the author of the *Oceana* confused the story. We shall probably never know whose share in the ideas put forward was the greater. There can be no doubt that Neville's later work gained a wider public for the *Oceana* than it might have had alone. The economic interpretation of England's troubles in the seventeenth century was reinforced by a second discussion of the relation of dominion and property. Eighteenth-century students of politics repeated with fatiguing regularity the more obvious aspects of this theory. As the century wore on they may have studied the work of either of them with less care, and the refinement and subtlety which appears in Neville's book was quite often overlooked.

Sidney

Closely associated with Henry Neville in his earlier career in the Interregnum period, Sidney,[16] unlike him, was to take an active part in politics in the 1680's. If he had not been arrested for his real or supposed complicity in the Rye House Plot, it is quite probable that his reputation would have been no greater than that of the author of the *Plato Redivivus*. Neville's experience which roughly paralleled that of Sidney, although his exile was shorter, had convinced him that civil war accomplished little that was permanent. His suggestions, therefore, were directed toward constitutional restrictions and readjustments which would rob the monarchy of any arbitrary prerogative and would rectify the balance in society by redistribution of political power in accordance with property. Sidney, although like Neville in his noble ancestry and his fervent support of the parliamentary cause, had drawn no such moral from the history of the Civil War. He and Neville had witnessed Cromwell's expulsion of the Rump. They had shared a distaste for his dictatorial methods. They had returned to public service on his death and had both been disappointed by the settlement of 1660. Nonetheless, their political treatises point different morals to the story of this epoch. Their contribution to the Commonwealth traditions of later generations was very different in character.

Algernon Sidney (1622–1683) was slightly younger than Neville, Marvell, and Nedham. His father, the earl of Leicester, was a diplomat during the boy's youth, and may have held somewhat similar political views. The bond between them seems to have been quite close. Sidney served in the parliamentary army. His forceful personality soon made him well known, but he refused to have any part in the court which condemned Charles I. His relations with the government in power, whatever its character, at no time were happy. When Charles II returned to England, Sidney was serving on an embassy to Denmark. Whilst there, shortly before the thirtieth of May, he had inscribed in the visitor's book at Copenhagen his famous motto proclaiming himself the foe of tyranny. News of this untactful inscription spread quickly and the earl of Leicester urged Sidney, in spite of his moderation in '49, to stay away from England. The years in exile were spent for the most part in Italy.

In 1677 his father was old and ill and his younger son, whose income was inadequate, was anxious to secure his share of the estate before the earl died. The generosity of Charles, possibly at the instigation of powerful men in France, allowed his return. Once in England, the temptation to take an active part in politics was strong. Sidney made several attempts to get into the House of Commons, but his elections were declared invalid even by the Whig Houses of 1680–81. Sidney did not get on with his brother or sister. His temper was famous. He seems to have become friendly with William Penn, but he does not seem to have found any general sympathy or support amongst the ruling classes of the day.

On the other hand, perhaps because of Milton's panegyric, his name had become "indissolubly attached to the interests of liberty" amongst those people who revered Commonwealth ideas. It is not surprising therefore to find him a member of that Council of Six debating ways and means in the winter of 1682–83. It would be more surprising to discover any evidence that he had converted the rest of the council to his own way of thinking. He was intransigent and inflexible and we have reports which suggest that his presence among the conspirators, if they must be called that, was almost enough to ensure that nothing would be agreed on.

The end of the story in one way was of course his arrest, the confiscation of his papers (among them his *Discourses* in manuscript), his trial, conviction, and death. In another it would be truer to point out that the court in which he was tried and the scaffold on which he met death bravely afforded him the opportunity for putting his views before the public which the publication alone of his long and learned book would never have equaled. He was forced to be brief. Circumstances enhanced the nobility of the grey-haired man of sixty, and the importance of his utterances to the court and on the scaffold. The government of Charles II realized too late that his martyrdom was more dangerous than his continued existence as a frustrated plotter could ever have been. Hampden was merely incarcerated and fined. He found no niche in the Whig martyrology.

Although Sidney was a violent man, his ideals were sometimes singularly simple as his posthumously published *Essay on Love* reveals. He never married. Much of his life was spent in camps, on embassies, and on his wanderings. These circumstances did nothing to modify his emotions or his nature. In exile he had plenty of time to read classical and Renaissance political treatises. He insisted that the documents seized from him and used in his trial were notes and reflections made in his retirement, but the passages of his book which comment upon England in the reign of Charles II could only have been written shortly before his arrest and are prejudiced and bitterly abusive. Jeffreys, summing up at the trial the character of the evidence against him, declared that hardly a line of the *Discourses* was not treasonable in itself. "This book," he said, "contains all the malice, and revenge and treason that mankind can be guilty of; it fixes the sole power in the Parliament and the people."

Sidney had devoted a great part of his work, in fact, to explaining his belief that rebellion was often necessary, and could effect improvement. He was prepared to illustrate the benefits so obtained from the history of the Romans and very many peoples since. Rebellion and freedom were linked in his mind. Men might rebel, indeed have a duty to rebel, whenever their liberties were threatened or attacked. Every man might kill a tyrant; anyone who has the virtue and the power to save the people need never want a right of doing it. Swords were given men that none might be slaves. He entirely disagreed with the idea that civil war was a disease; nothing whatever in the nature of monarchy or any government obliged men to bear them when tyrannical.

Free men who had overthrown tyranny and who had government of their own choosing were stronger than any others. The triumphs of the Roman republicans before luxury corrupted government and sapped their ancient energies, the victory of the free Germans, the successes of the Scots and the English against the Stuarts and against the foreign foes of the Republic, were noted by him as proof of the superiority of free states to any others. Sidney's attitude was extremely warlike. The

test of good government in his eyes was its success in war. By war he
not only meant war against oppression, foreign or domestic; he also
meant war against another state. The best government to Sidney was
the government which most effectively prepared the country for military exploits. When Capel Lofft, a late eighteenth-century radical, was
annotating his copy of Sidney with lavish evidence of approval and admiration, it was this passage about the state and war to which he took
exception.[17]

On December 7, 1683, Sidney gave to the sheriff on the scaffold,
as was customary, a paper concerning himself. In it he was able to put
succinctly in a few paragraphs the gist of what, in the printed *Discourses,*
runs to several hundred folio pages. "I am," he wrote, "persuaded to
believe that God has left nations the liberty of setting up such governments as best please themselves"; that magistrates were set up for the
good of nations, not nations for the honour or glory of magistrates;
that the right and power of magistrates in every country must be that
which the laws of that country had made it; that oaths taken to observe those laws had the force of contract and could not be violated
without dissolving the whole fabric. The king's most dangerous enemies were those who encouraged him to claim or exercise exorbitant
powers. Only a corrupt and lazy people had ever given away their fundamental rights to be governed well. It was, indeed, doubtful whether
such a right could be given or taken away. Neither conquest nor the
submission of a grateful people could bestow power on the ruler which
he could not justly exercise. When Sidney received sentence he cried
out that this was an age which made truth pass for treason. Among his
dying words was an entreaty to Almighty God:

> Grant that I may die Glorifying Thee for all Thy mercies; and
> that at the last Thou hast permitted me to be singled out as a Wit-
> ness of thy Truth; and even by the Confession of my Opposers, for
> that OLD CAUSE [that is to say of liberty against tyrants] in which
> I was from my Youth engaged; and for which thou hast Often and
> Wonderfully declared thyself.

Perhaps Sidney's evocation of divine approval for his cause was ultimately to have more effect than that of those who declared monarchy to have divine right. If one may judge by the event, God sup-

ported claims to revolutionary right rather than the hereditary rights of Stuarts, Bourbons, or others.[18]

Sidney's work and his legend remained for long sacred to revolutionaries wherever they might be and however good or bad their causes. Some of his other ideas are worth comment, though he is never constructive as Neville is. He was not particularly interested in the relations of empire and property although he likewise noticed the changing social pattern of the last century and a half. In this connection what is chiefly noticeable is his nostalgia for the medieval world in which master and man, landlord and tenant, formed a Gothic balance. As he described it, one wonders whether he did not really, in spite of his advocacy of change, think that the best times were in the past. On the other hand, he was said to know more history and more about governments of all kinds than any of his contemporaries.

On the whole, the study of history led Sidney into a belief in the necessity for constant change in government, as in clothes, in technology, and so forth. We did not need to cling to the style of garment which Adam wore nor to such political institutions as may have existed in his family, nor need we protect ourselves with bows and arrows. Times changed and with them institutions. Moreover, Sidney suggested that different kinds of men and varying climates demanded differences in their political systems. These differences, of course, would not in any way weaken those fundamental laws of nature which our reason readily discovered. Sidney perpetually reminded his readers not only of the importance of politics but of the difficulty of mastering its science. Only the wise and understanding could frame good governments. There was no universal pattern any more than there was a panacea for all distempers. Law must suit present exigencies. It must follow reason, nature, really common sense; obviously no one should live under a bad government or one that was deteriorating and failed to provide for current needs.

Experiment would be necessary to discover the best government. Good governments of the past should inspire faith only in fools, although their study would more readily enable the serious student to deal with current problems. Furthermore, the student of politics would have to weigh one set of imperfections against another. Parliament might be vicious and popular governments corrupt but if one had to choose, even the anarchy—which states ruled by imperfect popular institutions might suffer—was bound to be preferable to tyranny. A tyrant could not be restrained by law, nor could his heir be rejected for stupidity or failure. Sidney felt that popular governments in the long run would reform themselves if enough men interested themselves in public affairs.

Sidney's work continued to be read with care right down to the days of the French Revolution. His reputation rather increased than lessened as the eighteenth century wore on, in spite of the revelations of Dalrymple about the payments made to him and other Whigs by the French king. At the moment when these documents were published, Scotland was associated in the minds of those most likely to admire Sidney, with Toryism and with all sorts of nefarious schemes to undermine the British constitution. Dalrymple's charges, although amply documented, were discounted as the work of one hostile to all that Sidney stood for. During the American Revolution Sidney's *Discourses* was more of a Bible to the revolutionaries than any of the other works of his century, Milton only excepted. Germans and Frenchmen also read the book and applied its precepts to their own desires for freedom as they understood it. The continuing reputation of the chief of the Whig martyrs, and the effects of his influence may be found in nearly all the work of the eighteenth-century Commonwealthmen.

Ludlow and Nedham

Edmund Ludlow (1617?–1692) was a more determined and doctrinaire republican than either Sidney or Neville. It was not possible for him, like them, to return to England in the reign of Charles II. At his brief appearance in 1689, as already noticed, he found very few to support his suggestions. Yet the history of his *Memoirs* (1698) probably written between 1663 and 1673, shows an interest in his ideas very much greater than his misfortunes might suggest. The *Memoirs* are invaluable for the student of history. Although Ludlow is often dismissed as a man of narrow and unoriginal ideas, there seems to have been a fairly considerable public for these amongst the same eighteenth-century group who were reading Sidney and Milton and the rest. A modern edition, the work of the late Sir Charles Firth, appeared in 1894, and contained for the first time certain passages which earlier editors of Whiggish sympathies had suppressed. Firth's learned introduction and notes provide much information about the vicissitudes of the manuscript of the book. It also tells of some of the men associated with its various editions: Isaac Littlebury, an inveterate republican and translator of Herodotus; John Toland, editor of Harrington and active in many literary ventures of the first quarter of the eighteenth century; Richard Baron, responsible for so many mid-century reprints of the "Whig Canon."[19]

Ludlow's constitutional ideas were developed during the period of the Civil War, the Commonwealth, and the Protectorate. There seems no reason to suppose that because he wrote in exile, he had modified them in any way. He was against mixed monarchy, and in this respect out of line with a great many Whigs. His theory contained in a somewhat different form, suggestions which many of the eighteenth-century Commonwealthmen endorsed. He emphasized the separation of powers. He advocated a republican form of government in which a supreme tribunal safeguards the state against the usurpations of any single person or magistrate. He declared that all should enjoy liberty of conscience. Moreover, he instructed his readers in the evils that military dictatorship could bring to the "good old cause" of constitutional liberty. In Ludlow's model constitution there was to be no House of Lords although there were to be two councils chosen by the people, one to have the power of debating and proposing, and the other the power of resolving and determining. In each year a third part of both councils would retire from office. Some of these suggestions are not unlike those put forward in the *Oceana*. Ludlow's originality perhaps lies chiefly in his concept of a supreme court, "a select number of men in the nature of the Lacedaemonian ephori," who would deal with cases concerning other members of the government and would protect that government against any infringement of its fundamentals. Although Harrington is commonly thought of in this connection, Ludlow's proposals more directly anticipate American constitutional thinking than those of the *Oceana*.[20]

Whatever ultimate effect the circulation of Ludlow's *Memoirs* might have had overseas, there can be no doubt about their contribution to one controversy which recurred in England for a century or more after the Peace of Ryswick. The first edition of the *Memoirs* has on its title page, "printed at Vivay," but seems to have been produced in London in the establishment of John Darby in Bartholomew Close. Darby published Marvell's *Growth of Popery,* Lord Russell's *Dying Speech,* amongst other tracts of a similar character. In 1697 he printed the *Argument* against a standing army by Trenchard and Moyle. In rebuttals to this famous polemic, contemporaries did not fail to connect its appearance with the publication soon after of Ludlow, Sidney, and other works. The *Memoirs,* more than any of the other supposed publications of the group, afforded ammunition for the arguments against the maintenance of a professional army. These arguments now appear futile and anachronistic, bearing something of the same relation to certain political necessities, in this case the need for popular control of the military machine, as the excesses of the modern press bear to the question of untrammelled freedom of thought. Fuller discussion of this, however, belongs in the next chapter.[21]

The reputation of Marchamont Nedham (1620–1678)—a man in the judgment of his eighteenth-century editor, Richard Baron, inferior only to Milton—has suffered because he was a turncoat. He wrote frequently in the *Mercurius Politicus;* he translated John Selden's *Mare Clausum* in 1652, and in this same year *The Excellencie of a Free State,* published in book form in 1656, first appeared. Richard Baron, with some encouragement and help from Thomas Hollis, reprinted the tract in 1767, and an Amsterdam reprint appeared in 1774. The work did not enjoy anything like the continuing reputation of the philosophers Milton, Harrington, Sidney, and Locke. Baron's object in presenting Nedham's work to the public was indeed to increase the number of his readers and to suggest to his contemporaries political theories in it which he himself endorsed. His success is attested by Condorcet's tribute to the *Free State* in *The Progress of the Human Mind.* Much of what Nedham says is a repetition of familiar arguments about the advantage which freedom bestows on countries enjoying it over those ruled by tyrants or governments deficient in wholesome laws and "easy course of administration" and in a power of altering government and governors. To these three characteristics of the free state Nedham adds a fourth, an uninterrupted series of assemblies of the people, and a fifth, a free election of members for these parliaments under proper rules of election.

Nedham lists fourteen reasons why the people, or those elected to represent them, are the best keepers of their own liberties. The people, never defined by Nedham, would not usurp other men's rights. They would be concerned that public authorities would be directed for public ends. In a free state where a constant succession in power was assured, corruption would be impossible and faction unlikely to develop. Such a constitution would secure against self-seeking, liberty would be preserved since its protectors would be those themselves concerned in its advantages; there was less likelihood of oppression since all officers of such a state would be accountable for their misdemeanors. A free state was more valiant, as Sidney later attempted to maintain, and more fruitful. Reason and human nature found a proper expression, as Cicero long ago had discovered, under free institutions. Nedham pointed out that a free state was likely to be less luxurious, luxury and tyranny evidently having some connection with each other. On the other hand, though the excesses of wealth were avoided, a free state was the only preservative against levelling and confusion of property. Since all decisions in this state were made by common consent, every man's particular interest would be fairly provided for against the arbitrary disposition of others. "Whatever is contrary to this is levelling indeed; because it placeth every man's right under the will of another and is no less than tyranny . . . the very bane of propriety." [22]

A state of this kind was less likely to suffer civil strife. Nedham made suggestions, over and above his continued reiteration of the necessity for free suffrage, which would secure successive parliaments. He was convinced that the whole community should be instructed in the use of arms as a bulwark of their liberty and that moreover arms should never be lodged "in the hands of any but such as have an interest in the public." He was also insistent that children should be educated and instructed in the principles of freedom, quoting Aristotle in support of his idea. Legislative and executive powers should be entirely separate. This division, if maintained, might have preserved the free states of Spain and France. Charles I's attempt to seize both powers in his own hands brought a swift destruction upon him. The base of government should be large; office should not be restricted to a few. Party should be avoided at all costs; destruction by it in states like Rome, or in more modern times, Hungary or Genoa, of the liberties of the citizens was well known to all students of history.

Nedham put into succinct form many of the arguments against diseases of the body politic which were also current in the eighteenth century, and the reader of 1767 may well have found his treatises more immediately relevant to the situation of their own time than the *Oceana* or similar works.

Milton and Marvell

Two others amongst the famous writers of the seventeenth century continued to find readers throughout this period. The political writings of John Milton (1608–1674) and Andrew Marvell (1621–1678) are continually referred to and their arguments cited. How far their political notoriety was increased by the renown of their poetical talents is difficult to judge. To some extent it may be true to say that people separated them in their different roles as sharply and arbitrarily as Dr. Johnson's famous reference to "rebel and bard" would suggest. Another question may be raised in connection with their reputation—there is probably more relevance in this than in the other—how far do they become associated simply with an attitude or a very simple principle? How far did people really study their work in an endeavour to appreciate their individual political beliefs?

Milton was, of course, a gigantic figure in the seventeenth-century landscape. He enjoyed enormous celebrity on the continent. Toland wrote a famous life of Milton at a time when he was also interested in reissuing the prose works. He was more interested in the causes that the "rebel" supported than in the "bard." Milton stood first for a defense of free thought—of toleration; he passionately opposed censorship of all sorts. His eloquent phrases have continued to reach persons right down to modern times. Possibly the second contribution made by Milton which won most disciples was his tract on education. It is quoted endlessly by eighteenth-century readers, though its interest now seems slight compared to the work of the eighteenth-century experimenters, both in the British Isles and on the Continent.

Milton had moreover defended the establishment of a Commonwealth against the critics of his time who had been shocked by the execution of Charles and by the establishment of a republic. Toland referred to the *Defence* as his masterpiece. Both this and the *Eikonoklastes* provided ammunition for those who were anxious to get rid of tyrants. But Milton's justification of rebellion was not as forceful as Sidney's, though he was writing to defend an act in which Sidney himself had refused to have any part. Charles I, by his bearing on the scaffold and his patience before that at the hands of his very arbitrary judges, won for himself a place in the hearts of Englishmen of many generations to come, which his reputation as monarch could never have secured him. Long after the Revolution, when the Hanoverians were on the throne, sermons were preached on the thirtieth of January, deploring the dreadful deed on that day. Although a Stephens or a Bradbury or a Mayhew might rashly defend the principle of resistance to tyranny, defying the customary observance of the anniversary, they represented only a small minority by so doing. Milton's work, therefore, as it concerns king-killing, was not generally endorsed by Whigs. When approval is found, as in the case of Richard Baron who reprinted a part of the *Eikonoklastes* shortly after the hundredth anniversary of the martyrdom had been observed, it is almost certainly indicative of Commonwealth principles in the eulogist.

Associated with Milton in the Cromwellian Secretariat, and his loyal and affectionate friend thereafter, Marvell was more active after the Restoration than before. He produced three of the most significant tracts of the period and the best political satire before *Absalom and Achitophel*. His work became a part of every Whig history, his integrity the text of every diatribe against corruption. *The Rehearsal Transprosed* was a famous plea for liberty of conscience, praised for its wit and style long after the controversy which provoked it had died down. Reprinted in the eighteenth century, it found admirers among men unsympathetic to Marvell's politics. Marvell and Milton were not only linked by their pleas for liberty of conscience, they were also famous for their condemnation of popery. Over and over again the arguments which they used were reiterated in support of penal laws exempting Catholics from the privileges and duties of citizenship. Both men felt strongly that it was difficult to be a loyal subject and a sincere Catholic at one and the same time. Their well-known passion for free expression of opinion and freedom of worship for all only lent greater force to the exception they made of the Roman church. The work of men like Priestley in the latter half of the eighteenth century was necessary to bring about a change of attitude toward the problems of the popish minority.

Marvell emphasized the association of popery and arbitrary government in his best-known pamphlet. This tract appeared in part or in whole in many of the eighteenth-century histories of the reign of Charles II. The connection made between the Catholic religion and the growth of absolutism in France, a country represented as most dangerous both in foreign and domestic politics, was to find a wearisome echo in all Whig historical works for more than a hundred years. Since dislike of France was constant amongst the Whigs, Marvell's pamphlet found a popularity which it might have lost if a lasting entente between the two countries had developed from Walpole's determination to keep out of continental wars.

As Member for Hull for twenty years in the parliaments of Richard Cromwell, the Convention of 1660, and the Cavalier Parliament, Marvell was known to be rather lukewarm in his support of the restored monarchy, even in the honeymoon period of the Restoration, but discretion, talent, and friends secured him, in spite of service under the Protector, against any great inconvenience. Toward the end of his life he was drawn into the service of the Shaftesbury gang and is said to have written some party pamphlets for them. *The Growth of Popery* (1677) not only connected religion and absolutism; it also gave a rather one-sided account of the role played by the opposition in the parliament of that day. What is more, the *Seasonable Discourse* listed those members who had received government offices and pensions and had thus lost their independence as legislators. Accusations like these gave to the Cavalier Parliament its less complimentary name of "Pensioner." Marvell was a brilliant satirist and an able pamphleteer. His accusations were made with great skill and his victims have not yet entirely cleared their reputations of the crimes he listed. Moreover, his own fame has never been clouded by the faintest suggestion of dishonesty in an age when even a Sidney felt he could take money from the king of France. About Marvell there are many stories concerning his poverty, his excellent relations with his Hull constituents, his incorruptibility. His reputation as "honest Andrew Marvell" has endured. In the heyday of parliamentary corruption, Marvell's example and Marvell's diatribes against his less upright colleagues were a rallying point for all critics of the unreformed Commons.

General statements of the poet's political ideas were not particularly original though often worded with characteristic distinction of style and phrase. The prolegomena to the *Growth of Popery* summarized a concept of the constitution familiar to readers of Fortescue and Hooker as well as to the writers of the country party of their own day — the excellence of the courts, the laws which equally affected all and protected all, the king's power to do good and the responsibility of his ministers for any wrong decisions which were taken, and a legislature in which the meanest was represented. In general this account of the constitution would have been acceptable to all but the eccentric in the sixteenth, seventeenth, or eighteenth centuries. The emphasis upon liberty and property is faintly reminiscent to the modern reader of Locke and Fortescue. He repeated a passionate desire to see the purity of the constitution restored and to have a monarch ruling without a guard, that is to say, without an army or the councilors and placemen of whom Marvell disapproved, and in direct partnership with his people in parliament. Marvell himself most definitely belonged to a small group of members who long before they found powerful leaders were opposing various measures dear to the so-called "courtiers."

The *Last Instructions,* perhaps Marvell's earliest polemical work of any consequence, like his latest, *The Growth of Popery,* is an account of the many parties in parliament of which he disapproved. His highest praise was reserved for those who were "to no party sworn." This attitude toward party is quite typical of the age but is rather astonishing in a man of political acumen. He had shown in his description of Cromwell's regime as well as in his letters an appreciation of the function of difference of opinion in the fabric of the state. He watched men in the House of Commons change their seats as they changed their party, much as they would be obliged to do today, but he nowhere suggested a philosophy of party as an instrument of some use in a popular state.

Marvell's contribution to the Whig canon is threefold: denunciation of corruption and placemen, a plea for religious liberty, and the use of parliamentary reporting for party propaganda.[23] In the seventies, Danby wrote for Charles II a "Memo about the Booksellers." He said resolutions of parliament, speeches, and addresses were dispersed in certain booksellers' shops who thus "poison both city and country with false news," that is to say with "perfect true or artificially corrupted, or penned by halves on purpose as they make most for the faction."[24] Marvell's satire and pamphlets not only helped his party in this way, they also gained currency as reliable reports in the works of many later historians. His interpretation of the history of Charles II's parliaments in spite of frantic counterattacks from L'Estrange, Roger North, and other Tory commentators, remained the common and accepted view. "I fancy, Trimmer," L'Estrange prophesied in December, 1682, "that if You and I could but get leave to peep out of Our graves again in a matter of a hundred and fifty years hence, we should find *these Papers* in *Bodlies Library,* among the Memorials of State; and *Celebrated* for the *Only Warrantable Remains* concerning *this Juncture* of *Affairs.*"[25]

The Whigs of the Revolution and of the Sacheverell Trial

Whig and Commonwealthman in '88

The important actors in the drama of 1688 were great aristocrats and their confidants, churchmen, the ill-fated James himself, and his nephew, son-in-law, and successor, William of Orange. Historians have differed in their explanations and interpretations of the settlement peacefully achieved by the Glorious Revolution. Some have maintained that Commonwealth, almost republican ideas prevailed, disguised by monarchical forms and ceremonies. Others have argued that the Tory and churchly opponents of James's policies forced upon their Whiggish allies a considerable compromise with their principles. Leaving aside any attempt to adjudicate between different schools of thought, and ignoring all considerations of character and of conspiratorial activity, it may suffice here to note some matters on which there is fairly general agreement before analyzing ideas common among the Revolution Whigs.

The most important element in the contemporary scene was undoubtedly the fear, felt by nearly all Protestant Englishmen, of a Catholic king who increasingly showed a disposition to believe that his own ideas of right should prevail over all others—legal, religious, and parliamentary. The majority of Englishmen cherished a constitution which maintained a rule of law and in which a mixture of regal, aristocratic, and popular powers adequately secured their liberties and their property. Nearly all of them distrusted open party or faction, in court or country circles alike, declaring with varying degrees of sincerity or cynicism, their own lack of partisanship, and horror at the corruption it was thought to encourage among politicians. So much was common ground to an Evelyn, a Danby (whatever his own practice was), a Somers, a Shrewsbury, and a Wharton.

The theoretical basis or justification of the Revolution, however, was Whig. Tories might dwell on the event—on the danger to the church, on the dubious birth of the Prince, on the flight of James, on the unwillingness of his daughter, Mary, to accept anything less than regal status for her consort—but, outside of the "necessity" emphasized at the Sacheverell Trial and later by Burke in his *Appeal from the New to the Old Whigs,* produced no simple formula to explain the interruption of the succession. Explanations were, whether offered by Somers or Bolingbroke, inevitably Whig. The accomplishment of the Revolution for the Whigs rested securely upon a double basis of natural rights and contractual obligations. This was also true of Trimmers, like Halifax and Temple, standing somewhat outside the fracas but accepting its results without difficulty. Temple realized the need for variety in the forms of government. He saw virtues in many systems and theories. Although he emphasized the advantages of consent, he found distasteful any attempt to bring things "to the last extremity." Halifax, empirical in policies, but decisive in action, once convinced of necessity, declared his belief that:

> . . . there can be nothing *fixed,* but it must *vary* for the Good of the whole. A Constitution cannot make itself; somebody made it, not at once but at several times. It is alterable; and by that draweth nearer Perfection; and without suiting itself to differing Times and Circumstances, it could not live. Its life is prolonged by changing seasonably the several Parts of it at several times.[1]

Commonwealthmen found no difficulty in accepting revolution, but they had expected greater reformation in the governing system as a whole.

Commonwealthmen had had singularly little share in bringing William over in spite of the activities of Major John Wildman; of Charles Mordaunt, later earl of Monmouth and then of Peterborough; of Forde Grey, earl of Tankerville; and of the Hampden family, all of whom gave some signs of radical inclinations. Their hopes must have faded rapidly as the Convention debated. Popular enthusiasm had not been roused. When James, duke of Monmouth, had landed in 1685, he had attracted thousands of west country folk who were of a fanatic and republican temper. Many of them died in battle or by the vengeful sentences of Judge Jeffreys, leaving little but "dying speeches" behind them in a "Western Martyrology," and perhaps a legacy of political and religious dissent at such centers as Exeter and Taunton. There was almost no activity among their survivors in '88. Betrayed by Monmouth's kingly aspirations, by the misfortunes of war, poor leadership, and the enmity of their countrymen, they probably hoped nothing from the Dutch Deliverer. Farm labourers, artisans, and such persons as the men of Wapping of Rye House days no longer stirred.

In one sense then the Revolution might be said to end a political development. In another, by its success and by a general acceptance of its Whiggish rationalization, it made respectable eventually a large body of republican or Commonwealth writers. Even Burke paid a tribute to Milton. Locke and Sidney are often spoken of together. Summary consideration must now be given to the theories of the Revolution Whigs and those associated with them: the philosophers Locke, Newton, and Richard Cumberland and lesser luminaries like Tyrrell and the spokesmen against Dr. Sacheverell in 1710.

Locke and Newton

Locke was a determined Whig, though it is not easy to decide which of the many interpretations of his theories freely offered during the years since his death he would have endorsed. Nor can any simple progression or modification of his political theories be traced from his early association with the first earl of Shaftesbury, with Charles Mordaunt, and others of the more violent Whigs of the reign of Charles II, to his later intimacy with Somers and with Charles Montagu, earl of Halifax, the moderate statesmen of the reign of William III. He was a man of many friends at home and abroad, among politicians and among scientists and men of other learned interests. Among his acquaintance were Newton, Sydenham, and Molyneux; Thomas Herbert, earl of Pembroke; and the Mashams at whose house he lived. So were a host of younger people, for example Lady Masham's daughter; the

Clarkes for whom the *Education* was written; and Anthony Collins, the freethinker. Locke was an empiricist in more ways than one. Even in estimating his importance for a small fraction of his readers, the student is confronted by questions about his intentions, beliefs, and politics which cannot be answered certainly by a recital of his connection, or of the events of his life.[2]

Locke's education at Westminster and at Oxford was protracted. He enjoyed the teaching of such different men as Edward Pococke, Royalist and Oriental scholar; and John Owen, an important man among the independents. His father was on the parliamentary side, but his own reactions to the struggles of the Interregnum, save for an obvious impatience with Cromwell's dictatorial methods, are unknown. He was not a dissenter and may have contemplated at one time a career in the church. Not long after the Restoration, at the latest, he developed an interest in medicine which was to be lifelong. In 1665 he went abroad as secretary to Sir Walter Vane through the good offices of one of the Godolphins. On his return in 1666 he met Lord Ashley, afterwards the earl of Shaftesbury, and became his secretary, physician, and devoted adherent until death parted them in 1683. Even a prolonged stay in France from November, 1675, until May, 1679, interrupted only their personal contact and not their association.

The first draft of the *Letter* on toleration was written in the early days of this friendship and was certainly discussed by those persons in the earl's circle who were interested in better treatment for dissenters. Sometime before July, 1669, Ashley dictated to Locke *The Fundamental Laws of Carolina,* and some half dozen years later may have directed, if not actually dictated, the *Letter from a Person of Quality* (1675) which protested the second attempt of the government to impose an oath on Englishmen against innovations in church and state. During the early seventies Locke was already considering his own *Essay* on understanding, an enquiry into the problem of knowing, and discussing it with his friends. At an important moment in his own intellectual development he was closely associated with one of the most vigorous and versatile personalities of the day. Moreover his position at the Board of Trade in 1673 was due to Shaftesbury's influence and it was this that probably brought Locke to consider the problem of sound money and interest rates. On his return from France he rejoined the earl's "club of scribblers" which had produced the *Letter* in 1675 and with which such men as Andrew Marvell had been connected. He at once began to help with plans for the exclusion of James, Duke of York, from the throne.

It now seems reasonably certain that the earliest version of the *Treatises of Government*,[3] and a much longer one than that subsequently published, was written in connection with the controversy which produced such a wealth of important works and involved so varied a group. Locke was sufficiently implicated to find it expedient to leave England for Holland six months after the earl's death, during the discovery of the Rye in whose earlier stages his friend had certainly had a hand, and to remain there until the Glorious Revolution had been accomplished. Penn offered to secure his safety after James's accession, but he scorned a pardon for sins he felt he had not committed. He was interested in William's plans and intimate with men like Mordaunt, at this time perhaps as violent a Whig as anyone.

Locke came back after Somers and the Convention had offered the crown to William and Mary, and thus too late to have any hand in drafting the Bill of Rights. Lady Mordaunt wished her friend were there "to give them a right scheme of government, having been infected by that great man, Lord Shaftesbury." She, it seems, looked on the Convention as "an occasion not only of mending the government, but of melting it down and making all new." Yet there is no evidence that Locke saw either the opportunity or the occasion for radical change. On the eve of departure from Holland he wrote to Edward Clarke in terms which are Whiggish but not very revolutionary:

> People are astonished here to see them meddle with any small matters, and when the settlement of the nation upon the sure grounds of peace and security is put into their hands, which can no way so well be done as by restoring our ancient government; the best possible that ever was, if taken and put together all of a piece in its original constitution.[4]

Once settled in London under the rule of the Dutch Deliverer, Locke was openly a Whig and deeply committed to the cause of toleration. He probably hoped for a greater comprehension (as talked of in 1667) and for the safety and comfort of all god-fearing people whatever their shade of belief. His Latin *Letter* on toleration in duodecimo had been printed at Gouda earlier in 1689. Now an English translation appeared by William Popple—author of *A Rational Cate-chism*, nephew of Andrew Marvell, and later associated with Locke at the Board of Trade—no doubt with the intention of influencing the current discussions of what was to be done for the loyal dissenters from the Establishment. The act as passed had not "such breadth," Locke wrote to Limborch, "as you and true men like you free from Christian arrogance and hatred, would desire; but 'tis something to get anything. With these small beginnings I hope the foundations will be laid on which the church of Christ can be built up." Locke, with others, was obviously hoping that more concessions would be forthcoming, though he lived long enough to see an attempt at further constraint— the Occasional Bill of 1703—thrown out by a majority of twelve.[5]

Another aspect of Locke's public concern at this time was not only the drafting and publication of his thoughts on government in 1690, but his long memorandum, possibly for Somers, on the liberty of the press (dated by Fox-Bourne in 1694–95) which was probably a major factor in securing the death of the Licensing Act in 1695.[6] Both his literary and his public activities were largely devoted to the cause of liberty and his immense interest in its extension cannot be doubted. One of his later critics was to attribute to this insistence on religious freedom of thought and enquiry the revolutionary influence of his work in general.

Locke once more had friends high in the government. Somers and Montagu both carried great weight in national affairs. The former was distinguished by William's rare confidence, though he was not as influential in the years 1690 and 1691 as he was after he became Lord Keeper. Somers persuaded Locke to take the job of commissioner on the Board of Trade, not unlike his old position under Shaftesbury, and to keep it until his own fortunes were waning and Locke's health was failing in 1700. Another close associate was the Lord Privy Seal, earl of Pembroke. Locke was the confidant and adviser of the small Somers group or coterie in the Commons: Jekyll, Edward Clarke of Chipley (1651–1700), and Gilbert Heathcote, Member for London and a banker and merchant. He does not seem to have had any very close association with the discontented Whigs who began to attack Somers over the army business in 1697—Moyle, Trenchard, and their circle. It seems likely that he backed Somers in the controversy since William showed him signs of favour in that year. Locke concerned himself with economic and colonial problems, drawing on his earlier experience with Shaftesbury. He was free trader in money but a mercantilist in matters of trade. Perhaps he supported the Act against Irish Woollens which stirred his friend Molyneux to such eloquence in the *Case of Ireland,* but his attitude apparently did not mar the pleasure the friends enjoyed on their last meeting together later in 1698. Locke may have helped to prevent Molyneux's impeachment by the English Commons, but once more very little remains to trace his day-to-day reactions and activities in politics.[7]

Locke's health was poor though he survived the psalmist's allotted span by a year. He found a refuge from the air of London in the Essex home of the Mashams, where he resided when not obliged to be in the city about his business. There in 1704 he died whilst Lady Masham read the Bible to him. Locke's disciples, like Newton's, were often less than orthodox, though both sages were careful not to commit themselves to skeptical beliefs in their lifetime. Locke indignantly denied Toland's interpretation of *The Reasonableness of Christianity* (1695).

The body of works which occupied the philosopher in the seventies and saw publication in the nineties cannot be examined in detail. What must be established is Locke's connection with the Commonwealthmen of the generations after his own. A hundred years after his *Treatises of Government* were first projected, a work with a similar title was published by Dean Josiah Tucker, designed to expose the fallacies of Locke's politics and their mischievous effects. Tucker selected for quotation not only those passages he deemed specially relevant to his theme, but all those paragraphs from Molyneux, Priestley, and Price which revealed their indebtedness to Locke and thus illustrated the revolutionary character of his teaching. These were, he said:

> . . . Men whose Writings (we charitably hope, not intentionally, or maliciously;—though *actually*) have laid a Foundation for such Disturbances and Dissensions, such mutual Jealousies and Animosities, as Ages to come will not be able to settle, or compose.[8]

Tucker objected to what he thought a threefold fallacy—the theory of contract and its assumption that government was entirely artificial in origin; the belief that every individual had the inalienable right to choose or reject membership in a given society; the claim that everyone had the privilege of consenting or dissenting to all decisions of state. Moreover he felt that a "Lockian Republic" based on these delusions would not be content with their own form of liberty but would be indefatigable in disturbing the repose of others and incessant in exciting subjects to rebel. This may indeed, he prophesied, be the future role of the new American state. The Reverend Benjamin Turner not only attributed similar sentiments to Locke but connected him, though he was careful to say that his followers might have misinterpreted him, with the idea of universal suffrage. Both men deplored the extent of Locke's influence and the weight of his authority. In his anger at the American declarations of rights, Tucker failed to give Locke his due in achieving that English freedom of podium and press of which he was to boast in his conclusion that English slavery was preferable to American liberty.

> I find, that here in *England,* a Man may say or do, may write or print, a thousand Things with the utmost Security, for which his Liberty and Property, and even his Life itself would be in the most imminent Danger, were he to do the like in *America.*[9]

Before examining Locke's statements on natural rights and on government it should be clearly stated that he had no sentimental attachment to Commonwealth experiments, and he scarcely mentioned the classical republicans in his work. He was more obviously influenced by Hobbes than by Harrington or Milton. He probably never read Sidney's *Discourses.* Much of his theory was derived from English constitutional tradition and much from the "Judicious" Hooker. Though the *Reasonableness of Christianity* was somewhat unorthodox, Locke was not a dissenter from the Establishment. He owed something to the Latitude men, something to continental Arminianism. His belief in reason, the whole structure of his philosophic thought, left little room for the mysteries of priestcraft and anathemas for the damned. But his approach, for example, to censorship and toleration is different in spirit from Milton's and owes more to the skeptical tradition than to the poet's *Areopagitica.* Even his interest in biblical scholarship is different from the pieties of Praisegod Barebones. Typical of the age and day, but not especially Puritan, such pious researches distinguish English from continental rationalism throughout the eighteenth century. Though the doctrine of natural rights was to provide ample ammunition for reformers thereafter who might be considered democratical, there is almost nowhere in the *Treatises* any indication of interest in the "dregs of society." Locke, like his friend, Thomas Firmin, would put the poor to profitable work, and reorganize the century-old Elizabethan poor law. But he referred scornfully to Masaniello, the rebellious fisherman of Naples, and never to the egalitarian schemes of the Interregnum.[10]

His *Treatises* were more enigmatic than the longer *Discourses* of Sidney, in part because less lavish in illustration and reference. He was cautious nearly always where Sidney was rash. Both were believers in the natural rights of man; both believed in the need for careful readjustment of government when the balance of property had changed or when wastes had become powerful cities. Both emphasized the contractual nature of society. Locke seemed less interested in the warlike state than Sidney. He wished to avoid war, particularly civil war in which Sidney seemed often to glory, like Cromwell, regarding victory as a proof of divine approval. Though modern Marxists have strained interpretation too far in claiming Locke as their ancestor, especially in his doctrine of the value and rights of labour, there is some justification for stating that Locke's emphasis throughout is on the preservation of property, that is, on the economic motive in society.[11] But in this, as in his insistence on a rule of law, he is in direct descent himself from a long English legalist tradition upheld by Fortescue, Hooker, Hampden, Coke.

Locke stressed the natural equality of man, both in his psychological and his political pronouncements. He recognized the common obligations of all alike, rulers and ruled, to obey the law of nature, as well as the rules established by society after it has been formed. Once formed, that society chose its own particular form of government which might indeed have been of many kinds. On the whole that was best which best preserved property from depredation and which allowed some opportunity for the legislative body, the lawgiving organ, to be frequently renewed by the consent or franchise of the community it served. He admitted the need for a prerogative. He never suggested a fundamental unalterable system. The virtue of leaving something to the discretion of the ruler, granted recognition of the supremacy of natural law, was always understood. Sharply defined rules for the meeting and dissolution of the English parliament might be difficult to formulate.[12]

On the other hand a popular mandate, to use a phrase he would not have thought of, should be frequently renewed or the representative itself might be corrupted. Locke hinted, less frankly than Sidney, at the bribery and pensions of Charles's Long Parliament. The power of the people to elect a new legislative when the old has acted contrary to interest was the best fence against rebellion that could be set up. If the prince or the managers of affairs were guilty of a long train of abuses, prevarication, and artifices, and no other remedy existed— like a new parliament—trouble was likely to develop. Such "stirs" proceeded, not from variety of religious belief and worship, but from the "common disposition of all mankind who, when they groan under any heavy burthen, endeavour naturally to shake off the yoke that galls their necks."[13]

People were not so easily shaken out of their old forms as some were apt to suggest. They were hardly to be prevailed upon to amend the acknowledged faults in the frame to which they had been accustomed.[14] In the many revolutions in England, he noted, people had never changed the line nor departed from King, Lords, and Commons for long. There might have been less danger in encouragement of reform of grievances than in the apathy and submissiveness of the people under nearly all circumstances. The end of government was the good of mankind; and what was best for mankind? Should the people always be exposed to the boundless will of tyranny, or should rulers sometimes be liable to opposition when they grew exorbitant in the use of their power, and employed it for the destruction, and not the preservation, of the properties of their people?[15] This could as easily have been applied to James in 1680 or in 1689.

These, then, were the natural rights doctrines and implications full of potential timber for the revolutionaries. There was, more important after the eighteenth century than during its course, the Lockian theory of labour and the value it gives to products as well as the title it affords to property. This led to claims of egalitarian equality which perhaps Locke did not foresee and might not have approved had he anticipated them. Lastly, though it also sprang from the natural right to consent, must be considered his most specific discussion of conquest and government since it enormously strengthened his general, if often guarded, approval of revolution.

Conquest could destroy a commonwealth and thus make way for a new one. Without the consent of the people concerned, conquest alone could never erect a permanent, legal government. Conquest gave no title. In the most moving passage in the *Treatise* Locke entirely demolished the idea that "robbers and pirates have a right of empire over whomsoever they have force enough to master; or that men are bound by promises which unlawful force extorts from them." The only difference between a petty housebreaker and a crowned conqueror was that "great robbers punish little ones to keep them in their obedience, but the great ones are rewarded with laurels and triumphs because they are too big for the weak hands of justice in the world." Locke went on to say that the conquered could have no remedy but patience. They and their children "have no court, no arbitrator on earth to appeal to. Then they may appeal, as Jephthah did, to Heaven, and repeat their appeal until they have recovered the native right of their ancestors, which was to have such a legislative over them as the majority should approve." Conquest by an unjust war conferred no title to the obedience of the conquered.[16]

Locke then discussed conquest in a lawful war. He suggested that in some cases conquered and conqueror might incorporate into one people, as had the Normans and the Saxons. If they did not, the rule was purely despotical. Conquerors seldom troubled to make these distinctions, but they were nevertheless true. Moreover, though the lives of his victims might be at his disposal, the wives and children of the conquered could not be lawfully taken. Even in a just war there could be no right of dominion over posterity and these would have liberty if they had power to elect another government. The inhabitants of any country who were descended from conquered people retained a right to the possessions of their ancestors. Locke illustrated his remark by saying that no one could possibly doubt that Greek Christians, "descendants of the ancient possessors of that country, may justly cast off the Turkish yoke which they have so long groaned under, whenever they have an opportunity to do it."[17] Chapter sixteen contained in it, forcefully and clearly expressed, all the doctrine that revolutionaries needed. Molyneux was to write to Locke that he heard that the *Treatises of Civil Government* were his and that they were something no one need be ashamed of writing; what is more, the views expressed in them were the views applied not to Greek Christians, but to Anglo-Irishmen in his own *Case of Ireland* (1698), to be considered in its Irish context later.

Newton's achievement, like that of his friend and contemporary, was stupendous. Neither can be confined to one party or period. Nor can either be regarded simply as scientist, philosopher, politician, or heretic, to name but a few of the roles they played. Newton's authority was used to support a wide variety of arguments, not all of which were relevant. J. T. Desaguliers, chaplain to the Duke of Chandos and a scientist of some standing, wrote an allegorical poem, *The Newtonian System of the World, the Best Model of Government* (1728), which sounds promising. In fact, it was no more than a plea on the accession of George II for order and harmony in the ancient government of England currently disturbed by jarring parties. Newtonian science did not produce a universal political law, but it was constantly an influence on developing liberal thought.

The circumstances of Newton's career, the peculiarities of his character, and the contradictions that may be found in the legend of his fame have confused judgment about him and thus about his effect on succeeding generations. At all times the precise point of contact and relevance between scientific discovery and the ferment of political and philosophical speculation is difficult to place. Newton's timidity, his reluctance to engage in controversy, and determination to avoid trouble in his lifetime, have combined to complicate all considerations of his reputation.

His life was divided into two sharply contrasting periods. Before his illness in 1692 he had written not only all of the work for which he is famous, but had also committed to manuscript millions of words which were never published on matters theological and magical, which Lord Keynes's efforts recently restored to a resting place in a Cambridge repository.[18] The *Principia* appeared in 1687. Although the *Optics* was not to appear before 1704, it was composed in the twelve years after

1675. Newton's last lectures were given just before the appearance of the *Principia*. He was at that time obstructing the efforts of James II to nominate his candidates to positions at Cambridge. In 1689 he represented the university in parliament. His correspondence attests his interest in the success of the Revolution and his reflections upon de facto monarchs. He was a Whig.[19] His acquaintances, Locke, Somers, and Montagu, were successful in getting his appointment to the job at the Mint which he held the rest of his life.

At the Mint Newton was a conscientious civil servant and carried out the coinage reform already projected.[20] He became wealthy. Although he is said to have solved some difficult mathematical problems about this time and early in the reign of George, he does not appear ever to have made any very great intellectual effort again outside of certain revisions of his works. His niece, Catherine Barton, a brilliant and popular woman, looked after his domestic affairs. He in turn saw to it that when she became Montagu's mistress, she was properly provided for. When Halifax was dead and Catherine married John Conduitt,[21] Newton left his effects, including the manuscripts, to them. His disciples had meanwhile carried on his work. Dr. Samuel Clarke translated the *Optics* into Latin in 1706 and defended Newton later against Leibnitz. Roger Cotes, Henry Pemberton, and Colin Maclaurin edited and commented upon the *Principia*. William Whiston, his successor in the Lucasian chair, taught his system until anti-Trinitarianism resulted in expulsion from the university. Newton dropped his acquaintance and Whiston lived out a long life in London teaching mathematics and trying to push his less courageous friends into open avowal of their views.

Pemberton indignantly denied rumours that Newton had not understood his own mathematics in the years before his death.[22] Perhaps the younger enthusiast read into dignity and silence an intellectual activity which was in fact not there. Lord Keynes suggests that Newton was slightly "gaga" though perfectly competent to perform his job, to assume some public duties like that of the presidency of the Royal Society, and to invest his funds profitably. Whatever the case, Newton kept his counsel about the heresies he had written earlier in life. From his niece and her husband he probably had no secrets. His associates, like Hopton Haynes at the Mint, like Samuel Clarke, were not rash enough to follow Whiston's example, but they were certainly suspect to the orthodox. Nevertheless, as Newton's fame grew, the orthodox claimed him. He did nothing to contradict them, and the delays of the family after his death eventually resulted in a genuine conspiracy by the heirs to keep his heterodoxy hidden. Yet the manuscripts make certain what Newton's associations in his lifetime might, even without contemporary rumour and remark, have caused us to suspect.

Newton was, moreover, passionately interested in primitive Christianity and in biblical commentary. His letters to Locke, and *The Chronology of Ancient Kingdoms Amended* (1728) clearly illustrate this preoccupation of the first half of his life. Lord Keynes remarks on the combination in his personality of Faustus and Copernicus. Keenly curious about alchemy, he liked to guess, to intuit, in spite of his reiterated insistence upon the method to be followed in the pursuit of truth. These Socinian, Arian, and Unitarian beliefs did not preclude a vigorous piety and an insistence upon the importance of searching the Scriptures. Even the last was feared by the orthodox. The second half of Newton's life was to see a fierce pamphlet warfare between the Athanasians of the period and the searchers, like Whiston, for the truths of what they felt to be primitive Christianity. Whiston met with a group of his friends—among whom should be noted Arthur Onslow, the famous Speaker of mid-century—to discuss these matters. It is not without interest, therefore, that Onslow much later told Egmont that Sir Isaac Newton thought antichrist came in with the modern doctrine of the Trinity and that Dr. Clarke was of the same opinion. Was Onslow, too, among these prophets?[23] Were Jekyll and Peter King joined with them?

Whether the New Science, of which Newton was the chief oracle, was responsible for these heresies in himself and in so many of his followers, or whether both developments were simultaneous manifestations of the spirit of the age, may not be decided arbitrarily. Newton's discoveries endowed the universe with a general order. He connected earth and heaven in a vast unity working according to discoverable laws. Descartes had done much to free inquiry from restrictions. Newton freed scientists from Cartesian assumptions. His principles made dogmatism and intolerance impossible. They imposed upon philosophers new responsibilities and new methods. They must now reëxamine the unity of Creation. They must have courage to avoid arbitrary conclusions.

Newton's inspiration to others derived as much from his supreme faith as from his inventions and discoveries. In his first preface to the *Principia* he wrote with confidence in the eventual result of free investigation. "The errors are not in the art but in the artificers."[24] So he proposed to lay a "solid foundation to the most noble speculations,"[25] and was sure that these would be endlessly rewarding. God was in truth known by "his wise and excellent contrivance of things and final causes." To seek him "from the appearance of things, does certainly belong to Natural Philosophy."[26] He will be recognized by his deeds. The system Newton was exploring could only, he was certain, have proceeded "from the counsel and dominion of an intelligent and powerful Being."[27] He proved to his own satisfaction at least that truth was God and God was truth.

Freedom of opinion and enquiry thus became a necessity for the pious scientists.

> An entire liberty must be allowed in our enquiries, that natural philosophy may become subservient to the most valuable purposes; and acquire all the certainty and perfection of which it is capable; but we ought not to abuse this liberty by *supposing* instead of *enquiring,* and by imagining systems, instead of learning from observation and experience the true constitution of things.[28]

The rules of reasoning in philosophy laid down in the *Principia* are four in number, and are designed to show how far universals may be deduced.[29] Maclaurin, the Scottish disciple, thus described the groundwork of his master's philosophy:

> The tracing of the chain of causes is the most noble pursuit of philosophy; but we meet with no cause but what is itself, to be considered as an effect, and are able to number but few links of the chain. In every kind of magnitude, there is a degree or sort to which our sense is proportion'd, the preception and knowledge of which is of the greatest use to mankind. The same is the groundwork of Philosophy; for tho' all sorts and degrees are equally the object of philosophical speculation; yet it is from those which are proportioned to

sense that a philosopher must set out in his enquiries, ascending or descending afterwards as his pursuits may require. He does well indeed, to take his views from many points of sight, and supply the defects of sense by a well regulated imagination; nor is he to be confined by any limit in space or time: but as his knowledge of nature is founded on the observation of sensible things, he must begin with these, and must often return to them, to examine his progress by them. Here is his secure hold; and as he sets out from thence, so if he likewise trace not often his steps backwards with caution, he will be in hazard of losing his way in the labyrinths of nature.[30]

The limitations of our perception of God are many. Place and time perplex us.

These things, however, do not hinder but we may learn to form great and just conceptions of him from his sensible works, where an art and skill is express'd that is obvious to the most superficial spectator, surprises the most experienced enquirer, and many times surpasses the comprehension of the profoundest philosopher. From what we are able to understand of nature, we may entertain the greater expectations of what will be discovered to us, if ever we shall be allowed to penetrate to the first cause himself, and see the whole scheme of his works as they are really derived from him, when our imperfect philosophy shall be completed.[31]

Anyone who read Maclaurin on Newton, or who studied for himself the *Principia* and in particular its general statements about method, was likely, I think, to be encouraged in the free exercise of scholarly curiosity, and in claims for complete liberty for such activities. They were in general certain to be impressed with the unity of everything in God and from God. They might follow Newton in his courageous willingness to leave uncertain those matters he felt insufficiently proven. Though some commentators misunderstood his writing, Newton did not even make gravity a dogmatic principle, and was careful to notice the difficulty of explaining its nature as an attraction, a force or a property of some sort.[32]

His influence was twofold. His disciples looked for fuller explanations of the universe so immensely illuminated by his discoveries, and hoped to find by analogy and by similar methods, natural laws even in other than natural sciences. Then, in the second place they continued his faith that observation and experiment of the freest kind, and with as few presuppositions, would eventually redound to the glory of God and the clarification of truth and they were therefore prepared for skepticism of a most fundamental kind.

Newton made great and important scientific contributions. His faith encouraged optimism about all intellectual activity. His method, engaged in with supreme confidence, enforced the skepticism and empiricism of the age. The student into whose hands the *Principia* was placed was not only exposed to its mathematical contents, but to the enquiring philosophy of its author. He was likely, if his bent was in any way speculative, to explore the nature and validity of old and new beliefs with freedom. The Unitarianism or rationalism of the eighteenth century was encouraged by the study of the Newtonian Universe and the essential unity and harmony of all its parts, whether or no the true story of Newton's own theological conclusions was known. With this undogmatic but pious development also went inevitably the demands for the extension of civil as well as religious liberty. The dignity acquired by Renaissance man was immensely enhanced by the achievements of the science of the Enlightenment. Optimism increased. Without faith in individual reason and the likelihood of right action developing from its unhampered exercise, no movement for widespread political rights and privileges could gain many adherents.

James Tyrrell and Richard Cumberland, Bishop of Peterborough

James Tyrrell (1642–1718) was the friend and popularizer both of Locke and of Cumberland, as well as a polemicist in his own right and an amateur historian. He was the grandson of Archbishop James Ussher, a Londoner by birth, an Oxonian by education, and a resident of Buckinghamshire for long periods of his life. As already noticed, he started his literary career during the Exclusion controversy with *Patriarcha Non Monarcha* (1681); he continued it in 1692 with *A Brief Disquisition*, an abridgment and translation of Cumberland's *Laws of Nature*, and with his *Bibliotheca Politica* (1718 and 1727), first published shortly after the Revolution in the form of fourteen *Dialogues* between Meanwell, a Tory, and Freeman, a Whig. In this he puts forward Locke's views in simpler, though more verbose, terms and with an emphasis on the essentially moderate character of Whig policies. His work repays rereading for the light it throws not only on the governing Whigs, but on the social ideas of the period.[33]

The *Bibliotheca* is much more conservative than Locke's *Treatises.* Tyrrell asked whether or not monarchy be jure divino, or whether, from natural or revealed law, an absolute succession may ever be established. The crux of the question is not really the lawfulness of resistance, but as the endless dialogues between Meanwell and Freeman revealed, the antiquity, nature, position, and power of parliament. Ultimately, where does the supreme power lie? In parliament or in the king? Can they act separately or legally? Historical examples of changes in the English constitution from the days of the Anglo-Saxons are given. Even William, the Norman, used phrases paying lip service at least to the supremacy of English law. His descendants, John and his son Henry, a century and a half later agreed to the provisions of Magna Carta which, even Mr. Meanwell conceded, was hallowed by the veneration of many English generations. The argument of Freeman was that the royal oath obliged the king to keep his compact with his people. If he broke his word, valid steps might be taken by the Lords and the Commons to secure the country against tyranny or irreligion. The king of this realm was not the sole supreme power thereof. Neither had he ever been.[34]

Tyrrell is mildly convincing when he argues about the events in his own times. His presentation of Meanwell's argument is fair. The Tory maintained that in certain acts in the reign of Charles II, all resistance was expressly forbidden, that parliament had disclaimed coercive power over the king, and moreover, in the Militia Acts, parliament again not only denied its own right to levy war against the monarch, but imposed an oath to be taken by all lieutenants, deputies, and soldiers, which abhorred the traitorous position that arms may be taken up against him.[35] Freeman rather disingenuously replied that if you were going to take all that parliament did as sacred you would have to take the condemnation of Charles I by the fag end of parliament, a Rump, as sacred too. Freeman explained that oaths imposed at the

Restoration only included offensive action: they were never intended to turn the kingdom into a despotic monarchy like that of the kings of France or the Grand Turk. The Houses might very well have renounced the power of making war against the king, and yet have left themselves the right of resistance for self-defense.[36]

When religion, property, or the safeguards of law are in danger, then there is a right to take steps to secure them. Tyrrell did not subscribe to the doctrine that Sidney put forward, that any man may kill a tyrant. Indeed he went out of his way to say that individual resistance or assassination was not lawful. He does not describe precisely the combination of persons on whom such duties devolve. Certainly the "Immortal Seven," who invited William to come over, were wealthy and important enough to act as they did. Parliaments composed of lords and men of substance, speaking for the country as a whole, certainly had the power to legalize revolutions.[37]

No law or action could be legal without parliamentary sanction. It is rather surprising to find that Tyrrell did not feel that illegal taxation afforded a sufficient pretext for rebellion.[38] Hampden's case cropped up in the discussion between Freeman and Meanwell and, while Tyrrell quite obviously considered Charles arbitrary and the judge's decision unjust, he was still very careful to point out that the outbreak of civil war some years after the Ship Money case, was the result of parliamentary attempts to control the militia, legally a royal prerogative. Tyrrell may have been Cavalier in his sympathies. He may only have tried to avoid offending the old Royalist. Charles, he pointed out, though often wrong, was as frequently sinned against. He was very critical of rule by Independent and Cromwellian, though he did not admit that the Presbyterians were antimonarchical. When taxed with a parallel between the situation in '41 and in '89, he refused to allow its validity. A better comparison, he thought, could be found with the events of 1660, when a convention called by somewhat irregular parliamentary writs was legalized ex post facto by Charles II's government.[39]

This seems very mediocre Whiggery. The theory was aristocratic though Tyrrell emphasized a natural right to self-defense, even in the relations of wives with their husbands and children with their parents. He may on occasion seem rather revolutionary,[40] but he never considered in any detail at all the position in the state of men who were not gentry. It is quite obvious that he repudiated the idea that the meaner sort of person should have any power at all. Rebellions like those of Wat Tyler and Masaniello[41] were not the work of the major part of England or Italy. By this Tyrrell was not referring to the majority, but to those with whom the balance of land and other riches lay. He might include yeomen or substantial farmers, but villeins or cottagers were excluded from political power. The more vulgar or plebeian sort were represented in parliament but had absolutely no voice in it.[42]

The cautiousness of the Dialogues was typical of many who supported the Revolution. Here was the difference between a Tory revolutionist and a Whig resister, as John Withers pointed out in 1715. Harley and Shrewsbury had joined William in 1688; Harcourt had accepted the Settlement. The first Sunderland had lost his life at Newbury; Devonshire's grandfather suffered exile during the Puritan victory. Bolton's noble ancestor defended Basing House; Cowper's grandfather died in a republican prison. An earlier Derby had died on the scaffold in 1651. All the Godolphins were Cavaliers. Could these men be regarded as rebels? Tyrrell and many of his Whig associates felt that they could not. It was quite plain that resistance by such persons together with men like Tillotson and Tenison could only be for the happiness of the whole nation.[43]

Any sympathy with more radical ideas must be sought in *A Brief Disquisition,* but this is a philosophic discussion of the nature of man and the attributes of Providence based on the Platonism of Cumberland and the psychology of Locke. So far as Tyrrell himself is concerned, his politics were aristocratic and as little Whiggish as the circumstances of the Revolution would allow. The *Disquisition* admirably illustrates the close connection between even moderate Whiggism and the natural rights doctrines. These were bound to be regarded as strengthening Revolution politics and perhaps it was not quite as apparent to Tyrrell as later to Burke that this association with the "pretended rights of man" also reinforced the argument of those who equated Whig and libertarian.

De Legibus Naturae (1672) appeared as one of the many refutations of the theories of Thomas Hobbes. Its learned author, Richard Cumberland, was born in London in 1631, educated at St. Paul's and at Cambridge, and commenced his career in the church at a rather slow rate of advancement until the Revolution made his well-known sentiments against popery popular in government circles. He was promoted to the bishopric of Peterborough in 1691 and held it until his death in 1718, the year in which Tyrrell also died. Tyrrell's abridgment and translation, *A Brief Disquisition,* appeared twice in 1692 and 1701. The longer work was reprinted in Latin, German, English, and French at least seven times before the eighteenth century ended.[44] Only Henry More and Benjamin Whichcote among the Cambridge Platonists enjoyed as continuing a reputation, though they did not attract as large a public as Cumberland. The Platonists were optimists and interpreted both divine and human nature benevolently. They saw in the moral sense or conscience of man a force which needed only liberty and education to function in the regulation of social conduct as well or better than any dogmatic theological discipline. Cumberland in his vast disorderly book not only explained fully these ideas, but expanded earlier conceptions of the laws of nature. He was also claimed by the later utilitarians as one of their predecessors. Cumberland thus combined in his own philosophy theories which were to have immense influence over both natural rights liberalism and utilitarian radicalism.

Much could be said about his study of Descartes, of Gassendi, and Dutch writers of his century, as well as of the great classical tradition. His reading as well as his subtleties as a philosopher are both less important in the present context than his reflections on the nature of God, the laws by which he governed, and the character, objectives, and duty of mankind. Cumberland wrote to refute Hobbes's contention that the prime aim of man is to get what he individually wants, man in a state of nature being completely selfish. Cumberland, on the contrary, believed that mankind sincerely wanted to promote the common good. Sympathy was human and made society possible, man being a rational creature who saw in the identity of his own interests and the happiness of society a fundamental agreement. What we want and what we believe to be good, and this is self-evident, is that which enlarges the faculties and increases the happiness of all rational creatures. In this there is some agreement between Cumberland

and Grotius, but Cumberland emphasized rather more strongly the law of nature as the foundation of moral civil knowledge which may be deducted from its manifold effects. He thought Hobbes's principles were entirely destructive. The Bishop, with Grotius, felt that there was an essential morality, enforced by circumstance and conscience, which ensured a more solid foundation for civil government than Hobbes's formulae provided. Cumberland believed that the general principles of political action should be studied through our understanding of the nature of the Almighty and His creatures.

Cumberland was one of the earliest exponents both of the new optimism and of the utilitarian concept, that is, of the greatest good as the criterion by which government and human action must be judged. Earlier than Shaftesbury he propounded a concept of virtue, the identification of virtue, benevolence, or beauty, and a discovery of virtue in the harmony of nature. The sum of our pleasure must be found in the harmony of God's creation and the law of reason which preserved and motivated it. Cumberland exalted man, the only creature conscious of his own existence and thus able as a rational being to be aware of his place in the universe and his duty toward God. The law of nature was indeed revealed to him in the dictates of right reason. Happiness lay in association to obtain common felicity. Cumberland reasoned that even in a state of nature, possibly before civil government existed, there were obligations both to each other and toward the Creator.

Two things emerge from even the briefest summary of Cumberland's ideas: his emphasis upon the common good of rational beings, and his insistence on right reason. These were bound, as they were studied and accepted, to lead to further consideration of the vast numbers of common men, since the sum of their happiness was the criterion of good government. The emphasis on right reason, on the duty of developing that rational capacity which distinguished man from animal, and which enabled him to recognize the laws of nature, led to a greatly increased emphasis on the necessity of developing every individual understanding. Though Cumberland propounded no political plan for an egalitarian utopia, he provided almost as essential a part of the philosophical presuppositions of the reformers as his contemporaries, John Locke and Isaac Newton.[45]

John, Lord Somers, and the Whigs of the Sacheverell Trial

Somers was by no means anxious to combat the divine-right theories of Henry Sacheverell in the high court of Parliament. He regarded the impeachment in 1710 of that highchurchman as impolitic. Nevertheless, in considering the statements made in 1710 about the Revolution as expositions of accepted Whig theory, it is nearly impossible to omit some summary of what may be gathered about the ideas of the architect of the Bill of Rights, the Triennial Act, the Treason Act, and of at least parts of the Act of Settlement. Somers remains something of a puzzle. In mid-eighteenth century a fire destroyed many of his papers. The remainder were published by the Hardwickes but do not answer all questions. No good modern life or bibliographical study exists, although all works on the period refer to him. Brief memoirs appeared shortly after his death, and at the end of the eighteenth century. Tracts he is thought to have written achieved wide currency in England and in the American colonies, but conclusive evidence about his share in them is hard to find. The Exclusion tracts already mentioned are usually attributed to him; and *The Judgment of Whole Kingdoms,* connected with the trial of Sacheverell, though sometimes thought to have been from the pen of Defoe, nevertheless follows his theories, incorporates the Bill of Rights in its text, and may be considered here as a part of Somers's works.[46]

The Somers family owned White Ladies near Worcester and were from Gloucestershire. John's father, a lawyer, is said to have fired off a pistol in church as a protest against a sermon on divine right. His son sat under Dr. Bright at a school in Worcester, entered Trinity College, Oxford, in 1667, and in 1669 was entered at Middle Temple where he studied with Francis Winnington and with Joseph Jekyll who managed the Shrewsbury estates. Jekyll's son and namesake (1663–1738) married Somers's sister. Another sister married a Cocks and had a daughter who married Philip Yorke, the first earl of Hardwicke, eventually his uncle's heir. Somers briefly returned to Oxford, but qualified for the bar in 1676.

About this time he met Shaftesbury, Russell, Sidney, and Sir William Jones as well as the Onslow family and began his long association with and work for the Whigs. He was an exclusionist. He was employed in the trials for rioters in the London elections (1681). He acted as junior counsel for the seven bishops in 1688 and their acquittal is attributed in part to his skill. The historian Tindal included Somers amongst those privy to the plan for bringing William over and, as a friend of Shrewsbury, he may well have known of the letter sent by the Immortal Seven. It was in 1689 in the Convention that Somers began the most important phase of his career. He spoke on limited monarchy. He drew up the Commons resolution. He managed the conference with the Lords and successfully steered the Houses into the compromise statement which brought about agreement on the Bill of Rights and on the offer to William and Mary. He became Solicitor General and Attorney General in 1692. He was appointed Lord Keeper in 1693, and his influence over William smoothed the eventual passage of the Triennial Bill. His voice tipped the scales against a place bill and for a royal veto of a qualification bill. He was for moderation in the disbandment of forces after the Peace of Ryswick and almost certainly wrote the sensible *Balancing Letter* in reply to the cries of Trenchard's coterie against standing armies. The Treasons Act was supported by him. He and Montagu encouraged the reform of coinage and saw to it that the talents of Locke and Newton were employed by the government.

After the Tory reaction of '98 his influence was never the same, although the clause in the Act of Settlement about the tenure of judges is credited to him. His judgment in the Bankers Case was reversed. He regained some of the popularity he had lost during the disputes over the partition treaties by his work for the rights of electors, however humble, in the case of Ashby *v.* White. As the connection formed that supported the war and opposed Tory efforts to reduce the toleration granted in 1689, Somers's star rose again and, in spite of the Queen's dislike, he became Lord President of the council in 1708. He did not, as already noted, approve Godolphin's pushing proceedings against the Tory doctor, though it was at the time of Sacheverell's trial that *The Judgment* appeared and began its long career as a Whig manifesto.[47] During the remainder of his life he enjoyed poor health and was in virtual retirement, though he lived to sit on the Hanoverian Privy Council.

Somers was a statesman. He was a Whig, unwavering in his allegiance to Revolution politics. Much of the discussion of the time turned on the succession and divine right. Somers maintained that of course people could change their rulers if they were tyrannical. History supported their claim. The Jews changed their government. The English several times found it necessary to change theirs. God's blessing had rested equally on them under the Heptarchy and the Normans, as it had rested on the Italians under the Romans and under the multitude of modern states. Fifty kings and eleven emperors could be cited. "'Tis plain . . . that all Government Authority and Magistracy, proceeds from the People."[48]

The Judgment followed Locke—Somers's friend—in accepting limited government as most conversant with the laws of nature. Only those could be entrusted with government who,

> . . . having the greatest interest in the Nation, were most concerned to preserve its Power, Liberty and Welfare. This is the greatest Trust that can be reposed in Men. This Power was, by the *Spartans,* given to the *Ephori,* and the Senate of twenty-eight; in *Venice,* to that which they call *Concilio de Pregadi;* in *Germany, Spain, France, Sweedland, Denmark, Poland, Hungary, Bohemia, Scotland, England;* and generally all the Nations that have lived under the *Gothick Polity,* it has been in their General Assemblies; under the Names of *Diets, Cortes, Parliaments, Senates* and the like.[49]

This is the same argument fundamentally which Somers had used in the *Brief History of the Succession* (1681), that "the constant opinion of all ages [has been] that the Parliament of England had an unquestionable power to limit, restrain, and qualify the succession as they pleased." It is interesting to note that he there cites the Catholic martyrs, More and Fisher, who would not deny Papal Supremacy by swearing to Henry's, but were prepared to swear to the succession of any heir selected by Parliament.[50]

In none of the tracts nor any of those utterances which have come down to us does Somers appear radical in his ideas. His opposition to an increased property qualification for members of parliament in William's reign may indicate some concern lest the parliamentary system become too aristocratic, just as his stand in the case of Ashby *v.* White was on the popular side. As the friend of Locke he probably not only assisted in freeing the press from restrictions, but would have increased the freedom allowed rather grudgingly by the Toleration Act. He was interested in just and modest government by King, Lords, and Commons. Government was natural; it could be moulded to suit different nations, could be varied to suit time and circumstance. No nation needed to submit to a ruler of a different religion than their own, nor to a ruler that had violated the law by aiming to govern by despotic power. In everything we know about Somers we see the statesman and the temperate supporter of a constitution which secured lives, liberties, and properties, provision for common benefit, freedom for all men to speak what they pleased and thought, and a fair trial for all men accused of sins against society. Such sentiments must always be an honour to the Whig tradition.[51]

The prosecution of Sacheverell[52] ran counter to Somers's ideas of free speech but the arguments of the trial provide, as has long been recognized, a classical exposition of the politics of the warring parties. There is no need to do more than illustrate this. Dr. Henry Sacheverell had preached a sermon in which were propounded doctrines of divine right and passive obedience. The doctrine of the Church of England, dissent from which was a sin not to be countenanced by sincere believers, included belief in nonresistance to constituted powers. He had made hysterical remarks, which revealed misunderstanding of the nature of the English constitution, about the insecurity of the church, particularly under a Whig administration in 1709. What is more, he obviously disavowed any belief in the legality of toleration for Protestant dissenters, in spite of the act passed at the Revolution. Sacheverell tried to hedge in any remarks about the actual events of 1689. William came armed in the previous year, the doctor said, merely to defend his rights, and not to assist the English in any resistance. Reluctantly Sacheverell accepted the fact of the Revolution but not the logical justification for it. He did not admit the right of the subject, even *in extremis,* to resist established power. Yet, without this admission it was quite impossible to regard the government of his own day as anything but a usurpation.

Sacheverell, whatever the illogicality of his position, undoubtedly represented the ideas of the Queen and of many Englishmen. The sweeping victory of the Tories in the next election was in part due to a desire for peace and to public fatigue over even Marlborough's victories in the War of Spanish Succession, and in part to sympathy for Sacheverell. The victory of the Commons at his trial when they impeached him at the Bar of Westminster Hall before the Peers, was by no means paralleled by a wave of public approval for their action. Many Englishmen probably believed more strongly than earlier that church and state were separate parts of the same constitution and that the doctrines of one were essential to the preservation of the other. There was no logic in this position, but it appealed to many who never really dreamed of bringing back the Stuarts, or allowing their ruler to do what he liked.

At the trial no levelling or reforming Whig ideas were put forward. The Whigs merely contended that Sacheverell removed all grounds for support of the revolutionary settlement. He was said to have condemned the right to effect that revolution—that is, resistance rights—and to have denied the necessity of a legal toleration for Protestant dissenters. This denial involved a refutation of what had increasingly been English doctrine since the Reformation, the superiority of laymen over churchmen. The Elizabethan settlement was a settlement by statutory enactment and the same power that authorized it then had the power to modify the uniformity it insisted on in any way, whatever the belief of the highchurchmen might be.

If anything could ever have proved the perennial Whig claim that they represented no party in England, but merely supported the true interpretation of the constitution, it would be the basic assumptions and arguments put forward during the ten days' hearing. The account of the trial was published by order immediately after its conclusion, first in folio and then in octavo, and sold in very considerable quantities. However disastrous politically the decision may have been to proceed against Sacheverell, this publication by its circulation must have resulted in a more general understanding of English constitutional theory. Lechmere, the manager of the trial, described the excellence of the government under which Englishmen lived:

> The Nature of our Constitution is that of a limited Monarchy, wherein the Supreme Power is communicated and divided between Queen, Lords, and Commons, tho' the Executive Power and Administration be wholly in the Crown. The terms of such a Constitution

do not only suppose, but express an Original Contract, between the Crown and the People, by which that Supreme Power was (by mutual consent, and not by Accident) limited and lodged in more Hands than one; and the uniform Preservation of such a Constitution for so many Ages, without any Fundamental change, demonstrates to your Lordships the Continuance of the same Contract.

Lechmere continued,

> The Consequences of such a Frame of Government are obvious; that the Laws are the Rule to both, the common Measure of the Power of the Crown and of the Obedience of the Subject; and if the Executive Part endeavours the subversion and total destruction of the Government, the Original Contract is thereby broke, and the Right of Allegiance ceases; that part of the Government, thus fundamentally injur'd hath a right to save or recover that Constitution . . . look back on the history of *Magna Carta* alone, you can't doubt of the Sense of our Ancestors that they were Masters of Franchises that were truly their own . . . when the *last Extremity* called them to it, they never fail'd to vindicate them by the Arms of Resistance.[53]

On the second day of the trial, Sir John Holland pursued the same line of thought about resistance. Not only, he said, had God assured that the Sabbath was made for man and not man for the Sabbath, but government had been made for man, not man for government and general rules of obedience may upon a real necessity admit a lawful exception, and such a necessary exception we assert the revolution to be.[54] This absolute necessity of preserving law, liberty, and religion is what is meant when resistance is talked of—that is to say, as Walpole was to stress in a further argument, the resistance which maintains the very being of our present government. The argument for toleration in the trial was not based on complicated theories.

Benjamin Hoadly (1675–1761),[55] most famous of Whig Hanoverian bishops and already pretty well known as a pamphleteer before this trial, rushed into print against the divine right theories of Leslie and Atterbury, as well as Sacheverell, with those tracts usually known as *Hoadly on Government.* In them he did not go as far as later in his *Nature of the Kingdom or Church of Christ* (1717) when he committed himself to a position very hard for an officer of an established church to maintain. But Hoadly's weakness lay perhaps in his lack of interest in theological problems, revealed by his arguments attempting to persuade dissenters to conformity, as well as by his plea for toleration and the repeal of the Schism and Occasional Acts later.

He was a disciple of Locke and Hooker. Government was founded on consent and when the ruler broke his original contract with the people he might be deposed. The patriarchal scheme and the submission its proponents taught was nothing to Hoadly. He denied that the people needed a "bridle" of the sort the doctrines of highchurchmen would provide.[56] Moreover Hoadly had a belief in unrestricted private judgment. The efforts of some of the clergy to deny the validity of this essential Protestantism made him extraordinarily angry. Hoadly's writing brought him the plaudits of the Whigs in and out of parliament. Anthony Henley moved that he be thanked by the Commons for his work in 1710. Throughout the century Americans like John Adams and Jonathan Mayhew proclaimed their gratitude to him, placing him along with Cicero, Sidney, and Locke as preceptors of civil liberty.[57]

James Stanhope's arguments at the trial dealt, like Hoadly's tract, both with government and religion. These revealed the virtue of the brave soldier he was, and were typically Whig. The ultimate end of government, as Tully and Aristotle before him had written, was peace with reputation. Amongst those things which good governors should maintain to promote peace were good justice, sound finance, military virtue, and religion. He absolutely denied that support of the Church of England was the only course for men true to the government and that the sectaries were schismatics, heretics, and rebels. He advocated a truly Christian moderation toward those who were more loyal than some of Sacheverell's colleagues. Passive obedience, divine right, and hereditary indefeasible succession which nothing could ever invalidate, were tenets that should logically usher in the rule of one "on the other side of the water."[58]

Sir Peter King, Locke's nephew, followed[59] by showing that the Toleration Act, as commonly called, though not officially so designated, was an essential part of the Revolution and was accepted not only by

William and Mary, but in principle by the present queen when in 1705 she said in a speech from the throne that she would maintain the toleration. The Doctor's statement that heterodoxy in religion produced rebellion and treason in politics utterly misrepresented the English Establishment in church and state. Resistance had been justified not only in 1688 but many times before, and it might well be again. Where there was a right there was a remedy. The view that resistance was the essential element in revolution politics was clearly expressed at the trial:

> Whosoever, either Ruler, or Subject, by Force goes about to invade the Rights of either Prince, or People, and lays the Foundation for over-turning the Constitution, and Frame of any just Government, he is guilty of the greatest Crime, I think a Man is capable of, being to answer for all those Mischiefs of Blood, Rapine, and Desolation, which the breaking to Pieces of Governments brings on a Country; and he who does it is justly to be accounted one who resists the Ordinance of God, and the common Enemy and Pest of Mankind.[60]

The Whigs who conducted the trial emphasized resistance rights, not because they wished to alter society as it existed in England in their time, but because they realized that two principles at least must be recognized in civil society if it was to promote the protection and happiness men desire. There should be a possibility of change. There should be a law which was above the magistrate as he in his legal capacity was normally above the people. If there were no redress or security against the mischief the prince or governments might do, then everyone was in a state of nature. Those who were in authority had no power at all except what was theirs by the law of the country, and the makers of that law should then decide when it had been broken by any one of them or the magistrate himself. A monarchy limited in this way represented a medium between the mischief of arbitrary power and all unnecessary rebellion.

The Old and the New Whigs

A moderate Whig case was clearly presented at the trial. The Revolution Settlement as there interpreted was acceptable to the vast majority. But the popularity of Sacheverell's sermon revealed considerable Tory sentiment, and this in turn toned down the Whig defense. Edmund Burke looked on it as the great statement of those Whig ideas which he himself endorsed. His selection from it in his *Appeal from the New to the Old Whigs* (1791) further modified the interpretation.[61] He quoted Lechmere, Stanhope, Jekyll, and others of them in part, with his own emphatic approval of their reservations interspersed. It may be suggested that there was more resistance allowed, even in these statements, than his summary revealed, and that there was greater stress laid on toleration. These Whigs believed they had an almost perfect constitution defined by the Bill of Rights, the Statute of Habeas Corpus, the Toleration, and the Union. They did not advocate innovations, and were anxious to weaken the Doctor's arguments by dissociating themselves from them. They did not point out, as Halifax had done in the passage quoted earlier, the need for constant adaptation. Nor did the Whig spokesmen stress the natural rights of mankind. Cumberland had put forward philosophies based on the assumption of inalienable rights which Burke was at such pains to deny. Other evidence would suggest that the Revolution Whigs believed in their own right to influence affairs, to change the succession, to run the high court of parliament and even to dictate, as in the Act of Settlement, the movements and marriages of their monarchs. Nevertheless the great majority of them, as time wore on, spoke more of the excellence of the English system and the folly of even minor alterations in it. They concentrated on empire, economic stability, prosperity, and administration. Essayists like Addison and Steele spread mild Whiggery everywhere, but devoted almost as much attention to manners as to politics.

Among the Whigs, strengthened by certain arguments developed since the Interregnum and strengthened by the moral they drew from the Revolution, there were a few who wished to extend toleration, reform parliament, the universities, the poor laws, and even in some cases modify the mercantilist system and the dominion of England over other parts of the British Isles and her colonies. Natural rights doctrines were emphasized and applied in ways that might have surprised Cumberland and Locke. They absorbed Newton's new science and drew from it encouragement to greater freedom of enquiry. They found a revolutionary potential in Locke's philosophy, as well as in his *Treatises*. It is with them and their doctrines that the remainder of this book is concerned.

IV

Robert Molesworth and His Friends in England, 1693-1727

"Old Whigs"

For nearly four decades after the Revolution, a number of men connected in varying degrees of intimacy with Robert Molesworth worked to secure its benefits and extend its constitutional reforms. They produced a not inconsiderable body of political tracts and treatises which deserve to form a part of the English liberal tradition. None of them attained the stature of a Locke or a Sidney, but their publications attracted many readers on both sides of the Atlantic for more than a hundred years. They were in no sense an organized party. They shared many of the same ideas and engaged in many similar activities. They often referred to themselves as Old Whigs and were quite often praised or blamed as Commonwealthmen.[1] Most of them were members of the ruling class, and at least three of them—William Stephens of Sutton, Matthew Tindal of All Souls, and Benjamin Hoadly—were clergymen. One great magnate, Lord Ashley, looked to Molesworth as his mentor. Some of them were in parliament at different times. Toland and Thomas Gordon (Trenchard's partner in *Cato's Letters*) were outsiders and dependents, who attained an equal reputation in their own right.

No attempt will be made here to describe once again the political significance of such men as Addison, Steele, Defoe, and Swift—to name no more—controversialists familiar to every student of English literature and history. Nor will the policies devised by successive ministers and supported or opposed by members of either House be mentioned except where they directly relate to the Molesworth connection. These men were, it is true, associated at different times with statesmen like Somers, Godolphin, Sunderland (Marlborough's Whiggish son-in-law), and Stanhope, as well as with members of the Commons concerned in attempts to relieve the dissenters, a general naturalization and other reforming enterprises. A few of these were: Joseph Jekyll, already quoted against Sacheverell; Gilbert Heathcote, friend of the dissenting interest and writer on economic matters praised by Toland; Grey Neville, another proponent of toleration; and Wortley Montagu who brought in the General Naturalization Bill in 1708. The achievement of Molesworth's friends and admirers was to be found in their transmission of political ideas, rather than in parliamentary victories.

The year 1697 was marked by greatly intensified political speculation—the term political should be emphasized here since the debates were scarcely concerned with social conditions like those which stirred the interest of Thomas Firmin in 1678, and John Bellers in 1695. Molesworth himself was not insensitive to the state of the poor, but his chief preoccupation was political, not social. The constitutional revolution in Denmark in 1660, and the overthrow in a matter of days of the Gothic, German, or parliamentary system, seemed to him premonitory of a like fate for England if due precautions were not taken. Trenchard, in attacking the plan to maintain a standing force in peace time, related it to the decline of free government. He was followed by Andrew Fletcher and by Walter Moyle, the one considering chiefly the rise of absolutism since the renewal of letters and its association with armed forces; the other delving back into Greek and Roman history for more complex factors in the dissolution of free states, but also bearing in mind Denmark and other recent examples. Hotoman's *Franco-Gallia,* translated by Molesworth, was another moral story about declining popular estates. Mutiny, sedition, and treason all seemed less dangerous to these men than an acquiescence in any encroachment of the prerogative. Other topics recurred in the tracts, and especially in Molesworth's work—parliament, the separation of powers, the relation of Scotland, Ireland, and even the colonies with England. Finally a few reflections upon matters economic and social may be discovered. In the last two sections of this chapter the theories of Trenchard and Gordon, chiefly gathered from the *Independent Whig* and *Cato's Letters,* and those of Toland and Shaftesbury will be separately discussed, although many of the same themes recur in their works.

The violence and exaggerations of the free press, pulpit, and podium secured to most Englishmen after the lapse of the Licensing Act in 1695, often obscured the existence of common beliefs and attitudes. Some of these have already been noticed—the fears of illegal and thus arbitrary government as well as of popery. A fear of French ascendancy was general, though methods of combatting it might be debated. Whigs and Tories differed about the Toleration Act of 1689, but after some attempts to curtail it, it remained a part of the Settlement which included the succession, the independence of the judges, and the changes wrought in the character of parliament by the Union, by some clauses in the Act of Settlement and by such measures as the Qualification Act. A variety of motives lay behind many of the constitutional enactments of the years following the Revolution, but agreement on its virtues was widespread.

How many malcontents there were in England during the three reigns it is impossible to discover. There may have been rather more to the right of Sacheverell than to the left of Molesworth and Trenchard. The numbers involved were not great. Nor were they any more constant than the ranks of Whig or Tory. Nearly everyone owned to one or the other of the great party denominations, but few followed them consistently. Rigid definitions must be avoided. A group will be referred to here, but this is for convenience only. Coteries varied from year to year, and from place to place. All sorts of provincial, family, mercantile, and official influences affected their members. At the same time the essential homogeneity of English society must be remembered. Its cousinage extended not only through dissenters, merchants, officials, gentry, and aristocracy, but frequently connected even these apparently distinct classes in unexpected ways. Fundamental questions about social distinction were hardly raised. Discussions like those about the distribution of wealth, occasionally found even in Temple as well as in the works of the Commonwealthmen, were pretty closely limited to the relation of wealth to empire, that is, to the old question of the stable state, and were not much concerned with the welfare of the individual as such. The Commonwealthmen within the terms of their age, their class, and their education asserted liberty, talked about equality, and assumed the possibility of progress at a time when most Englishmen thought of the constitution as sacrosanct, and change as dangerous if not sacrilegious.

Robert Molesworth's Life and Friends

Robert Molesworth, in spite of the small number of his published writings and recorded speeches, was the most widely quoted and probably the most influential among the liberal Whigs, in his lifetime and for a considerable time thereafter. His acquaintance was wide. He had a violent temper, but he had also great charm and few who knew him well failed to respond to it. A Scotch-Irish disciple, James Arbuckle, said that no one who had known him could thereafter ignore politics.[2] His letters, written with the same ebullience and crispness that marked his tracts, seem to have been as effective. Had Molesworth added tact and discretion to his other talents, he might well have cut more of a figure on the parliamentary stage than his rare, often turbulent eruption of oratory achieved. Perhaps he attempted too much and allowed his interest in his estates, his children, his flowers, and his speculations to distract him from dedicated political service. He was, however, successful in broadcasting his theories, and in providing serviceable ammunition for liberal reformers.

Molesworth's father,[3] who died four days before his birth in 1656, was active in Dublin during the Civil War. His mother was Judith Bysse, the daughter of an Anglo-Irish lawyer. By her second marriage she had another son, Henry Tichborne, Lord Ferrard, who adored his half-brother. Robert was educated at Trinity College, Dublin. Nothing is known of any college friendship between him and his contemporaries, Trenchard and Molyneux. He married Lettice Coote, relative of Charles, Lord Mountrath, and of Richard, earl of Bellamont, sometime governor of New York and New England and a friend of John Locke. The Molesworths had a large family. Seven sons and three daughters survived childhood. They were related in one way or another to the Fosters, Ashes, Monks, Middletons, Boltons, Onslows, and Pulteneys. They owned estates in Ireland and bought land from the Wharton family at Eddington in Yorkshire. They were affectionate and gifted, as their letters testify, but were singularly unfortunate in the second and third generations, there being by the end of the eighteenth century but a single surviving branch of the whole Irish clan.

In 1689 Molesworth was among those proscribed by the government of James II. He fled to England with his wife and joined the circle around Anne of Denmark. William sent him to Copenhagen, perhaps to reward a good Protestant supporter, perhaps to please his sister-in-law, and certainly because he badly needed Danish mercenaries. The envoy secured these troops. He was clever and charming, but impetuous and irascible. He annoyed the Danes and was engaged in many fights with them. After his return he was unable to obtain any position in spite of help from Somers, Methuen, and Secretary Trenchard. William did not like him. Later his friendship with Godolphin and Stanhope failed to bring him into any prominent office. He was a member of Anne's Irish Privy Council until his insulting remarks about the clergy in 1713 resulted in dismissal. Appointed to the Board of Trade and Plantations by George I, he was at that time raised to the rank of viscount in the Irish peerage. With only brief intermissions, he sat for something like thirty years in the Irish and English parliaments. In 1722 he was invited to stand for Westminster, but eventually changed his mind, retired to his estates and enjoyed a circle of lively friends. He died in Ireland in 1725.[4]

Molesworth's acquaintance after the Revolution developed out of his family connections, his published works, and through his parliamentary associations in both Ireland and England. Information about his circle is uneven in spite of the vast numbers of his letters which survive. Enough material remains to show that his reputation was made with the publication of *An Account,* was continued by his often tempestuous activities in parliament, and was increased by the tributes of a remarkable list of contemporaries, both in William's reign and in those of his successors. In the last decade of his life his fame was enhanced by his vigour against the South Sea Company directors at the end of the first Septennial Parliament; by the publication of Shaftesbury's letters to him, and the preface to his translation of the *Franco-Gallia* referred to as the liveliest definition of a Real Whig; and by the appearance in his native land of his *Considerations for the Promoting of Agriculture* (Dublin, 1723). The latter occasioned Swift's well-known eulogy, in his dedication of the fifth Drapier's letter to the Viscount. What is more, some of the credit or blame for the immensely popular *Cato's Letters* went to the Irishman, though this was later denied by Thomas Gordon, never overready to acknowledge his literary debts. The Molesworth children reproached their father for his responsibility for some of the polemics. Anthony Collins, the freethinker, personally acquainted with Toland and Molesworth, shared their opinion. The fact that Molesworth was urged to stand for Westminster on the dissolution of parliament in 1721 attests his importance. The attempted election of the Viscount to the rectorship by the rowdy Scotch-Irish of Glasgow would be a testimony to his influence there, even if there were not the many letters and citations from his British admirers to suggest it.[5]

An Account, in the hands of an outraged Danish representative before the fifteenth of December, 1693, in spite of the date on its title page, brought many rejoinders.[6] Its popularity immediately enlarged the acquaintance of Molesworth, described by Locke as "so ingenious and extraordinary a man." Shrewsbury joined Somers and Secretary Trenchard in the summer of 1694 in recommending Molesworth to William as "honest and zealous for your government." His integrity was praised by John Methuen, Chancellor of Ireland, three years later. In his native land he made many friends, but these must wait for another chapter. In London his book was seized upon by the malcontent Whigs and quoted freely by Walter Moyle, by John Trenchard, and by others writing during the standing army controversy and meeting at the Grecian where Neville had lately sat and talked.[7]

Among others, Lord Ashley sought Molesworth out, and his protégé, John Toland, also made his acquaintance. Whether this was due to the common bond with Ashley, or whether they had met through Molyneux or in some other way in Dublin, cannot be certainly known, but the friendship then formed lasted throughout their lives. Shaftesbury cooled off in relations with the Deist, largely because of connections with Harley which lasted until 1710. Harley promoted Toland's publication of Harrington in 1700. Molesworth also knew Harley and expected services from him until the course of Tory politics of the great ministry became plain. The association was not close. With Toland the author of *An Account* was intimate and the letters and notes exchanged, though fulfilling all customary forms, seem singularly free from the tone of patron and dependent.[8]

With Shaftesbury also the friendship formed in the last decade of the seventeenth century continued to be warm. The *Letters* reveal the affection between them as well as the politics they shared. In the last years of Shaftesbury's life he became just as friendly and as frank about public affairs with John, his friend's eldest son. The friends regarded themselves as the Old Whigs, but, as Shaftesbury later recalled, their enemies dubbed them Jacobites. Their group was small but high-principled. Charles Davenant, himself a friend of Shaftesbury, in his *True Picture of a Modern Whig* (1701) described two unscrupulous men who plotted the overthrow of the Old Whigs and the ruin of the country as a means of advancing their own fortunes. The Old Whigs, it transpired, would sooner vote with Tories like Musgrave and Howe than with the gamesters, murderers, outlaws, and libertines then in control.

> They hated arbitrary government; We (the modern Whigs) have been all along for a standing army; they desired triennial parliaments, and that trials for treason might be better regulated; and it is notorious that we opposed both these bills. They were for calling corrupt ministers to an account; we have ever countenanced and protected corruption to the utmost of our power. They were frugal . . . we have squandered . . . the Old Whigs would have prevented the immoderate growth of the French Empire, we modern Whigs have made a partition treaty.[9]

Shaftesbury, though cool to the Junto, was ever an admirer of Somers, except probably in the matter of the armed force in 1697. Molesworth also distrusted the Kit-Cat and the Junto and thought a free nation ought to rely little upon them. He liked Wharton whom Shaftesbury also thought "true steel." Another common friend was Charles Montagu, earl of Halifax. Molesworth adored Godolphin and brought about a correspondence between him and the earl. He longed indeed for the earl to take a leading part in the government. He urged matrimony upon him because he thought the care of a good wife would improve his health. He would then be able to bring his influence to bear on public policies and give his support to the Lord Treasurer. Molesworth, in a letter of 12 November, 1709, explained why he so fully trusted and admired Godolphin in spite of his early Toryism:

I know there are envious persons enough who turn the best actions into evil and ascribe them to as bad causes as they can invent; but never shall any man persuade me that the publick minister who fixes a liberty of conscience, who unites two discording nations, who promotes public registers, procures general naturalisation, encourages the increase of people, the navigation of rivers, manages the public treasures so well, restores lost credit to a miracle, loves liberty, keeps secrets to a degree not known in England since Queen Elizabeth's time, provides for all the war in its distant parts, bears disappointment, lives frugally but not covetously, and gives not into the designs of Priestcraft of any kind, can do these through a bad intention, or be any thing like a Tory; I look upon him as a blessing fallen from heaven to us.

Godolphin, according to the Irishman, appreciated honest difference of opinion. When he and Sir John Cropley, Shaftesbury's best and oldest friend, had a private interview with the minister, Molesworth told him that he had recently voted against him in the House. To this the reply was: "'Tis gentlemen who are true to their principles and of such integrity as to do of themselves what they think well of, that I most esteem."[10]

In the next few years the fortunes of the Whigs declined. In spite of the care of his wife, Shaftesbury's health deteriorated and he was obliged to go abroad in search of a milder, easier climate. Harley proved to be the villain the earl had long ago suspected him to be. Toland eventually woke up with a shock to the fact and by 1714 was writing the vitriolic *Art of Restoring* against him. The Tories repealed the General Naturalization Act, persecuted the dissenters and endangered the Union by acts relating to Scotland, made a peace with France, and dismissed Marlborough. Gloom pervaded the correspondence of Molesworth and his friends. His son John, envoy to Tuscany, had become intimate with Shaftesbury, and they exchanged pessimistic reflections on events at home. Another son, Colonel Dick, had saved Marlborough's life at Ramillies and the personal connection with the

Churchills, which may have gone back to Anne's circle in 1689, lent bitterness to the General's disgrace. In 1712 Godolphin died. His death was reported with anguish by Molesworth to his wife, Lettice:

> My dear Lord Godolphin is dead! The greatest man in the whole world for honesty, capacity, courage, friendship, generosity, is gone. My best friend is gone . . . this great patriot could not survive the liberties of his country, whilst I, like a wretch, am to live like a slave, and have reared up children to no better an end.[11]

Perhaps Matthew Tindal, who went to stay at the Molesworth Yorkshire estate for two months at this time, managed to cheer his friend a little. The two men had probably known each other, at least by reputation since 1697. Tindal was an habitué of the Grecian, a proponent of a free press, of toleration, of the Hanoverian succession, and of the religion of nature. His most famous work, *Christianity as Old as Creation,* appeared in 1730, five years after Molesworth's death, but his deistical and political principles were well enough known long before. He was ordinarily classed with Shaftesbury as a major influence on the free thinking of his age. As a young man he had briefly inclined toward Catholicism, but his Protestantism reasserted itself completely. He was for most of his adult life a fellow of All Souls, though completely out of sympathy with the prevailing temper of the university. He was interested in Irish affairs, whether or not because of his friendship with Molesworth is uncertain, and a minor tract attributed to him defending freethinkers from the Irish convocation appeared in 1711–12. It is, incidentally, from his nephew Nicholas's *Continuation of Rapin* that the fullest account of Molesworth's battle with the Hibernian clergy in 1713 may be found.[12]

Also associated with this coterie was John Asgill. He had sat in both English and Irish Commons early in the reign of Anne and had incurred censure in both for his ideas about the translation rather than death of Christians. He ended his days busily writing in a room in the Fleet, the debtors' prison, where Anthony Hammond also took refuge. He wrote in support of the Hanoverian Succession in 1710. He was, he asserted, for divine right in the sense that David's kingship, although the psalmist was of a younger line, was divinely approved. In the same context he said he liked to read, but not to talk about, religion and government. He later supported the Peerage Bill, a scheme for new money, and a land register. He wrote about Charity Schools. He seems to have died a normal death, in spite of his beliefs, at a great age in 1738.[13]

Among the ruling Whigs some of Molesworth's acquaintances have already been noticed. For two others, however, there is evidence of approval though for one less than for the other. The Irishman thought of himself as on good terms with Charles Spencer, third earl of Sunderland (1674–1722), who was associated with Shaftesbury. His sons expected favours from the earl, and seem on the whole to have been anxious that he should escape without too much punishment from the South Sea scandal. Their cousin through their grandmother's second marriage into the Tichborne family was Judith, Sunderland's third wife, and their letters show some interest in her fortunes before and after marriage. John Macky and others, Evelyn among them, praised the learning and honesty of Charles Spencer. His admiration for Andrew Fletcher may well have indicated some early inclinations toward the Commonwealth side of the Whigs. He was immensely well read, and almost all contemporaries admired his talents. His library became famous, but from information remaining about it now, seems to have been the collection of a learned, curious, intelligent man, rather than a selection of the works relating to any one philosophy. Sunderland supported the Union and the Hanoverian interest, yet during the Harley administration he voted for the Occasional Conformity Bill and later induced Stanhope to modify liberal provisions in the bill for the Protestant Religion of 1719. He vigorously supported the Peerage Bill of 1719. It may well be that his subordination to Stanhope in matters of policy has been exaggerated, but there seems little doubt that even if he were as able he was not as liberal as the soldier.[14]

One or perhaps two of the Molesworths, Edward and Walter, served with James Stanhope in Spain. Their father and his friend Shaftesbury also had admired him. Probably Molesworth continued to support the general after he became a minister under the Hanoverians. Certainly Toland's *State Anatomy* (1716–17) was written to push some of the reforms then advocated and so far as can be discovered, Molesworth supported these in the Commons. Stanhope was not personally besmirched by the South Sea scandal in the parliamentary discussion in which Molesworth played so prominent a part in 1721. There is at least a suggestion that his cousin, Charles Stanhope, owed his acquittal to the absence from the division in the House of Molesworth, Jekyll, and Sloper. There is little direct comment on Stanhope in the Molesworth letters, but there is enough evidence at least to show that on the whole the Commonwealthmen upheld his policies in the Septennial Parliament, and were already suspicious of Robert Walpole in spite of his proven ability and his successes in 1720.[15]

An Account of Denmark

When Molesworth returned from Copenhagen in 1693, he shared in the general uneasiness of like-minded men about English affairs. This disquiet can be seen, for example, in the tracts of John Hampden, grandson of the Ship Money hero and himself involved in the Rye with Russell and Sidney—Hampden said that things were "in a state of unsettledness in all respects." He thought the conduct of the war and provision for its expenses, the whole question of trade, the procedure in trials for treason, the militia, the quartering of soldiers, all urgently in need of public discussion. Samuel Johnson, not long out of prison for diatribes against the Stuarts, was more concerned about parliament and urged a statute settling its meetings and duration.[16] His writing was vigorous as ever and as impatient of finesse. Molesworth's *Account of Denmark* was in part a contribution to the debates of these years.

He had several motives in writing it. There can be no doubt he was angry with the Danes and out of sympathy with their political or social customs. He was also immensely interested in their history, particularly that part of it which related to the Revolution of 1660 which had transformed their old Gothic constitution into a modern hereditary absolutism. He took great pains to discover its causes, course, and effects. His book, except for some comparatively minor errors and prejudices, remains the best account in English of the subject. Finally he was, as the admirer of old English liberties, worried lest his countrymen also allow their heritage to be diminished or lost through ignorance or indifference. "With a truly generous love to mankind,"

Shaftesbury said, Molesworth pointed out "the state of Denmark and prophesied of things highliest important to the growing age." Everything not purely descriptive or factual in the book relates to the main theme. Why and in what way did the Danes lose their freedom, and with what effects? In the answers to these questions Molesworth provided moral lessons for his times. When Morgens Skeel, the Danish representative, protested to William about *An Account,* he was undoubtedly right in suggesting that it was at least as much an attack on the shortcomings of the English as on those of the Danish government.[17]

The preface to *An Account* opens with a statement whose validity Molesworth was thereafter constantly to maintain:

> *Health* and *Liberty* are without dispute the greatest natural blessings mankind is capable of enjoying . . . Want of *Liberty* is a disease in any Society or Body Politick, like want of *Health* in a particular Person; and as the best way to understand the nature of any Distemper aright, is to consider it in several Patients, since the same disease may proceed from different causes, so the disorders in Society are best perceived by observing the Nature and Effects of them in our several Neighbours.

In short, a study of Denmark revealed the nature and development of absolutism, just as the reading of Hotoman's *Franco-Gallia* showed the slower processes by which France had reached the same condition. Such investigation was useful. So was travel. The Russians under the dominion of a Czar and an oppressive ecclesiastical hierarchy with the monopoly of education in their hands were not allowed to leave their country, nor to discover how others live. Englishmen could and often did. This led into a discussion of the value of journeys abroad and how they might best be utilized. This in turn introduced what is really the main theme of the preface, the matter of education.

The proper education of youth was the foundation of liberty. When its direction was in the wrong hands, as in Russia or Denmark, the effects were far-reaching. Molesworth was inclined to condemn the English system. His prejudice against Oxford highchurchmen is obvious. Priests, whether Lutheran, Anglican, or Papist, inculcated doctrines of slavish obedience and did little to stimulate the search for truth, or the development of public spirit, courage, honour, and enterprise. The curriculum, with its false emphasis on dead languages, was designed for the cloister rather than the world. Englishmen should learn to love their country and study its history and literature as well as its political advantages, and this, before they went abroad. Otherwise they might be led into mistakes, and even the idea that "princes have acquired a right to be absolute and arbitrary where subjects have given up their liberties," as in Denmark.[18]

Molesworth greatly admired Locke. Molyneux reported to his friend the Irishman's reverence before a portrait of the philosopher hanging in his Dublin study. Yet it is quite possible that he had not read the *Letters on Education* before he wrote this preface. His reflections sprang out of his subject and out of his immense distrust of Tory clericism. He looked back to the Greeks and Romans and wished that Englishmen were educated by philosophers rather than priests. In Denmark he attributed the stagnation he observed in intellectual life to uniformity in religion, and to the official character and privileges of the Lutheran church. They were supporters of the new regime and through their control of opinion, from the cradle to the grave, made mutiny against it and relief from it improbable and almost impossible. Molesworth wanted education to encourage active virtue and curiosity about the needs of one's country.[19]

Whether *An Account* owes anything to Locke or not, it must be placed beside the *Letters* and Milton's tract as one of the important stimulants to new educational ideas in the period. Among the experimenters in England, Scotland, and America Molesworth's ideas were common currency. He was to be quoted by Fordyce and Turnbull, in turn drawn on by Franklin in his plans for the College of Philadelphia. Over and over again there are echoes of his phrases or references to his *Preface*. Moreover, amongst his contemporaries, like John Toland, Matthew Tindal, and Walter Moyle, there can be found similar suggestions about the importance of education in a free state, about the need for a new curriculum, about the contrast between the education of Greece and Rome and that of Oxford in objectives, methods, and the virtues developed.[20]

Some of the Whigs would have liked to reform the universities by statute. Scotsmen, whose revolution was of course at once a defeat for

the Stuarts and a triumph for the Presbyterian party, expelled supporters of the old order and appointed professors favourable to the
new. But the English Revolution was neither a party nor a sectarian triumph, and it would have been dangerous to appear to follow James's
example of interference with the privileges of the dons of Oxford and
Cambridge. Jacobitism would have been strengthened. Bitterness persisted against highchurch Toryism. Men remembered the Oxford de-
crees of 1683, the most violent expression of English Toryism, published on the day of Russell's execution for his part in the Rye. Lord
Macclesfield, the Whig lord who took John Toland abroad with him
in 1701, devised a scheme of university reform. After the accession of
George I, Lords Stanhope and Sunderland were very much interested
in the matter. A bill was drafted to deprive the universities of the right
of appointment and patronage and vest these for a term of years in
royal commissioners. In his *State Anatomy* (1717), as well as in his *Memorial* (1714), Toland endorsed university reform as desirable. References
to "University Monks" may be found in such tracts as Molesworth's
Count Patkul, which came out in 1717. Stanhope's scheme was dropped
after 1719, though dissatisfaction with not only the politics of the professors, but with the education offered can be traced for a long while
afterwards.

One explanation offered by Molesworth for the Danish estates' mis-
calculations about their revolution was to be found in a poor educational system, the monopoly of clerical instructors, and in so severe a
censorship in their land that all speculation about religious and political questions was prevented. Three other important factors described
in *An Account,* contributing to the dissolution of the old Danish parliamentary or Gothic constitution, were the lack of balance between the
different parts of the constitution, the wealthy and nonpublic-spirited
nobles, and the existence of a standing army controlled by the king.
According to the theories of Sidney, Fletcher, Trenchard, and Molesworth, the nobles should form a safeguard for the liberties of their
country. They should be armed against both invaders from abroad and
overpowerful monarchs at home. When they shirked their duties, as
in Denmark, when they refused to bear a due share of taxation, they
endangered the government provoking an alliance of clergy and common against their privilege. These two estates therefore called on the

king to assert his authority and offered him an hereditary title instead of the elective crown he already wore. The court, taking advantage of the situation and of the presence of troops in Copenhagen, devised the famous oath of allegiance which in fact bestowed an absolute power on the king entirely unforeseen by the estates. "Had the King not had an army at his command, the nobles had never delivered up their government." Had the nobles behaved better, had they not abused their position, the crises could not have arisen.[21]

The Danes were to find that their victory over the selfish nobles was dearly bought, and that the little finger of an absolute prince was heavier than the loins of many nobles.[22] In England the balance lay among three estates, but one of these was the king himself. The hazards of an elective monarchy had been avoided whilst—according to revolution politics—the advantages of change when events made it desirable were retained. But whatever the precise bodies were which acted as checks upon each other, the principle was the same, a balance of constitutional power. Molesworth's *Account* was to be studied, not only by his contemporaries, but by Americans like James Madison (the Virginian) and John Adams, when they were considering problems of the New World. Their concern reminds the modern student of the regard for balance in government to be found in the controversies of the eighteenth century.

The Peerage Bill merits discussion in the light of these tracts and the disputes about the preservation of the best form of mixed government. Denmark and its lessons were cited on both sides during the debates about the bill in the first Septennial Parliament of George I. Moreover Molesworth's authority was freely claimed in pamphlets for and against the bill. He has been credited with *The Patrician,* as well as with a tract Walpole almost certainly wrote, *A Letter to a Member.* Molesworth's name does not appear in the division list of the vote in the Commons which defeated Stanhope's bill. His attitude cannot be certainly ascertained. Yet the evidence would seem to point to his approval of the measure. He was always keenly critical of any encroachments by royal prerogative. Anne's creation of twelve peers to strengthen her interest in the Lords in 1712 was resented by the Whigs. Although Stanhope's opponents were ready enough to point out that the action was exceptional and that royal powers were diminished and unlikely to revive in the future, his supporters lacked their confidence and professed considerable anxiety over the quite recent precedent set by the queen. Sunderland, Peterborough, and Addison supported the bill. Toland had anticipated its provisions in his *State Anatomy,* which may indeed have been designed to sound out and prepare opinion. The Whigs were hopelessly divided on the issue, some arguing that the bill restricting royal creations for the future would ensure the preservation of the balance; others that it would unduly increase the powers of the aristocratic element and thus upset the balance. Molesworth may well have aligned himself with the Stanhope connection on this occasion. Walpole proved in this, as in many other debates during his career, that he was skillful in his appreciation of the Commons' wishes. It is not proven that he thereby displayed greater public spirit than Stanhope, though purely political motives may have influenced both of them.[23]

The standing army controversy, provoked by William's wish to retain some mercenary forces after the conclusion of peace in 1697, was to be echoed at each succeeding debate on the armed forces during the century. The tracts of Trenchard and Moyle, Toland, Tindal, and Johnson, as well as those of Andrew Fletcher, were probably all the result of discussions amongst their authors. Many of them were often to be reprinted, in part or in whole, in collections and separately. At the time, the argument against mercenary forces was already unrealistic. It ignored the exigencies of contemporary warfare and failed to appreciate the safeguards afforded by parliamentary control of taxation. Somers's *Balancing Letter* pointing out the harsh facts of the case annoyed, at least for the time being, his friends among the Old Whigs, but provides further evidence for students of his character, of his extraordinary good sense and his understanding of the foreign and domestic issues involved. Nevertheless, his opponents deserve rereading. They may have been confused about the immediate problem, but their reflections on government and upon the fortunes of free states were frequently judicious and penetrating.

Molesworth had stressed the importance of the armed force in Copenhagen in 1660. In the Preface to his translation of the *Franco-Gallia* he recurred to the relation between mercenary troops and absolutism, and these remarks gained force from Hotoman's story of the decline of the ancient liberties of France. He was not entirely unaware, later in life at any rate, of the changed circumstances of defense for England in relation to the continent. In 1718 when the matter of armed forces was being discussed in the Commons, his book on Denmark was quoted to show the dangers of a standing army. He then spoke on the government side against auditor Harley, and stated his belief that the situation in Denmark in 1660 was not analogous to that of England in the reign of George I. Professional troops, as well as a good navy, were essential and were most unlikely to prove a weapon against the liberties of the country.[24]

In the standing army discussions there was always an attempt by opponents of professional forces to emphasize the importance of the navy to England's defense. This need not be reiterated here. It ought also to be realized that though their arguments so often seem futile in view of the immense changes in military science that had taken place, they themselves admitted the antiquated organization, weapons, and equipment of the militia about which they wrote so much. They argued that the militiaman needed as good arms as the "poor swaggering idler in a red coat"—that is, the professional soldier—and a thorough reorganization of the national system. Fletcher produced a complicated scheme for this purpose. Nevertheless, they maintained, nothing could equal in fighting potential the man defending his estate, wife, and country. Molesworth pointed this out in the Preface to the *Franco-Gallia*. Trenchard waxed eloquent upon it. There was more than a hint of nostalgia for the good old days of feudalism when the gentry led out their loyal tenantry to defend their country's liberty and the "nobility" secured "the people against the insults of the prince and the prince against the popularity of the commons." In the past, moreover, Englishmen had not only taken up their swords against tyranny but also had fought most successfully against their country's enemies. The militia should "consist of the same persons as have the property; or otherwise the government is violent and against nature." Sidney had written in this vein. Harrington was thought to have provided support for the arguments.[25]

The emphasis in the discussion, however, was upon the danger to internal security from royal power rather than upon necessary protection against external attacks. Over and over again the connection between absolutism and mercenaries was pointed out. Commines, Machiavelli, and Boccalini were cited. Trenchard and Moyle reviewed both ancient and more recent history. Fletcher briefly surveyed the decline of the old estates system—the Gothic governments. All deduced the same moral: "He that is armed is always master of the purse of him that is unarmed." Even the admitted right of the English Commons to raise taxes might fail to be respected by a would-be despot had he at his command soldiers to enforce his wishes.[26]

Fletcher's arguments are interesting and must be considered again in a later chapter.[27] Those of Walter Moyle, in 1697 the associate of Fletcher and Trenchard at the Grecian and probably joint author of the famous *Argument* against a standing army, are worth some further attention here. A Cornishman, he was Member for Saltash in 1695–98, a justice of the peace, a dabbler in literature, antiquarian studies, and the study of government. At the request of Charles Davenant he translated Xenophon's *Discourse upon Improving the Revenues of the State of Athens* (1698), and in the same year he wrote *An Essay on the Lacedaemonian Government*. It seems likely that the *Essay upon the Roman Government,* though not printed until five years after his death in 1721, was written while the standing army controversy was raging—perhaps in 1699—and was circulated in manuscript among his friends.[28] Moyle considered in the works for which he was solely responsible many aspects of political science besides the relation of absolutism and armed forces. His friend, Trenchard, in his preface to *A Short History,* had written of the mistaken notions current about government and especially one, that reformation was impossible. Government was a mere piece of clockwork acting after the manner of its construction. The art of the politician, therefore, was to insure that it moved to the public advantage.[29]

Moyle, at greater length and throughout his two essays on Greek and Roman Commonwealths, considered the mechanism of other constitutions—how they had failed and where they had succeeded—and pointed out to his own countrymen the lessons of their history. In the essay on Sparta the Cornishman revealed himself as the disciple of Henry Neville, of Locke, and of Sidney, whose discourses against Filmer had just appeared. "I am," Moyle said, "on the side of liberty," which he explained meant the Revolution and the government by

King, Lords, and Commons. He used Sparta to show the value of government by consent to a free maritime people who refused to be dominated by clerical faction.³⁰ In the *Essay upon the Roman Government* Moyle found even more relevancy to the situation in England. But in both he discovered that true constitutions consisted in a "proper distribution of power into several branches, in the whole composing as it were one great machine," and, he pointed out, "each branch was a check upon the other; so that not one of them could exceed its just bounds, but was kept within the sphere in which it was circumscribed by the original frame." In Lacedaemonia the distinct functions of each were known. In England, unfortunately, this was not the case.³¹

In Rome the early rulers instituted a liberty of conscience, a general naturalization of foreigners, and a clergy who "served the gods for naught" instead of taking tithe. Numa also allowed the people some freedom through his institution of diviners, and a careful use of nobility gave the old Roman monarchy some strength. Monarchy in turn gave way to an aristocracy and then to a commonwealth, supported by a numerous militia and founded on freedom and property. Moyle traced the period and revolutions of empires—the common circle in generation and corruption of all states—but differed with Polybius in thinking them due to changing balance in property, not to vices and oppressions. Land was the center of power, he said, as great Harrington had demonstrated. Thus aristocracy was usually founded on the shattered balance of monarchy, and a commonwealth upon the growth of great possessions among the commons and their independence of the nobles.³²

The Romans were "reasoners" in matters of politics and government and impatient of any insolence and oppressions; an "empire of laws" gave them the right of appeal from the tyranny of any governor, and made them disdainful of all subjection. Moyle traced the rise of the popular government and its victories. He noticed independence, erection of tribunes, a standing body of laws, the exclusion of diviners or clergy from counsels, the agrarian law, the increase in population by "promiscuous naturalization," the weakening of class distinctions, and finally the right to be elected into the government. Good laws against bribery, against profit in government service, against usury, as well as provisions for rotation in office and voting by ballot, made the fabric of state "immortal," free from inward disease and invincible to outward attack.[33]

In his second essay Moyle attributed the decay of this admirable government to a failure to "return to its original," that is, to reinforce or renew old principles of balance. The Roman commonwealth lasted for two hundred and fifty years, made many conquests, and was troubled by fewer seditions than the succeeding empire. The Romans made great progress. From all of which Moyle concluded that there was a vigour in all free states—Athens, Carthage, Sparta, Rome—flowing from courage, liberty, and equality. Their eventual decline, Moyle concluded with Machiavelli, came from an alteration of their way of living and a failure to return to first principles.

The people often dispensed with fundamental laws. They kept magistrates in office too long. They failed to bring to account or impeach men who harmed the state. Earlier Scipio, Cato, and others had acted as defenders of laws. Later few would do so. Voluntary exile was allowed. Moreover there were fewer men of superior virtue and merit. It is easy enough to read into the essay the current politics of England, and many of Moyle's implied recommendations were those of his associates. Later *Cato's Letters* were to demand public enquiry into the South Sea directors' great wealth and to use similar classical analogies. But Moyle's support of an Agrarian, his turn of phrase, his emphasis on equality—not common at this time—gave his work a democratical flavour which is rarely found in Molesworth, Trenchard, or Fletcher.[34]

In Rome the people grew careless. In Denmark the nobles failed to see dangers ahead. In Francis Hotoman's *Franco-Gallia* the French seemed unaware of what was happening to them until their liberty was gone. It followed therefore that constant vigilance was necessary. Citizens must warn their fellow countrymen of dangers they see and point out usurpation and tyranny. Parliament, like the ephors of old Sparta, was the guardian of liberty and must exercise the right to inquire freely into administration. The Justiciars in Aragon had formerly performed this function. In Rome under the kings no such official or body had existed, so frequent seditions were necessary, indeed helpful, as Moyle pointed out, in obtaining redress of grievance. There were fewer disturbances in the Commonwealth simply because the people now had their representatives to take action. Great dangers, like Cannae, might also provide an opportunity for reform.[35]

Molesworth maintained the same doctrine. To expel "a tyrant or an idiot" could never be treason. His argument is rather more subtle than that of Samuel Johnson who believed the people always had a right to put out a prince they disliked. Molesworth felt that motive determined whether a rebellion was treasonable or lawful. "When Subjects take up arms against their *Prince*, if their Attempt succeeds, 'tis a *Revolution;* if not, 'tis call'd a *Rebellion:* 'tis seldom consider'd whether the first motive be just or unjust." Molesworth, it may be remembered, gave greater currency to the story of Sidney's motto, "This hand to tyrants ever sworn the foe." He reflected upon so-called traitors and suggested that to visit the father's sins upon the children was unfair. It is surely "enough to hang or behead the *Offenders*" without penalizing their families. Treason can be the sin of rulers as well as subjects.

> 'Tis certainly as much a *Treason* and *Rebellion* against this *Constitution* and the *known* laws, in a *Prince* to endeavour to break thro them, as 'tis in the *People* to rise against him, whilst he keeps within their Bounds and does his Duty. Our Constitution is a government of *Laws,* not of *Persons* . . . Our Constitution considers no *Power* as *irresistible* but what is *lawful.*

In other words, kings and ministers must be called to account by the constant vigilance of the people. Molesworth and Trenchard relentlessly pursued the South Sea Company directors for actions in effect, they thought, if not in law, treasonable. The twelfth of *Cato's Letters* made a case for this attitude. Molesworth had complained that one of the troubles in Denmark was the absence of nonconformity in every sense of the term. The minds of the people were of one caliber. There were no intestine commotions, no mutinies and libels. "You never hear of any Person guilty of the Crime of Treason against the King; the Government has riveted itself so fast upon the Bottom it now stands, that no Body offers to wag so much as the Tongue against it." No one could have said that the Real Whigs did not wag their tongues loud and often![36]

Projects and Reforms

In England, as in all old Gothic or German countries, parliament was responsible for watching over the liberties of the people. "Frequent meetings of the Estates was a part of the very fundamental Constitution" of Denmark. All matter relating to good government was transacted in them. They removed kings whose character and talents were not equal to their job. They debated all problems.[37] Frequent meetings were, of course, desired in England. "High Whiggism," Molesworth declared, was for annual parliaments. The Reverend Samuel Johnson published a tract on the matter in 1693 boasting of the fabulous history of Saxon assemblies, but in the same year a Triennial Act limiting the duration of the Commons (which Molesworth attributed to "Low Whiggism") was consented to by the reluctant William. Annual meetings were expected to take place. All the Old Whigs supported the bill but hoped for even more frequent elections in the future.[38]

Yet the period was to see a Septennial substituted for the Triennial with both Molesworth and Moyle supporting Stanhope's government. Moyle amusingly described to a friend the changing reactions of his associates to this bill. He was writing in April, 1716.

> No motion was at first treated with more coldness, the politicians of the Grecian and the neighboring coffeehouses, fired with uncommon warmth, bellow'd aloud against it, but time and good arguments make them espouse the quite contrary opinion . . . the chief arguments used on the Whig side, were the present situation of our affairs, an enemy at home in open rebellion . . . that the Triennial Act never answered the ends at first proposed by it, . . . that it serv'd for no other end but to keep alive our animosities . . . ruined the gentry . . . hinder'd the due administration of justice.

Stanhope was meditating repeal of the Septennial by the autumn of 1719, and there can be no doubt that once the crisis of 1716 was past, the Commonwealthmen among the Whigs always declared themselves of the same sentiment.[39]

Trenchard, in Cato's sixty-first letter in 1721, could see no means of preserving public liberty with any monarchical form, save by frequent fresh elections. "The possession of power soon alters and vitiates" the hearts of members and ministers. A rotation in power and magistracy is essential in a free government. Parliaments cannot bind their successors. Molesworth thought taxes should only be voted for the life of the parliament then sitting. He also wished to see not only frequent and cautious parliaments, but parliaments elected from new and more representative constituencies. Like Locke, he deplored Old Sarum. He suggested in his *Considerations* enfranchisement of leaseholders.[40] He never referred to unrepresented persons in the sense that Neville had done in his *Plato Redivivus,* or Robert Sawyer's speech to the Convention of '89. Cato emphasized only the general rights of the people, and never criticized the actual distribution of the franchise.[41]

The reform of parliament chiefly insisted on by all the Molesworth connection was the separation of office holder and parliament man. If the House were eased of members that had offices and employments or pensions from the court, corruption, election briberies, and bitterness in party conflicts might also diminish. John Toland brought out *The Danger of Mercenary Parliaments* in 1695 with the approval of Shaftesbury, and it was reprinted in 1722 with the elections to the second Georgian Parliament in mind. Trenchard prefaced the *History of Standing Armies* with what was always to be known as his "incomparable" remarks on government containing a bitter attack on the development of a cabinet. Shaftesbury, writing at the time the Act of Settlement was being debated in the Houses, emphasized the clause about places as all-important—especially since earlier attempts, that in 1696, for example, had proved abortive. Somers, whose influence had prevented the earlier bill, may indeed have realized something of the advantage of having ministers in the House readily available for rebuke or comment. But the development of the English ministerial system was to take place without the blessings of political theorists. Scipio Maffei, an Italian visitor in 1737, who noticed and explained the English practice with respect to the relation of executive and legislature a good deal more accurately than Montesquieu a decade later, seems to have been exceptional in his recognition of recent administrative history. The men who were in office no doubt saw certain necessities which Molesworth and Trenchard, who never held any, entirely failed to appreciate. The virtue of these Commonwealthmen was in holding ministers to account for their failings, and in keeping the public informed about politics in general. Already by 1700 and before the Act of Settlement, Parson Stephens could notice amongst the restraints on the English monarchy the popular control of ministers through parliamentary legislation.[42]

Government in a free country must be by laws to which the people have consented. Molesworth therefore, like his countryman Molyneux, and like the Scotsman, Fletcher, was much interested in the relation of the different parts of Great Britain, and the degree to which a government centered in London fulfilled the demands for natural rights. His opposition to the act against woollens which provoked Molyneux's famous *Case of Ireland,* and the act of the Sixth of George I declaring the dependency of Ireland, will be discussed in a later chapter. It sprang, of course, from his experience as an Anglo-Irishman, unwilling to be deprived of the inherent rights of an Englishman. His support of the Union with Scotland which Fletcher opposed was less due to a divergence of principle between them than to a difference of temperament. Fletcher, like Archbishop William King in Ireland, feared a government centered in London. Other parts of the island would suffer. All interest and wealth would crowd there. Fletcher would only have consented to a Union on "equal terms," by which he meant federal terms, and he insisted on certain limitations on prerogative as an essential part of the settlement. Molesworth also wrote of "equal terms" in which he would have included his native land, the Principality and the Northern Kingdom. Other Irishmen, like Henry Maxwell, shared his views, but were prepared to accept the settlement of 1707 as a benefit.[43]

John Trenchard was probably of a similar opinion. After he left Dublin, he studied law in London, but a fortunate marriage and rich inheritance made him free to neglect it as a career. He was appointed one of the commissioners of the forfeited estates in Ireland in the reign of William, and made a success of the job. The English voted him a reward of one thousand pounds. The Irish respected his consideration of their claims. Long after his death Samuel Madden, in his *Reflections and Resolutions Proper for the Gentlemen of Ireland* (1738),[44] spoke of him as one who understood Ireland better than most who had no estates there. Trenchard devoted the one hundred and sixth of the letters by

Cato to the matter of colonies and plantations. In it he animadverted upon the English policy toward Ireland. Like Molesworth, he pointed out the expensive character of government by force. All profits from overseas possessions might be swallowed up by the expense of maintaining them. Attempts to restrict colonial enterprise might result after all in illicit trade antipathetic to English interests. As Molesworth had pointed out, "'Tis so much more desirable and *secure* to govern by *Love* and *common Interest,* than by *Force;* to expect *Comfort* and *Assistance* in times of danger . . . than to find them at such a time a *heavy Clog* . . . or to have as much need of entertaining a *standing* Army against our *Brethren,* as against our known and inveterate *Enemies.*"[45]

Molesworth ignored other plantations than the Irish, but Trenchard, though Ireland was probably most vividly in his mind, deliberately turned to the whole colonial problem. He outlined the advantages to England of colonial commodities which could not be produced at home. Supremacy in world trade might well be ensured by imperial experiments. Nevertheless, he continued, the colonies will grow up and cannot be expected "to continue their subjection to another only because their grandfathers were acquainted." It would be their desire to gain independence when the need for protection had disappeared. Only mutual interest could be relied upon to retain their allegiance. They would not seek any change while they had full employment and could maintain themselves comfortably. The North American colonies would grow too powerful to be governed for English interests alone. Their climate and soil would enable them at length to compete on equal terms. "Men will always think they have a right to Air, Earth, and Water, a Right to employ themselves in their own Support . . . to make the best of their Soil and to work up their own Products." Better to take them into partnership than to drive them, as we had the Irish, into rivalry. All would gain and England, the rich and opulent country, would gain the most. Trenchard, of course, put forward in much extended form suggestions that can be discovered in Charles Davenant and in Josiah Childs. His interest and acumen had been much sharpened by his Irish experience.[46]

Trenchard may be regarded as a moderate critic of the mercantilist system, and Davenant thought along somewhat similar lines. Shaftesbury suggested that "impositions and restrictions reduce trade to a low ebb. Nothing is so advantageous to it as a *Free Port*." Molesworth was preoccupied with civil liberty, and hardly mentioned trade except to declare himself against monopolies.[47] However, he believed in government action to foster prosperity and encourage population. Credit should be extended. Public works, buildings, and highways, as well as the improvement of waterways, should be undertaken. Public servants and seamen should be well paid. Idlers should be put to work or punished. In Ireland relief from the tithe, public granaries, schools, and instruction in industrial techniques should be provided. He spoke with some indifference of the game laws, though in the context—the necessity for a national militia and the arming of free men—perhaps this should not be taken too seriously.[48]

Molesworth feared depopulation and was anxious to see foreign Protestants encouraged. An Irish tract of 1697 on this subject was dedicated to him. He put his ideas into practice by employing Huguenots on his Yorkshire estates. Cities prospered, he had argued, which did not close their doors to strangers. There was in them a greater consumption, and freer circulation of coin.[49] A general naturalization, actually implemented by the Godolphin administration in the Act of 1708, was endorsed by almost all the Real Whigs except the Reverend Samuel Johnson, who had argued in a tract of 1698 along conventional lines that immigrants would take the bread out of Englishmen's mouths. In *The Rights of Mankind* Tindal supported the naturalization. Toland would have extended it to Jews. Moyle, in his study of ancient Rome, attributed a part at least of its prosperity to a generous welcome to foreigners. "A Genuine *Whig*," Molesworth maintained, was "for promoting a *general Naturalization,* upon the firm Belief, that whoever comes to be incorporated into us, feels his Share of all our Advantages and Disadvantages, and can consequently have no Interest but that of the Publick; to which he will always be a Support to the best of his power, by his *Person, Substance,* and *Advice.*"[50]

There were suggestions in the Preface to the *Franco-Gallia,* as well as in *Considerations* and *Denmark,* that Molesworth thought about the poor. Poverty, popery, and wooden shoes were popularly associated in the minds of Englishmen who were wont to contrast the plenty enjoyed by them with the scarcity abroad. In Denmark the boors were wretchedly off. Taxes were heavy. There was moreover no yeoman class. In

cities where local restrictions by laws prevented competition and forbade the entry of strangers, except upon too hard terms, decay was
likely to set in. They might become wastes. "New villages not incorporated, or more liberal of their Privileges grow up in their stead."[51]

On the whole, Molesworth was inclined to blame poverty in part on
original sin or idleness, and in part on inadequate political liberty. He
wanted to renew and improve the old mixed constitution. He wished
to secure greater liberty of speech and religion. This was his constant
concern, as it was that of his associates. Uniformity of opinion in Denmark, as already noticed, impressed Molesworth unfavourably, and it
is not therefore surprising to find that he advocated the most sweeping
kind of religious liberty for all sorts of sects and opinions. As a young
man he was passionately antipapistical and pushed for the penal laws
in Ireland. By the time he wrote *Considerations* (1723), he had come to
a saner view of the rights of the Catholic majority in Ireland. In England, with all his friends, he supported a greater toleration than that
reluctantly conceded in the Act of 1689 and opposed the bills against
occasional conformity and the schism.[52] His distrust of the clergy was
enhanced by their real or supposed interference in Dublin politics on
behalf of Tories and Jacobites in 1712. He made himself notorious by
an ill-advised aside as he watched the Irish convocation come to pay
their respects to the government. As the clergy appeared in the Castle
on 26 December, 1713, Molesworth was heard to exclaim, no doubt
with his accustomed vehemence, "They that have turned the world
upside down are come hither also." The Irish Lords condemned him,
classing him with Toland and Asgill who had already been expelled
from the country for their unorthodox views. The queen dismissed
him from the Council, but the Irish Commons refused to act further
in the matter.[53]

After George I's accession the dissenters began to press for the repeal of some of the laws against them, particularly those of the last
years of Anne, though they would also have liked the Test abolished
and the Corporation Act repealed. The matter dragged and much
paper and ink was consumed in debating the position of the sectaries.
Finally in 1718 Molesworth was chairman of a large meeting to expe-
dite progress on the bill brought in by the Stanhope administration,
and he materially assisted the good work. The greater relief was not

obtained. But the Schism and Occasional Conformity Acts were repealed and the dissenters credited Molesworth with a good part of the achievement. He deserved their gratitude. He believed that the state should not enforce belief. "To stretch or narrow" any man's conscience to the standard of our own was unforgivable. None could engross heaven "by way of *Monopoly* to their own *Corporation*."⁵⁴

Trenchard and Gordon, Two Independent Whigs

Among the most widely read and important polemical works of the reign of George I were the series of essays known in their collected forms as the *Independent Whig* and *Cato's Letters,* appearing in London from 1720–23 and many times reprinted during the next twenty-five years. Although Molesworth and others were credited with some part in the enterprise, it was known to be chiefly the production of John Trenchard and Thomas Gordon. The former was already famous for his diatribes against standing armies in the reign of William III. He was a wealthy west countryman married to Anne Blackett, daughter of a north-country baronet related to the Buchans. On Trenchard's death in 1724 Anne married Gordon, who thus became possessed of a house and considerable wealth. Gordon's antecedents are obscure. He seems to have met his patron and partner in a London tavern and to have become his amanuensis and collaborator as the Bangorian controversy spread and as the malfeasance of the South Sea directors discredited the ministry. For four years the essays and letters attacked the divine righters and Tories in the church, and the wealthy malefactors in the state. For the rest of his life Gordon wrote less violently—it is suggested as a result of Walpole's efforts, though it is hard to see why the husband of Anne Trenchard should have been bribed—and devoted himself to his translations of Tacitus and Sallust, and to commentary upon them which was hardly less controversial than his earlier journalism.⁵⁵

In general the *Independent Whig* was anticlerical and antipapistical. He demanded general freedom of thought and no interference with its expression by censor or church. A general optimism throughout the essays and letters produced a belief that if liberty were achieved, progress must follow. Political conditions changed and these changes needed study unhampered in any way. Magistrates must be criticized, exhorted, and if necessary discharged. Brutus was the subject of one of *Cato's Letters.* The moral was obvious. The illiterate and underprivileged sections of society were not much considered, though the constantly reiterated appeal to the people sometimes suggests to modern readers, and probably to those of the eighteenth century as well, more of a democratical inclination than in fact may have existed in Cato's mind.

The anticlericalism of the *Independent Whig* is its most striking characteristic. This, too, has already been seen in the work of Molesworth and Moyle. It could be traced back to Marvell and to Milton. But at the time of its publication the *Independent Whig* was undoubtedly entering into a whole complex of disputes not necessarily connected with each other, but all concerned with ecclesiastical discipline. First of all, so long as the exiled Stuarts continued to exist and to profess Catholicism, there persisted a strong and vigorous prejudice against the Protestant but Highchurch group that were suspected of Jacobitism and of a belief in divine right. No such theory, of course, was acceptable to the authors of the *Independent Whig* and *Cato's Letters.* What is more, there seems to have been a suspicion in the mind of Benjamin Hoadly when he preached his famous sermon in 1717, "The Nature of the Kingdom, or Church of Christ," that even the Whig clergy were contemplating a revival of discipline in the Establishment. That Wake and Gibson were considering strengthening episcopal authority over matters spiritual in a manner certain to prove inconvenient to men like Hoadly and obnoxious to all who were hostile to clerical powers, now seems proven. But the violence of Hoadly's attack, whilst it prevented an extension of the sort desired by Gibson, also embittered and confused relations between church and state. It may have injured rather than helped the cause of the dissenters during and after 1718.[56]

In addition to continuing fears of popery and suspicion of Highchurch politics, there was a revolt among Episcopalians and the old sects alike against subscription to any statement of dogma, articles, or confession. A discussion of this must wait for another chapter, since it involves references to all sorts of arguments—quarrels among churchmen, quarrels between churchmen and freethinkers, quarrels over the Trinity. Trenchard and Gordon, whose theology was less than orthodox, were frankly against all authority in matters spiritual but that of the individual conscience. In a complacent age this bickering, these fears of pope and bishops, these disputations about dogma averted stagnation, maintained freedom of opinion, and thus encouraged sentiments later favourable to reforms. The fulminations of a Tindal, a Hoadly, or a Stephens continued Revolution politics, anathematized absolutism and its apparent support in anniversaries like that of the death of Charles I, and prevented the Establishment from becoming merely a sectarian group. The churchmen, however, who wished to preserve the church as a fundamental part of the constitution, were for the time being completely successful.[57]

Antipopery agitation was of course an old story. Few before Priestley late in the eighteenth century could be brought to admit that Catholics should have charitable treatment. Locke feared them. Memories of the dragonades and the Revocation of the Edict and of other continental persecutions were fresh. Popery and arbitrary government, Catholicism, censorship, and inquisition were associated in the minds of most people. The chief, the only universally valid reason for rejecting the Stuarts, was their religion, believed to be incompatible and irreconcilable with English liberties. Moreover the old cry of "abbey lands" was still astoundingly frequent and shrill. The Hollises, the Pelhams, the Russells, and many other noble families enjoyed property that once belonged to the church. Were a Catholic to mount the throne, their property would be endangered. Harrington and Temple referred to it. In 1687 James II thought it expedient to direct Nathaniel Johnston to write a tract reassuring owners of such lands about his policy even if England should return to the old church. William Coventry and Gilbert Burnet questioned his sincerity. Father Paul (Sarpi) was cited on Catholic claims. Bishop Sprat attributed Russell's role in the Rye House Plot to his fear for his family possessions. Others voiced the fears attributed to the Bedford clan. As long as there was a pretender, and even when there was no immediate danger from one, the matter was raised. Cato in 1721 warned that a popish administration would strip them "to the skin and reduce the English laity to be once more humble cottagers and vassals to the monks, friars and other ecclesiastical gluttons." This echoed the cry of Colonel Titus nearly fifty years before: "Is it for one to expect Moderation again! For our souls we are

Heretics, they will burn and damn us; for our Estates, they will take our lands and put Monks and Fryars upon them."[58] In 1734, *The Free-holder's Alarm*, and in 1745, *A Serious Address* both stressed the dangers to property owners of a Stuart return.

No one can read the *Independent Whig* or *Cato's Letters* without being impressed by the genuine fears of the authors. They looked on all churchmen but respectable freethinkers, and on the dissenters whose cause they espoused, as the chief menace to the liberties they were asserting so loudly. They feared Tories, even if they were Protestants. They disliked the highchurchmen within the Establishment as much as nonjurors outside it. Dr. Brett with his enthusiasm for ceremony, and "Bungay" with the Arminian intolerance of which he was accused, were both condemned.[59] Was this just the prejudice of a small coterie noted for its speculative enterprise? Or did it reflect anxieties which were more general and which can be justified from a study of the situation? On the whole the Whigs had some grounds for their apprehensions. It would be rash to assume that because the Stuarts never had anything but fleeting success in attempts to return, and the government until the days of George III was ostensibly Whig, there was no danger that England would lose some of the freedom achieved so painfully in the seventeenth century. A growing conservatism for a country earlier torn by so many commotions was not likely to continue reformation of grievances or to extend privileges. The passionate refusals of all English parliaments of the Georgian age to repeal Tests or reform the franchise of constituencies show the increasingly reactionary feelings shared by a significant number of eighteenth-century churchmen.

The critics of the church wished to lessen ecclesiastical influence. They argued, like the wise Marquis of Halifax, that "the mists of superstition" of the past which have made "a horizontal hat, a starched band and a long petticoat" pass for essential marks of wisdom and virtue must be dispelled. The claim of churchmen that their church was a fundamental part of the constitution, untouchable and unchangeable, was more strongly urged than ever before. Amongst lawyers or physicians, soldiers and mechanics and professors no one minds the exposure of fools and knaves, but if you so much as touch upon the meanest of the clergy, the whole order regards itself as divided and religion itself in danger.[60] The *Independent Whig* was against all divine right.

The victory that was doubly secured by agitation within and without the church was not a fuller toleration but a complete freedom to ask for it and to criticize everything. Tindal, who had advocated a free press and unrestricted speculation about all matters of religion from 1698 until his death, may have been overconfident about the effect of the unrestrained workings of human reason. Shaftesbury's work was filled with the same presuppositions. Only tyrants and oppressors were afraid to allow freedom. Bigots were slaves and slaves bigots. Even Cromwell, "high as he carried authority, allowed people to talk and rail." In *Tacitus* Gordon argued that complaint was less dangerous than secret execrations. Speech and press should be free. Any attempt to direct opinion was futile.

> Religion is a voluntary Thing; it can no more be forced than Reason, or Memory, or any Faculty of the Soul. To be devout against our Will, is an Absurdity; and it is ridiculous in others to hope to make us so, in Spite of ourselves. We have no Power over the Appetites of others, no more than over their Consciences. Neither a Man's Mind nor his Palate, can be subject to the Jurisdiction of another.[61]

Christ's kingdom was not of this world nor could it be confined to those who agreed to a few dogmas. Given freedom of belief and liberty to speculate, however, men would arrive by themselves at truth, beauty, and goodness. They should be educated, but educated to think freely. They should be imbued with a proper reverence for the right of others to speculate for themselves.

The Independent Whigs—as Trenchard and Gordon were called—were perpetually concerned to show the necessity for discussion of everything political as well as religious. The Independent Whig,

> . . . scorns all implicit faith in the State, as well as the Church. The Authority of Names is nothing to him; he judges all Men by their Actions and Behaviour, and hates a Knave of his own Party, as much as he despises a Fool of another. He consents not that any Man or Body of Men, shall do what they please. He claims a Right of examining all publick Measures and, if they deserve it, of censuring them. As he never saw much Power possessed without some Abuse, he takes upon him to watch those that have it; and to acquit or ex-

pose them according as they apply it to the good of their country, or their own crooked Purposes.[62]

On another occasion Cato maintained that parties in England varied and changed their character just as they were in or out of power. His argument is worth noting, since a difficulty in any discussion of English parties is the extraordinary similarity in positive reactions to an unpopular government. The passage from Cato is worth quoting as a shrewd appraisal of the position even as early as 1721, right after the failure of Atterbury's Jacobite plot.

> The *English* Climate, famous for variable Weather is not less famous for variable Parties, which fall insensibly into an Exchange of Principles, and yet go on to hate or curse one another for those principles. A *Tory* under oppression, or out of a place is a *Whig;* a Whig with power to oppress, is a *Tory.* The *Tory* damns the *Whig* for maintaining a resistance, which he himself never fails to practise, and the *Whig* reproaches the *Tory* with slavish Principles, yet calls him Rebel if he do not practise them.

Cato maintains that,

> . . . the Truth is all men dread the Power of oppression out of their own hands, and almost all men wish it irresistible when it is there . . . the original principle of a *Tory* was to let the Crown do what it pleased . . . of a *Whig,* was to be no further for the Interest of the Crown than the Crown was for the interest of the people. [Both change out of power] . . . The *Tories* therefore are often *Whigs* without knowing it, and the *Whigs* are *Tories* without owning it.[63]

The Whig of these *Letters* emphasized the adaptability of both national and political bodies. There is something to be said for the definition of a Whig as one who was prepared for any change that might seem to be necessary in the constitutional fabric. That by 1721, most of the "party of movement" had abandoned utopian schemes, or new constitutions of their own contriving, as Swift had recently said they wanted, hardly alters the importance of the maintenance amongst the Whigs of the principle that change was legitimate and could be brought about even in a country so fortunate and so free as England.

Cato denied that he was a Republican because in his thirty-seventh essay he had quoted at length from Algernon Sidney's character of the good and evil magistrate. There is nothing particularly republican in these passages "unless virtue and truth be republican . . . Mr. Sidney's book for the main of it, is eternally true, and agreeable to our own constitution, which is the best republic in the world, with a prince at the head of it."[64]

What did the authors of *Cato's Letters* think of the people? They thought men by nature were alike. All were made of the same materials, nor was there greater difference between lord and slave than that which proceeded from chance or education. Many a Cicero had kept sheep, many a Caesar had followed the plough and many a Virgil had foddered cattle. All men were the same to begin with. There was less difference in their talent than some believed. Government should provide public education. According as that were good or bad the people under it would be wise or foolish.[65]

The people, one of *Cato's Letters* pointed out, were nearly always right except when they had been misled by wicked men. Popular judgment in the matter of Gibraltar, a war with Muscovy, the education of the Prince of Wales, the character of the best ministers, were cited in support of this extremely optimistic view. These opinions coincided with those of the authors. The people were by nature honest. A story from Sir Paul Rycaut's *Present State of the Ottoman Empire*,[66] about a poor Turkish cook who became Grand Vizier and justified his master's confidence, was told to illustrate this statement. People had no "bias to be knaves." They realized that government should be for the general good. If the government were corrupted by force as in Denmark, or by pensions as in the England of Charles II, the people surely had a right to resist its enactments. Gordon in his *Tacitus* suggested that the people were apt to be peaceful, grateful, and more moderate than their rulers. Naturally conservative, bound to old names and habits, the people were only unreasonable or turbulent when they had been oppressed. Princes who were not beloved by the people were in a weak and precarious position, although the desire to keep quiet as long as possible might permit their rule over dangerously long periods.[67]

"After so much said about the people it may not be improper to add something concerning the nobility. As by the people," a revealing paragraph continued, "I mean not the idle and indigent rabble under which name the people are often understood and traduced, but all who have property without the privileges of nobility; so by the latter I mean such as are possessed of privileges denied to the people." Nature, in other words, produced no nobility, but education and property combined to endow certain classes with political rights, privileges, and duties. In society no man should be higher than others but for the good of others. A civil establishment could make a noble, but could not secure a soul to fit the title, or ensure descendants who would deserve the same privileges. Reverence paid to title and rank was of little account and must be regarded as flattery by all wise men. To be great was not in every man's power, but to be good was in the power of all; "thus far every man may be upon a level with the other, the lowest with the highest, and then might thus come to be morally as well as naturally equal." The first springs of inequality were in some measure to be found in human nature but the most important factor was the nature of society. No one wished to be equal with anyone to whom he could be superior. Self love was always accompanied by hope. An ambition to excel might be too much discouraged, as in Venice, or too little as in places like Turkey.[68]

One of *Cato's Letters* occupied itself in speculation about what would happen if all magistrates, all priests, all officers, were dismissed. Some people at least would feel that the government would be improved. Yet the filling of those vacancies might be difficult and this provided an opportunity for the discussion of the complexity of political science.[69] Every ploughman, of course, knew a good government from a bad one, and whether or not he had peace and security under it. Every man should know about the government. Public truths should never be kept secret. Government was a trust committed by all, or nearly all, to one or a few who ought to be bounded by restraints. Some people had thought that once the government had been so committed, private men ought not to bother with it, but this was foolish. To say that private men have nothing to do with government was to say that they have no concern with their happiness and their misery. "A whole country can never find an equivalent for itself and, consequently, a whole country can never be bribed . . . while the public voice is pretended to be declared by one or a few for vile and private ends, the public know nothing that is done till they feel the effect." Hence the necessity for public information and public interest in current events. Cato constantly pointed out the necessity for education and interest in political science.[70]

Cato raised the difficult question of who should judge when the magistrate had done ill. He concluded that neither magistrate nor people had such a right restrictive of the other. Every man should act according to his own conscience. "In truth, I think it is much the right and business of the people to judge whether their prince be good or bad . . . as to judge whether he be dead or alive."[71] Cato goes on to say that where the interest of the governors and the governed clash, there could be no judge between them. No foreign power could arbitrate, no doctrine of complete submission could possibly meet their case. He dismissed as absurd the idea that this doctrine of resistance was likely to lead to anarchy or worse. People were unlikely to rebel until public grievances were so enormous that there could be no question about them. "Upon this principle of people's judging for themselves and resisting lawless force, stands our late happy *Revolution*."[72]

The natural power of the people checked the magistrates by tumults and insurrection. Cato suggested that these were a poor way of subduing and disciplining the government but he was completely convinced of the rights of resistance. He admired Brutus and Algernon Sidney. He despised a doctrine of passive obedience since certainly "no man will suffer injustice and violence when he can help himself." The twenty-eighth letter defended the reputation of the Roman hero whose name provided the pseudonym of the authors. Cato contended that great traitors ought to be hanged. Cato had written against all sorts of tyranny and therefore Cato was said to have been an incendiary and an enemy of the constitution. The attitude of the churchmen and their condemnation of rebellious subjects was noted in this letter. Princes had run into wild wars without consent, "yet if their subjects oppose them they are guilty of resistance which is reckoned a rebellion, a very terrible and trying crime . . . what strange Doctrine is this? that every Man in a Nation shall suffer for the Sins of one Man whom they could not restrain; or that any Man shall suffer for the Crimes of another?"[73]

Without the right of resistance men cannot defend liberty, the chief topic of his letters.

> All Men are born free. Liberty is a Gift which they receive from God himself, nor can they alienate the same by Consent, though possibly they may forfeit it by Crimes. No man has Power over his own Life, or to dispose of his own Religion, and cannot consequently transfer the Power of either to anybody else; much less can he give away the Lives and Liberties, Religion or acquired Property of his posterity, who will be born as free as himself was born, and can never be bound by his wicked and ridiculous Bargain.
>
> The Right of the Magistrate arises only from the Right of private Men to defend themselves, to repel Injuries and to punish those who commit them . . . every man is answerable for the Wrong which he does. A Power to do Good can never become a Warrant for doing Evil.[74]

Liberty would bring all benefits with it:

> Liberty naturally draws new People to it, as well as encreases the old Stock; and Men as naturally run when they dare from Slavery and Wretchedness, whithersoever they can help themselves. Hence great Cities losing their liberty become desarts, and little Towns by Liberty grow great Cities.[75]

Cato paired liberty and equality. Equality could not long be preserved without an Agrarian. When men were too rich, and at the public expense, with monstrous fortunes, when courts were too luxurious and people too poor, then it was the right of the people to rebel against their condition. On the other hand, in "happy Britain" the distribution of property was adapted to its government. There was general liberty, security of property, and private virtue. The time had not come for a more equal commonwealth:

> It proceeds from a consummate Ignorance in Politicks, to think that a Number of Men agreeing together, can make and hold a Commonwealth, before Nature has prepared the Way; for she alone must do it. An Equality of Estate will give an Equality of Power; and an Equality of power is a Commonwealth or Democracy. An

Agrarian law, or something equivalent to it, must make or find a suitable Disposition of Property; and when that comes to be the case, there is no hindering a popular Form of Government.[76]

In the gradual development of greater equality and property liberty played a considerable part. The Romans owed the great progress they made to the freedom enjoyed under their commonwealth. Improvement of knowledge brought neither terror to the magistrate nor danger to the people. Freedom protected the state. It stimulated its citizens to greater exertions. Nothing was too hard for liberty. Great discoveries in arts and sciences occurred in countries where free enquiry was allowed. Preservation and extension of liberty was all important.[77]

Toland and Shaftesbury

Both Toland and Shaftesbury have attracted more attention from philosophers than from historians. Their significance for the student of libertarian thought is not inconsiderable, but neither is it easy to define. Perhaps Toland's service lay in his definitions of politics and in his interest in the preservation of the theories not only of his patrons, Molesworth and Shaftesbury, but of their seventeenth-century predecessors, Milton, Harrington, and Sidney. Shaftesbury's contribution must be sought in his philosophy and its libertarian potential.

Modern work on Toland has come from continental rather than English scholars.[78] His philosophy brought him notice during his life from men like Leibnitz, and since his death has secured him a place in most histories of the thought of the eighteenth century. A genuine freethinker, he was passionately curious about, though consistently opposed to, superstition of all sorts. He studied pantheism, Jewish theology, the Druids, and he was a keen observer, quick to note analogy. Some illustration of his talents and his methods may be found both in his antiquarian studies and in those notes exchanged in manuscript between Molesworth and Toland which were written by each as they read Martin's *Description of the Western Islands of Scotland.* Toland was most commonly regarded as a deist, largely on the evidence afforded by his *Christianity not Mysterious* (1696). His religion was eclectic. He may have been brought up as a Catholic. He was educated first among the dissenters and at Glasgow. He then studied both at Oxford and abroad. With the exception of his own prejudice against authoritarian theologians, retained until he died, Toland never found it difficult to alter and amend his beliefs.[79]

Toland was early in life a recipient of the bounty of some Protestant sectaries. A little later he became a protégé of Shaftesbury and of Molesworth. Harley used him for a while. He was employed in the mission of Lord Macclesfield to Hanover at the end of King William's reign, and not very long after revisited the continent in the years 1708–10. Since he had attracted the interest of certain royal and wealthy Europeans, he was probably supported by them during these travels. In England, besides help from Molesworth, he may have picked up some profits from his many publications, but he was never in receipt of a secure or large income.[80]

Toland cannot be cleared from a charge of ingratitude to many that helped him, but his politics seem to have been consistent whether he was working for Shaftesbury or Harley, or later with the Stanhope Whigs. He supported the campaign of Trenchard and Moyle against a standing army. He attacked the Stuarts in *The Art of Governing by Partys,* and pointed out, probably at Shaftesbury's suggestion, *The Dangers of Mercenary Parliaments.* He also criticized Protestants and Whigs, but was entirely loyal to the Revolution and the Hanoverian succession. The many times reprinted *Gentle Art of Restoring,* written in the heat of his disillusionment with Harley, certainly helped to excite public opinion at a critical time against supposed Jacobite designs. His commentaries on both Milton and Harrington did a good deal to spread their ideas. The prefatory note to the *Shaftesbury Molesworth Letters* was as fair a statement of the politics of the friends and their coterie as may be discovered. This publication, it is true, annoyed the family and widow of the third earl who could not be expected to enjoy seeing Shaftesbury's hesitations and questions about his marriage made public. But Molesworth was alive and knew about Toland's intentions. He would certainly have protested at any misrepresentation of fact. *The State Anatomy* may be regarded as a manifesto of the Molesworth connection. Toland had no personal influence. Nor does he seem to have

had many intimate friends. John Raulins is mentioned as one by Desmaizeaux; Molesworth was another. Anthony Collins was on visiting
terms with him, but on hearing of his death expressed no sorrow, only
anxiety lest he should not manage to secure the return of books that
had been borrowed from him.[81]

Toland's excursions into contemporary controversy were for the
most part for causes which would now be considered good. He was for
the rule of law rather than the biased will of any prince, for security
of judges and for fair trial for those accused. He was against the corruption of electors or elected. He supported the claims of the Irish to
have laws of their own devising, claims of the Jews to equal civil rights,
as well as demands of dissenters of all sorts provided they were not
themselves intolerant. His emphasis on property was typical of his age
though perhaps ludicrous in a man like himself. He was not democratical. He believed in the use of reason, the right of all men alike. The
best of all governments was the English Commonwealth.[82] That word,
often associated with anarchy, confusion, levelling, and sedition, really
signified liberty and order, equal laws, strict impartial justice, a wise
and liberal education, economy, an upright administration, a nursery
of capacious, daring, and gallant spirits, and a national religion duly
maintained but tolerating innocent dissenters. Toland defended himself against his detractors in *The State Anatomy*. He declared himself a
friend to religion which he was not, an enemy to superstition which
he undoubtedly was, a supporter of good kings, and where there was
occasion, a deposer of tyrants.[83]

Last among the Real Whigs to be discussed in this chapter, Shaftesbury is the best known and yet most difficult to analyze. There have
indeed been many studies of his life work and influence. Yet his politics have escaped definition. That he was keenly concerned in current
problems and that his philosophy was liberal have been recognized. A
summary of the politics of the *Characteristics* must be attempted.

Shaftesbury's record is simple enough and very well known—his
early education by Locke, his unhappy schooling at Winchester; his
travels with a tutor and Sir John Cropley, a lifelong friend; his brief
years of political activity interrupted by increasing ill health and journeys to relieve it; his happy marriage of convenience advised by Robert
Molesworth; his last voyage after the birth of a son in 1710, to Italy; his

two Italian years cheered by the devotion of his wife and servants, and by the friendship of Molesworth's son, John, then envoy at Florence. His last energies were devoted to his *Characteristics* which were indeed to bring him continuing reputation and an influence he might never have enjoyed, in spite of his wealth, position, and ability, had health allowed him to follow a public career longer.[84]

During the years that Shaftesbury was at all active in English politics he had, he later wrote to Molesworth, but a small following.

> For saving yourself, and perhaps one or two more (I speak the most) I had none that acted with me, against the injustice and corruption of both parties; each of them enflam'd against me, particularly one, because of my pretended Apostacy, which was only adhering to those principles upon which their party was founded.

In these active years his estates and position ensured him some influence in certain constituencies.[85] His personality also had its effect, though he would not appear to have been a ready speaker. The well-known story about his share in passage of the Treason Bill of 1695 suggests that his emotional intensity rather than his eloquence carried the day. With Molesworth and Trenchard, he seems to have been discouraged by the standing army controversy. But it could not have marred his relationship with Somers for long. The Whig lawyer recalled the earl to his aid during the crisis in politics, 1699–1700, when the Tories were in the ascendancy, and when both feared for the future of the Protestant succession. Shaftesbury was a firm believer in the clauses about placemen in the Act of Settlement. Together with Somers, he also supported the Kentish Petitioners of 1701—voted scandalous, seditious, and insolent—against the attack of the malignant party upon the "ancientest and greatest" of the English privileges, the right to address and petition the throne. As important, perhaps, as the support by the Whig lords of the popular party, was the aid rendered by Daniel Defoe. The victory was due to the journalists rather than to the politicians.[86]

Shaftesbury was depressed by the rise of Tory sentiment in the next few years. He traveled. He returned to live in or near London, 1705–08, to support the Union and to advise with Godolphin and with Somers. But his health was poor and never enabled him to fulfill the hopes of friends like Molesworth that he would join with the Lord Treasurer to bring about a thorough reformation in public affairs. By the time that Harley had more than confirmed their worst suspicions about his integrity, Shaftesbury was obliged to seek health abroad. He was as shocked as others by Sacheverell, that "seditious" priest, and the rabble that followed and supported him.[87]

Shaftesbury often made statements typical of the aristocratic Whig of the day. He was "truly monarchical" in his principles. He distrusted those who incited their fellows to rebellion. The resulting confusion might convert good governments into absolute tyrannies. He thought England was as free as the existing balance of power between her estates would bear. He distributed Toland's *Harrington* among his friends in 1700,[88] but any commentary from him is lacking. He was not democratical. Like the aristocrat he was, he referred to "laborious hinds." Nonetheless both his activity and his writings combine to suggest optimism, liberality, and a kind of realism in his approach to politics not at once apparent in the *Characteristics* or the edition of Whichcote's sermons.[89]

In the *Characteristics* his theories tend toward the liberal and reveal an insistence upon the social and moral instincts of man and upon the universal good; upon the necessity for freedom for any kind of achievement, scientific, aesthetic, or political; upon an optimistic view of the possibilities within every man given the proper circumstances. Attempts to resolve the relations of science and revelation, science and art, reason and emotion are not to be found in Shaftesbury who combined an empirical approach to political and theological problems with an immense self-reliance on matters of taste and morals. He rejected the authority both of the schools and the churches, but substituted the still, small voice of taste and sense. Was he reasonable or romantic? The question is inappropriate. He was immensely sensible in every way, not least in his illogicalities.

Over and over again in Shaftesbury there is a realism in what he says which sharply divides him from partisan writers. This was true when he talked about immediate political issues, and regretted the selfishness of those who avoided taking sides as well as the wickedness of troublemakers who created schism. He saw in party cabal as well as in religious societies a natural expression of the social instincts of man. He realized that the greater community "fell not easily under the eye"; that the universal good was to many a distant affair. He advocated the study of the general welfare, the interests of the whole world, and he wanted all to love the public and seek its greatest happiness. He deplored savage and destroying wars and saw the dangers of large imperial systems. He laid most stress upon the removal of restrictions, the free development of man's potential benevolence, and upon the natural fulfillment of herding instincts.

Thus Shaftesbury recognized in the community the proper outlet for man's disposition "to cantonize" into groups or states or societies. Confederation had a charm. The highest genius often showed an inclination to combine. The human infant was the weakest of animals, from birth dependent upon society. If bred to slavery man would naturally be less enterprising than if born to freedom. His instincts were good. He was benevolent, and, unless artificially restricted and intimidated, would seek the happiness and well being of his community. Shaftesbury regretted the absence in English of a word like "patria" to express the love of country. He himself was patriotic and appreciated the advantages of focusing affection and endeavour upon the beloved country. Where the state was vast and public affairs seemed the interest only of a few, the combining principles of man could be satisfied only in cliques and cabals.[90]

Shaftesbury's attention and endeavours were for England. Neither he, nor Molesworth, nor Trenchard, nor any of their friends, spent much time in speculation about the reasons for development of free institutions in one state rather than another. They were immensely interested in the processes of decay which brought about the dissolution and decline of once happy nations. Shaftesbury denied that soil or climate affected law and government. The English climate was worse than most, but Englishmen had been fortunate in their ancestors and in the government and laws devised by them. He was refreshingly free from sentiment about old customs. England had, he believed, improved since the days of good Queen Bess.[91] He ardently wished for further improvement. What he feared was that past achievements should be undone by intolerance and by restrictions on the free exercise of virtue and genius for the extension of happiness. Both

Locke, his own teacher, and Hobbes were greatly to be blamed for denying the moral sense of man and thereby throwing morality to the winds. Shaftesbury, in spite of the philosophies of the Oxford Tories, had confidence in his fellow countrymen. Fundamentally they all loved freedom. Differences between them, Whig or Tory, Anglican or sectary, were not very considerable.[92] He sought to remind them of the benefits they enjoyed and of the possibility of achieving even greater happiness in the future.

The good life, whether of the universe or of the smaller community within it, could not exist without liberty. Sound education and free opinion were emphasized. Anthony Collins, the younger friend of Locke, was also a disciple of Shaftesbury. Like him, Collins refused to confound licentiousness with liberty in thought.[93] How else than by taking thought could man arrive at perfection? All great men from Socrates to Tillotson had supported this demand. Dogmatical churchmen or determined atheists were equally to be eschewed since man could be born into slavery or deflected into injustices. With freedom, however, a balance between interest and benevolence could be maintained.[94]

Shaftesbury's preoccupation with the fine arts led him to stress the advantage to them of political freedom. He wanted a public for his own work and he had confidence in the public taste. With the growth of liberty greater genius would appear in Britain. In *The Moralists* he had argued that as yet man had not enjoyed the full opportunities to establish virtue. Christians absorbed with another world had seldom preached the possibilities of progress in this. Yet true religion and right judgment were most likely to appear in the good state where just laws promoted the public welfare. In the future anything was possible for free countries. Shaftesbury did not restrict this improvement to any one class or group; genius would flourish with the general liberalizing of public and private life:

> In reality the people are no small parties in this cause. Nothing moves successfully without them. There can be no public, but where they are included. And without a public voice, knowingly guided and directed, there is nothing which can raise a true ambition in the

artist; nothing which can exalt the genius of the workman, or make him emulous of afterfame, and of the approbation of his country, and of posterity.

Shaftesbury continues in the vein which makes us regret that he wrote so little directly on political theory:

> For with these, he naturally, as a freeman, must take part; in these he has a passionate concern and interest, raised in him by the same genius of liberty, the same laws and government, by which his property and the rewards of his pains and industry, are secure to him and to his generation after him.
>
> Everything cooperates in such a State, towards the improvement of arts and science . . . when the free spirit of a nation turns itself this way, judgments are formed, critics arise; and the public ear and eye improve; a right taste prevails and in a manner forces its way. Nothing is so improving, nothing so natural, so congenial to the liberal arts as that reigning liberty and high spirit of a people, which from the habit of judging the highest matters for themselves makes them freely judge of other subjects, and enter thoroughly into the characters as well of men and manners, as of the products or works of men, in art and science.[95]

Attempting to determine the difference between Whig and Commonwealthman in, say, 1727, is somewhat like trying to distinguish between northern and southern Democrats, or the Republicans of New Hampshire and those of the Dakotas. All pay tribute to Revolution politics, that is, to an established constitution, now expressed not only in immemorial customs, but in the statutes and declarations of the last quarter century. Most Whigs thought change had gone far enough. They maintained a right to resist the pretender and his claims of divine right. They were warmly attached to the Protestant religion and realized the value of the support given to its cause by the old sects. They did not want a monarch who pushed his own policies or interfered with the monopoly in government of the ruling class. Considerable deference was paid to the king as a support to aristocratic status. There were some dangers in their complacent assumptions about their almost complete control of church and state.

Foreigners remarked that despotism might well have been established in England, as in France, if it hadn't been for the existence of parties amongst the men who dominated public life. The Jacobites moderated the influence of the Tories, and moreover, as Lord Shelburne was to observe, ensured a measure of union in the kingdom. The republican fringe stirred up the Whigs. Had one side or the other prevailed, the anarchy of the Interregnum or the tyrannies of the French monarchy might easily have upset that wholesome equilibrium which distinguished the Augustan Age.[96] The Whiggish malcontents or Commonwealthmen in varying ways provided a deterrent to complacency, and reminders of the need for improvement and the continual adaptation of even good governments to economic and political changes. Like the sects and the party system, they prevented stagnation in church and in state. In an age when Englishmen stressed the sovereignty, not of a divinely appointed king but of a triumphant parliament, the Real Whigs reminded them of the rights of electors and of the unenfranchised, of the virtues of rotation in office and of the necessity for constant vigilance against the corruptions of power whether wielded by king, ministers, or estates. Molesworth and his friends admonished their countrymen about present dangers. They called attention to the lessons of history and the possibilities of the future.[97]

V

The Case of Ireland

Liberal Ideas Before Grattan and Tone

Irish history between the Boyne and the accession of George III was uneventful, but Ireland was miserable and downtrodden. The case of Ireland (title of Molyneux's famous tract) was hard. Torn by internal feuds between conquered and conqueror, as well as by rivalries in the Protestant Ascendancy, administered and restricted by a government external to the country and unsympathetic to its troubles, Ireland was unhappy and without means to help herself except by individual sacrifice and self-discipline. Open oppression and widespread poverty stimulated some thoughtful and brilliant men to consideration of both political and social problems. All Irishmen were sharply aware of the difficulties of their relationship with England. The sentiments and aspirations of the old Irish, except for an occasional complaint or comment, remained hidden. Perhaps they still cherished hopes of an independent kingdom under a Catholic king, but they made no overt attempts to secure one, nor did they support the risings in England of the 'Fifteen or the 'Forty-five. The discontent of both the ruling Episcopalians and of the less privileged Presbyterians, that is of all Protestant Irish, was obvious and found frequent expression. Protests were rendered less than effective because the protection afforded by London against the real or supposed Jacobitism of the Catholic majority was still felt to be necessary to their continued existence in Ireland, and to the security of their lives and estates.

The Irish Protestants were not republican, or with very few exceptions, Commonwealthmen, but their own situation forced from them expression of ideas potentially revolutionary and useful to rebellious colonists, to critics of mercantilism, and to supporters of full civil and religious liberties for all mankind. Irishmen in the first half of the eighteenth century protested the status and character of their parliament and denied England's claims to overrule its wishes and judicial decisions. They urged the employment in Ireland of men of "English blood and Irish birth," rather than officials lacking all knowledge of Irish problems. They hoped to ameliorate their economic condition either by an equal Union, similar to the Scotch arrangements of 1707, or by persuading England that her interest as well as theirs would be better served by relaxation of commercial restrictions. They were appalled by the poverty of their country and shocked by the luxury of most of their own class as well as by a general absence of public spirit. They sought to improve the situation by examining the causes of scarcity and destitution in a land of plentiful natural resources. Many suggestions were made about the possibility of improvement which depended upon Irish resolution rather than English concession: a public bank, premiums for technological and agricultural inventions and methods, various self-denying ordinances were all proposed. Moreover, serious consideration was given to the problems of the working classes and to concessions to religious and social needs which would encourage greater industry and contentment among them.

Such proposals were not confined to either Whigs or Tories. The Whigs in Ireland supported the Revolution and the Protestant succession. Tories were as usual suspected of Jacobitism by the Whigs. Not all Whigs were reformers, not all Tories proponents of passive resistance; and practically none of them were adherents of the exiled Stuarts. Amongst men of all political prejudices may be found critics of the existing order. Swift was a Tory, an Irish nationalist prepared to use Whig arguments against English tyrannies and a keen observer of the poverty and the virtues of the Irish poor. Berkeley supported authoritarian theories and wrote in support of passive obedience. This lost him the sympathy of men like Molesworth and William King whose ideas about economic, and even political, remedies for Irish miseries were in fact very similar to those put forward in *The Querist.* Molyneux, Molesworth, and Swift were more outspoken about English policies than Samuel Madden, Dobbs, and Berkeley. All advocated antimercantilist ideas, and urged reconsideration by the London administration of the Irish situation. All attempted to persuade their countrymen of the necessity for residence and for determined attacks on the appalling conditions around them. All condemned the absentee, the self-indulgent, and the unenterprising amongst their fellows. Prejudices against the subject Irish softened and proposals to help Catholics circulated. Presbyterians, more liberal in their purely political speculations, were also at this time inclined to urge greater concessions to nonconformists of all religious persuasions, and as the century wore on, showed a tendency shared by a few liberal Episcopalians to make common cause with the Catholic Irish in demands for self rule and Catholic emancipation.

Irish circumstances in this century stimulated the development and spread of liberal ideas. Since the same situation also resulted in a large emigration to the New World, these ideas reinforced colonial theories and assumptions. The persons who left Ireland were not all men of the same political persuasion, but among them were some at least whose role in the country they adopted was significant, both in the achievement of independence and in drafting of a new constitution. Irishmen also left Ireland for Scotland and England, to be educated, to seek new careers, or, in the case of many Presbyterians, to enter educational institutions.

Hutcheson's influence in Scotland was such that his ideas must be described later in connection with Scottish liberalism, but his Irish life and friends must not be forgotten. Nor can the influence of men like the Viscount Molesworth and the saintly Berkeley over their readers and admirers in Scotland be ignored. The theories of *The Querist* and of *An Essay on Trade* by Dobbs, as well as of a number of disciples of Molyneux, contributed to the developing economic liberalism of the later half of the eighteenth century throughout the British Isles. English radicals were influenced by Molesworth and during the eighteenth century were in touch with other Irish writers and thinkers. During the reforming campaigns of Cartwright, Jebb, and Wyvill, Irishmen like Grattan and Drennen, confessed heirs of the Irishmen to be discussed, were in close communication with both Scottish and English reformers as well as with Americans, and in considerable agreement with most of their aspirations.

A rather arbitrary arrangement of material follows. Molyneux's work must come first with some commentary on its contribution to Irish nationalism and to antimercantilist arguments. A group of men who carried on his protests at English claims and legislative enactments must next be described. Archbishop King was a prophet of philosophic optimism, yet he provides a useful example of discontent among the ruling Anglo-Irish, and in his long career he was connected with many controversies and with a variety of persons. Maxwell and Arthur Dobbs, two younger contemporaries, worked to promote a Union and a relaxation of restrictions by England. Dobbs also considered the whole matter of subject races. Swift, a friend of both King and Molesworth, supported and shared their concern about Irish economic conditions in spite of the political differences about Whigs and Tories. His use of the Whiggish canon in this connection was as wholehearted as that of a famous agitator of mid-century, Charles Lucas. Both called on the authority of Molyneux, Sidney, and others to further their campaigns against external oppression and internal malfeasance. A group of reformers, most of whom would have shrunk from any connection with radical ideas—Madden, Prior, and Berkeley, classmates at school and at college and friends throughout their careers—admonished their fellow countrymen about their faults and tried to persuade and encourage them to do all that was possible to remedy Ireland's troubles. Though they refrained from all but the mildest criticism of English policies, they will be found to share many of the reactions of the more violent Molesworth and Swift. They advocated much the same policies and reforms at home and in England. Finally the Scotch-Irish asserters of civil and religious liberties will be briefly described.

William Molyneux and His Case of Ireland

In his own lifetime, William Molyneux (1656–1698) was widely known for his scientific and philosophical activities. Since his death as much or more of his reputation has rested upon the tract published in the last year of his life. *The Case of Ireland,* reprinted at least eleven times in the next century, was to be cited whenever Irishmen wished to refute English claims of ascendancy. As time wore on it become the accepted manifesto of anticolonialism and of antimercantilist ideas. It was widely read by all sections of Irish opinion and found a public in America besides. The circumstances of its author and the occasion and method of its composition are therefore of considerable interest to the student of developing liberal ideas.[1]

The Molyneux family moved from England to Ireland in the sixteenth century. Sir Thomas was Chancellor of the Irish Exchequer and died in 1697–98. His grandson lived in Dublin and fathered a large family of four girls and five boys; only three besides William need be noticed. One daughter married Anthony Dopping who became a bishop. Another married into the Madden family and was the mother of Samuel, author of *Reflections and Resolutions*—to be described later on. Thomas was an antiquarian of note, and a friend of both King and Berkeley who cared for his son after his death.

William, author of *The Case*, was born in the same year as Robert Molesworth and attended Trinity College, as well as Inner Temple in London. His tutor at Trinity was William Palliser, later Archbishop of Cashel. In 1678 he married Lucy, daughter of Sir William Domville, Chief Justice of Ireland. Her health was delicate and she died soon after their return from England where they had taken refuge during the troubles of James II's reign in Ireland. Molyneux twice represented Dublin University in parliament after the Revolution. He was active both before and after the Revolution in starting a philosophical club which is regarded as the precursor of the Royal Society founded by Prior in 1731. He knew Molesworth. He formed a warm pen friendship with Locke and much enjoyed meeting the philosopher shortly before his death in the October of the year in which *The Case* appeared. An early death, at forty-two, left his fame to the continued enthusiasm of his readers, rather than to any organized coterie of disciples.[2] In *The Case* Molyneux adopted the revolutionary theories he had discovered in Locke. He was largely responsible in his alma mater for the study of the philosopher's work and the early adoption of the *Essay* as a text.

The Case of Ireland was planned in the first instance to help William King, at that time bishop of Derry and involved in litigation with the Londonderry society. The English House of Lords had overridden earlier Irish decisions, anticipating somewhat the situation of 1719, in which year the case of Annesley *v.* Sherlock was decided. In spite of Irish protests that appeals lay only to the Lords in Dublin, a statute asserting the dependency of Ireland was then passed in London to remove all possible doubts about the powers and pretensions of England over Ireland. While Molyneux was collecting material for his friend in connection with the earlier dispute, which would support claims for the antiquity and independence of Irish institutions, he was further roused by news of the bill against Irish woollens which was passed by the English Commons in 1698. Both grievances were mentioned early in his tract. *The Case* was therefore concerned with legal, political, and economic relations with England. Throughout Molyneux sought to demonstrate from natural and constitutional law, from history and from political science that Ireland, though united through the crown, was independent of the English parliament.[3]

Earlier writers had anticipated much of both theory and precedent cited in *The Case*. A debt to Locke's *Treatises*,[4] was warmly acknowledged, though these essays were not acknowledged by Locke. Passages in *The Case* on consent and on conquest are reminiscent, in phrase as well as sentiment, of Locke's work. Thus the revolutionary potential in the Englishman was perpetuated in part at least by the popularity of a tract occasioned by mercantilist policies the philosopher had endorsed or even originated at the Board of Trade in London. *The Case* had many Irish precursors. Professor McIlwain long ago examined some of these in his study of the American Revolution. Patrick Darcy in a widely circulated speech in 1641 had attempted to distinguish between the regal authority of Charles, which the Catholic Irish were prepared to acknowledge and utilize, and the dominion claimed by the English parliament against which they were in rebellion.[5] Not a little of the historical and legal material used by Darcy was itself derived from Sir John Davies's authoritative *A Discoverie of the True Causes Why Ireland Was Never Entirely Subdued*. This book, objective in a fashion rarely followed in the period among English administrators, was later singled out by Hugh Reilly in *Ireland's Case* (1695) as the only Protestant writing which did not try "to stifle or disguise the truth."[6]

It seems likely that Molyneux derived much of the material presented by both Davies and Darcy from a manuscript drawn up for the use of James, Duke of Ormonde, Viceroy of Ireland, by his father-in-law, Sir William Domville, in July, 1660. Irishmen were uneasy about their status. Domville's treatise used most of the precedents of earlier works and much of its argument reappears in Molyneux's *Case*. The two were copied one after the other into a volume now among the manuscripts of Trinity College and clearly indicate the extent of Molyneux's indebtedness. Domville concluded his observations by maintaining that the independency of Ireland was established by common law, statute law, the practice of former ages, and by royal recognition shown by titles and by prerogative act. Domville,[7] Anthony Dopping, and Molyneux shared an interest in the Irish *Modus* which afforded them evidence of the antiquity of Irish institutions. To these arguments and examples Molyneux added some further reflections upon recent events and some of the theories about government he had derived from his friend, Locke. The resulting heady mixture was eagerly imbibed by Irish readers. An Oxford diarist, Thomas Hearne, wrote of Molyneux that he was an ingenious man and a good mathematician, but a "downright republican." Yet the evidence on which Hearne based this condemnation was a diatribe, not against regal powers, but against the growing claims of the English parliament over plantations and colonies.[8]

Much of *The Case* tiresomely reiterates legal and historical arguments. These had some basis and cannot altogether be ignored by the historians of law. Molyneux's fame as an advocate of independency rests, not on his precedents which could be offset by others damaging to his theory, but on a few striking paragraphs and phrases revealing his belief in "the inherent rights of all mankind." He wished to give, and many Irish wished to find, "modest, dispassionate, irrefragable proof" of the rights and liberties of his native land. He could not, he claimed, believe that Englishmen could ever think of making "the least breach in the Rights and Liberties of their Neighbours." No one could be a sincere believer in freedom who is not in favour of all men enjoying its blessings. Those who attacked freedom anywhere were likely, themselves, to suffer by the weakening of this good old cause. All over Europe the noble Gothic institutions which once preserved German liberties were vanishing. England retained hers; Poland had some slight remains. He could not imagine that the English, "those great asserters of all liberties," could really mean to abolish the rights of parliament in one kingdom of the three.

Not only was it dangerous to the parliamentary cause everywhere to weaken the authority of any one legislature; it was entirely against reason and the laws of nature as laid down or explained by Locke, Puffendorf, and Grotius. Man had a fundamental right to property and conscience. A tax without consent would be little better than robbery. Laws without the knowledge or agreement of the governed could have no validity. All men by nature were in a state of equality in respect to jurisdiction and dominion. Molyneux quoted Hooker in this connection. He not only denied that precedents in law and history could give this right to England; he also discussed how far it was reasonable to treat a conquest or a conquered country. Ireland was not a colony, nor had Ireland been conquered. He strengthened his argument by discussing the nature of conquest and the rights it conferred on the conquerors. It was these statements that were peculiar to his book, and acceptance of these assumptions removed any possible grounds for oppression. A military victory might give certain privileges to the victor. Persons not involved in the struggle (or their children) could be punished for faults not their own. Thus, even if it could be argued that Ireland was ever conquered, it could never be shown that the posterity of a conquered people could be deprived of the inherent rights of man.

No country had a right to injure another unless an actual state of war existed. Prohibition of the goods even of competing woollen manufacturers could in no way be justified by statements that they hurt English industry and commerce. This claim struck at the whole basis of regulation of the economic life of colonies and plantations by England, and at the mercantilist theories of the time. In the long run Molyneux argued the general good would be better served by a strict regard for the rights of man everywhere, than by selfish restrictions which eventually would work to the detriment of both the state which imposed them and that against which they discriminated.[9]

The Case of Ireland put forward a theory of natural inherent rights of man which excluded all possibility of dominion by one country over another, and stated with great forcefulness arguments against the

Navigation, Cattle, and Woollen Acts restraining Irishmen from freedom in the development of their own economic possibilities. A long series of tracts echoed Molyneux's principles.[10] Many English and a few Irish attempted to refute them. William Atwood, later Chief Justice of New York and not very popular for his insistence there on English rights, wrote against Molyneux in terms contradictory of every argument about inherent rights. Moreover, he claimed that English colonies and dependencies compared very favourably with those of other countries. Like John Cary, he thought Ireland should be grateful for the protection she received and that all colonies should pay something for the security enjoyed. He disliked what Cary called Molyneux's "Trumpet of Rebellion." Its principles, he alleged, if carried to their logical conclusion, would result in a restoration of the native Irish to their lands.[11]

Most of the antimercantilist tracts which considered *The Case of Ireland* devoted some attention to the whole problem of colonies and dependents, and urged the advantages of love and gratitude over fear and helpless subjection as security for English dominion and empire. The general theme was bolstered by analogies from Scottish and Welsh history. The growth of British towns and counties, it was argued, had not adversely affected the prosperity of London. Moreover, as time wore on the evil effects of continued restrictions—the poverty of Ireland, the loss of manpower due to emigration and the general torpor of the country—were all pointed out. A few people like Berkeley suggested adaptations to conditions rather than revolt from them, but he, too, gently asked if Union and freer trade would actually hurt England.[12]

The Case of Ireland influenced the course of Irish protests against dependency in a political or legal as well as an economic sense. It was not the first protest against parliament's claims to rule Ireland as a province, but it was one of the most effective, and included nearly all arguments past or present, legal or philosophical, which were to be used in the struggles of the nationalists.

Brisk Asserters of Irish Liberties: King, Maxwell, Dobbs, and Swift

During the thirty years following the publication of *The Case of Ire-land* the political prospects for those who shared its views grew darker. Restrictions were increased, and claims were enforced by statute without any compensating concessions whatever. William King seldom received any favourable attention from the English church; his advice was nearly always neglected. This was certainly due to his endorsement of the views of Molyneux and opposition to English claims. Maxwell wrote on behalf of Union, hoping thereby for relaxation of the Navigation Acts and other restrictive measures. Dobbs, his junior, wrote later in similar vein, though he did not publish all his reflections. He continued in his *Essay on Trade* (1729–31) the attack on mercantilism. He also considered the problem of the Irish native in relation to his experience at home and also in America, where in mid-century he was Governor of North Carolina. Swift, often at variance with Molesworth and King before the accession of George I, and bitterly opposed to a project for an Irish bank which Maxwell favoured in 1720–21, was closely allied with all of them in opposition to the act of George I asserting the dependency of Ireland. His vitriolic campaign against Wood's Halfpence, and many proposals for the betterment of the state of Ireland involved the acceptance of doctrines about the rights of man which his earlier Toryism had rejected. Even Charles Lucas, a mid-century rebel against the Dublin oligarchy, and against the status, character, and duration of the Dublin parliament, used no more telling quotations of English political theorists on the side of liberty than the Dean of St. Patrick's.

William King (1650–1729) was prominent in more than one field of activity. His *De Origine Mali* (1702) at once attracted the serious attention of thoughtful continental and British scholars. After his death a translation by Edmund Law attracted many more readers. Its optimism and its emphasis on true notions of liberty must be analyzed in considering liberal theories during the reign of George II.[13] In his lifetime King was a vigorous and upright churchman, interested in the improvement of ecclesiastical property and learning, conscientious about the duties of his high offices, and willing to rebuke even his intimate friends for any lapse from Christian or public rectitude.[14]

King's parents were Presbyterians of Scottish ancestry. He was educated at Trinity and profited by the teaching and friendship of Henry Dodwell and John Christian. He took his bachelor's degree in 1671, his master's three years later, and was appointed to a charge at Tuam in 1674. His autobiographical notes do not reveal when or why he left his father's church for a career in the Irish Establishment, and whether this was the result of a change by the whole family. What is certain is that he was unsympathetic to the Presbyterians and engaged after the Revolution in controversy with Joseph Boyse (1660–1728) over the services and dogmas of their respective churches. King considered the Episcopal church nearer than the Presbyterian to scriptural precepts and practice.[15] He was never favourable to any relaxation of the acts which prevented Irish dissent from full civil participation in the affairs of their country. On the other hand there is some evidence that King was not prepared to persecute deserving and clever dissenters, like Francis Hutcheson, whose school in Dublin continued to operate in the twenties with no noticeable inconvenience. King feared the ambitions of Presbyterians and the substitution of their system for the Anglican, but he himself was not intolerant. His philosophy was not narrowly dogmatic. He saved his anathemas for Toland, whose philosophy he condemned, and he utterly refused any concession to freethinkers like him.

> As to Toland's concern, there is a great difference to be made between a man that differs from others in the manner and method of worshipping God, and another that denys any God at all, that has no principles of Morality, nor owns any obligations on him besides his present interest, that holds falshood, perjury, murther, etc. to have no evil in them besides the opinion of the world nay that denys there is any Such thing in nature as virtu or vice. 'Tis to these principles that we owe all the mischiefs and villanys that have disturbed the world, and they never were received or countenanced in any commonwealth, but the destruction of it followed, now this I take to be avowed by Tolands case . . .[16]

King's career was interrupted by the troubles of King James's reign, and he suffered imprisonment because of his determined Protestantism. After William's victory at the Boyne he was rewarded first with the bishopric of Derry, and then in 1703 with the archbishopric of Dublin, which he held for the remainder of his life. His politics and his Irish nationalism never commended him to London or Canterbury and prevented his becoming primate. In Anne's reign the Tory churchmen attempted, during the years of the great ministry in London, to dominate Dublin politics. Molesworth bitterly condemned the bishops for their activities and suspected them of Jacobitism. His sentiments were shared by his friend, William King. This particular dispute was ended by the accession of George I. Thereafter King and Molesworth both were to find plenty in English policy toward church and state in Ireland to irritate them and to stimulate them into frank criticism. Molesworth's ready tongue and independence were well enough known, but his friend the Archbishop was also astonishingly frank, both in his private correspondence and in his letters to Archbishop Wake. He took no pains to conceal his annoyance at English policies and, though he occasionally felt obliged to explain his freedom, he continued to exercise it. He was not slow to show his annoyance, sometimes in ways scarcely becoming a high ecclesiastic of the Establishment, to the English clergy and officials who came over to Ireland. He had not approved the appointment of another Englishman to the Bishopric of Derby after the accession of the Hanoverians, but in spite of his opposition, William Nicholson, then bishop of Carlisle, was translated to Derry and in due course appeared in Dublin to take his place in the Irish House of Lords. He then found that King expected him, as the most recent appointee to the Irish Bench, to sit in the lowest place despite his English service. Both men wrote to Archbishop Wake about the matter; the *Journals* of the Irish parliament are also full of it. The incident was unimportant except as revealing the gulf between "English blood and Irish birth"—a reigning toast Nicholson reported in one of his letters—and the English fresh from England. This gulf was not lessened by the conflict over jurisdiction and the bitterness of the Anglo-Irish over the Dependency Act of 1719.[17]

Charles Leslie accused King of "old republican principles" in politics, but this was certainly unjustified. The Archbishop admitted the fundamental equality of man, but saw in present inequalities the provision of providence for the public service. Rich men must have leisure to serve the state; the poor, industry to do its menial tasks.[18] King firmly believed in the rights of Englishmen, wherever they were, to be governed by laws to which they had themselves consented. Old English principles, he once told Molesworth, "were love of their country, a great value for Liberty, a passionate esteem of honour and glory, and strict adherence to honesty and justice." The proper principles were, he felt, all-important in the "raising and destruction" of empires. Cromwell had found parliament beaten by the King's forces until he inspired his men with principles as strong as theirs, putting war "on the foot of religion," with the result that cobblers and draymen "spirited with that principle soon beat the men of honour."[19]

King condemned English policy on grounds, therefore, of right and of expediency. Tyranny betrayed their beliefs and was likely to alienate those otherwise friendly, and to ruin rather than enrich England.

> It is plain that England fears Ireland though without cause, but the way to secure of it is not to oppress it, witness the Romans oppressing the Germans, and Pharaoh the children of Israel. If the English in Ireland be treated as Englishmen, they will be Englishmen still in their hearts and inclinations, but if they be oppressed, they will turn Irish for fellowship in suffering begets love and unites interests.[20]

Another letter noticed the illegal but prosperous running of Irish cattle and Irish wool and woollens. "Your observations," he told his correspondent, "that Ireland has gained more by projects that appear fateful to her than by any other way is just; witness the Cattle Act, which was designed for our mischief but has proved the foundation of all our trade, riches, and improvement, and although the Woollen Act was of great danger to us, yet we have gained this by it that we now wear our own stuff."[21]

He was immensely angry at the revived claims of the English House of Lords to adjudicate for Irish matters. The case of Annesley *v.* Sherlock was settled in London, though there really seemed no good reason for the judges to make it their business. King wondered why they bothered. Perhaps, he speculated, they wished "to put us into a rebellion, that they will have the forfeitures of estates?" When the decision was followed up by the passage of the Act declaring Ireland dependent upon England (6 Geo. I), "the enslaving act" as he dubbed it, he particularly resented the reference in it to the recalcitrancy of the Irish. The country had never been quieter, though England had been disturbed by the rising of the Fifteen. He and Molesworth exchanged gloomy letters, and the Viscount when in London was kept informed of Irish developments by the Archbishop. Their anger and depression was not helped by the fact that neither had any real solution for their difficulties, though Molesworth was more optimistic about the possibilities than his clerical friend. All the protests since the Revolution had achieved nothing, and this act further depressed the status of the Protestant Irish.[22]

Some persons urged a Union of Ireland with England, and later with Great Britain. King did not share their hopes nor their confidence in the good results a Union would bring. He opposed the proposals in Anne's reign, and he never changed his mind. The Act of 1711 raising the property qualifications for candidates for election to Westminster presented further problems since under its provisions few Irishmen could qualify. His considered opinion was that a Union would work more to the interest of England than Ireland, but that if this subjection was the order of the day, then there should be in London some "that will speak for us."[23]

There were others throughout the first half of the eighteenth century who supported a Union. Molesworth has been mentioned. A friend and fellow member of the Irish parliament, Henry Maxwell of Finnebrooke, was a well-known proponent of the idea, and two others of his acquaintance, Synge and Dobbs, were to leave some evidence they supported Union as a solution for Ireland's ills. Maxwell (1680–1729) was active in parliament, was to be one of the enthusiastic supporters of the project for a bank in 1719–21—another matter in which King's sympathies ran contrary to his—and appears, through what we know of him and of his brother John, to have been a disciple of Molyneux, whose *Case* the latter was responsible for reprinting at the height of ill feeling about the Dependency Act. John was also to translate Cumberland's *Laws of Nature* during the twenties and to publish it in

1727. The Maxwells were cousins of Lord Farnham. They were Whig and Protestant Episcopalians, somewhat antagonistic toward their Presbyterian brethren, though Henry was willing that dissenters should enter the army when troops were needed. He shared King's wish for an Irish rather than an English official class. Various tracts and pamphlets show his concern with a variety of schemes for increasing agriculture and improving credit.[24]

Maxwell had probably studied Petty's *Anatomy of Ireland* (c.1672). Speaking of the inconveniency of "not union," Petty had written, "It is absurd that Englishmen born, sent over into Ireland by the commission of their own king . . . should therefore be accounted aliens."[25] Maxwell served in parliament with Molyneux whose views were well known. His own tract came out in 1703 and 1704, both in London and in Dublin. Union with Scotland was already being discussed. It is certainly in this period that Molesworth made remarks about the matter in his Preface to the *Franco-Gallia;* they could not have been written after 1707. Several excellent pamphlets followed Maxwell's *Essay,* and "Thoughts" on Union appeared sporadically thereafter. Those favourable to the ideas pursued much the same arguments as Maxwell, but frequently expressed them less well.[26]

Maxwell freely admitted the power of England to enforce any claims her parliament might make about the regulation of trade or any other matter in which Ireland was concerned. His argument rested chiefly on the analogy with the situation in Wales, on the disadvantages accruing from the existing system, and on the advantages to both countries a Union might be expected to bring. Wales, he pointed out, had been incorporated into England in Tudor times and had since developed a visible interest in preserving the English government. Fletcher referred to this in less favourable fashion in his discussion of the Scottish Union. Thomas Talbot left a manuscript describing the changes brought about in Wales and the precedents thus afforded for other such unions. Wales had been an open enemy, had had a different law and language. Wales had become loyal. Ireland as he wrote was poor and under oppressive laws. The Irish would never love those who enslaved them and might feel that their condition could hardly be worse under French or Spanish dominion. The Irish tried to secure wealth through a clandestine trade, and its profits were lost to England. With a Union, wealth would increase and the yield from Irish taxes with it; Irish trade would be largely confined to England. In the event of foreign invasion it would be to the interest of all to defend the united kingdom. Self-love was a principle ingrafted in men's nature. A desire for security led men into society. Once Ireland found that her connection with England was profitable and her grievances were removed, Irishmen would give their loyalty and service to those who benefited their interest.[27]

Much the same argument occurred in "Some Thoughts in Relation to a Union," a manuscript left among the papers of Arthur Dobbs (1689–1765). Dobbs was much franker in his condemnation of English policies in this unpublished work than in his *Essay on Trade*. Many unthinking English people had wished Ireland sunk in the sea, and had done their best to keep her poor. Dobbs, like Maxwell, however, tried to demonstrate that both countries would benefit from Union. Writing considerably later, he was able to point out that Edinburgh had not in his opinion suffered from the removal of parliament to London, nor would Dublin. Absentees would be tempted back by better conditions. These better conditions would bring greater returns from Ireland than were possible in a country impoverished by restrictive legislation. The wealth of England had been increased by the growth of cities like Manchester, Birmingham, and Sheffield, and would further multiply with the enrichment of Ireland. Discontent would decrease in Ireland when she had representatives in London who could explain her needs.[28]

Dobb's best known work is the *Essay on Trade*, published in two parts (1729–31). In this he did not dwell to the same extent on Union, but he used similar arguments and even phrases. He was very cautious in his references to English policy. He was lavish in his analysis of the political arithmetic of the Irish situation, and in his suggestions about policies, both Irish and English, which would improve the situation of the one and add to the revenues and power of the other. Dobbs not only saw economic advances which would be achieved, he also saw in improved conditions the best likelihood of the native Irish leaving the Catholic church for the Protestant.

In the *Essay* Dobbs stated that all men desired affluence and prosperity; there was therefore a duty to promote happiness. A flourishing commerce would increase happiness. The prudent and industrious might be able to enjoy more of the innocent pleasures of life. In his consideration of public welfare Dobbs discovered trade to be an all-important element in the contented society. Trade united distant nations as well as members of the same community.

> As the Soul, animating the natural Body, makes all the Members of it useful to each other, in Subservience to its Maintenance and more comfortable Subsistance; so Trade, in the Body Politick, makes the several Parts of it contribute to the well-being of the whole, and also to the more comfortable and agreeable Living of every Member of the (com)munity. Every Nation, every Climate from the Equinox almost to the very Poles, may partake of the Produce of all the rest, by means of a friendly Intercourse and mutual Exchange of what each has to spare.

English policy, however, had caused the value of land and rents to fall, increased the poor, and made necessary the keeping of a military force in Ireland to ensure public order. In spite of legislation and administration, Ireland had found a "stolen trade" with France and Holland profitable. England had gained thereby no advantage. Ireland was losing the Protestants, the very persons on whom the English government ought to rely for loyal cooperation. England had claimed that frequent disturbance in Ireland had made their oppressive policies necessary. "On the other side, we reply [he wrote] that the Hardship is laid equally to the Conquerors and to the conquered without regard to their own Offspring, and of those that bore the brunt of the War." The only profitable course was to adopt a more liberal policy and remove the obstruction to Ireland's wealth and happiness.[29]

There were faults within the governing class. Mines and fisheries were neglected. Good tillage was not studied. Too many proprietors lived abroad. Landlords failed to give tenants good treatment. A secure rental system and an allowance for improvements might encourage the development of a yeoman class. The establishment of granaries could provide against famine. Frugality was a very desirable public virtue. Increased scientific investigation, technological advances, and the establishment of boards and trusts which would develop national resources and new industries as the Linen Trust had done, should be promoted.[30]

The native Irish were Catholic, and Dobbs shared the prejudices of his age against their religion. He did not concern himself with the right to liberty of conscience as did Molesworth or Synge. He was, however, prepared to ameliorate the burden of tithe and to help those Catholics who would abjure any acknowledgment of papal claims to interfere in domestic politics. He pointed out the virtues of Catholic family life, and contrasted their large numbers of children with the reluctance of Protestants to marry young or to produce children.[31]

Dobbs took an active part in Irish life. He was sheriff of Antrim, and represented Carrickfergus in parliament in the twenties. He was interested in the same schemes for a bank which Maxwell supported. He took part in the establishment of the Royal Dublin Society. He acquired about two hundred thousand acres in North Carolina to which he went as governor in 1754, dying there in 1765. He had the habit, as the reflections on Union show, of writing down his thoughts. Among his manuscripts is a "Scheme to Enlarge the Colonies" which, though his colonial activities need not be described in a chapter on Irish liberalism, is in fact revelatory of an Anglo-Irishman's opinion on subject peoples. The "Scheme" is mercantilist in tone, more so than his *Essay,* and he perhaps felt the situation of colonists was less comparable to that of Ireland than did later American admirers of Molyneux and Lucas. In the "Scheme" he discussed with a sensitivity rare in that day alternatives to contemporary policy toward the Indians.[32]

The establishment of colonies was due to overpopulation and thirst for dominion. Commerce had little enough to do with it, though dominion could include an increase of national wealth. It was at this point that he portrayed a keener sensitivity than his contemporaries. Land in America was taken regardless of the rights of native proprietors. Much trouble ensued and much expense was incurred by the crown in the protection of the colonies. Dobbs suggested that it would have been better to have united with and incorporated the native tribes instead of forcing them away and laying waste to their country. They should have been civilized, converted, and instructed in the arts, science, language, and the manners of Britain. They would then have bought more manufactures and slaves would not have been necessary. Nothing could justify dispossessing the natives except gaining their consent by giving them an equivalent, by instructing them, and by sharing the benefits of the country with them. Yet they were deprived of all the conveniences of life and of hope for a better world hereafter. Christians should practice what they preach. Indians ought not to be despised by them. In many ways the customs of the Indians were more in accord with the law of nature than those of their conquerors.

Dobbs proceeded to develop three schemes which could make amends for past mistakes. Young women should be offered premiums to go and marry natives and thus bring civilization to them, in the most direct fashion. He saw no reason to suppose that any colour distinction was necessary. In the second place, he would send out traveling ambassadors, men learned or skilled in different ways who would not only observe what could be done, but also instruct the Indians and establish towns and schools. Dobbs thought that by heaping favours on the Indians, many subjects would be added to Britain who would increase her wealth, secure her against the French and the Spanish, and present to the world an edifying spectacle of a thankful and free people.

Two more of Molyneux's disciples must be mentioned, the one a genius, the other an inspired propagandist. Swift was a Tory. He had pilloried Molesworth and King for their politics at the end of Queen Anne's reign. He had hoped for advancement in England and been disappointed in this as in other matters. His work for Ireland has been dismissed by some as merely a manifestation of hatred for England. The motives of so complex a character cannot be disentangled, but it should be remembered that the care of the church fabric in his charge, a concern for the sick, and a passionate preoccupation with the impoverished surely had little to do with frustrations in London. Prejudices against Presbyterians, dislike of projects associated with the official Whig government, impatience with pride, corruption, and with endless discussions of the whys and hows of policy—these must all have been intensified by English experience, and the chance to annoy English ministers at the time of Wood's Halfpence was welcome. But Swift was brought up in the house of Temple, by no means a Tory, even if no other party can claim his allegiance. Swift's library contained Harrington, and he was familiar with the works of Sidney and Molyneux. An awareness of the failings of governments and distaste for the pretensions of the great lent even to his unpolemical work a revolutionary character. Swift denied that Ireland was a "depending kingdom." He asserted that all government without the consent of the governed is the very definition of slavery. He admired those who talked "of liberty as a blessing, to which the whole race of mankind hath an original title. Whereof nothing of unlawful force can divest them." Freedom consisted of being ruled by laws made with popular consent. This, of course, was all in defense of Ireland against England.[33] In his sermons and in his *Gulliver,* he anathematized wealthy and pretentious people. Readers of his works, listeners to his sermons, were likely to derive liberal rather than Tory politics from them. Henry Yorke (1772–1813), a radical at the end of the century, and protagonist of the French revolutionary movements, declared that his republicanism had been enforced by reading Swift. Thomas Spence, an egalitarian contemporary, in his anthology of the "lessons of liberty" he wished the "Swinish Multitude" to learn, included passages in the penny numbers from Swift on bribery and on the blessings of mediocrity which sit well with their levelling fellows. Whether anyone became a Tory because of contact with the Dean is doubtful, but it was not only Irishmen who drew Commonwealth morals and Whiggish precepts from his work.[34]

The politics of Charles Lucas (1713–1771) were no less violent in expression than Swift's, but they were also much less complex and original. He was an able, aggressive, blunt reformer. He was bullet-headed and he was crippled. Able throughout his life to write thousands of words without any effort, he was concerned in two campaigns: municipal integrity and parliamentary reform. The gradual corruption and deterioration of the city government of Dublin troubled him and he determined in his first public effort to do something about it. The corporation had gradually become unrepresentative even of Protestant citizens. Lucas gained considerable popular support, but made himself so objectionable to the administration that he was brought to trial in 1749 and accused of trying to overthrow the government. He fled to the Isle of Man, then made his way to London where he made many friends, including Dr. Samuel Johnson. In 1763 Lucas returned to Dublin and began to fight the abuse of "standing" parliaments. At this time there was no stated term to Irish parliaments, which often lasted throughout the better part of the reign, losing in the course of years any possible connection they may originally have had with the public of the constituencies. Almost the first reform of Irish policy in the eighteenth century, Townshend's Octennial Act of 1768, regulated duration.

Lucas's ideas, as revealed in his many tracts and pamphlets were not new nor were they clearly presented. He won adherents by vigour, and swamped opponents by the floods of constitutional examples from English history with which he filled his treatises bolstered by the authority of Milton, Sidney, and Russell amongst the English; Molesworth and Molyneux amongst the Irish. He was obviously a devout admirer of all of them. Claiming to be an Irish asserter of liberty and true principles, he quoted Magna Carta and extolled parliament and the noble British Constitution. Very few of the popular phrases of the constitutional documents of the seventeenth century escaped use during his efforts to promote the cause of truth and liberty in Ireland. He consistently maintained that private persons, for example the wicked aldermen of Dublin, were acting against the English constitution. Defiantly confident of this, he dedicated one of his volumes to George II. The chapters of his journal were embellished with quotations from Milton and classical authors like Cicero. His service was to remind his public of the views of Molyneux and the lessons Molyneux had drawn from the Danish revolution, as well as to revive all the common arguments used by asserters of liberty in protection of their rights. He does not seem to have apprehended the problems of the native Irish, but he certainly resented, as King and Swift had done, the subjection of the Anglo-Irish population to corrupt and tyrannical administrations. Lucas died before the American Revolutionary War had commenced, but a letter to him from the town of Boston about the massacre of the fifth of March 1770 was printed, and English radicals like Hollis included his works in their collections of liberty tracts and sent to him publications of their own of which they thought he would approve.[35]

Endless other Irish tracts about the situation of Ireland afford much opportunity for illustration of the spread of the doctrines of independency and the agitation against mercantilism. One anonymous pamphlet of the year 1757 — *Northern Revolutions: or, the Principal Causes of the Declension and Dissolution of Several Once Flourishing Gothic Constitutions in Europe in a Series of Letters from the Ghost of Trenchard, Once a Free Briton*

(Dublin, 1757)—epitomized the spirit of the discontented Anglo-Irish. In the advertisement the author professed to have seen ghosts of the past: Hampden, Sidney, Russell, Cromwell (apparently because of his capture of Dunkirk), and Trenchard. Trenchard was described as a very odd sort of a fellow whose general knowledge made him the best patron of science, whose love for virtue and for liberty made him write or dictate the best parts of *Cato's Letters,* and whose incomparable *Independent Whig* laughed out of countenance superstitions in religion. But, though the preface thus concentrated on Trenchard, the rest of the work revealed at least as much or more reliance on Molesworth and his *Account of Denmark* and its declension. The tract attempted to reveal the relation of the degradation of provincial Norway to the ills of Denmark, and drew a parallel with Ireland's situation in the British Isles. "The subjugation of Nordweg to Danemarch," as he humorously spells them, was then amply described; all laws from Poynings on, including commercial restrictions and the "enslaving act," were described in scarcely veiled terms. Liberty, trade, and most industrious sons were lost to Nordweg. Danemarch itself, such was the excellence of its ancient constitution, bore a greater weight of corruption than any government. Even the subversion of its ancient laws was slow. At last, however, the kingdom fell. Virtue was lost and with it liberty. In that disaster the infamous practices of Danemarch upon the poor people of Nordweg, reducing them to a beggarly state and then to bondage, eventually riposted upon her own constitution.[36]

Reflections and Resolutions Proper for the Gentlemen of Ireland: Molesworth, Madden, Berkeley, Prior

If the ruling classes in Ireland failed in their duty in the eighteenth century, it was not for want of admonition and criticism. These came, not from the native Irish nor from outside observers, but from their own countrymen. Swift's ironic *Proposal,* Molesworth's frank *Considerations,* Madden's *Reflections,* Prior's savage exposure of absentees, and Berkeley's gentle but penetrating *Querist*—all pointed out faults and shortcomings, all admonished them to do better. Even their novelists, Henry Brooke (1703–1783) and Maria Edgeworth (1767–1849), took up the same story and emphasized its moral. These were not attempts of Commonwealthmen to alter the government and level society, but the effect was to introduce new ideas in politics and economics, egalitarian and often nationalist in character. The duty and obligation of the rich, the proper development of the country's economy, the improvement of the standards and status of the poor—these subjects received attention from able and articulate men. In some respects their efforts met with success, and improvements in Ireland during the period owe much to contemporary investigations of resources of technology and good husbandry. Population increased. Toleration was extended and by the last quarter of the century England's policy was at last modified, though this was due as much to events overseas as to the efforts of polemicists nearer home. But the fatal divisions in Ireland and the unfortunate nature of the Union, when at long last it was forced on men whose grandparents had begged for it, led to further disasters and not to the more comfortable future for which the eighteenth century hoped.

English policy was of course the easiest target for the Drapier, the author of *Denmark,* and for the nephew of Molyneux. "Tis true we are told we are slaves," wrote Molesworth, "but it must be our care not to deserve being so." He attacked tithes. He defended the Irish poor from the charge of indolence. He condemned the landlord system and the harsh treatment of leaseholders penalized for improvements. He compared, much to their disadvantage, agricultural methods of the Irish with those of the English. He advocated the establishment of schools of industry—instruction in husbandry would be more useful than "precepts of distinctive religion." Granaries should be provided, fisheries encouraged, roads developed, and the problem of unemployment attacked.[37] *Thoughts on Tillage* (1739), often attributed in catalogues to his pen but certainly the work of a later admirer, endorsed such suggestions. They are to be found in the aphoristic reflections of Sam Madden who paid tribute to the Viscount; in the work of Thomas Prior; and, though without acknowledgment, perhaps no conscious obligation, in the writings of Berkeley.

Sam Madden (1686–1765), a clergyman and a classmate of Prior and Berkeley at Trinity, inherited the ability of his family and asserted sympathy with his uncle William Molyneux's theories, as well as with those of John Trenchard. Like so many other reformers, Madden laid great stress on the importance of Irishmen mending their habits. Like Molesworth in the Preface to *An Account,* he thought education should train for citizenship rather than for classical scholarship. Boys should study the noble maxims and sentiments in the classics, rather than merely grammar. Training in oratory would fit them for parliamentary service. Education should be varied. Those with a genius for science should be separated from the classical scholars, and others removed to trade and industry. "Duller Boys, as we call them, may if another term be given them become infinitely more useful as merchants or men of business . . . it is mere loss of time to force all our young gentlemen thus to drudge at languages as the Turks do at Trades." He thought some geography, astronomy, and civil law might be taught. He deplored the habit of sending lads abroad on the grand tour before they were mature enough to profit by it. Madden is thus to be numbered among the progressive educators of his age, along with Locke, Molesworth, Fordyce, and Franklin.[38] He advocated the establishment of premiums and prizes for both young and old, to encourage them to engage in work profitable to their country in practical science, in philosophy, and in art. He was keenly interested in the work of the Royal Dublin Society founded by his friend Thomas Prior. He adopted Molesworth's various suggestions about husbandry and the treatment of tenants, and he repeated the admonitions of the Dean of St. Patrick's and the Bishop of Cloyne to spare the use of luxuries and encourage the purchase of native goods. Sumptuary laws, he felt, might enforce good resolutions. He hoped to increase population and raise standards of living.[39]

Madden was very forthright in complaints about the treatment of his fellows by England. In the fourteenth resolution he said:

It cannot but seem hard to be used and considered as aliens by those, who, by rewards and favours, persuaded members of our people now living, or their ancestors, to come over hither, and spend their blood in their service to extend their empire, commerce and power. Shall not even their descendants as justly claim the privileges of Englishmen as do the children of ambassadors, who were born in the most distant kingdoms, where their fathers remained in the service of their prince and their country? And may not the children of those Englishmen, who have planted in our colonies in America, be as justly reckoned Indians and savages, as such families who are settled here, can be considered and treated as mere Irishmen and aliens.

A little later he asked, "have we not the same Prince, Church, Laws and Constitution derived to us by our forefathers, and have we not (the great cements of national friendships), the same principles, affections and interests in religion and government?"[40]

Madden supported, together with "many of the best English patriots as well as the best writers and judges in politics, a union." He regarded the situation in Ireland as perfectly odd, "a people that like amphibious animals are envied as Englishmen in Ireland and maligned as Irish in England." He went on to suggest that bodies politic, like natural ones, were prosperous only so long as all their branches were nourished. Surely no one could be jealous of Ireland's wishing a share of the rights and privileges enjoyed in England, Wales, and Scotland, "since there is room enough in the world for five times the commerce we could all carry on were our stocks and labors joined by a union." Ireland could be a support instead of a burden to the Empire.

He ended his plea by a reference to the famous *Essay on Trade and Plantations* in *Cato's Letters,* and copied Trenchard's words entreating his fellow-countrymen, if they wished to keep Irish friendship, "to imitate the Example of Merchants and Shopkeepers; that is, when their Apprentices are acquainted with their Trade and their Customers, and are out of their Time, to take them into Partnership rather than let them set up for themselves in their Neighborhood."[41]

A List of the Absentees of Ireland and the Yearly Value of Their Estates and Incomes Spent Abroad . . . was published by Prior in 1729. It at once found many readers. Thomas Prior (1682–1751) had been educated with George Berkeley, not only at Kilkenny but at Trinity College, Dublin. He had later visited England where he stayed with an uncle at Cambridge, at Oxford where he obtained an M.A., and in London where he may first have met Swift and where Berkeley was staying at this time, 1712–13. Throughout their lives Prior acted as Berkeley's adviser and, from 1723, as his business manager. They shared the same opinions about Irish conditions and the same hopes for improving them. They were both men of very wide interests. Prior studied coinage and advocated the establishment of an Irish mint. He castigated in his most famous tract those men who complained about English policy but never thought about their own duties and spent their money on foreign luxuries in a foreign land and condemned those English officials who drew salaries from Ireland but never resided there. He pointed out the possibilities of using Irish wool at home, and suggested that some grazing lands could profitably be put under cultivation.

It was to investigate all the possibilities of increasing Irish wealth, even within contemporary restrictions, that Prior and thirteen others founded the Royal Dublin Society in 1731. Some of these men were of the Molyneux connection; others were writers and administrators like Arthur Dobbs and Justice Michael Ward. Bishop Edward Synge and Dr. Stephens, who was a lecturer at Trinity, a chemist and a doctor, were in the group. Sir John Perceval, later earl of Egmont and a friend of Berkeley, was to be a member. During his brief term as Viceroy in 1745, Philip Stanhope, earl of Chesterfield (1694–1773), supported every good work in Ireland. On his return to England he secured for the Royal Dublin Society a small government subvention and continued to follow its activities.[42]

George Berkeley (1685–1753) returned from his sojourn in Rhode Island in 1732. In 1734 he became bishop of Cloyne and resided in his diocese, though he kept up with Prior, Madden, and other friends through correspondence and visits. *The Querist* appeared in 1736. An earlier work on *Passive Obedience* had incurred the enmity of the Molesworth Whigs in 1714.[43] An opponent of the philosophy of the third earl of Shaftesbury, he attacked its precepts in *Alciphron* in 1732. Berkeley was an enemy to freethinkers, though he was not intolerant of honest differences of opinion. Charity forbade cruelty to those of other beliefs. A state church was desirable; atheists and blasphemers should be punished. In the *Discourse to Magistrates* he emphasized the necessity for an "awful" sense of religion and said that "religion is the cement which unites several parts of a political body." Berkeley was not a Jacobite. He believed in authority, order, and the adoption of opinions acquired either by private reason and reflection, or taught and instilled by the law of the land. He did not believe that savages were necessarily virtuous, though their opportunities for certain kinds of wrongdoing were fewer. He warned Commonwealthmen, "asserters of liberty," that damaging established prejudices might be more dangerous than retaining them.[44]

So far Berkeley would seem entirely antipathetic to the Whiggery of Molesworth or even to the violent partisanship of national rights by Swift. He disliked innovation. Yet he studied history and realized that strong constitutions, natural or political, did not feel "light disorders," and he felt bound to show his fellow countrymen the lessons he derived from observations of the fate of Gothic countries and the growth of states. *The Ruin of Great Britain* is full of passages which might have come from Molesworth's pen. Dangers to the English system were marked. Improved education and investigation of political and social disorders could avert disaster.[45]

The Querist is a series of rhetorical questions of a strangely disjointed character, but in it may be found a whole program for the improvement of Ireland, by her own endeavours and by the altered policy of Great Britain. Liberty for Berkeley might consist of a mean rather than the ebullient emancipation of a utopian dreamer. Prejudices and authorities were cherished, but as he ranged over the problems of his time, he developed innovating theories in matters economic. They spread more widely than some of the effusions of self-confessed Commonwealthmen. His latest editor, Mr. Luce, quotes Maynard Keynes's unpublished remark that Berkeley wrote the shrewdest essays of his time.[46] On money, credit, banking, and on incentive he was in advance of his time. He was passionately interested in the problem of poverty. Like others already mentioned, he condemned luxury and pressed the gentry to do their duty. Ireland was full of poor people, yet a small class lived extravagantly and were apparently insensible to the needs of the country. Surely, Berkeley asked, the wants of the majority should be considered before the indulgences of these few.[47]

Berkeley, like others before him, suggested that English policy might be modified and that changes in it could improve the situation of both countries. It might be to their mutual interest to be united, and to befriend each other. He favoured greater attention to education at all levels, and suggested that Catholics should be admitted to Trinity. Like Swift, he advocated sumptuary laws and the encouragement of the use of Irish rather than foreign goods. He criticized the behaviour of the ruling ascendancy, both with regard to their luxury and to their failure in Christian duties. They had not, for example, studied the old language in order better to instruct the Irish in the Protestant religion. So far Berkeley seems no more, no less, enlightened than his fellow countrymen already described. His examination of poverty and his suggested remedies, however, show his great originality and his practical knowledge of both domestic and foreign economic problems.

Poverty in Ireland was due to mistaken policy. It could not be blamed on the religion of the Catholic majority. In Europe Berkeley had observed the industry of Sardinians and French. He saw no reason to suppose that Irish Catholics would not work as hard. Robert Molesworth had indeed noticed the industry of his tenants and defended them against the usual Protestant charges of sloth, but Molesworth was more interested in the improvement of agricultural techniques and in reform of the relation of landlord and tenant than in monetary policy. Berkeley was extremely anxious to induce policy makers to consider credit, money, profitable work, sound distribution of industry and its rewards, and wished them to review the whole matter of incentive.[48]

The Querist was enormously interested in the establishment of a bank with capital raised out of taxes and controlled in the public interest against the possibility of manipulation by private speculators and profiteers. The need for credit for the development of industry and commerce had been recognized in an earlier abortive movement for the Irish bank supported by Henry Maxwell and pushed by the earl of Abercorn and others in 1719–21. That effort had failed. Many, like Swift and King, had opposed it, the one because he connected banks and Whiggery, the other because he feared that it would be difficult to keep out those interested only in making a large profit out of loans. Berkeley published a brief synopsis of his suggestions in a letter of 1737 following the appearance of *The Querist*. A tax on wine might raise the capital, parliament should make good any deficit, paper money or notes should be issued, and distributed in cash or on the security of individuals or public institutions. Such a bank situated in Dublin should be organized with inspectors amongst other officials, to secure the public interest in the bank. There were to be no shares, no profits except to the public, no possibility of bankruptcy. This would restore credit, without which the natural resources of the country could not be properly developed. Money to Berkeley was a counter or a ticket, gold and silver were useful only for the industry they bought—that is, they were credit and not the most convenient form of it. Berkeley also wanted a mint, and small coins which would circulate freely. Statistics should be kept to see what was actually happening to the circulation of wealth and to the expenditures of the country. All this was proposed as a matter of public policy and national control, a necessary monetary reform to implement the attack on poverty.[49]

Berkeley considered the poor, the majority of Irishmen whose work would create wealth. How to persuade them to industry was an important consideration. Berkeley felt that incentive, beef and good shoes, higher wages, would all act as a spur to endeavour. Emigration would not tempt if home conditions were improved. He admired the industry he saw in other lands, though praise for child labour in Holland strikes a less modern note than his other suggestions. Like Andrew Fletcher, he approved of forced work by criminals. A prisoner had lost his liberty. He might as well work for the public benefit as suffer transportation. A country full of well-fed, well-housed, and adequately clothed persons would increase in population and in wealth. Workers would become more enterprising, and new arts and improved industries would result.[50]

Not only should the poor be encouraged to associate comfort and industry; the manufacturers should be induced to extend their scope. Irish woollens might be restricted by English legislation. They could be used at home. But other products might be substituted, for example, tapestry and carpets which would not compete with English products. Berkeley urged a variation in the pattern of economic activity, both in country and in urban districts. He pointed out many opportunities. He wished these to be studied by the Royal Society, and he foresaw an increase in the production of works of art if a National Academy were founded. Here *The Querist* was supporting the aims of friends, Prior and Madden, and he undoubtedly helped them obtain wider membership.[51]

There were ten issues of *The Querist* before Berkeley died in 1753. As a result of reading it many must have reconsidered the problem of poverty and the desirability of the "moralisation" of wealth, as Mr. Luce has described it. Practical results, except in such support as the Royal Dublin received, were nil. The general influence is hard to estimate. Certainly Berkeley's Scottish correspondents, Wallace, Wishart, Maclaurin (1698–1746), and Andrew Mitchell, must have read and discussed it. Wallace had once thought of accompanying Berkeley to the New World. All had admired Berkeley's philosophy and, as young members of the Rankenian club,[52] had sought his advice. Scotland had also to combat the problem of poverty. There *The Querist* should have contributed to the awakening consciousness of the importance of the labouring poor, if not in England where exaggerated complacency over the Poor Law system was apt to stifle speculation about improving the poor by any means but exhortation to charity or medical attention in hospitals. Berkeley found readers. Thomas Spence, in those penny numbers designed to promote the proper ideas among labourers, reprinted, besides extracts from Swift already noted, some dozen and a half of Berkeley's questions—whether men do not top the tree to make the lower branches thrive; whether as seed equally scattered "produceth a good harvest," even so an equal distribution of wealth does not cause a nation to flourish; whether the vanity and luxury of a few ought to stand in competition with the interest of a nation. In such ways even the Tory Bishop of Cloyne contributed to the development of a sense of responsibility amongst all members of society and an equalization of the evaluation of those different sorts of men within it.[53]

Shrewd observation, wide experience, and public spirit led these reformers to the promulgation of theories of great importance in the development of liberal economic and social ideas. They were not without influence upon the situation of their own times. They cannot be ignored in considering the antecedents of the extreme natural rights doctrines of the American colonists, or of the growing numbers of antimercantilists. Their importance, however, is antiquarian or historical in the sense that they did not leave behind them a legacy of revolutionary literature in Ireland. That was chiefly to be found in the classes and the pamphlets of the dissenters—those dissenters who were divorced from some of the often narrow orthodoxy of their forefathers and who had drunk in the philosophy of Shaftesbury and the politics of Molesworth—the relatives, friends, and students of Francis Hutcheson.

Civil and Religious Liberty

Three quarters of the population of Ireland in the period follow-ing the battle of the Boyne suffered varying degrees of religious and civil disabilities because of their failure to conform to the Established Church. Improvements came slowly in the last half of the eighteenth century, effected as much by external events as by the softening of prejudices within the island. That story has often been told. Much of it relates only incidentally to the history of liberal ideas. Nor need the heresies of such men as Rundle and Clayton within the Establishment form a part of this chapter. Thomas Rundle failed to obtain present-ment to a rich English bishopric because he was suspected of Arian-ism by Bishop Gibson. He was instead given the bishopric of Derry which he held for the last seven years of his life. Always against undue severities to dissent in all parts of the British Isles, his Irish experience came too late to affect his already emphatic Whiggery.[54] Robert Clay-ton, Bishop of Clogher, was a graduate of Trinity. His extraordinary *Essay on Spirit* is described by Leslie Stephen as metaphysical fetishism. Not long before he died he spoke in the Irish House of Lords, violently pressing the obliteration from the church liturgy of Articles and both Nicene and Athanasian creeds. He propounded a more extreme ver-sion of ideas which were being put forward in England by Jones and Blackburne and which would, if adopted, have reduced, indeed almost annihilated a disciplined dogma in the Church. Such efforts were part of contemporary movements common to England and Ireland.[55]

The most vigorous statement of the case for toleration from an Irish churchman was made by a native and was based upon experience of problems peculiar to Ireland. Edward Synge, later Bishop of Elphin, preached a sermon on 23 October, 1725 (anniversary of the Irish Re-bellion), published as *The Case of Toleration* and productive of much comment. The Synge family was full of bishops and was prominent in the eighteenth-century church, as it still is in other activities. His father wrote a popular work, *A Gentleman's Religion* (1693), designed to explain Christianity both to the rational philosopher and to men of mediocre intelligence. Edward Synge the younger was the friend of Hutcheson, Molesworth, and George Berkeley. He shared their aspirations for an equal union of Ireland and England—or if that were not possible, an amelioration of mercantilist restriction—and with hopes that Irishmen themselves would do all possible to develop and profitably use the natural resources of their country.[56]

A good many tracts have been attributed to Synge, but his fame need rest only on the sermon upon the text, "Compel them to come in." It followed closely upon Molesworth's *Considerations* with its defense of the poorer Irish Catholics, its attack on tithe and ecclesiastical courts, and its suggestions for the payment of the Irish Catholic clergy by the state. Synge devoted himself chiefly to denials of both the propriety and the usefulness of "racks and torments." No one had a right to persecute. Once admitted, such a power might be used in Catholic countries against Protestants, as in Ireland against Papists. Penalties imposed in France and Poland would be recognized as legitimate. While acknowledging that certain papist tenets and practices had in the past afforded grounds for doubting their loyalty in Protestant states and therefore seeming to necessitate a measure of restraint, Synge still felt strongly that force made hypocrites and seldom effected real conviction. That was more likely to result from the good example of Protestant Christians, who should always bear in mind the effects of their behaviour upon the Catholic population. Moreover, care should be taken to educate children, if not in the nonsectarian manner proposed by Molesworth, at least in such fashion as would leave no doubt of their duties as citizens. He also proposed allowing Catholics to disclaim the doctrine that the Pope may depose heretical princes or release subjects from allegiance to them.[57]

The cause of the Catholic population before the formation of the Catholic group in 1759 was kept before the public eye by pamphlets like *An Axe Laid to the Root* (1749). *A View of the Grievances* (1745) proposed that they should be allowed to own land under the old law of gavelkind—equal distribution among children at the death of the owner—which would effectually prevent large accumulations.[58] Henry Brooke, the writer, whose *Farmer's Letters* (1745) were antipapistical, suffered a change of heart in mid-century and pled for the redress of

Catholic grievances in 1761. Brooke had been associated with William Pitt and the opposition politicians at the court of Frederick, Prince of Wales, and was a violent Whig. His novel, *The Fool of Quality* (1767–1770) contained a long disquisition (on the English constitution and on the nature of regal power and aristocratic privileges), which, though not republican, was certainly suggestive of the radicalism of Richard Edgeworth and others. He was a supporter of Irish nationalism of about the same caliber as Lucas's, but by the time his best-known work, *The Fool*, appeared, his radicalism was already less apparent than that of Thomas Day and the English rational dissenters.[59] At no time does Brooke seem to have been an originator or reformer.

A curious story in the sad history of persecution in Ireland has some relevance to the present chapter. Bishop John Law, son of King's translator, the saintly Edmund Law of Carlisle, abandoned all attempts to convert his flock in his Irish diocese and began to instruct them instead in the mysteries of the Catholic religion using a well-known text by Gother as his guide. When questioned about this extraordinary behaviour, he remarked only that since Protestant missionary work was uniformly unsuccessful, he was at least endeavouring to make good Catholics of the population.[60]

Catholic writers were not prolific. Not much of importance came between Hugh Reilly's defense, *Ireland's Case* (1695)—which may have suggested Molyneux's title, and which repudiated current Protestant charges—and the equally well-known work of Nicholas, Viscount Taaffe in 1769, *Observations,* urging, in view of half a century of peaceful behaviour, better treatment of his coreligionists and instancing continental and overseas precedents for this. "Let *North America be* the mirror to reflect the benign face of universal indulgence to conscience, that monitor *within,* which, when it suggests our proper duty, as members of the community, *ought to remain uncontrolled from all human restraints.*"[61]

Synge, perhaps most tolerant of churchmen, had consorted under Molesworth's roof with Presbyterians. He formed friendships there which continued after the death of the Viscount. Hutcheson's son dedicated the posthumous *System of Moral Philosophy* to Synge, who had earlier read, and perhaps commented upon, the manuscript circulated during the late thirties. The Bishop's views on civil and religious liberty may have been only less liberal than those of the philosopher. Hutcheson, discussed in connection with Scotch thought of the period, was not the only Presbyterian in the Molesworth circle; James Arbuckle and Sam Boyse the poet were in it. Molesworth's influence had been manifested in Scotland by persons like George Turnbull, briefly chaplain to Rundle at Derry, by Arbuckle, by William Wishart, later Principal of Edinburgh. Wishart and Wallace, another Edinburghian, brother-in-law of Turnbull, acknowledged their debt to Molesworth and Shaftesbury[62] whose philosophy permanently influenced their own beliefs. There seems no reason to doubt that other contemporaries and relatives of Arbuckle and Hutcheson (who had married the Wilson sisters), Abernethy, Haliday, Drennen, Duchal, and Bruce, shared the politics of the Molesworth connection. They not only came under those influences, but were permanently affected by their activities and studies at Glasgow in the period when the Scottish enlightenment was just beginning, and when the influence of English and continental philosophy, science, and literature were powerful, modifying traditional custom and belief.

The Scotch-Irish in the early eighteenth century, before numbers emigrated to America, about half the Protestant population of Ireland, produced many talented men. Some were to adopt the ideals of the nonsubscribers and to approach the theological position of later Unitarians. Emlyn, at the beginning of the period, was roughly handled by Joseph Boyse and the orthodox of Dublin, whom Toland had also shocked. But by 1726, when an open split occurred in some twelve congregations, the schism was visible. In the long run it weakened Irish Presbyterianism. But before this had become apparent, the New Light group had preached and published sermons that were widely read, had contributed a quota of tracts and pamphlets to contemporary controversy, and handed to a second generation a patriotic spirit that included all Irishmen in its loyalties, and diffused a liberal philosophy throughout more than one city and country.

The liberal Presbyterians might almost be described as a colony of the city of Glasgow whose university most of them had attended. Many of them kept up the college friendships throughout their lives. Turnbull conformed, but when he visited Ireland as chaplain to Thomas Rundle in the thirties, he was greeted with open arms by Arbuckle and sent on to other friends as an old intimate.[63] Bruce kept up with the careers of Wishart at Edinburgh and other classmates.[64] Many of them were related—a web of kinship bound together Arbuckle, Abernethy, Hutcheson, Bruce, Drennen, Haliday, and Smith. They witnessed each other's wills,[65] they often educated each other's children, and they read each other's books. They delighted in conversation. They exchanged letters and books. William Drennen, credited with authorship of the phrase "Emerald Isle," wrote about his forefathers with pride. He gloried in being a Protestant dissenter.

> I am the son of an honest man; a minister of that gospel which breathes peace and good will among men; . . . a Protestant Dissenting minister, in the town of Belfast; the friend and associate of good, I may say, great men: of Abernathy, of Bruce, of Duchal, and of Hutcheson.

He described Alexander Haliday, friend of his youth and maturity as:

> a Genuine Whig . . . nurtured under the philosophy of Hutcheson, and early inspired by the poetry of Akenside, the study of the former gave him that chastity of the moral sense which binds political and personal duty in the same strict tie of honesty and honour; and the divine muse of the latter, threw that sacred flame of liberty into his breast, which burned while he continued to exist. In the principles of civil and religious liberty he lived and in them he died . . . these were the associating principles of Maclaine, Bruce, Wight and Plunket; the principles of the venerable Camden, and the amiable Charlemont, of the untitled Stewart, and the unpensioned Burke.[66]

Among the earlier generation so vividly portrayed were to be found ministers in Belfast and in Dublin; Abernethy and Duchal; Drennen and Haliday; publishers like Bruce and Smith of the Philosopher's Head on the Blind Quay; writers and custom house officials like James Arbuckle. The most famous of these was Hutcheson, who spent his student days and the sixteen years of his professional career at Glasgow. In the twenties, he had a school in Dublin which he and Thom Drennen ran, and whose most famous pupil, perhaps, was William Robertson, later known as the first Unitarian. He returned to Dublin after his appointment in Glasgow but he maintained his connection and sought their advice, and as freely gave his aid and comfort to Scotch-Irish in Glasgow.[67]

John Abernethy (1680–1740) and Samuel Haliday (1685–1739) were the oldest of this connection listed here. Both studied at Glasgow about the time that James Kirkpatrick and John Simson were also enrolled. Abernethy spent some time in Edinburgh, Haliday on the continent and England, after their days at Glasgow were over. Haliday occupied himself in working against the passage of the Schism Bill. Abernethy was briefly at Wood Street, Dublin, with Joseph Boyse, and then at Antrim. He took some interest in missionary work among the native Irish and returned to Dublin where he remained until his death in 1740. He was the leader, Wodrow reported, of his party—that is, the liberal nonsubscribing group. Haliday encountered some criticism at the hands of the orthodox Samuel Dunlop, but in spite of doubts of his orthodoxy, he eventually became minister of a Belfast congregation with whom he, too, remained until his death in 1739. With Abernethy, John Mairs, and Kirkpatrick, he formed the vanguard of New Light belief. His sons, Robert and Alexander, were both educated by Hutcheson at Glasgow.[68]

The Wood Street congregation were fortunate in the preaching ability of John Abernethy.[69] His sermons were widely read and admired, even by those unsympathetic to the preacher's more advanced theological views. He was learned and he also loved to talk. To him moral and civil liberty were intimately connected. Liberty was equally the right of all. Conscience should be exempted from all control. A church was a spiritual organization for mutual worship. Hoadly's Sermon on *The Nature of the Kingdom or Church of Christ* was a favourite with Abernethy. Christ came to set men free in every sense of the word. Man was born with a capacity for knowledge and for choice. Unless he were allowed to exercise his reason freely, and use his own discrimination, he could not attain happiness. The duty was not to compel people by tests and oaths. Judge not that ye be not judged. Persuasion was the only proper weapon for Christians. Persecution violated the natural genius of man. Every man should worship as he pleased.

Magistrates should only restrain disorder. They had no right to restrict the conscience. Subscriptions and confessions, Anglican and

Presbyterian alike, were more likely to make hypocrites than keep men from wrongdoing or encourage man to good. What was more, civil disabilities hurt Ireland as much as the individuals concerned. Emigration to America might be curtailed if tests were repealed. Abernethy's views and those of his associates in the writing of certain tracts against tests, Bruce and Haliday among them, were to circulate and to be reprinted in 1751 by Richard Baron, the student of Francis Hutcheson who had earlier suggested this project to him. Abernethy's sermons, published in London in the same year as the tracts, filled four volumes and achieved as many as three editions. They are much better reading than might be expected, and amply explain his reputation. The influence of Shaftesbury, Hoadly, and Locke is manifest throughout.

Before turning to James Duchal, Abernethy's younger partner at Wood Street, and his memorialist after his death, something more should be said about the Presbyterians at Swords, Lord Molesworth's house near Dublin. To what extent men like Arbuckle and Hutcheson and Boyse the younger associated there with Molesworth's Episcopalian friends is uncertain. Certainly Edward Synge, the youngest, formed there his lifelong friendship with Francis Hutcheson. Possibly Henry Maxwell, though somewhat older, also mingled with the recent graduates of Glasgow. His ancestry and his politics might make this likely, though he was never a proponent of concessions to Presbyterians of more than a limited character. King, as mentioned, protected Hutcheson's Dublin school from the penalties it might otherwise have legally incurred. Whether he or Swift discussed those problems of politics with the coterie of disciples at Swords cannot be discovered, but seems most improbable. What is certain is that the Presbyterian group spent much time there, wrote and received the advice of Molesworth upon their work and encouragement to further activity. Hutcheson mentioned this in his *Inquiry*. *Hibernicus's Letters,* dedicated to Molesworth's son, makes plain that the essays this contains were the work of people closely associated with the father.[70]

Molesworth became the mentor and patron of these men whilst they were still at Glasgow. Surviving letters to him reveal their admiration and his interest in them, that is, in Turnbull, Wishart, among the Scotch, Arbuckle and Smith among the Scots Hibernicus. These were the moving spirits in *The Case of the Students* who, as the tract of that title reveals, attempted to honour their Irish patron at their university but met with some discouraging results. Hutcheson was a little older than Arbuckle and may have encountered Molesworth earlier. It seems likely that Arbuckle lived in the household. He was left ten pounds by the Viscount in his will and this may be a reward, not only of affection, but for some medical services rendered to the aging and ailing nobleman. The young man had studied divinity at Glasgow and started a literary career, and at some stage had deserted divinity for the study of medicine. He was the editor and chief contributor to the venture known as *Hibernicus's Essay* undertaken under Molesworth's patronage. He went into the Customs House at Dublin, perhaps as a medical officer, and his letters from there to Drennen survive. He married Hutcheson's wife's sister in about 1742, and his son James continued the family friendship with his cousin Francis throughout the century. James Arbuckle's will was witnessed by Hutcheson's widow, by James Duchal, and by Alexander Stewart, the grandfather of Castlereagh and the devoted intimate of Bruce and Hutcheson over whose tomb he erected a monument.[71]

Arbuckle wrote poetry and continued, as his letters show, to produce it even when at the Customs House. His philosophy may be most conveniently gleaned from *Hibernicus's Letters,* a major share of which was his, though it also contained essays by Hutcheson, by Samuel Boyse, and others. Arbuckle had early fallen under the spell of Shaftesbury's *Characteristics.* He never escaped from this and it may have been responsible for his abandoning the idea of the Presbyterian ministry. He also absorbed much of the philosophy and of the politics of Molesworth. *Hibernicus's Letters* were obviously designed to be an Irish "Spectator." They were not primarily concerned with political questions, but they attacked Mandeville's *Fable,* they elaborated a theory of education for a free state and they constantly reiterated the connection of freedom in society and right-thinking among the individuals composing it.[72]

The good life was, in fact, defined according to the precepts of Shaftesbury. Beauty, virtue, and imagination were stressed, as well as intellectual recreations, castle building in Spain, laughter, and good fellowship. Literary taste should be developed. This, it may be remarked, did not include popular ballads or stories like Moll Flanders, but the study of Temple, Milton, Fénelon, Montaigne, Grotius, Longinus, and Machiavelli, besides such obvious works as those of Shaftesbury, Molesworth, and Locke. Arbuckle wished to think philosophically. All important in any state, but in Ireland in particular, good education and the encouragement of learning were necessary for those who wished to improve conditions. Health and liberty were stressed and the value of individual effort. A healthy, well-educated, and right-minded individual would not be easily corrupted in the realm of politics. Self-denial was urged on Irishmen. They should patronize home goods, not foreign luxuries. Increased trade would help the poor much more effectively than charity. A severer regime for the rich would lengthen their lives and the increased consumption they would therefore bring about would be more profitable than that of the merely selfish and luxurious. A sound economy at home secured a better life for the Swiss, as contrasted with the misery of Denmark and of France. *The Letters* were not specific about political questions of their time. They simply reflected the doctrines of the Swords circle about the social character of virtue and the importance of the sharing of pleasure and wealth in a free society. Social duty was in part discipline, in part reflection upon the harmony and order which would induce industry and increase happiness. Tyranny, bigotry, and persecution should be avoided.[73]

Arbuckle did not make any kind of mark in contemporary politics in Dublin. He kept his circle of friends by letter and visit. He evidently enjoyed some wealth and was able to send Bruce money when he needed it. A prejudice against Tories can be illustrated by a rather spiteful reference to a compliment Swift had apparently paid to some verses by Arbuckle published in the Dublin papers.[74] He, Bruce, and Duchal discussed books and philosophy and strengthened the liberal dissenting group in the capital city. Arbuckle seems to have followed a line of thought, similar but not identical with that of his brother-in-law, putting greater emphasis on beauty and almost none on the moral sense.

William Bruce (1702–1755), the publisher, was, like his friend, a writer who had assisted Abernethy in tracts against the Test. Trained at Glasgow, he was always a passionate dissenter. Dissent was, he thought, a most impregnable barrier against the encroachment of tyranny. After

Bruce's student days it is not easy to establish the chronology of his career. His deep thinking and interest in ethical problems was noted by contemporaries. In about 1728 he went into partnership with Smith at the Philosopher's Head on the Blind Quay. By July 1742, he seems to have been the tutor of Robert Henry, son of a Dublin Banker. He went north in 1747, and shortly afterwards was back in Dublin and supporting the campaigns of Charles Lucas. He was reported to have written several tracts at that time in addition to those produced with Abernethy in the thirties. He is known to have helped in the establishment of a very useful widow's fund for the Presbyterians. There seems to be no doubt that he and his partner published books in tune with their own prejudices, like Dobbs on *Trade; Persecution Contrary to Christianity;* and *An Examination of Church Power*. A letter from Bruce to Drennen describes their Harrington of 1737. "Our subscriptions to Harrington go on apace. It will be the prettiest and cheapest book that has been printed in Ireland." It was a reprint of Toland's edition, and among the subscribers may be found nearly all the names in this chapter. Harrington was a favourite of Hutcheson who endorsed many of his suggestions in lectures on polity to his students. John Smith, Bruce's former partner, once expelled for lighting a bonfire in honour of Molesworth in Glasgow, wrote a poem on the cousins who were in 1755 lying in the same grave under the monument erected by Stewart.

> Still anxious for his country's good, he knew
> No danger of his mistake, he felt it true,
> That *Happiness* and *Virtue* are the same,
> And only flourish in fair *freedom's* soil.

His services as publisher obviously outweigh his merits as poet! [75]

Like Abernethy, whose partner he became and with whom he lived, James Duchal (1697–1761) was a Glasgow student. He followed his friend at Antrim before joining him in Dublin. He seems to have been a classical scholar and to have had some medical knowledge. His sermons found admiring readers in England and Ireland. In the collected edition there is a brief memoir by James Wodrow, in addition to which some of his letters to Thom Drennen may still be read in Belfast. His closest friends after Abernethy were Drennen, Bruce, and Arbuckle.

In the year he died one of Duchal's letters maintained once more the principle of acting only by conscience. "Civil and religious liberty," he wrote, "is certainly our most valuable possession in this world . . . whatever a man can do for liberty, it becomes him to contribute." He was a disciple of Shaftesbury. Freedom was everyone's birthright. Enslaving anyone else was an outrageous violation of a fundamental human right. Moral perfection was attainable by all, but in order to achieve reason conscience must have perfect freedom of choice. Duchal's biographer concludes that he was "Warm and unbiased in his affection to the cause of truth and liberty . . . utterly adverse to the imperious, narrow, bigoted spirit which has wrought such mishaps in the Christian world."[76]

After helping Hutcheson (whose cousin, Alexander Young, had married his sister), with the Dublin school, Drennen went to Belfast in 1736, first as Haliday's assistant and later as his successor. A very sociable man, he apparently enjoyed his freedom as a bachelor and attracted a good deal of wit when he finally married and produced a family. His capacity for friendship and communicative temper is attested by his correspondence. Hutcheson wrote to him; so did Bruce, Duchal, and Arbuckle. This, in spite of the fact brought out by their frequent complaints that he himself was not the most conscientious letter-writer. He does not in fact appear to have written much at all, though his influence was a factor in the growth of liberal ideas in Belfast.[77]

The son's tribute to his father's circle, already quoted, explained their influence. William Drennen was connected both with Belfast and Dublin. A sister married Samuel McTier in the former city. He worked with McTier, with William Dickson, and with some of the Joy family, printers in Belfast for the relaxation of penal laws and for the abolition of dependency. They associated with Catholic Irish in the United Irishmen movement at the end of the century, and Drennen wrote manifestoes as well as poems and other pieces for them. At the end of his life he attempted to maintain the liberal tradition of his own forbears in Ulster by support of the Belfast Academy where rational Christianity and liberal politics would be taught. With his demise and the establishment of Queen's College — less favourable to liberal ideas — that tradition almost died out.

The problem of the relationship within Ireland between nationalists of different background and religion was not solved in the eighteenth century or since, but a few among the New Light Presbyterians identified themselves with a United Irish sentiment and program, and received some recognition for this at the time. Wolfe Tone (1763–1798), wholehearted supporter of Catholic and nationalist aspirations during the French Revolution, shortly before his tragic death in 1798 analyzed the situation in his native land in a manner laudatory to this minority of dissenters:

> The situations of England and Ireland are fundamentally different in this: The Government of England is national; that of Ireland provincial. The interest of the first is the same with that of the people. Of the last, directly opposite. The people of Ireland are divided into three sects, the established church, the Dissenters and the Catholics. The first, infinitely the smallest portion, have engrossed, besides the whole church patronage, all the profits and honors of the country, and a very great share of the landed property. They are, of course, all aristocrats, adverse to any change, and decidedly enemies to the French Revolution. The Dissenters, who are much more numerous, are the most enlightened body of the nation. They are devoted to liberty, and, through all its changes, enthusiastically attached to the French Revolution. . . . In Ireland the Dissenters are enemies to the English power, from reason and reflection; the Catholics from hatred to the English name.[78]

The reason and reflection to which Tone referred, and the principles which two generations of Drennens upheld, appeared in the sermons and tracts of Dublin and Belfast. They were, however, much more fully developed in the work of Francis Hutcheson, in whom the liberal ideas of Ireland and Scotland blend and to whom, after some remarks on his Scottish precursors, attention must shortly be given.

VI

The Interest of Scotland

Scotland in 1700

The upheavals of 1688 in Scotland revived a revolutionary tradition which went back to George Buchanan and the troubles of the sixteenth century. It also brought the Scots into touch with the English political writings of Harrington, Sidney, and Locke, as well as the philosophical works of the Platonists, More and Whichcote, and their disciple, Lord Shaftesbury, to list no more of the literary influences which spread from south of the border. Continental legists like Grotius and Puffendorf continued to be studied, and the works of classical Stoics and Epicureans. Dogma remained an important field of study and argument, but philosophical speculation became increasingly prevalent. The many political and economic problems at home stimulated enquiries and provided the brilliant generations of the eighteenth century with a wide field of endeavour.

The two parts of the kingdom united in 1707 presented striking contrasts in circumstance and in habit. In Scotland itself the ignorance and superstition of the Highlands, which was popularly blamed for their prevailing poverty, challenged the wealthier, more stable south. The development of philosophy, political theory, and the sciences of political economy and sociology was hastened and immediately conditioned by the state of Scottish society in its largest sense. After surviving the Darien disaster and achieving the difficult adaptation to the exigencies of Union, a part of Scotland prospered exceedingly. Even the American war in the last quarter of the century only momentarily retarded progress. The northern section of the country remained politically and economically backward and out of tune with the vigorous south. Both the material gains and the persistent losses of the different areas had their effect on the theories of the time. Some of these found practical expression in, for example, the Act against Heritable Jurisdictions after the rebellion of the 'Forty-five, and in the encouragement of emigration to the New World. Partisan and ephemeral political disputes drew, as always, expression of theoretical rights and wrongs. A brief survey here will be confined to that segment of Scottish opinion which continued a revolutionary tradition and added something important to it.

In Scotland it is rare to find a teacher, preacher, or controversialist who was not concerned both with political and economic problems. Buchanan in the sixteenth century shared the limitations of the English classical republicans, and was wholly occupied by the question of who should rule. Fletcher, a century later, though anxious to limit monarchical power, to regulate the relations of different parts of the British kingdoms, and to revive a national militia, was also immensely interested in the poor and the hungry. Hutcheson, a much-admired professor at Glasgow for fifteen years; Wallace, a minister who mixed in the brilliant Edinburgh society of mid-century; Smith, the father of classical economy; and even the conservative Adam Ferguson, Hume's successor at the Advocates Library and a government servant of George III—all were sympathetic with the "dregs of society" at a time when almost none of the English devoted a page to their plight. Property in land, sacred south of the border, here found critics of whom the most striking was William Ogilvie, a teacher at Aberdeen, who endorsed Harrington's suggestions.

Another current problem was the matter of public education, always important to Presbyterian Scotland, and freed by the spirit of the Scottish enlightenment from some presuppositions which had heretofore hampered its development. Scottish universities were much more progressive in method and curriculum than the English. Scots, like the English, but with much more urgency and enthusiasm, were talking about charity schools and other provisions for general instruction as a remedy for some of the problems of the Highlands. The economic liberty allowed by the Union achieved a phenomenal success in Scotland and impelled the Scots to advocate a more general relaxation of the whole mercantilist system. On the purely political aspects of discussions the most interesting development was the fact that long before any serious movement for parliamentary reform in England the philosopher, Hutcheson, was advocating drastic changes in the system of representation. Finally, on the matter of inherent rights of the sort Molyneux and Trenchard had discussed, the Scots were on the side of the colonists so far as the speculative philosophers were concerned. Not all supported the Americans, but an astonishing variety did: luminaries like Hume and Boswell, lesser folk like Charles Nisbet, and ministers like John Erskine and William Thom. Hutcheson had foreseen and justified the break. Burgh, active in the Price circle in London, wrote wisely on colonial problems as they appeared to him in 1774.

Buchanan and Fletcher

Scots of the eighteenth century turned to Buchanan rather than to Knox when they sought encouragement and inspiration for liberal ideas. The father of the Presbyterian church continued to be a force, but the royal tutor, less important in everyday life and worship, had more adherents amongst the men of the Scottish enlightenment. Dugald Steward, in his *Progress of Metaphysical, Ethical and Political Philosophy,* emphasized this:

> The dialogue of our illustrious countryman Buchanan, *De Jure Regini apud Scotos,* though occasionally disfigured by the keen and indignant temper of the writer, and by a predilection . . . for forms of policy unsuitable to the circumstances of Modern Europe, bears, nevertheless, in its general spirit, a closer resemblance to the political philosophy of the eighteenth century, than any composition which had previously appeared . . . The political reflections, too, incidentally introduced by the same author in his history of Scotland, bear marks of a mind worthy of a better age than fell to his lot . . . In reading them, one would almost imagine, that one is listening to the voice of Beccaria or of Montesquieu.[1]

Buchanan's influence was secular. His most important early disciple was Montaigne. James VI imbibed little of his instructor's spirit, though he may have profited by his learning, but Montaigne was ever to remember the Scotch preceptor. In seventeenth-century England the *Dialogue* was twice printed in translation, in 1680 and 1689. Oxford burnt it as subversive in 1683. It became a favourite work with William Pitt, Lord Chatham. The arguments in it became a part of the Real Whig creed and so passed into American thinking in the eighteenth century.

Buchanan emphasized a society which was natural to man. God created human beings as social animals and endowed them with social instincts. Thereafter, they were left free to develop the institutions which suited them and which brought the greatest measure of happiness to them. Governments existed for the people and should be changed if they failed to help them. Kings were for the people, and not vice versa. When necessary they might be deposed. The decisions of the people in their representative assemblies should be reached by majority vote. How could a whole people agree on what is right? Buchanan maintained that scarcely any law could be made but which bears down on some, nor any magistrate chosen who is not unpopular with a few.

> What is sought is that the law shall be of advantage to the majority of the people, and that the majority have confidence in the person chosen. Then, since a majority of the people may decree a law or create a ruler, why should a lesser matter—viz., that the public should hold the ruler accountable and should set judges over him—be forbidden? And, if the tribunes of the Roman people and the Lacedaemonian ephors were needed to limit the exercise of public authority, ought it to appear wrong for a free people, either for a like reason, or for a different one, to cast about for a way to restrain the unreasoning violence of tyranny?[2]

Buchanan's insistence on a self-governing society, based on its natural right to live as well as possible, and on the rule of law established by the majority of the people in and applicable to all, magistrate or citizen alike, was, as Stewart said, essentially modern in the attitude it revealed. His interpretation of Scottish history was along similar lines, and his countrymen did not fail to honour and appreciate his philosophy.

It seems less than just to the writers of the seventeenth century to pass immediately to Andrew Fletcher of Saltoun, but in eighteenth-century Scotland his work was next in importance to that of Buchanan. He was unsuccessful in much he attempted. He opposed the Stuarts and suffered exile. Returning with Monmouth, he was prevented by an unfortunate quarrel from sharing the rest of that adventure. The Revolution brought him back but he soon became disillusioned with the new order. He joined the fight against a standing army in 1697 and consorted with the club at the Grecian. Though William was forced to disband some troops, no scheme for a national force such as Fletcher had proposed was adopted. The disasters of Darien and the discussions about the relations of Scotland and England in the early years of Anne's reign afforded an opportunity for Fletcher to point out the danger of the "preëminence" enjoyed by London, to suggest a federal system for the kingdoms, and to urge the adoption of "limitations" upon royal power. But the Union achieved in 1707 was far different from that for which he had hoped. Fletcher retired into private life, but his writings and published speeches continued to circulate and appeared in collected form four times in the eighteenth century. Biographical notices and encomiums were written about him by David Erskine, eleventh earl of Buchan and by Richard Watson, Bishop of Llandaff.[3]

Educated by the Whig historian and churchman, Gilbert Burnet, Fletcher traveled and read widely in Italian authors. He later published an essay in that language. He was deeply interested in history and particularly in the vicissitudes of European governments since the revival of learning. The old Gothic balance he had studied with his tutor had been destroyed; the feudal system based on land and service had disappeared, leaving the way open for absolutism. The vassal had been dependent on baron, rather than king; in contemporary Europe the princes possessed the sword and monarchies were changed into tyrannies. England and Scotland still retained some ancient liberty. Fletcher felt they should be warned that changes came from negligence rather than from the contrivance of ill-designing men.[4]

Fletcher thus illustrated the subject:

I shall deduce from their original, the causes, occasions, and the complications of those many unforeseen accidents; which falling out much about the same time, produced so great a change. And it will at first sight seem very strange, when I shall name the restoration of learning, the invention of printing, of the needle, and of gunpowder, as the chief of them; things in themselves so excellent, . . . might have proved of infinite advantage to the world, if their remote influence on government had been obviated by suitable remedies.[5]

When Constantinople fell to Mahomet II, he continued, "many learned Greeks fled over into Italy." They introduced the study of Greek at about the time that the learned began to "restore the purity of the Latin Tongue." Even more important was the art of printing, which made classical learning and arts familiar to many. From a natural propensity to pleasure Italy imitated the luxury of the ancients and was presently filled with architects, painters, and sculptors. "Thus the Italians began to come off their frugal and military way of living." This infection spread, but would not alone have worked so great a change in government if the invention of the needle had not greatly improved navigation so that a passage to the East Indies was found and a new world discovered. "By this means the luxury of Asia and America was added to that of the ancients." Europe sank into "an abyss of pleasure." Fletcher argued that "these things brought a total alteration in the way of living, upon which all government depends."[6] Expenses fell on the barons, and they turned military service into money. Diets and parliaments also voted great sums upon "a people grown rich by trade and dispirited for want of military exercises." So came about the decline of freedom in Europe.[7]

Fletcher emphasized the relation of government to economic and cultural developments. In putting forward his account of a series of accidents to explain the change from the medieval or Gothic world to that in which he himself lived, he used examples which textbooks have made commonplace and which many historians of ideas have modified or pushed aside. In the context in which he used them, however, as important factors in the emergence of absolutism, they still retained considerable validity.

Fletcher did not, in suggestions about the current situation in Scotland and England, bring forward what could be called a democratic plan. His contemporaries considered him republican—a Common-wealthman. He brought in suggestions for limitations to secure the liberty of the kingdom, which were not unlike those proposed by Henry Neville. He wanted annual parliaments meeting at stated times, and in no way dependent on royal whim, and an increase of lesser barons or of English knights in the composition of parliament. He wished to abolish the royal power of war and peace, as well as appointment to all offices, and the disposition of all military forces should be under parliament. He was prepared for drastic measures against any king that would upset these arrangements.[8]

Fletcher was interested also in a federal union, since small, independent states could not easily subsist in the British Isles. Molesworth advocated something similar in the Preface to *Franco-Gallia* and may have been inspired by the Scottish republican.

> The Ease and Advantage which wou'd be gained by *uniting* our own three Kingdoms upon equal Terms (for upon unequal it would be no *Union*) is so visible, that if we had not the example of those Masters of the World, the *Romans,* before our eyes, one would wonder that our own Experience (in the instance of uniting *Wales* to *England*) shou'd not convince us, that altho both Sides would incredibly gain by it, yet the rich and opulent Country, to which such an Addition is made, wou'd be the greater Gainer.[9]

The Conversation Concerning a Right Regulation of Governments for the Common Good of Mankind (1704) showed that Fletcher had read and endorsed the sentiments of Molyneux's *Case.* The Union Fletcher demanded would make due provision for decentralization of government and prevent such injuries as the Irish were suffering, and even remedy the "great imperfections and inconveniences" of Wales. Trade was not the only consideration in government. Justice was due from one nation to another. Unjust usage would tempt separation.

By an equal Union, Fletcher hoped that "we shall then be possessed of liberty; shall administer our own affairs, and be free from the corruptions of a court; we shall have the certain and constant alliance of a powerful nation, of the same language, religion and government." He feared that, "if in the Union of several countries under one government, the prosperity and happiness of the different nations are not considered, as well as of the whole united body, those that are more remote from the seat of the government will be only made subservient to the interest of the others, and their condition very miserable."[10]

Fletcher lost his fight. The Union of 1707 opened English trade to the Scots, not all of whom were as indifferent as Fletcher to its advantages. A measure of security was obtained for the Presbyterian church. The United Parliament sat in London, not even occasionally in some Scottish city. Fletcher had been willing to abandon Edinburgh, as unsuited for a capital city, but he was not willing to give up the claims of Scotland as a seat of government. There can be no doubt that some, though not all, the evils Fletcher feared developed from the arrangements of the Union.

Fletcher was not merely a student of absolutism and of prerogative; he was a keen observer of social conditions. He saw in the poverty of his country a challenging problem and proposed solutions for it. He blamed the Scots, themselves, for their failure to provide against the evils of the union of the crowns while they could, for their iniquitous rental system, for their laziness and a failure to make the most of resources on land and at sea. The remedies he suggested for the economic situation were as drastic as those for the political.

Landed property should be limited to an amount which could be cultivated under an owner's supervision. Slavery could solve the problems of unemployment and hunger. In this way the rich would assume responsibility for the poor, would be provided with industrious labour. Thus the real happiness of Scotland would be increased. Abuses of slave-holding would be prevented by regulation of a paternal nature.[11]

In spite of the wild temper which disturbed his youth, his later years were remarkable for philosophic acceptance of defeat and an attempt to make his own property a good example of estate management. Always sharply critical of ambitious, self-seeking men, his own behaviour lived up to the ideals of public spirit he professed, and he was long respected in his native land. Few of his suggestions were carried out. Throughout the eighteenth century, however, Scotsmen studied the ills of society, particularly with relation to the poor, to increasing the wealth of nations, and to the redistribution of political power in accordance with property.

Frances Hutcheson and Adam Smith

Francis Hutcheson, the famous philosopher and teacher of Adam Smith, was amongst those men whose influence in eighteenth-century Scotland was greatest. He was born in Armagh in Ireland in 1694 of a family who, early in the seventeenth century, had come from Ayr in lowland Scotland. His father, John, had followed the same profession as his grandfather, a Presbyterian minister, and is said to have been responsible for securing for his church a moderate annual subsidy, the regium donum, from the English government. Francis was educated at a grammar school near Saintfield and then at a dissenting academy in Killyleagh, whose teacher, James McAlpin (fl.1700), had a reputation for learning. About 1710 the philosopher, excluded by his family's Presbyterianism from Irish or English universities (like so many who swelled Scottish enrollment), went to the University of Glasgow and remained there six years. Before leaving Scotland he tutored the young William Boyd (1704–1746), later fourth earl of Kilmarnock. Hutcheson was licensed soon after his return to Ireland as a probationer in his father's church and was invited by the congregation of Magherally to be their pastor. He decided, however, to accept another invitation to Dublin where some of his friends urged him to set up an academy of his own. Hutcheson married Mary Wilson, the daughter of one of King William's soldiers, in 1724, and by her had one son, Francis. They lived until 1730 over the school at the corner of Dominick and Dorset Streets, and had many friends in the Molesworth circle and among Glasgow classmates. Hutcheson was elected to a professorship at Glasgow in 1729 and took up residence there in 1730. Robert Wodrow heard his inaugural lecture, delivered in a low and hurried voice. He died whilst on a visit to Ireland in 1746 and was buried in St. Mary's churchyard, Dublin.[12]

During his years in Dublin he published *An Inquiry into the Original of Our Ideas of Beauty and Virtue* (1725). This and the other essays of his sojourn made him known both "abroad and in Dublin." Continental and American libraries bought this, his best-known work. During the sixteen years in Glasgow he translated, edited, and wrote a Latin "Compend," or, *Short Introduction,* and the long "System" which during his lifetime circulated only in manuscript among his friends, Drennen, Bruce, Synge, Abernethy, and Rundle.[13]

Hutcheson's portrait was painted by Allan Ramsay the Younger and from the portrait a wax bust was modeled by Isaac Gosset, which enabled several sculptured likenesses to be made for admiring pupils like Dunbar Hamilton, earl of Selkirk (1722–1790), and Brand Hollis.[14] These bear out the statements of both Leechman and Carlyle that he was handsome. Hutcheson was above middle height, fair-complexioned with red cheeks. His features were regular. His whole person raised a "strong prejudice in his favour at first sight." He talked well and there can be no doubt he was an enormously effective lecturer, though his writing is undistinguished. As he walked up and down the classroom, his manner was informal, but the words were eloquent. Like Gershom Carmichael (1672–1729) and others before him, he lectured in English.

Students visited his house, sought his advice; and parents entrusted him with funds for their children. Hutcheson's letters are witty and they are full of that immense interest in his pupils which has been the secret of so many successful teachers. He encouraged Foulis to leave his barber shop for the University, helped him start his famous publishing house, and suggested books for him to print as he did with another pupil, Richard Baron, who faithfully carried out his suggestions. Probably his cousin's firm of Bruce and Smith in Dublin received advice of the same kind. In the books he selected may be found further evidence as to his politics—civil war tracts, the great seventeenth-century classics of English political thought, and contemporary works by his friends like Abernethy. Hutcheson's personality, appearance, and activities as a widely read and respected writer and popular teacher combined to make effective his presentation of radical ideas—of that liberty which he espoused.[15]

Hutcheson spent thirty years including infancy in Ireland, twenty-two in Scotland. His forefathers (with the possible exception of an English mother) were Scottish, though long domiciled in Ireland. Although his environment and the circumstances of these two countries greatly affected his thought, English influence was enormously important in determining its direction. In Robert Molesworth, Hutcheson had a friend at a very important period in his development, soaked in the theories of Milton, Harrington, Sidney, and Locke, and acquainted with all the most important like-minded Englishmen of the Augustan age. To say that, however important, Hutcheson's contribution was but a part of the whole achievement of his contemporaries is not to belittle, but to comprehend it.

Hutcheson's politics were based upon his philosophical assumptions. A balance between liberty and the necessity imposed by the Golden Rule and determined by the criterion of utility was to be achieved by the moral sense of man. This sense would harmonize our own and the general good. Virtue and happiness were closely dependent upon one another. The social impulse was important for the grand determination towards our general happiness and towards the greatest general good. Man naturally admired virtue, even that not immediately profitable. In the exercise of social duties was displayed, at once, self-love and universal benevolence, since the sum of all was the greatest good. Illogicalities were easy to find in the idea of this infallible inner light or moral sense, reflecting an omnipresent natural reason; and in the concept of a more passive reception of beauty, reflecting the eternal harmonies. In environment improperly conditioned, the explanation of individual infringements of the general good could be found. Education should provide that knowledge, without which the fullest liberty and happiness could be enjoyed. An improvement in situation and in training would cultivate our moral sense. The study of history, poetry, music, and art would develop just notions of virtue and abate those desires and opinions which would hinder ultimate contentment. Hutcheson hardly faced the problem of those interpretations of good which ran counter to the general welfare. He was much more concerned with the altruism and goodness revealed in the deeds of fellow men than with the question raised by such qualities as selfishness or cruelty found at times even in children. In the development of democratic ideas, this faith in the nature and reasonableness of men was likely to be more stimulating than the realization of man's many failings.

The preface to the *Compend* announced that it was written, not for the learned, but for those anxious to study that way of life which right reason required. The application of his theories to particular political and social problems was extraordinarily clear and explicit. A rule-of-thumb common sense dealt with objections that might be raised to the rights of man enumerated and the political reforms advocated. In spite of the great debt he so freely acknowledged to others, Hutcheson's most original contribution to eighteenth-century thought was undoubtedly made in the field of politics.

Most important was his whole-hearted endorsement of the right of resistance. He fully admitted the advantages of civil union. He had lived through two rebellions and was aware at first hand of the disruption such strife can bring. He recognized the duties of servants to their masters, children to their parents, wives to their husbands, subjects to their rulers. Yet Hutcheson, even when stressing obligation and peacefulness, always reserved a right of defense against private or public tyranny. Thus, his doctrines of individual rights connected with his notions of political behaviour. Children could not be bound forever to obey parents. Servants might leave unjust masters, the conquered might demand consideration from the conqueror, and the subjects of the most absolute monarch could not be tied down forever, and in all circumstances, even by oaths and contracts. Nor, therefore, could colonists be tied by sentiment or past agreements to the mother country.

Hutcheson absolutely dismissed Aristotle's famous statement that some men were naturally slaves. He denied that slavery could descend a generation, even if imposed by the circumstances of any given moment of time. He saw in slavery only an involuntary state, brought about by wicked men or sometimes by wrongdoing. For example, he conceded that the idle might be enslaved for a term or for life, but only as a punishment from which release could be sought in reformation of manners. There was nothing natural in a state of slavery as such.[16]

Arguments in the *System* against an absolute private dominion of any one over any other, are extended to the married state and to family life in general. In his remarks on a sensible balance of power in the family, he suggested an ideal to which, on the whole, practice still presented an unpleasant contrast. Authority in the family should rest with that member best able to exert it wisely. It should at all times be used with discretion and with the assent of all members of the group. Men were stronger than women, but on that account should not necessarily usurp all rights in the education of the children or in the disposal of common property. The same standards applied to men and to women, though the results of departure from them might prove more embarrassing to one party than to another. Children, too, had valid rights. They, too, were rational agents. John Witherspoon (1723–1794) reminded his readers that children were not slaves and he may have been thinking along lines laid down by his erstwhile teacher. The rights of heads of families should depend on consent and on voluntary continuance in the family unit. Though Hutcheson emphasized filial obedience he insisted on the rights of young people. With respect to servants, he was equally explicit. They should have a right to something more than a bare maintenance, even to something for pleasure, gaiety, and a little stock for themselves and their families.[17]

The rights of resistance to tyranny of a magistrate were early propounded in *An Inquiry*. Civil war might be a lesser evil than subjection to a bad government. The only possible good that might derive from passive obedience would be patience. But men have generally been a "great deal too tame and tractable"; hence, the enslavement of nine-tenths of the nations. These were, of course, different notions of happiness. Thus, in one country there prevailed a courageous disposition, where liberty was counted a great good and was an inconsiderable evil—in others, the spirits of men were more abject and timorous, where civil war appeared the greatest natural evil and liberty no great purchase. Yet Puffendorf and Hobbes exaggerated the burdens imposed by the state. Generally speaking, men "have sufficient motive to submit to any tolerably contrived plan of polity."[18] States, justly administered, have a right to expect obedience, whatever their origin. Hutcheson was obviously impatient with fine distinctions between different types of authority or between the law of nature and that of nations. On the other hand, he always insisted on the limits of obedience and the rights of all to withdraw from the country. Subjects might be bound to bear mistakes for a "distant utility" or out of public duty. Subjects might submit to conquest; it might sometimes be the duty of a former ruler to give up older claims. On the other hand, tyrants and limited monarchs alike could be resisted. The criterion of virtue in a trust or delegation of power was the prosperity of the whole, and of any failure to achieve this the people as a whole must be judge. No conveyance of power, however complete, could be valid when the government seemed not to be acting for the general good. Colonies could separate whenever they felt this was to their advantage.[19]

Though an extended survey of Hutcheson's colonial public would take up too much space here, it may be noticed in passing that the seventh chapter of his third book, "The Rights of Governors" and their limitations, was felt by the New Englanders to be appropriate to their situation with respect to Thomas Hutchinson (1711–1780), Governor and Captain General of Massachusetts Bay. A very large part of the chapter was reprinted in the fiftieth number of *The Massachusetts Spy* on 13 February, 1772.[20]

Laws, Hutcheson felt, were so far from excluding liberty that they were its surest defense. No divinity could make just a tyrannical ruler. The people had a right to dethrone a prince perfidious to his trust, or an heir apparent whose theory seemed to threaten the liberty of the subject. Ultimately, Hutcheson's theory of when it was that colonies might turn independent rested upon his assumption that a power to resist actions inimicable to their general good rested with any community of persons. Just as a child might oppose an unjust parent, or a servant a bad master, so might the citizens of any country, province, or plantation oppose governors whose actions ran counter to their welfare.[21]

Hutcheson's discussion of the nature of civil society in the *System* owed much to former writers. In its analysis of the different forms of states, the *System* followed the classical lines laid down by Aristotle and modified by Polybius. Naturally enough, the best form was the mixed state. In his analysis of the foundations of the best state, as in his recommendations for its mechanics, Hutcheson followed Harrington. "That state is best," he wrote, "which depends upon its natural bottom of property." Property could give no absolute right to monarchy, for example, but no monarch could last for long without a due proportion of wealth. A democracy could not exist without a wide distribution of wealth among its members.[22]

Hutcheson's emphasis upon the economic foundations of power was due to his enormous interest in the nature of money, the problems of value and price, and the division of labor and its relation to the formation of civil society. Adam Smith's debt to his thinking has often been investigated. It is important, however, in the present connection, to notice the common sense that distinguishes Hutcheson's often apparently casual dicta. His remarks on luxury compare favourably with those of most contemporaries who wasted much time in lamenting the vice which indulgence caused, and failed, as he did not, to examine the very real benefits that follow from increased consumption on the part of a vigorous, long-lived population. He distinguished between the evils that might come from wealth and the good that might be enjoyed as a result of industry. Sober, plentiful consumption should not be condemned as luxury. The goods likely to be used by the artificer class should be allowed to come in freely. So should goods or exports be freed from "all burdens." Duties should not in any case be high enough to discourage consumption. Raise the demand; if goods were expensive, people would work harder to obtain them. On the other hand, the "lower and more numerous orders of the people" should be discouraged by the price from the use of foreign goods. Population should be encouraged by lower taxes on the married and, as Molesworth had suggested, by the general and easy naturalization of foreign labourers. Hutcheson in general was for an extension of economic freedom, though he was by no means completely rid of social and mercantilist presuppositions.[23]

In the discussion of property, he admitted the rights of free enterprise and a due profit from it, but was specifically against community of property. He had some reservations about wealth which are very interesting and have very radical connotations. He suggested an agrarian law,

> . . . as will prevent any immoderate increase of wealth in the hands of a few, which could support a force superior to the whole body. 'Tis in vain to talk of invading the liberty of the rich, or the injury of stopping their progress in just acquisitions. No publick interest hinders them acquiring as much as is requisite for any innocent enjoyment and pleasures of life. And yet if it did, the liberty and safety of thousands or millions is never to be put in the ballance with even the innocent pleasures of a few families; much less their vain ambition . . . or external pomp and grandeur.

In the last phrases he would seem to agree with Wallace who wrote that even the poor had immortal spirits and could not be maintained for the grandeur or interest of a few. Hutcheson and Wallace also agreed about the necessity of abolishing that ignorance which was always so favourable to poverty and thus to tyranny.[24]

The general good should be the end of political association, rather than the exaltation of a few; thus privilege, for anything but merit, is inadmissible. Office should not go by inherited favour. No one had a right to power, nor a right to inflict misery on others, unless the public interest required it. Not even superior wisdom gave a right to rule. Government, indeed, should be so planned as to prevent mischief when it fell into bad hands. We could not expect that the wise or good would always rule. A rotation in office might deprive the state of the prolonged service of a good man, but it would also be a safeguard against all evil men. New talent would be brought forward. Corruption would be prevented since long continuance in office would be impossible. The people who would select officers might not always choose well, but would be much influenced by the character and reputation of the wise as they made their choice.

A popular elected assembly and a senate with a limited term would provide security against tyranny. Both bodies would have a rotation, though somewhat differently arranged in each. The senate, as in *Oceana,* should deliberate, concert, propose. The Assembly, informed before they met of the matter coming up for consideration, since wise decisions were difficult to come to during keen debates, would decide upon the measures drawn up by the upper house. The regal element, working with the senate and assembly and dependent upon them for money, could either be an hereditary monarch subject to the law, or it could be a small council elected for a term by the senate. It may be noted that an elective monarchy or presidency was not suggested. Hutcheson thought in republican terms, but seemed not to have had any very definite preference as to the precise form of the monarchical element in his state. In concluding remarks on the structure of the state, in the sixth chapter of the third book of his *System,* Hutcheson once more recommended study of the constitutional laws most suited to each kind of state as considered by Aristotle and Harrington.[25]

The Scottish professor believed in as wide a reform of representative systems as his mentors, Molesworth or Harrington. Like them, he endorsed the ballot and frequent elections. He was not, like Molesworth, concerned with the landed property of the representative. He was anxious to see what Molesworth called "wastes and desserts," like Old Sarum, deprived of their privilege. "A constant door to corruption must be open if small or poor districts and cities have representatives quite beyond the proportion of their wealth to the rest." Bribery must be made impossible. He expatiated on the advantages of a rotation in senates, councils, and assemblies, in which a third or fourth part go out at one time. A fixed law favoured no one, so neither representatives nor magistrates who went out from a fixed term need feel affronted. They might, indeed, help their successors with advice. Censors created by the senate should degrade all who were dissolute or dishonourable.

It is odd that two suggestions for parliamentary reform should appear in Scotland in mid-century, a considerable time before Baron, himself a Glasgow student (1739–1742), brought forward his scheme for a "representation by counties" in London. Not only does Hutcheson make these drastic demands, but a tract called *Liberty and Right* (1747), appearing at the time of the 'Forty-five, proposed a plan that might have come from a nineteenth-century Chartist, advocating payment of members, a readjustment of constituencies, more frequent elections, the ballot, and the abolition of primogeniture.[26]

Hutcheson endorsed a very wide freedom in religion. He was cautious, perhaps as minister and professor in a touchy established church, about restraints of any kind. He was discreet when he talked with Wodrow, who, as champion of orthodoxy, tried to see how far he shared the views of friends among the near-Unitarian Irish. The job at Glasgow, as Simson's Case had earlier proved, depended on ability to avoid controversy with the Kirk. Discretion, popularity, and perhaps a greater sympathy with moderate views than many dared admit, saved Hutcheson from the consequences of such criticism as he could not entirely escape. In the *System,* he condemned the contests and claims of the rival sects. Calvinist and Arminian, materialist and metaphysical, orthodox, Arian, and Socinian: "The warm zealots of all sides have represented all schemes of religion opposite their own, opposite also to all goodness. . . . Virtue ever was and will be popular, where men can vote freely," he continued. Then goodness and virtue will reign. Any obstacle to this freedom would be a deterrent to morality. Some power of censorship might be conceded. Honest freethinkers could hardly have been annoyed by the magisterial powers Hutcheson was prepared to allow.[27]

The last part of Book III described both the defense of the realm against external foes and the courts of justice in which domestic enemies or criminals would be tried. The admiration for a citizen militia was reminiscent of, and perhaps roused by, the pleas against standing armies of Fletcher and Walter Moyle. He was certain that military service for as many as possible of the population would promote industry and provide a stock of sober, virtuous veterans for emergency service. This force would be served by a rotation of officers in the higher command and so the nation would also be well served with a good supply of officers and generals. James Burgh, in his *Political Disquisitions* (1774), had expressed a somewhat similar idea derived from the same sources.[28]

Like Sidney and Molesworth before him, Hutcheson was enormously interested in plain and uniform laws which did not present an endless labyrinth. Laws should be readily understood by all. The courts should be open; high ideas of justice should prevail. The most severe punishment by the courts should be reserved for crimes against the public interest on the part of either private men or magistrates. Punishments should be devised to increase the general good and security. They should be proportioned to guilt. If fines were imposed, the pecuniary scale should be adjusted in relation to the wealth of the criminal. If "corporeal" punishment were to be used, then it should be adjusted to his health. Torture, if indeed it were ever justifiable, should be most rarely inflicted. It could only be used to deter crime but even then was likely to corrupt the torturer. Beccaria may not have read these passages, as well as the earlier *Inquiry* with the famous utilitarian formula which Bentham adopted from him, before his *Dei Delitti e delle Pene* appeared in 1764, but there is a very astonishing coincidence of thought between the Glasgow philosopher and the younger Italian.[29]

The ideas of the *System* on international relations, like its concept of natural law, owed much to Grotius and Puffendorf. Hutcheson departed sharply from their views with respect to the rights which conquest conferred and decisions about peace and war. His ideas on the limits of the rights of conquest have been noticed. When he defined just and unjust war, he was conventional enough, but he applied, here as everywhere, the criterion of the greatest good.

> . . . nor has anything occasioned more misery in human life than a vain and indolent ambition both in princes and popular states of extending their empires, and bringing every neighbouring state under subjection to them; without consulting the real felicity either of their own people or of their new acquisitions.

In short, in foreign as in colonial policy, that is best which considers most fully the welfare of all mankind.[30]

Hutcheson's definition of when it was that colonies might turn independent, his defense of liberty and of human dignity, his teaching that the standard of moral goodness was the promotion of the general happiness, his whole idea of the state, were significant not of his single genius, but of the environment into which he was born and in which he lived, and of the tradition he inherited. Ill-judged policies, by a distant government, ran counter to those rights for which Englishmen of an earlier generation had fought and about which they had written. Those battles and books were infinitely important to all those whose position was less favoured than the Georgian English. "Tyranny, faction, a neglect of justice, a corruption of manners and anything which occasions the misery of the subjects, destroys this national love and the dear idea of a country."[31] Hutcheson was conscious of the emotions and experience of his fellows in his own age.

Perceptiveness and intensity of emotion explain much of his success as a teacher. Evidence of his influence on his students, as well as of the spread and use of his writings in his own century, is overabundant. Parliamentary reformers, antislavery propagandists, supporters of colonial aspirations, as well as early utilitarians, all found inspiration in Hutcheson's pronouncements. Liberalism at Glasgow, at Aberdeen and wherever his disciples may be found, was a vital and a growing force.

The position of Adam Smith, greatest name in the Scottish enlightenment, in a study of developing Whig theories and radicalism, is much more difficult to delimit and describe than that of his beloved teacher. His *Wealth of Nations*—the *Principia* of the social sciences as Governor Pownall called it—provided the foundation for modern economic thought. Many opposing interests have found in Smith justification for enterprises of widely different social effects. Very few nations or persons have yet tried to work out the whole of the implied program of the *Wealth of Nations*. A business proponent of individual enterprise may use Smith against government restrictions of his acquisitive instincts, while entirely ignoring or combatting Smith on the freeing of international trade. Smith was concerned with the larger workings of an economic natural law. He was not by disposition a revolutionary, nor was he moved to eloquence, as were so many of the Real Whigs, by the political considerations of the social contract, or of justice. His *Moral Sentiments* lacks the ardent love of liberty which marked Hutcheson's *System of Moral Philosophy*. He was a professor and beloved by his students, but his effect was intellectual, rather than emotional, as Hutcheson's had been. He could talk without bitterness of Cromwell's military rule or James's expulsion. He was convinced of the merits of the Revolution Settlement including the Union, but he had not the missionary zeal of a Priestley or a Burgh.

What deeply stirred Smith's sympathy was the condition of the lower ranks of society. He not only examined the needs and rewards of the working poor; he also considered their leisure and the disadvantages of a scanty education. He attributed drunkenness or disorderly conduct, not to viciousness, but most literally to ignorance which left no other recourse open to young men at work from their earliest years. His most striking passages were devoted to sympathetic consideration of the workers. An examination of the liberties of Greece and Rome led him, not to the ecstasies of Moyle and Trenchard, but to the statement that such liberty was founded on slavery. Societies of free men have different institutions, different occupations, less time for public business. Slavery was an unprofitable use of labour. Slaves were very seldom inventive; all important discoveries had come from free men.

Smith was not especially interested in slavery as such. His attention was chiefly focused upon the workingman. Labour determined the value of goods. The labourer produced food and clothing for everyone in the nation. There had been complaints that high wages for the labourer meant higher prices, but so did higher profits for the manufacturer. Which was worse, he asked? Smith answered that improvement in the circumstances of the lower ranks, far from being an inconvenience, was a definite advantage to society.

> What improves the circumstance of the greater part can never be regarded as an inconveniency to the whole. No society can surely be flourishing and happy of which the far greater part of the members are poor and miserable. It is but equity, besides, that they who feed cloath and lodge the whole body of the people, should have such a share of the produce of their own labour as to be themselves tolerably well fed, cloathed and lodged.[32]

Smith therefore dismissed as disingenuous the complaints of merchants about high wages, while they ignored "the pernicious effect" of high profits.[33]

Smith was not only interested in a fair return for labour; he was also observant of the effects of poverty upon population. He noted with sorrow the mortality among the poor in spite of large families. He outlined no general scheme for a welfare state, but his remarks drew attention to the need for a consideration of national health. He studied the poor laws of his age. He wished for the free circulation of labour necessary in the industrial development he desired. He stressed equity in this matter as he never did in the purely political aspects of his lectures. The removal of a person from one parish to another under the law of Settlement was a violation of natural liberty. He expressed surprise that the English, so jealous of their liberty, had for want of due understanding allowed these oppressive laws to remain in force.[34]

Education, whilst in many branches better handled privately by endowments, or by these and a system of fees, should also, so far as the labouring poor were concerned, be a matter for state action. Elementary instruction at an early age should be provided through schools not unlike those of his native Scotland. Ability to read and write should offset the natural tendency of the division of labour in modern industrial processes to deaden mental activity. Education at a higher level should be further removed from clerical control and its curriculum should be revised. Students should be discouraged from too early excursions to foreign parts and stimulated to attend university classes by the improvements in pedagogical methods.[35]

Smith was interested in the history of the relations between poverty and wealth. He concluded that it was in the progressive state while society was advancing to further acquisitions, rather than when it had attained its full complement of riches, that the condition of the labouring poor seemed to be happiest and most comfortable. The increase of wealth had released Europeans from tyranny and had brought with it order, good government, and the security of individual freedom. Freedom, as its advantages were realized, should be extended. Old regulations about apprentices, about the poor, about prices and wages, should be discarded.[36]

On the international side this would also lead to freer trade and intercourse between nations. Endeavours should be made not to keep colonies in a state of subjection, but to grant them representation and freedom from restrictions. Ancient empires knew nothing of representative institutions. It would be wise to extend what was regarded as an inherent right to colonists. They would feel of no account in their own lands, if policy were decided elsewhere, and their own institutions were subordinated to the mother country. In the long run both England and America would gain by freer trade and a more equal consideration of the interests of each.[37]

Smith has been regarded as the spiritual father of both Marxism and Capitalism. The *Wealth of Nations* has commonly been thought to afford the theoretical basis for the activities of robber barons of a later period, even whilst Communist philosophers have seized on the theory of labour to support very different but also predatory claims. Surely the impartial reader can find in his pages little advocating a doctrinaire system of any kind. Men should be free in order to develop their capacities. Such development in a properly constituted political society would be of advantage to that society, to the world. In no sense was it a demand either for thoughtless exploitation or for conscious regimentation of the "laborious majority."

Ferguson, the Rankenians, Wallace

Adam Ferguson (1723–1816) was a member of the Edinburgh Philosophical Society at a time when Hume, Smith, Robertson, and Wallace also were members. He shared with Hume an interest in history; with Smith and with Wallace an interest in the nature of the classes of society. He was the least gifted among them, but his continued emphasis on inequalities of rank and his strictures upon slavery have led to a sometimes exaggerated estimate of his liberalism. He modified his views as he grew older. The *Institutes* (1769), first product of his Edinburgh classroom, laid much more stress on the equality of man than his later *Principles,* published in 1792 after his retirement. Ferguson's contribution to the Scottish liberal school of thought lay chiefly in penetrating observations on history, on reasons discovered for the rise and fall of states and the relation of stability and security to liberty and policy. Man was a product of environment; that in turn could be greatly affected by the members of the community in which each lived and a general recognition of the necessity of right action.

Ferguson was educated at St. Andrew's and then became chaplain to a regiment commanded by Lord John Murray. He was with this troop at the Battle of Fontenoy and accompanied them to Ireland and to France, though he left the service when they were ordered to America in 1755. He succeeded David Hume at the Advocate's Library in 1757, and became professor at Edinburgh University not very long after, holding first a chair of natural philosophy and then of moral philosophy. He retired in 1785. Lord North sent him to America in 1778–79 on a commission to negotiate with the colonists. In spite of the ill health which occasioned his retirement, Ferguson continued to write history and philosophy, and lived to the ripe old age of ninety-three. He was humorous and a brilliant lecturer, but difficult, jealous, and overbearing, and readily offended.[38]

Ferguson's politics, those of a conservative Whig, reveal no patience with utopian schemes, and nothing but abuse for the claims of natural rights by the Americans. Both these and their defender, Richard Price, were attacked in a vigorous pamphlet in 1776. The colonists owed everything to England, he felt, and should be prepared to pay for it. On the other hand the increase of English obligations and responsibilities, as well as the enlargement of the population and wealth of the empire, made new policies necessary. Ferguson hoped for success for British arms overseas, and for a reconsideration of the problem of empire when success made it possible.[39]

Both *On Civil Society* (1767) and *The Roman Republic* (1782) examined the reasons for the rise and fall of states. Those who knew Rome knew all mankind. Certain developments in Society followed clearly on circumstance and period. Society, natural to man, gradually produced wealth and inequality of status. This in turn resulted in social differences. Ferguson believed in an evolution, was a philosopher of gradualness and disclaimed any credence in the accomplishments of single lawgivers like Numa or Lycurgus. Frequent and drastic changes were undesirable. On the other hand tumults, factional strife, resistance might occasionally be necessary to prevent despotism and the sacrifice of the many to the few. He was by no means pessimistic about the result of the efforts of gifted and industrious individuals to improve their own fortunes and the laws and policies of the state under which they lived. Freedom lay more in the opportunity for talent to succeed, and in equal laws providing protection for the innocent, than in certain punishment for the guilty, or in any attempted redistribution of wealth or power.[40]

Ferguson was much interested in the development of national character. Human beings infected one another with both virtue and with vice. A high prevailing standard would bring conformity, even from men of lesser caliber. In a degenerate age good men had less success, though in their efforts lay the hope of eventual regeneration. Political institutions might not inspire talent, but where they did not impede it, improvements were likely to be effected. During the Roman Republic good regulations, like rotation in office (abolished by Tiberius), were made at a time when individuals had opportunity to achieve wealth and power. The expanding state stimulated prowess in battle and enterprise in other fields of endeavour. This in turn brought its own changes. Success brought luxury and great inequality. Rich and poor soldiers and citizens were sharply divided in addition to those differences which talent, occupation, and inheritance might bring about at any time. The role of slavery in the Roman state was stressed by Ferguson, and he described the competition between slave and free labour and the effects of the manumissions of slaves on the society which they then entered. This kind of historical analysis not only illuminated the relation of the nature of society to its circumstance and developing policy; it also showed in a manner typical of the century that certain evil results followed from certain social changes.[41]

He was therefore anxious to show the moderate courses that might stifle resentment at the accumulation of property, so favourable to the rich, so often felt an injury to the poor. Abolition of entail and primogeniture might lessen jealousy. Some variability of fortune was inevitable, however much the fact might be regretted that this often brought luxury to the idle and indigence to the industrious.

> We are therefore obliged to suffer the wealthy to squander that the poor may subsist; we are obliged to tolerate certain orders of men, who are above the necessity of labour, in order that, in their condition, there may be an object of ambition, and a rank to which the busy aspire. We are not only obliged to admit numbers, who, in strict economy, may be reckoned superfluous, on the civil, the military, and the political list; but because we are men, and prefer the occupation, improvement, and felicity of our nature, to its mere existence, we must even wish, that as many members as possible, of every community, may be admitted to a share of its defence and its government.[42]

The decline of states, he said, came from a lack of vigilance which allowed corruption to develop and private vices to flourish. Ferguson almost suggested in the second volume of his Roman history that a study of the wrong philosophy might be a factor in decline. Cato was a stoic recognizing no good but public good. Whereas Caesar was an Epicurean who knew no good and evil save pleasure and pain. Nations seemed to follow a circle; emulation might lead to corruption and corruption to despotism. Eminent men would become scarce, factions and mutinous peoples would endanger the state. There could be many fluctuations. Man could live under a wide variety of constitutions. No nation ever suffered internal decay but from the vice of its members. Men of fortitude could help their countries survive even bad periods and prosper. There was no inevitable period to the life of a society. If men were to become generally corrupted, then the end was certain. In

Rome human nature "fell into a retrograde motion, which the virtues of individuals could not suspend! and men in the application of their faculties . . . suffered a slow and insensible, but almost continual, decline."[43]

Ferguson's contribution to liberal thought was somewhat indirect, though none of his readers could fail to reflect upon the distinction between rich and poor and the difficulties which arrive in certain stages of prosperity in great empires. Caution and an increasing fear of change robbed the *History*, the most liberal of his works (after the early *Institutes* was replaced by the *Principles*) of the moral that might have been drawn from it. Robert Wallace, his colleague in the Philosophical Society wrote much more directly on the desirability of levelling out distinctions and sharing the world's drudgery more fairly.

Wallace's connections at different stages of his career must be briefly described before his work is analyzed. He was one of a brilliant generation of Edinburgh students, a member of the early "Rankenian" Club, whose membership embraced the avant-garde of religious and political speculators. The Rankenians met in a tavern whose master's name they adopted. The club was formed in 1717 and consisted of: Dr. William Wishart, later Principal of Edinburgh, a disciple of Molesworth and of Shaftesbury; George Turnbull, his friend and Wallace's brother-in-law, who taught six years at Aberdeen (1721–1727) before traveling abroad and moving into Anglican circles in London and Ireland; John Stevenson (1695–1755), a professor at Edinburgh as famous for his interest in belles-lettres and politics as for the logic he was supposed to teach; Colin Maclaurin (1695–1747), mathematician and popularizer of Newton, whose influence was extended beyond the classroom through his book in spite of his early death; John Dick, related to the heretical Simson; Charles Maitland M.P. (Aberdeen 1748–1751, died 1751); and Andrew Mitchell, Ambassador to Berlin. These and others, about twenty in all, disseminated throughout Scotland "freedom of thought, boldness of disquisition, and liberality of sentiment."[44]

In later life Wallace, who was licensed to preach in 1722, enjoyed an even more brilliant circle in Edinburgh and engaged in friendly controversy with David Hume. His reputation as a young preacher had been felt by Wodrow to be marred by heretical ideas derived from too many *Spectators* and the works of Tillotson and Shaftesbury.[45] Wallace was not a freethinker of the category of Matthew Tindal, and in 1731 his first publication was a rebuttal of Tindal's work. Soon after, he achieved fame and power for his opposition to Sir Robert Walpole's severity toward the murderer of Porteous. Gaining the confidence of Tweeddale, chief government minister for Scottish affairs in the early forties, he wielded considerable influence. Together with Doctor Webster he started a fund for the widows of the clergy similar to that started by his Irish friend, Bruce, in Dublin.[46] After Tweeddale's retirement, Wallace continued to enjoy the best society of Edinburgh in his day and the respect of all classes of the community. He published sermons; *A Dissertation* on population for which he was best known; an attack on the pessimism of John Brown's *Estimate; Various Prospects,* a utopian series of essays; and other works. He was both a mentor and a Maecenas to his younger brethren.[47]

Both Wallace and his friend, Wishart, were taken to task for supposed heresy, but both managed to escape censure after the examination had taken place. That they were liberal in their theology, that they believed, as Wodrow once reported, that there could be legitimate differences of opinion among Christians, is certain. They were confident that the Deity was benevolent. They were loath to stress hellfire. Wallace believed in Christian teaching and paid regard, as Tindal, for example, had not done, to divine revelation. Free thinking was noble, but should not be an excuse for denying the precepts of Christianity. We might not always see the reason for things; but the revelations of God must not be rejected. Reason was intended as a means of testing divine truth. Wallace succeeded in avoiding serious trouble with the church because he was a very sincere Christian.

Wallace's sermon on *Ignorance and Superstition,* preached in 1746 on behalf of charity schools, on a text in Psalms 74:20, was designed to show that ignorance was contrary to rational nature, and that education was necessary for liberty and happiness throughout the land. Wallace was preaching whilst the threats and fears of the rising of the 'Forty-five were still fresh in everyone's mind, and he blamed a good deal of the trouble in the Highlands to the condition of the population, who were for the most part ignorant and poor. He felt that the more people knew, the more likely they were to be orderly, and to respect the laws of society, the less likely they would be to form trouble-some coteries or become subservient to absolute government. Want of knowledge was much more dangerous to society than learning could ever be. Wallace was attacking the ideas commonly associated with Mandeville in his *Fable of the Bees* where Mandeville had suggested that a certain amount of ignorance was necessary to provide a labouring class and that charity schools were likely to do harm. Clear and extensive knowledge, Wallace maintained, was the glory of man. "Mankind cannot cultivate and subdue the earth to so great advantage separately as by their joint and continued labours. "Society ought to be constituted in such a way that the labour of mankind may not be so hard, severe and continued as to become mere drudgery." Trade and agriculture, he maintained, would flourish as the intelligence of the population increased. Wallace endorsed More's utopian concept of a land where all would share in the drudgery, and praised Harrington's *Oceana*.[48]

Wallace was convinced of the dignity of labour and of something due to the lowest of mankind. All had a right to liberty of conscience, freedom of speech, freedom from violence or repression, and a knowledge of the nature of society and religion. With such knowledge, that is, without ignorance and superstition, the Highlands would not have rebelled.

In *Various Prospects* Wallace again suggested that More's *Utopia* ought to be taken more seriously than heretofore. As in *Ignorance and Superstition,* the question of equality and of the dignity of labour was raised, as well as the question of a stable society, the greatest obstacle to which, he thought, was to be found in a state of war, in poor education, in equality, and in bad government. The greatest protection could be found in the diffusion of enlightened ideas as to what is best for the happiness of the whole. In *Various Prospects* Wallace quoted from Rousseau and from Maupertuis, and he was obviously familiar with the work of the contemporary philosophers. The evidence of his earlier sermon and an examination of his theories show that his own originality and an intensive study of More and Harrington sufficiently account for his radical ideas, and that he took nothing new or significant from French sources.[49]

In the advertisement to *Various Prospects* the author's design was described. He wished to offer support for religion and virtue. "The following Speculations are chiefly designed for the Free thinkers who have not so high a relish or so steady a faith of religious Doctrines." The four hundred six pages of the text were divided between twelve sections, the "Prospects." Prospect One concerned "a general view of the imperfections of human society and of the sources from whence they flow." Prospects Two, Three, and Four outlined "the model of a perfect government not for a single nation only, but for the whole Earth," and discussed how far such a model was practicable. Prospects Five, Six, and Seven discussed the beauties of nature, the distresses of mankind and the brute animals, and presented a comparison of the happiness and misery of the world. Prospect Eight concerned the ticklish problem of liberty and necessity, and the last four Prospects vindicated Providence and offered some advice to sober freethinkers.[50]

Wallace examined the defects of society with some care, though his natural optimism prevented too gloomy a view of the progress of human affairs. He continually reminded his readers of things as they were, but nevertheless betrayed as often a belief that they could and would be improved. The combination of shrewd observation of the prospect of society in his own time and an ebullient belief in progress typical of his age makes Wallace's book extraordinarily interesting. He was convinced that mankind had not taken full advantage of the opportunities afforded for happiness here. Nature, he felt, was "abundantly stored for supplying all their necessities and satisfying all their desires." Indeed, man had refined human nature, adorned the earth, and made many useful inventions. Progress made encouraged the belief that much more could be made "if men cultivated their genius with due care, and if they made a proper use of those riches which are in nature."[51] Wallace felt that if proper care were taken the population could be increased, the amount of food could be much enlarged, and all could have a much higher standard than they enjoyed at the time. He felt that the advancement of knowledge had been in great measure left to chance. Men's enquiries had been perpetually interrupted. He realized how much of the world was yet to be discovered, how little was cultivated, how backward were medical studies and all sorts of other skills which might increase man's capacities and enjoyments. The earth could never be fully peopled or cultivated until it became the abode of peace, security, and plenty. Every man should be able to marry to his

liking, maintain his children comfortably, and enable them to do likewise. This should be possible "where not only poverty, but the fear of
it is banished, and where the noise and alarms of war are not heard."[52]
Wallace's model was intended

> . . . for uniting all mankind under governments which shall pre-
> serve the same language, maintain an universal correspondence
> among the most distant inhabitants of the globe, and raise the whole
> human race to the highest perfection. Let us not immediately take
> it for granted that such a government is utterly impracticable. Let
> us suspend our judgment till once we have considered whether we
> can conceive a consistent idea of it.

He outlined eighteen points reminiscent of More's *Utopia* which he
summed up:

> That there should be no private property. That everyone should
> work for the public, and be supported by the public. That all should
> be on a level, and that the fruits of everyone's labour should be
> common for the comfortable subsistence of all the members of the
> society. And, lastly, that everyone should be obliged to do some-
> thing, yet none should be burdened with severe labour.

Wallace went on to suggest that care should be taken that the new
world state be founded on federal lines. He suggested that each state
within the greater union should be neither too small nor too large, that
regular migration of inhabitants from one climate to another should
be arranged to the great pleasure and profit of the citizens, and he
pointed out that "knowledge is most successfully acquired by united
endeavours." Mankind could not cultivate the earth separately to as
great advantage as by their joint labours. There were difficulties in
establishing such a system and on an equal basis. It was not likely to be
formed very soon, since there were many governments already in existence, men were loath to yield up superiority to others and in general
showed no enthusiasm for reform. Governments declined and fell, and
this might make possible future improvement.[53]

The chief enemies to an egalitarian state—emulation, the love of
liberty, and interfering passions and appetites "which excite violent
struggles by men's fixing their attention on the same objects which can

only be enjoyed by one or by few"—might be overcome. These, he concluded, were the only obstacles to "an equal distribution of labour among mankind and to their equal enjoyment of the advantages which flow from it." In spite of this statement, later readers of Wallace's *Prospects,* like William Godwin (1756–1836), were to recall a further and much more serious obstacle described—in *A Dissertation on the Numbers of Mankind* (1753) as well as earlier in *Various Prospects*—the possibility, as knowledge grew, of a vastly increased population. This argument, Godwin suggested before demolishing it to his own satisfaction, destroys the whole scheme for common property and the betterment of mankind. Wallace may have forgotten his own predictions. In his third *Prospect* he dismissed all difficulties stemming from love of liberty and emulation. These were unlikely to trouble his utopian constitution under which the "whole earth would become a paradise."[54]

Few people, he thought, had hitherto enjoyed freedom. In his "new modelled" state men would be free enough compared with their present circumstances. Destructive liberty would not be allowed, that is, freedom to be idle, lewd, and voluptuous, to educate or not to educate themselves, to spend our money as we pleased, for or against the public good. Real liberty, that is, freedom to indulge ourselves in everything agreeable to nature and reason, would be permitted under the utopian government. In an interesting note to this passage[55] Wallace proclaimed his admiration for the English constitution, but deplored its lack of provision for the proper education of youth, for regulation of manners, and extravagancies of humour. None of the things which he had outlined need be so destructive to the stability of his egalitarian state as two defects which he observed in the existing system: "(1) the great inequality among mankind, and the advantages enjoyed by a few, which they neither deserve, nor employ for good purposes. (2) The want of a proper education and discipline of the youth."[56]

Wallace was concerned to find a remedy for discontent and a preservative of public spirit. He was extraordinarily anxious that no one should be distinguished by marks of honour, by their clothes, food, or houses. All the infirm, sick, and aged should be maintained at public expense. A great deal of discontent, "frequent murmurs," and "fatal revolutions" came from the revolt of men of sense and spirit against rule by persons not fitted to govern. Only those who were clever and wise should be selected to rule. An equitable distribution of labour and profits from it, together with all private property, would remove hardship and the possibility of theft and robbery.

Wallace recurred in all his writing to the importance of education: "It is the want of a proper discipline and education of the youth which is the second great source of our vices and wretchedness, and which renders our governments so changeable and unsteady."[57] Men were shockingly careless about the education of their children. Those who were careful were often frustrated "by the poisonous examples of other children who are ill-educated." He believed that "with proper management, good dispositions might be so effectually instilled into youth, as would prevent such a deluge of vice as has overwhelmed the world."[58]

Wallace by no means endorsed the contemporary encomiums of a state of nature as set forth in the *Discourse Upon Inequality*. Like George Berkeley, he looked upon the original status of nature as stupid and savage, and he could never persuade himself, he said, that Providence intended men to remain in this state. Were his utopia to be established, he wondered how long the earth could nourish the populousness which would inevitably follow on the removal of the inconveniences of having a family, though he did not believe that Nature herself would bring to an end a constitution which made the earth a paradise and human society flourishing in all respects. In other words, he argued, that it was unnatural to set bounds to human knowledge and happiness. Wallace fell back rather surprisingly at this point in his argument on his belief that Providence or nature would set due bounds to the establishment of any government unsuited to a limited earth.[59]

The second half of Wallace's book, or rather more than the second half, was devoted by him to an almost Shaftesburian rhapsody on the beauty, magnificence, and wisdom of Nature. He exclaimed:

How grand is that prospect which is set before us during the solemn silence and shade of night! The luminaries of Heaven shine forth with majestic pomp and form a glorious spectacle to the eye. To the contemplative mind they appear still more wonderful, and afford a delightful subject of speculation. Reason comes in aid to the feebleness of sense.[60]

He continued his soliloquy about the delightful prospects of the earth diversified with hills, valleys, woods, rivers, lakes, and seas, and proceeded to reflect that nature had made ample provision for all our needs, in the soil, the vegetation, the waters of the earth, and the animal creation. He concluded his very rapturous prospect with the Psalmist's statement that the earth is full of the riches of the Lord. In contrast, he examined the distresses of mankind and of brutes. He found it difficult to explain Nature's design in the constant killing and destruction of animal life. He examined more carefully the only rational animal within his view, and once more concluded that art was long and life too brief to acquire a proper knowledge of it. We might see darkly through a glass that there might be a greater share of happiness than misery, but perhaps not so much as we should expect from the goodness of Almighty God. He devoted Prospect VII to showing that notwithstanding all the difficulties and vices of mankind, man was on the whole happier than he was miserable.

Wallace throughout defended the Christian position, that is "that the author of nature is not responsible for those calamities which do not arise from the claim of nature, but from the perverseness and folly of those creatures that have abused that liberty with which they have been imbued." In other words, to contrast the rapturous prospect of nature with the difficulties and vices of man and of animals was to lose sight of the balance of happiness and misery. Human liberty "necessarily supposes a future state after death . . . else God may be said to abandon his creatures, at least to give up the best of them on many remarkable occasions, to cruel treachery and oppression from the vilest and most contemptible."[61] Great comfort may be found in belief in a law propounded by a benevolent being and governing our universe. Virtue, justice, equity, and benevolence were irradicably imprinted in men's minds and did not depend on fashion or on education. Some freethinkers like Shaftesbury recognized this. Others, whom alone he condemned amongst skeptics and atheists, looked on all as the effect of chance. Their ideas were mischievous. The doctrine of a future state was calculated to support the good and sober the vicious. An ardent desire for mortality existed in all human beings, and the lower animals, according to Wallace, might also enjoy life after death. God would never condemn anything created to complete destruction, nor would he neglect to reward equitably the good and evil doers. Philosophers might extol virtue for its own sake, as the author of *Characteristics* had done.[62] The idea of virtue might inspire heroism for the common good, but so might the doctrine of a perfectly just, wise, and powerful governor of the universe.[63] Wallace saw evil around him, yet his temperament and his faith made him optimistic. In his argument there is sometimes a suggestion of a conflict between divine and philosopher, bon vivant and sage.

Was Wallace in these speculations writing his *Various Prospects* to convert his friend Hume, or was he writing to present his fellow countrymen with a more sensible political system than that which Rousseau and Maupertuis had recently made current? Possibly the answer is to be sought in the reports about Wallace which have come down to us, which depict him as a lover of argument and conversation with men of very diverse ideas. A series of such arguments of a friendly sort might have resulted in his decision to publish those twelve essays. They illustrate the distinction between the thought of the continental men of the Enlightenment and Britons of the same period, the Briton being distinguished by readiness to speculate freely, and also by a basic piety and by his conviction that he was, in spite of the many criticisms he levelled at contemporary conditions, fortunate in his own situation. At the same time Wallace's work provides evidence of the existence of radical thought in Scotland.

Later Republicans at Aberdeen and Glasgow — Blackwell, Ogilvie, and Millar

All Scottish universities had their share in the awakening of the period 1660–1780. In many cases, however, as with John Simson at Glasgow, or with Archibald Campbell at St. Andrew's, the teachers stimulated pupils like Hutcheson, or possibly James Burgh, to heresies of other kinds than the religious tenets which they themselves embraced. It is impossible here to include all of even the important names. Aberdeen had an interesting and influential role in the period, not only in Scotland, but in America. William Smith, first provost of the College of Philadelphia and William Small, beloved instructor of Jefferson during a temporary stay in Virginia, were both graduates of the Scottish institution. Smith threw in his lot with the revolutionaries. Small returned to England and became a part of the Birmingham circle of Day, Boulton, and Edgeworth to which he was introduced by his friend, Benjamin Franklin. At Aberdeen George Turnbull, who has already been mentioned (as an early correspondent of Molesworth and a later assistant to Bishop Rundle), taught philosophy long enough to instruct Thomas Reid, later a professor at Glasgow. Thomas Blackwell spent a long career there, teaching Greek and history and becoming famous for republican sentiments. His nephew, David Fordyce, who predeceased him, studied and also taught there the philosophy he had learned from Shaftesbury, Molesworth, and the republicans of the seventeenth century, as well as from Hutcheson of Glasgow. George Campbell disseminated Shaftesbury's ideas on beauty and virtue among the local literati, as well as among his readers. John Gregory studied there before he practiced in London, and taught at Edinburgh. These men determined the flavour of mid-century Aberdeen.[64]

The Homeric scholar, Blackwell, seems to have been as much disliked as his nephew was beloved, and not only by persons like Dr. Samuel Johnson who detested his politics. He was naturally quarrelsome. He wrote no political treatises, but produced works on Homer and on the court of Augustus which enjoyed some popularity. In these Shaftesbury's ideas on human nature, on the connection between liberty and virtue, and on the advantages of free constitutions for the development of genius were followed. British advances in science attested the happiness of its government, and the connection between liberty and learning. Corruption would bring dictatorship. Violence might be necessary to stimulate free and active spirits.[65] Blackwell's republican views seem at this distance to have been those common to most admirers of Locke and Newton.

His nephew, David Fordyce (1711–1751), achieved in his forty years a considerable reputation, and was regarded by John Ramsay as already the equal of Stevenson at Edinburgh when the accident at sea ended his career. Two volumes of *Dialogues* and an essay in Dodsley's *Preceptor* show the influence of Turnbull, whose *Observations on Education* only preceded the *Dialogues* by a few years; and of Hutcheson, whose *Compend* is indeed summarized in the essay, and whose acquaintance he is reported to have made. He is also said to have known Butler.[66] Since his moral philosophy coincided with that of the Glasgow professor and his posthumous works were not primarily political, his contribution to Scottish liberal thought may best be illustrated from his work on *Education* which was widely read and quoted. Franklin was amongst its readers very soon after it appeared.

The Dialogues started with an encounter in a stagecoach of some travelers, including a woman brought up on a new plan by a very wise guardian, who were all going to visit a modern academy. They talked throughout as acquaintance developed. Education was to train for life, not for bookish pursuits. They despised the "Studious Drudge." Education should be carried on in the vernacular and by visual as well as oral means. Lecturers should watch their classes, encourage questions and discussions. They would determine the results of debate by ballot. Public virtue and liberty would be stressed and those authors studied, from Plato to More, Harrington, and Sidney, who had emphasized them. History could be important, both of revolutions in government and the many changes and translations of property that accompanied them. Students should learn to think justly. They should have enlarged notions of human nature, of government and religion.[67]

Fordyce proclaimed himself the disciple of the immortal Harrington, the great oracle of modern politics, who had decided the general laws which governed the grand crises and revolutions of the world. Since the breakdown of Gothic systems, several persons were now doing what one formerly did for himself. Education was therefore necessary to enable man to maintain freedom under changed circumstances. Once again the economic and contemporary problems seemed to have infected even a visionary like Fordyce.[68]

Another famous name in the Commonwealth tradition was connected with Aberdeen. William Ogilvie was a fellow student of Reid. He was at King's College, 1755–59; he studied at Glasgow, 1760–61, and at Edinburgh the following year. He returned to Aberdeen as professor of humanities. He is chiefly famous for *An Essay on the Right of Property in Land,* written between 1776 and 1781 and published in 1781. He presented a copy to the Library Company in Philadelphia in the hope that Americans might profit by its ideas in their own constitutional experiments.[69]

If the power of the people predominated in a country, it might be able to change the whole system of landholding. The existing system in Europe, Ogilvie thought, was not derived from a good period of history. There was therefore a chance to develop a method of land-holding which would be equitable and would extend to everyone the advantages of a country life. The English farmer was known to be in-dependent in his ideas. The rural labourer was poorly treated. Two principles must be assumed: the natural right of all to an equal share, and the right of those whose labour had increased fertility to a share in the profits from this increase. In these introductory pages Ogilvie stressed the poor conditions, the poor farming, the imperfect develop-ment of English lands, quoting Franklin and also *Letters from a Farmer in Pennsylvania.* He wanted to fix farm rents permanently, providing for reassessment every thirty years. A board might be set up to pur-chase estates and divide them, or there might be a progressive agrarian law. Certainly North America should have such a regulation. He did not think egalitarian division practicable, but he felt that an overall plan and considerable regulation of absenteeism and poor agriculture should be attempted. Ogilvie admired the small farms of Prussia. He realized that only a completely despotical or democratical state could effect the changes he desired.

Ogilvie condemned riches, especially hereditary riches; the la-bourer performed the duties and the wealthy spent the income. Were his system to be adopted, improved cultivation would support an in-creased population at a better standard of living. He thus suggested a remedy for the growth of population foreseen under certain circum-stances by Wallace.[70]

A greater influence on Scottish radicalism, though less forthright in suggesting innovations than Ogilvie, was John Millar (1735–1801), professor of law at Glasgow for forty years, and author of *The Origin of the Distinction of Ranks* (1771), and *An Historical View of the English Gov-ernment* (1787–1803).[71] Like an earlier professor at his chosen univer-sity, Hutcheson, Millar was more highly esteemed by contemporaries than by nineteenth-century students of the eighteenth century. He was the son of a much-respected minister. He was educated in Glasgow, in a grammar school, in Hamilton where his father was parson, under Mr. Pillans, and at the University of Glasgow, which he entered in 1747.

After a considerable course of study, Millar acted for two years as tutor to the son of Henry Home, Lord Kames, and there made the acquaintance of David Hume. He prepared for the bar, but in 1761, to the surprise of his friends, applied for the chair of law at Glasgow and retained it the rest of his life. He occasionally defended felons in the courts. He occupied himself in the duties of a professor, and increased the number of students attending law lectures. The rest of his time was spent in the composition of his works and in the conversation of the brilliant group of friends he made: Baillie, a Professor of Divinity and a neighbor at Whitemoss; Dr. Wight, professor of history at Glasgow; Thomas Reid, with whom Millar's admirer, Hume, had many arguments; Professor Jardine who taught logic at Glasgow; and other members of the Literary Society founded in 1752 and flourishing when he came back to his alma mater in '61. Fortunate in his private circumstances, the loss of a son in America, and of his wife, cast a shadow over his late life. He was survived by three sons and six daughters.

The Professor, in the words of his biographer, was "a steady and zealous Whig." He supported various reforming movements of the day. He urged a change in representation. So long as prerogative was balanced by nobility he felt that the faults of the old system were not serious. He was not a proponent of a universal suffrage as such, but of a wider and fairer franchise. He was much concerned to remove patronage from ministerial hands. He felt that a swollen bureaucracy had immensely increased royal power since the Revolution, and many of the most interesting passages of his *View* are devoted to this theme. He would have liked to see offices filled by some sort of freehold vote. He opposed slavery. He welcomed the French Revolution. He was in short a fairly typical Commonwealthman of the late eighteenth century. His original contribution may be found in his historical work, in many ways the most distinguished of the great Scottish school.

No one can read Millar's *View* or his *Origins of Ranks* without realizing that as an historian he had imagination, detachment, and learning above that of his contemporary, Hume. His style did not equal Robertson's, but his judgment about the development of the English Constitution still merits respect. He examined those factors, domestic and foreign, which worked for and against individual liberty. Republican sentiments, if they may be called that, in no way affected his account of King Alfred, nor his observations upon earlier Gothic governments. Hume's reflections upon events and persons are often penetrating, but his narrative of the course of events is commonplace and was based on very inadequate reading of material ready to hand. Millar, by contrast, appears to have had greater mastery of his subject and a much more original view of its nature and content.

The *View* described not merely the sequence of political events and persons, but the play upon each other of economic and social developments. Institutions changed with the changing situation and occupations of the people who lived under them. Barbarous hunters would have less need of government than the modern population of commercial and industrial countries where the need for laws protecting freedom of each from the other and from the magistrates was so essential. Millar was a careful student, not only of the work of Harrington, but of Rousseau and Montesquieu, but he was less dogmatic and more scientific than any of them. And although a social determinist, he was not of the doctrinaire persuasion. Climate and soil affected the growth of nations. Individual differences, as well as circumstance, began the distinction of ranks. A member of the natural law school, he endorsed the idea of progress wholeheartedly. Nevertheless, he was also aware of accidental circumstances which drastically altered man's fate and the casual interposition of particular persons. Millar has been enthusiastically discovered by the Marxists, but they are forced to admit that far from anticipating the master's view of a classless society, he regarded rank as an inescapable and indeed a necessary feature in human society at any time. He thought any attempt to abolish it would be dangerous.[72]

As disciple of Harrington, though very far from being a utopian, as his views on rank and suffrage reveal, Millar had a keen sense of the dynamics of history—the relationship of property and power, the pull of a commercial state toward a popular system, and the attraction toward despotism of a large, wealthy state where standing forces and increased resources gave the monarch patronage and weapons against individual liberties. He was keenly aware of the effect of character and circumstance as his tribute to the parliaments of the early seventeenth century shows. If the House of Commons had not stood on guard under the Stuarts, it too might have been "one of the ghosts of national councils." As he examined the civil wars, he applied his theory of economic influences. Greece and Rome provided, he said, no real parallel. Their democracy, when it existed, had been for city-states. Harrington's solution of democratic problems was adapted to England's situation, providing against a large tumultuary assembly on one hand and despotism on the other. Such a government would be supported by middling and inferior gentry together with the inhabitants of towns "lately raised to independence." The nobility feared loss of property in the anarchy that must follow the overthrow of monarchy. Millar noticed the existence of many speculative systems during the Interregnum, and attributed their appearance to the stimulus of the troubled times. He virtually ignored the Levellers. His sympathies were with the classical republicans, with Harrington more than with Milton, whose ardent love of liberty he thought marred by partisanship. Sympathy for the French Revolution was typical of Millar and many of his students. "Jupiter" Carlyle, diarist, told of a parent who planned to send his son to Glasgow but thought better of it as Millar's politics were described to him—this, in spite of the professor's justly deserved scholarly reputation.[73]

In Millar's history or discussion of society, little evidence can be found that he cherished egalitarian ideas. He belonged, it seems, entirely with the Commonwealth group and was as much and as little republican as they. He advocated an equal right to enjoy all privileges under the constitution, but not an equal right of the wise and the ignorant, the rich and the poor, the clever and the foolish, to rule the whole. His plan for election to office by freeholders was very seventeenth century in character, and his endorsement of wider suffrage was made with many reservations.[74] Millar's revolutionary contribution lies in his philosophy of history and in his awareness of the changes brought by developing commerce, rather than in emphasis on resistance rights, although of course he assumed these. Republicanism may have been more marked in his private conversation. He never wrote as revolutionary a statement as Hume's pronouncement that "a constitution is only so far good, as it provides a remedy against maladministration," nor did he dwell, like the philosopher, on the fact that intolerable tyranny need never be borne.[75] But Millar's teaching encouraged radical politics and his writings increased the vogue for the economic interpretation of history, stimulated by Smith's *Wealth of Nations* and Ferguson's *Civil Society* and *Roman Republic.*

It would be pleasant to dwell on Hume, on his Cromwellian parliament without bishops or Scottish peers, his nonhereditary second chamber, his insistence that government may be changed as the good of society demands, his wish to control the variable and uncertain arrangement that prevailed with regard to royal prerogative, his views on party—all these seem to place him near to the Commonwealthmen. Moreover, suggestions about law and conquest seem to have echoed Hutcheson's lectures. The examination of the durability of large republics, once achieved, was penetrating, as were the original economic ideas. His support of the colonists is well known. Party prejudice, as shown in the *History,* was a surface irritation, a taste. Hume's Toryism was more superficial than that of a Burke or a Bolingbroke, even if his writing strengthened Tory sentiments about English history for a long time to come. His political ideas, like his philosophy and his religion, showed the wisdom and detachment of a skeptic whose chief motive was not to lead or convert, but to reflect, ponder, doubt, and stimulate the like in others. In this last Hume was entirely successful.

If Hume must be excluded from this survey, so must James Boswell (1740–1795), though for a time his zeal for Corsican freedom made him an asserter of liberty. He sent to Paoli the works of Harrington, Sidney, Addison, Trenchard, Gordon, and others in favour of liberty, though only a short while before he had expressed dislike of the chief martyr of the Rye. Boswell was sentimental. His occasional Jacobitism, his enthusiasm for his encounter with Rousseau, his inclination towards the ancient church—all rested on the same basis, emotion of a romantic kind. He supported the Americans, perhaps as a result of his talks with Sir John Pringle (once a Rankenian); more probably because he was a Scot and inclined to resent English dominion. He was much disappointed in not being appointed to the job Adam Ferguson gained on the commission sent to America in 1778, though Lord North cannot be blamed for his choice. In 1765 Boswell felt like a hero of austerity in a dissolute age. He probably felt the same way in 1775–1783. Romantically, Boswell was never slow to help the cause of liberty against tyrants.[76]

Two Scotch eccentrics should be mentioned in closing this chapter: William Thom (fl.1720–1790) and David Erskine, eleventh earl of Buchan (1742–1829). Both were liberals of some consequence, though the achievement of the noble lord is easier to assess than that of the disgruntled minister of Govan. William Thom seems to have been somewhat older than his colleagues when he went to Glasgow in the 1740's. He did not share the popular enthusiasm for Hutcheson. He bore the university a grudge for some trouble over the stipend he was supposed to draw from his church at Govan. He pilloried Glasgow and its professors in *The Trial of a Student in the College of Clutha in the Kingdom of Oceana* (1768). Eight years after his death, his sermons and tracts were collected and printed.

Thom thought education should be fitted to the new needs of his age. He urged the establishment of a business school in Glasgow. He sympathized with American grievances and wholeheartedly supported their cause, though he also hoped for reconciliation. He pitied his compatriots who farmed and suffered from Scottish landlords. Even the English treated their tenant farmers better, an admission that must not be undervalued at this time and from this minister. He urged compatriots to emigrate while there was time and so to secure a place in the future center of empire and government. He advocated kind treatment of the native Americans—the Indians—by those he encouraged to emigrate.[77] Thom, therefore, whatever his personal differences with Hutcheson, belonged in fact to the same school of political thought, and may have owed more than he cared to admit to classroom inspiration.

Lord Cardross, later earl of Buchan, also a Glasgow alumnus, instructed by a mother who had studied with Maclaurin and by James Buchanan, attended Smith's lectures and was elected to the university debating society of "Oceana" in 1761. In 1764 he joined the Chatham circle in London. After his father's death in 1767 he devoted much time to the education of two able half brothers: Tom (later chancellor) and Henry Erskine. He was a pro-American and later, claiming relationship on the slenderest of evidence, corresponded with Washington and sent his essays on Fletcher and Thomson to Jefferson. In 1780 he published "a speech intended to have been spoken" against the system of electing the sixteen Scottish peers to the House of Lords. It had been usual for the London administration to select and circulate the names before the election took place, thus ensuring additional ministerial support in the upper chamber. Buchan wholeheartedly condemned the practice and criticized the Union as a whole. His protests resulted in rather less obvious ministerial dictation at succeeding elections, but he himself never voted again.

At the same time he supported Wyvill's associations for parliamentary reform which were so lively at the end of the American war. He welcomed the French Revolution. His brother, Tom, gave legal assistance to Tom Paine. But the political activity of the earl, in spite of a long life, was extremely slight. He wrote not only the essays mentioned, but other antiquarian notes, and he encouraged such projects as the festival, inaugurated under his patronage in 1791, honouring Thomson, and the collection of material for a national biography. He hoped to bring men of liberal sentiments together in philosophical societies. He was interested in labour-saving devices to improve the lot of the workingman. He adopted somewhat freethinking and Unitarian ideas. His influence cannot ever have been very great and diminished as he grew older, but his sentiments and projects reflected all that was liberal in his country's political tradition.[78]

The Scottish Commonwealthmen looked back to their own republican writers, Buchanan and Fletcher chief amongst them. They derived principles favourable to political liberty, and likely to include, as time went on, greater recognition of the rights of a larger proportion of the population. Their chief contribution to the thought of the period lies in their realization of the injustices of a world where the labourer's toil was poorly rewarded and his stake in the share of land and wealth less than his activities and his rights deserved. They studied the wealth of nations and the laws of political economy. They had seen in two generations an immense extension of prosperity in their own country. But they never lost sight of the ignorance and superstition of the uneducated Highlanders, nor of the difficult conditions an ancient system imposed on their farmers. It is no accident that classical economy and much of modern socialist philosophy alike look back on these thoughtful Scots. They were Harringtonian in their interest, but greatly changed and extended the lessons he taught. They were not very democratical, perhaps, but they realized some problems which were neglected by the English at this time. The fairly simple notion that luxury corrupted virtue did not satisfy their curiosity which was roused to examine the relations of commerce, industry, rank, and society with each other, within a single country, and throughout the world.

VII

The Contribution
of Nonconformity

Unpopularity, Schism, and Decline; Social and Legal Status

Much was said by contemporaries, as well as by later historians, about the decline of dissent in the eighteenth century. No group can be regarded as altogether negligible which includes the men to be discussed in this chapter. For the gradual enlargement of the idea of liberty, and for the maintenance of the ideal of a loyal diversity of belief and practice, these generations of nonconformists deserve praise. Their history repays scrutiny. Isaac Watts early made clear his resolution of "taking his lot" with the dissenters. "Such he was," Dr. Johnson continued in the *Lives,* "as every Christian Church would rejoice to have adopted."[1] He steadfastly claimed for himself and his associates, as well as for his opponents, liberty of thought. He always refused to believe that "those Penal Laws," from which all outside the Anglican communion suffered "are now, or ever were either Holy, Just or Good."[2]

Like a friend and contemporary, Philip Doddridge of Northampton, Watts observed a rule of universal charity and enjoyed the friendship of Christians of every denomination. The preaching of James Foster of Pinners Hall attracted the admiration of many not of his religious persuasion, including Dr. Johnson and Alexander Pope. Henry Grove, contributor to the *Spectator* and later master of Taunton Academy, carried into the West the learned traditions of Theophilus Gale, Thomas Rowe, and of many classmates at the Academy founded by them. Industrious historians like Daniel Neal and William Harris endeavoured to do justice to the virtues of their Puritan forbears, and to examine impartially the good and the bad of both sides in the civil wars. Wealthy laymen not only worked for the less well-to-do among their coreligionists in England, but made magnificent benefactions to academic institutions at home and overseas. These men and many more lived, worked, and cherished civil and religious liberties between the Revolution and the death of George II.

The attitude revealed in the lives and works of the politically conscious among the dissenters is important in a study of Commonwealthmen. The differences between the new tolerance manifesting itself among nonconformists and the Latitudinarianism displayed by many Anglicans will be discussed later in chapter VIII. Only the very briefest summary of the legal situation of dissent need be given. Distinctions between the old sects will be largely ignored. Their academies have already been the subject of learned works. The Society of Friends and the followers of Wesley and Whitfield have enormous significance for the history of humanitarian and religious reforms, but in a discussion of eighteenth-century arguments about the constitution they can be safely neglected. Some of the sectaries still conformed to the practices and precepts of an earlier period. The particular Baptists, some of the provincial Independents, and a few Presbyterians remained faithful to Calvinist and Brownist confessions of faith. Their continued existence was a reminder of a demand for greater liberty, but they took no great part in political agitations of any kind. There were, however, a growing number among the old sects and even among Quakers and Anglicans who were infected, as the phrase went, with Arian, Socinian, or Unitarian ideas. An increasing proportion of the dissenters now looked back to the intolerance of the Puritans with distaste. These refused to support any demands for tests or subscriptions to confessions or articles, and professed an increasingly liberal theology which scarcely confined itself even to the old insistence upon the Scripture as the rule of faith.

Two volumes, *Religious Liberalism in Eighteenth Century England* (1954) and *Religion and Learning* (1935) have recently been published by Roland N. Stromberg and Olive M. Griffiths respectively. These describe what were different products of the same movements noticed by Leslie Stephen in his monumental work on thought of the period. The growing intellectualism and libertarianism of the English Presbyterians explains their strength and their weakness. Miss Griffiths also examines the many philosophical and theological divergencies amongst the group. Mr. Stromberg discusses the problem largely in terms of the Deists versus the Christians and clarifies the position of many of the orthodox. This chapter assumes familiarity with the finding of such writers as these, and attempts only to disentangle the political interests of dissenters per se and the manner in which these were manifested.

The social status of dissent had deteriorated. By the reign of George II dissenters were represented in the Lords only by Willoughby of Parham, himself too poor to do much for them save lend his name to dedicatory pages of discourses and sermons, or to the boards of charitable foundations. Wealthy dissenters were still to be found, but it was rare, as Mrs. Barbauld pointed out, for the second or third generation of the prosperous to remain outside the church.[3] Dudley Ryder and Joseph Jekyll continued to be sympathetic, and even generous, towards the dissenters, but they conformed in order to continue in their chosen profession. A number of ministers, especially among the Presbyterians, went into the Establishment,[4] which has always attracted men of this denomination. Even today men may be found in the hierarchy who look back to the manse rather than to the parsonage. Not many statesmen were interested in the nonconformists. When the question of further concessions to their demands came, it met with surprisingly small response. The victory of the *status quo* seemed inevitable. Along with the growth of rationalism went a certain contempt for differences in worship and a considerable emphasis on uniformity.

The legal position of dissent was little changed between the repeal of the Schism and Occasional Conformity Acts in 1719 and 1812. The Toleration Act of 1689, never again seriously challenged, allowed Trinitarians who were willing to assent to thirty-five of the Thirty-Nine Articles to preach and teach freely. A license was supposed to be obtained, though these conditions were seldom enforced as time wore on and were abolished entirely in 1779. Such laxity made the forming of Unitarian churches possible in the last quarter of the eighteenth century. Definite but modest advances were made. The decision that fines could not be exacted from conscientious dissenters who refused office rather than take the necessary oaths, was one; there were some concessions to Catholics. On the other hand Hardwicke's Act of 1753 obliged all nonconformists to marry in the parish church.

Dissenters were certainly more comfortable during the period, but this ease depended entirely upon the continuance of mild administration of the law. Doddridge suffered in 1732 from the intolerance of a local clergyman. Lindsey and his Essex Street Unitarian chapel could at any time after it started in 1774 have been legally prosecuted.[5] The steadfast opposition of the Episcopal bench in the Lords to any manner of abatement of tithe or reform of the ecclesiastical courts, as well as to pleas, even of their own clergy, for some minor changes in the service and in subscriptions required for priests and students, was not such as to encourage hopes of any success in the future. The Commons always contained a few members willing to bring in a bill or vote for a petition, but never before the reign of George III in sufficient quantity to upset current arrangements. Even then, the episcopal barrier in the Lords long remained firm. Legal, political, and economic privilege remained the exclusive preserve of the Establishment. A determination to maintain this was obvious. For one, Hoadly, willing to make concessions at the beginning, there were three—Law, Shipley, and Watson— at the latter end. All were from Cambridge where conditions encouraged heterodoxy. The Church's cherished privilege was on the whole supported by public opinion. No popular pressure on the Commons or the Lords in behalf of dissent existed. The old, faulty, unreformed parliament probably represented well enough majority opinion on this matter.

The explanation may be sought in several directions. This period emphasized both uniformity and the preservation of the status quo. There was nervousness about the possible repercussion of changes in the position of any group or in the workings of any part of church and state. Before the Civil War a proposal to change the Articles, the service, or even the position of bishops in the body politic would not have been disposed of by the argument that such a change was likely to endanger political security. Indeed, during the debates in Charles II's reign on the repeal of the act abolishing episcopal temporal power, it was pointed out, though without effect on the vote, that the exclusion of abbots during the Reformation afforded an excellent precedent for keeping the bishops out of the Lords. By that time the troubles of the Interregnum had turned the current of opinion against change.[6] The dissenters' reputation thus became confused with all memories of the difficulties of the Long Parliament, all innovations of the Interregnum, and all intolerance manifested by Puritans at any time. This association was constantly recalled to explain the conservatism of the eighteenth century. There were two other factors in the continuing failure of dissent to obtain full civil rights. Dissenters were unpopular with the crowd; they were also thought to be fast declining and thus politically unimportant. It was not necessary to placate them. A further imponderable in this discussion was the spirit of the dissenters themselves which had changed a good deal. They were more liberal, and less able to combine effectively for the purposes of propaganda. There is no question that their new reasonableness and susceptibility to persuasion by government leaders lost them opportunities to press their case.[7] Before discussing the lives and works of a few rational nonconformists in the period, some of these obstacles must be described a little more fully.

Many men not reactionary by temperament nevertheless believed in this period that church and state were inseparably a part of the constitution; the stability and prosperity of the kingdom depended on the union. The Tories' views on this matter need not be considered; they were for a long while without a recognizable philosophy of conservatism. Those who followed Filmer, who had real genius, were men of mediocre ability. Bolingbroke's attempt to supply the ideological vacuum was brilliantly conceived but less effective, during his lifetime at least, because of his own lack of integrity.

More significantly, some Whigs—like Anthony Ellys, Bishop of St. David's, a kindly and moderate churchman; like John Perceval, first earl of Egmont,[8] an independent, tolerant gentleman; and like William Hay, would-be reformer of the Poor Laws—all considered uniformity desirable and further concession than that afforded by the Toleration Act dangerous. There was, Ellys argued, a necessary bond between church and state. Even the classical republicans like Harrington, Neville, and Moyle, he pointed out, saw the need for a public religion. Countries like Holland and Prussia had such entirely different constitutions that their greater tolerance hardly afforded a precedent. But if the church were endangered, the English Gothic balance of king, lords, and gentry (or "people") would be upset. The popular might then submerge the noble or gentle element. The only church that was suitable to the English was the one already established. Changes advocated by men like James Peirce, author of *A Vindication of the Dissenters;* by Daniel Neal, the historian; and by Samuel Chandler of the Old Jewry Meeting, a prolific tract-writer—were bound, he thought, to bring disaster. These men said they were working for political rights. Were these obtained, they would then withdraw state support from the church and abolish the episcopal order. To Ellys the maintenance of the status quo meant the preservation of everything he valued: true religion, the power of the gentry, the English constitution. He did not even wish to see such concessions as might encourage a comprehension of any of the dissenters within the church. Modifications would, he quite rightly thought, alienate as many within the Establishment as they would draw into the fold.[9]

William Hay, another Lockian supporter of the Revolution and to a moderate degree of Walpole's administration, argued in a somewhat different way, but to the same end. Some liberty must be conceded to opinion. This must be carefully limited and the government should do its utmost, though he did not make clear in quite what way, to ensure a considerable measure of uniformity. This would be its best support. His *Essay on Civil Government* appeared in 1728 and contained several reflections upon this matter. Egmont also wrote against the granting of further privilege and the repeal of the Test and Corporation Acts. These three men were high-principled and thoughtful Whigs. It becomes absolutely clear in studying their ideas that they never dreamed of the possibility of a separation of church and state, that they had no conception of that loyal diversity we have shown to be an ideal of some of the dissenters.[10]

Proponents of uniformity feared the swamping of Anglicans by the dissenters who would attain office were the penal laws repealed. They feared that once in power they would disestablish the church and would give rein to levelling and republican ideas. How many dissenters would have obtained office or power had the penal laws been repealed in 1718 or 1732 remains doubtful. Ellys obviously believed that there would at any rate have been enough to secure their supposed ends.

Mrs. Barbauld, at the end of the eighteenth century, thought that few would have entered public life.[11] The events of the period since 1812 or 1832 would seem to support this judgment rather than that of Ellys and his friends. Nonconformity not only obtained the franchise in the nineteenth century; it also increased its own numbers. Disestablishment never seriously threatened the English church. The situation of Wales and Ireland was entirely different. Disestablishment in both countries was, of course, a victory in one sense for nonconformity over Anglicanism; in another it was only a triumph for the doctrines of majority rule and national separatism.

Some prominent men of the eighteenth century made their sentiments public. Watts disliked the privileges of the Episcopal bench and in general the official connection between church and state. Towgood, in his *Dissent from the Church of England Fully Justified* (1753), many times reprinted on both sides of the Atlantic, attacked not only the record of Anglicans in public affairs, but the character of their church system. He disapproved of their methods of appointments, and favoured a much more popular arrangement, granting some consideration to the wishes of the people, the congregations. God had left men freer, he thought, than the churchmen liked to believe. He could see no justification for the English system.[12] Priestley, another determined dissenter, not only argued that the connection of church and state was unnecessary and undesirable, but also that a disestablishment would in fact bring more strength to Christianity.

> I have even no doubt, but that, as Christianity was promulgated, and prevailed in the world, without any aid from civil power, it will, when it shall have recovered its pristine purity, and its pristine vigour, entirely disengage itself from such an unnatural *alliance* as it is at present fettered with, and that our posterity will even look back with astonishment at the infatuation of their ancestors, in imagining that things so wholly different from each other as *Christianity* and *civil power,* had any natural connection.[13]

Such statements supported Ellys's beliefs about dissenting objectives, but they were not particularly common. Their chief significance, as their full arguments are studied, seems to lie in the evidence they afford of the changed complexion of dissenting ideals. In 1640 there were a number of men who wished to alter the church. In 1645 English Presbyterians had hoped to set up their own national system. Later some Independents were found who hoped under Cromwell to discover a simple formula from Holy Writ to which all could subscribe in one visible church. A considerable body of Puritans wished to impose an ethical and social code on the country through Protectoral ordinance. Important during the next fifty years or more was the growing belief that all establishments and all regulation of a public kind, beyond a few safeguards against atheists and some more stringent controls on papists, was undesirable. This was true of Presbyterians, as well as of Baptists and Independents. The eighteenth-century dissenter advocated an ideal separation of church and state. On the practical level he wished for equal political rights; he had no intention of setting up a new national system. Even admiration for this ideal separation was much less important than the demands for the rights of Englishmen and the abolition of every kind of penalty for difference of opinion. To achieve this was, he thought, more important than the destruction of the privilege of the majority, if it continued to support episcopacy.

The extent of levelling and republican ideas among nonconformists was much exaggerated by their oppressors and opponents. That there was something popular in the churches of Baptists and Independents from the beginning was true, but that there was much that was revolutionary or subversive of property in the ideas of most of them before the late eighteenth century was quite false. The reformers wished to improve the constitution, a radical suggestion at the time.[14] Their critics concentrated on miscellaneous abuse, rather than on any very serious consideration of what it was the dissenters meant by civil and religious liberty. Nicholas Amhurst, afterwards connected with *The Craftsman,* but notoriously a Whig at Oxford, addressed some mediocre verse to Lord Stanhope in 1719, a member of the Constitutional Club to which he also belonged. This provides a pretty good account of the type of attack the nonconformists put up with.

> Long the *Dissenting* Protestant has born
> Malicious Slander and imperious Scorn,

Reproach, ill nature and licentious Rage,
The Subject of a Tribe for half an Age,
No solemn Marks of Sorrow can atone
For Crimes long since, and Madness not his own:
While the *Conforming* Zealot is allow'd,
To mix at Pleasure the seditious Crowd,
To act with Pardon each flagitious ill,
To Plot, Rebel, Assassinate and Kill,
Broils for the Church unsinning to foment,
To laugh at Oaths, and solemn Lies invent;
No crimes can his *establish'd* Goodness taint,
Tho' *Regicide,* a Martyr, and a Saint;
Proudly he glories in the Traytor's name,
And ev'n the *Gallows* vindicates his fame
On Guiltless men the Guilt of Bloodshed lies,
And once a year for Vengence loudly cries,
Past woes are call'd to mind and present fears,
And *Forty One* still rattles in our ears.[15]

The Dissenters were unpopular; whether more or less than Catholics and Jews, it is difficult to decide. Probably the former were more feared, and the latter less generally thought about. A plebiscite would hardly have obtained relief for dissent. The mob rioted against Jews in mid-century and Catholics in the days of George III. It burned meetinghouses on several occasions, from the days when Bradbury's chapel was attacked during the Sacheverell riots, to the disturbances of 1715 and 1737, through to the demonstrations which led to Priestley's exodus from Birmingham and later from England. At certain moments hunger, ignorance, and Jacobite influence may account for these. But nothing but prejudice of an unpleasant kind can have explained the action of the Cambridge undergraduates who disturbed local congregations at worship,[16] nor that of the many pamphleteers who printed unprovoked attacks on dissent.

Other reasons sometimes cited for keeping dissenters out of political life were that they were declining,[17] and that growing rationalism made all their many conscientious scruples meaningless. The possibility has been entirely overlooked that to some these differences in worship and dogma were enormously important, and the Test an insuperable obstacle. The right to pursue free inquiry was vital to the happiness of many sectaries. Growing public indifference meant less active persecution, but often resulted in less consideration for the conscientious nonconformist. That there was some decline in dissent, or at least in its striking power, seemed obvious, not only to Anglicans but to dissenters themselves, and much was written about it. Precise statistics may be disputed; the divisions and controversies must be admitted.

The proportion of dissenters in 1715 has been estimated as about two hundred and fifty thousand to the five and a half million total population. At the end of the century it was suggested that they represented about a fifth of the nation, that is, about two million. Unfortunately, in the absence of precise information, much of this is guess work. By the time the later figures were calculated Methodists were included, so that actual calculations for the old sects remain unreliable. There seems to have been some indication of a fall, and then a recovery, in the numbers of congregational licenses issued down to 1740. Thereafter there were signs of renewed growth. The proportion between the old sects had undoubtedly changed. Presbyterians, formerly two-thirds of the dissenters, had shrunk to barely a twentieth. Baptists and Independents had not weakened so much, but showed at the time little vigour. The revival in the next century was largely due to the vitalizing influences of Methodism and of evangelicalism, and not to the missionary efforts of the eighteenth-century sectaries.[18]

One of the explanations for decline of dissent of the older kind was found in the rise of the Unitarian movement, and in the many controversies which accompanied it. A Unitarian at this time was generally a liberal in politics as well as in matters theological. These Unitarians represented the very quintessence of dissent, the right of anyone to think as he pleased, to worship as he pleased, and to resist all attempts at definition and subscriptions, both by church and by state. The English nonconformist had always been divided between two points of view. The one found in some biblical texts support for the beliefs of strict Baptists, of Congregationalists, for independent covenant or Calvinist creed, and all derived spiritual and moral stimulus from their communion which strengthened their determination to suffer anything for their beliefs. The second stressed the rights of all

Protestants to question and to probe, and represented the intellectual tradition from Milton to Lindsey and Price. Both represented a minority demand for tolerance. Both groups included saints, but political activity and a constantly restless search for truth was most marked among the intellectuals. In the eighteenth century there were commonly to be found in rising proportions Baptists, Independents, and Presbyterians infected with Unitarian ideas. A few of the orthodox were noted for their politics, but the great majority of those interested in this study will be found among the heretics. Controversies eventually helped the cause of religious liberty, but weakened dissent and lessened its influence. This is particularly true of the battles of Salters Hall, but also applies to other wrangles throughout the period.

Timidity, or readiness to listen to ministerial advice, which might be due to the long discipline of being an unprivileged and persecuted minority, may be ascribed to a certain slackening of enthusiasm. Attempts at union, at organization (like the London Dissenting Deputies),[19] or the activities of small societies meeting in coffee houses and the writing and talking about their problems—all seemed ephemeral and rather futile efforts. Whatever dissent had gained in liberality and in comprehension of different points of view, it had lost in fighting power. Men seem to have found it easier to fight for a dogma or a creed than to fight for the right to have many or none.

In a study of the Commonwealthmen sect is unimportant. Foster was a Baptist; Hunt, Watts, and Priestley Independents; Grove, Towgood, and Doddridge Presbyterians. Price was an Arian and libertarian; Priestley at the last a Unitarian and necessitist, though the political ideas of these friends were indistinguishable. Emlyn found a refuge at the Barbican; Whiston was baptized by Foster at Pinners Hall, though abandoning none of the doctrine that had made them notorious. The Hollises, prominent among dissenting laymen throughout the eighteenth century, came from Yorkshire, and had leased Pinners Hall for the Baptists. There they continued to support them until the lease ran out, but those then remaining attended Lindsey's Essex Street Unitarian chapel in the last quarter of the century. Groups which took little part, literary or active, in politics, might be expected to give some sympathy to more interested and aggressive dissenting societies in their demand for the right to worship, even when they deplored their particular interpretation of that right. Evidence must be drawn from the articulate. As their utterances are studied, they will be found to dismiss as unnecessary and irrelevant, differentiation in matters of religious dogma and discipline.

The dissenters were not strong in parliamentary circles. Debates yield little of interest up to the reign of George III, but a vast amount of material for the study of dissenting ideas is available elsewhere. Sermons continually referred to civil and religious liberty; treatises on moral philosophy concerned themselves also with such problems; letters and reported conversations recurred to them. There is a plethora of material in funeral orations of the time, and in introductory biographies prefaced to collected works. Eighteenth-century dissenters occupied themselves with history and with editorial work. No one who has studied the productions of Thomas Birch and of Richard Baron in succession can fail to notice the difference in approach to the period of their chief interest. Textbooks and accounts of the academies are valuable, as in general are all works on matters educational by dissenters. The century had hardly ended when *The Protestant Dissenters' Magazine* (1794–1799) and *The Monthly Repository* (1806–1837) began to print data of political and theological interest. Historians like Walter Wilson, David Bogue, James Bennett, Joshua Toulmin, John Rutt, and William Godwin were pouring out books on the period 1640–1800. Some of these were themselves manifestations of early nineteenth-century radicalism. Others were pious efforts to preserve a record of the personalities and adventures of the old sectaries.

A few individuals, noted in their lifetime for their activities on behalf of civil and religious liberty and familiar through their works, will be described. Many of them will be clergymen and teachers. They did not, of course, outnumber the laymen, but they were on the whole more articulate. A few journalists, who might well have been treated as Commonwealthmen, like Ralph Griffiths of *The Monthly Review*,[20] were almost too careful to keep their journals out of controversy, though the *Review* constantly supported the Americans. Others, like Dr. Benjamin Avery,[21] of amateur status, entered journalism for dissenting propaganda. At least two poets and some vigorous women must be mentioned. A large family connection, amply documented, is that of the Hollises.

A clear pattern does not emerge from the following sketches. In times when major political disputes and crises are not developing, sharp distinctions do not appear. This was an age of reason, of prosperity, of complacency. The dissenters described were neither complacent, nor were they desperate. They were all convinced of the desirability and of the ultimate possibility of improvement in their status and that of the country as a whole. They could not entirely endorse the satisfaction of the majority of articulate Englishmen with the present, since defects seemed obvious to them. They were themselves apart and excluded, for example, not only from office, but from universities in England. This gave them time to consider their lot. Their bonds with the Americans were close. Neither severely persecuted, nor completely secure, the dissenters could only with difficulty obtain a hearing for their grievances. A free press and a remarkably tolerant government afforded opportunities for propaganda. They wanted to improve education, and had an immense respect for its possibilities. They wished to amend the representative system. They feared the growth of ministerial power and its use of reward and persuasion among the parliament men. They looked back with sympathy to Commonwealth legal reformers and innovators. This was not a very dangerous or radical movement. Any association with Interregnum anarchy in popular parlance seems during most of the period to have been pretty far-fetched. At the end support given the French Revolution in its earlier stage, as well as the enthusiasm for the American claims, seemed to confirm the connection of dissent and rebellion. Yet this was not really their chief disadvantage as a political group. Their weakness was brought about by the perforcedly academic nature of their activity.

Schism: Barrington and Bradbury

Dissenters of the early eighteenth century will be passed over briefly here. They were on the whole at one with their Anglican fellow Whigs, Hoadly, Molesworth, Trenchard, and Tindal in their support of Revolution principles. Some of their works are still read. Defoe, whatever the political exigencies of his struggle for existence, was always faithful to the dissenters. George Ridpath and John Dunton were well-known journalists on the same side. Dunton had taken part in apprentices' riots supporting Whig principles in the eighties, had visited New England, and became after the Revolution "the Athenian Oracle," a marked eccentric and a great collector of the tracts of the seventeenth-century controversies.[22] John Shute (afterwards Lord Barrington) as a young man became a follower of Locke and wrote on behalf of the right of dissent and of Revolution principles. An occasional conformer, he was pressed by Somers into the campaign for the Union with Scotland. He had American connections and his son visited Massachusetts. In 1723 he was allegedly involved in a scandal which brought about his expulsion from parliament. The remainder of his life seems to have been spent writing and talking. His Sunday evening suppers with Jeremiah Hunt and Anthony Collins have already been mentioned. The two nonconformists are said to have convinced the Freethinker of the truth of some miracles reported in the Bible. Barrington's tracts and utterances show him to have been a strenuous advocate of liberty, with a distaste for fanatical zeal, though he belonged to the period of turmoil and continued parliamentary activity, rather than to the mid-eighteenth century on which attention will be focused.[23]

Barrington's great achievement for dissent was his work for the repeal of the Schism and Occasional Conformity Acts brought about after much delay on 18 February, 1718–19. Not all the concessions sought by Stanhope or by Barrington and other nonconformists were achieved, but the Act for the Encouragement of the Protestant Religion—as the measure was called—at least allowed the advantages obtained by the Revolution settlement to be enjoyed without curtailment. Rejoicings were diminished by the troubles at Salters Hall, where a conference or assembly of the Old Sects met the day after parliamentary victory, to discuss grave differences about discipline within dissenting ranks. Whilst Barrington, Bradbury, Calamy, and others of the best-known nonconformists had been at one about the repeal, they were by no means united in other ways, not least on the whole policy of the Salters Hall meeting. Neal, Calamy, and Watts, with half a dozen others among the Presbyterians, refused to have anything to do with the matter.

The year 1719 marked a great divide in nonconforming history.

Arian or Socinian ideas were to be found at Cambridge where Newton and Whiston had been suspected of heresies; in Ireland where Emlyn had suffered for his opinions at the hands of the orthodox; they impeded the rise in the Established Church of Samuel Clarke, one of the most learned men of the day. In Exeter in dissenting circles Joseph Hallett and James Peirce were known to be sympathetic toward such tenets. In 1718 an attempt was made, first in a general assembly of the ministers of Devon and Cornwall—an organization that harked back to the seventeenth century—and then in a committee of lay dissenters, to force a public confession of faith in the Trinity upon all pastors and thus to prevent heretics from holding pastorates. During the debates, the advice of London friends, both lay and clerical, Barrington's amongst others was sought. Barrington first suggested a meeting at Salters Hall, probably to postpone discussion until the parliamentary struggle was over. At the conference it soon became apparent that deep differences divided the Old Sects. Their advice to their Exeter colleagues was not unanimous and failed to settle the matter. Salters Hall voted by a majority of four that subscriptions to confessions or creeds were not desirable. Further votes were taken on what advice to send Exeter. It seemed to be agreed only that ministers and their congregations could part company if their views on the Trinity differed, with the result that each church became judge of its own situation. Any vestige of the old assemblies was over, though in the London area groups existed to administer funds or to push certain public campaigns. In doctrine and discipline, the individual church was thereafter autonomous.[24]

Salters Hall marked the cleavage in the sects between the old fanatic and the modern rational dissenter. Barrington was a moderate man. He had conformed to enjoy the political role for which he felt fitted. He studied and he talked albeit, as his efforts with Collins show, he was by no means a skeptic. Thomas Bradbury, his chief opponent, was a Calvinist with no sympathy for the fine distinctions made by anti-Trinitarians of all kinds. The fight between the two men reveals some of the problems created by any attempt to delimit the political dissenters to any category of religious denomination. Bradbury so annoyed Barrington at Salters Hall that the wealthy layman left Bradbury's congregation for Pinners Hall, already a center of moderate or rational theology.

Both Barrington and Bradbury were passionate proponents of Revolution politics. They opposed passive obedience, and persecution of dissent, denying that there was either a divine form of church or national government. In spite of common political beliefs, Bradbury hounded the anti-Trinitarians as dangerous characters and would have excluded all of them from communion with the sects. Bradbury was a Yorkshireman educated at the Leeds school. He had held a variety of pastorates before his long, active career in London commenced. In the metropolis he preached in four different series of weekday lectures besides his labours on Sundays. Pinners Hall, Old Jewry, Weigh House, and Salters Hall employed him. His wig in younger days, his dark skullcap in old age, his tall commanding figure and his vigorous personality impressed his audiences. He preached on all the Protestant holidays, never hesitating to quote violent phrases against popery or the diatribes of Sidney against tyranny. After the fifth of November celebrations he invariably repaired to a tavern and joined in with the singing of "The Roast Beef of Old England." He collected books and particularly Civil War tracts, and some of his collection was inherited by his younger friend, Richard Baron, also a Yorksman from Leeds. He reprinted one or two favourite ecclesiastical pamphlets. He was dogmatic and quarrelsome. He and the saintly Watts engaged in public controversy. Even queens were not spared by his oratory, and he publicly rejoiced at the death of Anne. No wonder that so redoubtable a fighter was attacked by the Tory crowds during the Sacheverell troubles, and that his meetinghouse was sacked.[25]

Bradbury's sermons show vigour and passionate Whiggery. It is not easy to judge how far this defense of Revolution politics (the righteousness of deposing James) carried the Independent toward levelling politics. Archdeacon Blackburne, who knew much about Baron, if not so much about Bradbury, declared that both men were antimonarchical in sentiment. There can be no doubt about Baron's politics. Those of the elder dissenter, though certainly Whig, cannot be proved to have been republican. In his sermons he attacked the luxury of the Establishment and of some richer men. He deplored the taxation of the poor and their meekness under tyranny—the theme of *The Ass: or the Serpent*. He deeply regretted the failure of "the Good Old Cause" and attacked its betrayers of the reign of Charles II. But whether this implied approval of levelling experiments, or only of the rule of the Saints and the toleration of Cromwell is not now clear. He certainly welcomed the Hanoverians, but they represented the Protestant religion and the overthrow of the Stuarts for whom he had no good word. Royal power was more than offset after the Revolution by the increased role of the people in parliament. Bradbury's Puritanism more than lived up to the popular conception of dissenter:

> We know your pretence, you for liberty howl
> But had you your will, you'd destroy Church and all.

Against the Establishment, he believed in the old rigid Calvinism of the early Interregnum.[26]

After Salters Hall, more and more London ministers leant toward the nonsubscribing side. One of the influences in this seems to have been the academy of Thomas Rowe at Newington Green and those at Exeter and Taunton.

Rowe[27] came from a famous family of ministers and writers including the famous Elizabeth Singer, Mrs. Rowe, a rather gloomy poetess of the early eighteenth century who was married to his nephew. He was related to the Munckleys, the Wrights, and the Groves of Taunton. He had been educated by Theophilus Gale and by Thomas Doolittle. Gale, the learned author of a work, *The Court of the Gentiles* (1669–1677), tracing all languages to Hebrew and all ancient culture to that tradition, was a remarkable teacher. He used the comparative method. The arguments of all sides were laid before the student, who was encouraged to form from them judgments of his own. Gale was a Platonist. Rowe studied Descartes and became a Cartesian. His students, Watts and Grove, a generation later became Newtonians. Rowe used Locke's work in his classes, and was himself a brilliant teacher of advanced ideas and tolerant methods.

His teaching was rewarded with an unusually brilliant group of students: John Hughes, the poet, who later conformed; Daniel Neal, the historian, connected by marriage with the Lardners, Hunts, Listers, and Jennings; Henry Grove, himself, a relative of Neal and a cousin of

Watts, a teacher at Taunton. A poet and a staunch dissenter, Samuel Say (1676–1743) was also a student and was connected with the Cromwell family through his aunt, Mrs. Bridget Bendish, Cromwell's granddaughter, of whom he later told a famous story. Mrs. Bridget was said to have been a great favourite, as a baby, of her grandfather whom she strikingly resembled. She was suspected of having sheltered Rye House plotters, but escaped their fate. She married Thomas, related to Ambassador Bendish, and herself had a son, Henry (died 1741), a nonsubscribing layman at Salters Hall. Thomas died in 1707 leaving her a widow and the manager of his salt pans. Thereafter she ran them herself, traveling in informal dress and alone, but singing, to and from her business. She became a notable eccentric. Hearing some passengers in a stage coach abusing the Protector, she became angry. At the next stop, dismounting and drawing a fellow traveler's sword, she challenged the offender to a duel. The gentleman, impressed by her sex or ferocity or both, withdrew his statements and made his peace.[28] Stories and characters like these would be current among the students and their friends. The Interregnum would be discussed and its battles fought over again. Milton was studied and became, as in the case of Say, a favourite poet. The atmosphere of schools like Newington Green was conducive to maintenance of Commonwealth tradition and the extension of its liberalism, both political and theological.

Historians, Preachers, and Tutors

NEAL — THE HISTORIANS AND JOURNALISTS

Daniel Neal[29] became a London minister and studied the history of Puritanism. His work on New England appeared in 1722; the history of the English Puritans in the thirties. In the latter he attempted a friendly but candid review of the work of his ancestors and predecessors. Besides his friends at Rowe's academy, Neal's marriage into the Lardner family brought him a host of others. He was related to the Hollises and the Sollys. He was an intimate of George Benson who had correspondents all over the world—America, Germany, Ireland, and Scotland. Benson also enjoyed a London circle of friends which was extremely active and consisted of Dr. Avery, the editor of *The Occasional*

Papers of 1717, supporting repeal of the acts of Queen Anne's reign against dissent; Dr. John Ward, a famous teacher at Gresham College; Philip Glover, Jeremiah Hunt, and Nathaniel Lardner. "Why should the gates of the church be narrower," he asked Fothergill later in the century, "than the gates of Heaven? I would as soon give up my Bible as the right of private judgment!" Benson had been trained at Glasgow and officiated at Old Jewry, a Presbyterian church.[30] Neal was an Independent, with as wide an acquaintance, and had greater talent than his friend.

Neal's preface to the fourth volume of his *Puritans* was dated March 1738, and summarized his conclusions about his studies. Uniformity in religion could not be attained, nor would a comprehension be a service to the cause of truth and liberty without the toleration of all other dutiful subjects who did not wish to enter into it. Wise and good men had found truth in different forms. All kinds of tenets had occasioned mischiefs. All parties in power had been guilty of persecution — Catholics, Anglicans, Presbyterians. No clergy should be given power to punish and penalize. Reformation, when it came to Protestant England, was the work of pious laymen supported only at the last by clergy. Freedom of religion was essential. An establishment might be allowed so long as it was stripped of civil powers. No church should be allowed to act against the interest of society and independently of the state; otherwise great and powerful religions swallowed up all others. Dissenters in England should be thankful for what they had achieved and stand fast in the exercise of social virtues and the pursuit of Christian freedom. Joshua Toulmin (1740–1815), a later editor of Neal's *Puritans* and himself a historian, judged that this "work has on the whole, a liberal cast; it is on the side of civil and religious liberty; it is in favour of the rights of Englishmen, against unconstitutional prerogative; it is against an imperious and persecuting hierarchy, whether Episcopal or Presbyterian; it is in favour of the great interests of mankind."[31] This review of the record of both sides in the Civil War is probably the most interesting revelation of dissenting ideas in a secular work in the second quarter of the eighteenth century.

Edmund Calamy (1671–1732), another historian and London Presbyterian minister, and prolific writer, from whom we derive much of our knowledge of the ejected ministers, was a moderate man who withdrew from the Salters Hall controversies, but who ventured into print a good many times against the Tory historians and on behalf of dissent. He considered the government of England "Godgiven." In preaching at the ordination of John Munckley in 1717, Calamy made clear his attitude to variety in religious discipline and dogma. His politics were almost entirely confined to the drive for religious liberty. Isaac Kimber, a London Baptist minister, wrote an early life of Cromwell (1725) which was on the whole favourable to the Protector and entirely favourable to the Puritans. On the Levellers, after giving their program, he pronounced the judgment that they were wrongly accused of being against all degrees of honour or riches.[32]

Michaijah Towgood (1700–1792), whose *Dissent* from the Church of England has already been mentioned, and William Harris (1720–1770) were both students of Henry Grove, though at different times, and both were interested in historical writing as well as the ministry. Harris wrote a series of biographies, starting with Hugh Peter in 1751. Among them was *Cromwell* (1762), the first scholarly life, containing new material and evidence of research. He and Towgood, in addition to other activities, were writers on the American side in the controversies of George III's reign. Towgood was sure that Pym and Hampden would have supported the American cause. Both were quite sympathetic toward the republican experiments and reforms of law and parliament in the Interregnum period. Towgood wrote *An Essay Towards Attaining a True Idea of the Character and Reign of Charles I* (1748) about the time Mayhew, who was an admirer of his work, was preaching his famous sermon, *Discourse Concerning Unlimited Submission* (1750) in celebration of the hundredth anniversary of Charles's death. Towgood admitted the illegality of the court which tried Charles, but saw in the king's own acts the real explanation of the tragedy which befell him. He entirely denied charges against the Puritans that they had destroyed Christian fellowship. They stood for the uniformity of Christianity amidst variety.[33]

Some of the dissenters tried their hands at periodicals, in the manner of the *Spectator*, but perhaps more nearly akin to that of Trenchard in the *Independent Whig*. Two of the best known, *The Occasional Papers* (1716–19) and *The Old Whig* (1735–39), were directed by Benjamin Avery.[34] Ben Grosvenor, a London minister, had a hand in both. The first was directed toward repeal of the Occasional Conformity and Schism Acts, but contained besides the arguments of the fourth paper about the dissenters' dilemma, general examinations of the old Puritan record for the advancement of liberty. It was not diversity, but refusal, of liberty which caused trouble. *The Old Whig*, perhaps stimulated by the campaign of 1735 which failed to obtain repeal of the Test and Corporation Acts, was somewhat broader in its scope, although it also emphasized religious liberty. Its second number speaks of "inalienable rights" in a manner suggestive of the Declaration of 1776.

"The Old Whig," composite author of the periodical bearing this name, regretted the postponement of William Hay's Poor Law reform. He defended Rundle. He attacked Oxford University for shackling the understanding. The cause of liberty was the cause of God. Consistent Protestants were strenuous asserters of their own rights, and zealous advocates of those of others like the Quakers. They wished to leave the job of making converts to others and concentrate on spreading the principles of Hampden, Russell, and Sidney, who lived asserters and died martyrs to the cause of liberty, public and individual. God had endowed everyone with the privilege of private judgment. The government needed to secure property; it did not need to trouble about beliefs, only about actions which endangered the state. "The Old Whig" suggested that office should be open regardless of rank or creed. He also suggested, in a passage it would be easy to translate wrongly, that sometimes an agrarian law was necessary. Men could be obliged to give up wealth if the government needed it, but never their right to judge for themselves. "The Old Whig" believed tyrants were as fallible in judgment as the bulk of mankind. Even the common man might choose. The Whig should consider how to strengthen and secure his boasted liberty. His principles could be nothing but just conclusions from knowledge of natural rights.[35]

One of the contributors to *The Occasional Papers* was Moses Lowman (1680–1752), for many years a minister at Clapham in Surrey. He was a contemporary of James Foster, and was educated at Inner Temple, at Utrecht, and at Leyden. He had much less renown for his support of civil and religious liberty than, for example, Thomas Bradbury, but his *Dissertation on the Civil Government of the Hebrews* (1740) affords us a most astonishing example of the vitality of Harringtonian ideas, and in it the *Oceana* and ancient Israel become confused. Lowman obviously regarded Harrington's plan as entirely practicable. The connection of property and power was stressed, and the importance of agrarian laws providing for redistribution of land to preserve the balance of the state and prevent the development of faction and party was noticed. The restrictions placed by Israel upon the priesthood, and the supreme court which defended the purity of the constitution were admired. Idolatry was forbidden to Hebrews as popery was to the English. A rotation in office safeguarded the land from evil ministers. A national militia defended the realm. Debtors were humanely treated. The *Dissertation*, while concentrating on the Hebrews, was quite obviously a moral story for the times.[36]

FOSTER

A famous contributor to *The Old Whig*, James Foster (1697–1748), was, like Lowman, a contemporary of Towgood, though he did not enjoy so long a life. Foster attended the same academy at Exeter as Locke's nephew, Peter King; James Hallett, one of the rebels in the discussion which led to Salters Hall; and Nicholas Billingsley, said to have been a republican. After serving several very small congregations, Foster became chaplain to Robert Fulton. Then in 1724 he went to London and soon became one of its famous preachers. His reputation for learning and for oratory earned him a D.D. from Aberdeen through the good offices of Fordyce and Blackwell. Foster was well liked by a wide variety of persons, and Pope eulogized him as "gentle Foster." He eschewed persecution and protected Emlyn and Whiston, early sufferers for their Socinian beliefs. Offered preferment in Ireland by Thomas Rundle, like Watts, he was too determined a dissenter to accept.[37] Besides his contributions to *The Old Whig,* his publications included sermons, tracts, and two volumes of *Discourses* dedicated to Lord Willoughby of Parham. Foster was first of all a great preacher and, even in his *Discourses,* much of what he wrote was merely hortatory. In his audience at Pinners Hall and among the readers of his printed exhortations, his liberal ideas excited some sympathy.

The philosophy he preached was not profoundly original, and much of it derived from Cumberland and Hutcheson. Throughout there is an emphasis upon the dignity of man, the value of free enquiry, and the obligations of society toward every individual within it. Self-love, Foster said, was inseparable from nature. Nevertheless private interest should not dictate every action. Men should love the public, and aim at universal good as the highest expression of wisdom and virtue. A general public spirit in the civil community to which all belong was the only effectual way to contribute to the happiness of man. A particular love of country and its laws and liberties should be subordinated to the general good of all mankind. A concern for universal liberty, the happiness of the whole, public order, and harmony, was the real test of virtue. The brotherhood of man was emphasized. Thinking only in national terms was to be deplored.[38]

Foster emphasized the freedom of the individual. Arguments for this were based on a belief in a universal sense of good and evil. Whatever could not stand the test of free discussion and enquiry could not be the religion of reasonable beings, nor proceed from the wise and beneficent Governor of the universe. Man's nature, a reflection of God's, was fundamentally good. There might be an abuse of freethinking, but within proper limits, which with Foster were extensive, much freedom could be the basis of social happiness. Study and worship were regarded as equally necessary. Virtue was not much stimulated without confidence in the existence, wisdom, and goodness of God, which provided reasons for its exercise. The belief in future reward and punishment dictated a vast number of actions, good and bad, for which civil law could not legislate. A future state seemed justified in general by the fact that on earth virtue and vice were not duly rewarded or repaid. The liberty to choose was the foundation of human morals and the basis of judicial retribution for choosing wrongly. If we were not responsible for our actions, punishment would be as foolish as praise.

Society was natural to man, essential for his moral character, and his happiness in society was important to God who was Governor of all. It would be quite impossible to separate morality and religion. Even in the lowest offices of life it was necessary to have social justice, although it was sometimes overlooked. The relation of master and servant, husband and wife, subject and magistrate, each brought their social duties. The chief requirements were a benevolent, honest heart, and an awareness that such relationships existed, since all men have a right to happiness, just as much for the welfare of the inferior as for the superior party.

The *Discourses* devoted a great deal of time to the relationships of individuals with each other. The duty of a husband as well as his authority should be remembered. Subjection was equally irksome to both sexes. Men were not all upon a level. There were differences of rank and station which the providence of God and the wisdom of society had ordained. Parents were reminded not to treat their children as slaves or with even an appearance of arbitrariness and tyranny. Example was important. It was better to inspire the child with sublime sentiments of morality than to use the rod. Discipline might occasionally be necessary; the rod would never convince, only terrify. Extreme severity in paternal government, like tyranny of other kinds, depressed and sometimes broke the spirit. Religious instruction should represent God as an attractive, not a gloomy, figure. A wise selection of Scripture should be made. Children had natural rights. The obedience expected from them should be limited. It was not, for example, just that they should be forced to marry people if they did not want to.[39]

Men were equal at birth. It was not perfectly certain that they were equal in a state of nature, though it was certain that inequality did exist. Some variations of station and of office could be regarded as accidental, caused by greater or lesser improvement of the understanding, different degrees of diligence or prudence. Rich men endeavoured to secure the service of people more indigent than themselves. Some inequalities would arise whatever the form of society might be. Servitude was of two kinds, free and perfect. In other words, the hired servant and the slave represented two different types of subjection. Foster then discussed the matter of slavery in the best-known passages of his work. Thomas Clarkson's *History* of the abolition of the slave trade, published at the beginning of the nineteenth century, listed less than a dozen names of those before his own time who condemned this traffic, amongst them Hutcheson and Foster. Foster said such perpetual, even voluntary, servitude (that is, transfer of oneself into slavery) seemed to be a plain deviation from the general scheme of the God of nature, who intended that all His reasonable creatures should be free. Trade in slaves, a sordid game, was unnatural and wrong. Even though the Bible spoke about slaves, we should remember that they were common then, but that in our time and country the "heart of man beats, by nature, most strongly for *liberty*."[40] Every man had an equal right to his conscience, an inalienable right common to all, but inequalities in the level arising from genius, passion, folly, and so forth, were nonetheless bound to occur. The just regulation of government should not be neglected, and it should always be remembered that the higher the station the greater the duty. The responsibility of the master was thus greater than that of the servant.

Not only was slavery repugnant to Christianity; so also was tyranny. How far was government ordained of God? Obviously the ruler could not be entirely uncontrolled. Yet, there was no express command of God instituting a particular form of government. Men were induced to settle under any government by a desire for social harmony, security, and defense. All governments came from voluntary arrangements, or from usurpation. Whatever the form of government, no man could really alienate his own rights to life and liberty. The magistrate was a part of, and not divided from, the community. In matters merely religious God might be the sole arbiter; in a civil dispute it was difficult for one man to be possessed without another being deprived. Different religious opinions hurt no one. The duty of the State was to do justice both to merit and to infirmity. No one should be prevented from serving his country merely for dissenting principles.[41]

WATTS

Isaac Watts, the hymnologist, was the most famous of this group. Almost every Protestant still uses some of his verses, but perhaps not one in a thousand associates anything else with the poet's name. Yet, in his lifetime, and for many years after he died, Watts was well known for his hymns, for his textbooks used in a wide variety of institutions on both sides of the Atlantic, and for his devotion to civil and religious liberty. He was born in 1674 at Southampton. His father may have been in prison for nonconformity at the time of his birth. His mother came from a family of Huguenots long settled in England. After leaving Rowe's Academy he retired for two and a quarter years to his father's house. He then became tutor to the son of Sir John

Hartopp of Newington, a rich city dissenter. This family was connected with the Cromwells. Watts himself, indeed, was to dedicate poems to Mrs. Bendish; to her son; to the Fleetwoods; to David Polhill, grandson of Ireton; and to Fleetwood's grandson, John Hartopp. He may have known Richard Cromwell. At this time he started writing textbooks. From 1699 he was connected with the Mark Lane Meeting, founded by Joseph Caryl, and continued by John Owen, and by Isaac Chauncy, son of a president of Harvard. He took up regular duties after the church had also considered but rejected Thomas Bradbury. In 1702 he moved to the Minories to the house of Thomas Hollis, the father of the benefactor of Harvard, and stayed there until 1710. In the church he was assisted by Sam Price, uncle of Richard, the Arian of late eighteenth-century fame. In 1712, after some disagreement with Hollis, Watts went to stay with the Abneys, cousins of the Barringtons and also connected with his church. Watts was independent financially, with his salary and the revenue from his books, but he never married. The Abneys were fond of him; he remained with them until he died. He always considered himself a semi-invalid. If he did less than his congregation would sometimes have liked among them, he cannot be accused of idleness in the study. His literary achievements brought him two D.D.'s from Scotland and offers of advancement in the Establishment. Watts was short, five feet two, had a small, oval face, grey eyes, and had an agreeable voice. He seems to have been greatly beloved by all but Bradbury.

Like Newton, Watts became a favourite of the orthodox. The hymns revolutionized services. His understanding of young people and his provisions for their instruction in Christianity were appreciated widely. The timidity which is said to have marked both his pulpit utterances and his conversation, may also be found in his cautious generalizations. He was not disputatious; he had great learning and tolerance.[42]

Benjamin Colman of Harvard once sent him his picture, and Watts hung it with Cotton Mather's and his father's in the front of his study.

I have there (he wrote) near eighty philosophers and divines surrounding me; their spirits are copied in their books, and their faces adorn my beloved place of retirement. There Heathens and Christians, Papists and Protestants, Calvinists and Arminians, Presbyterians and Episcopalians all meet in silence and peace. Were you to see my co-habitants, you would say I was a man of catholicism. Most of them I hope to meet in the regions of peace and love.[43]

With all his charity Watts was a vigorous dissenter in every sense of that term, and held opinions of a distinctly radical tendency. Some of his ideas may be derived from his early schooling with Rowe, some from a later study of Hutcheson, "the ingenious author of *The Nature and Conduct of the Passions.*"[44] More undoubtedly came from his own reflections in that quiet study he loved so well. Distinctly averse to all tests and restriction upon free thought, he may have been less than orthodox in theology. He was interested in the poorer members of society. He had a philosophy of education which had great influence on Doddridge and is still worth studying. A Whig in his admiration of the mixed government of England and in his opposition to tyranny, he had scant sympathy for Charles I's fate. His radicalism was most noticeable in his pronouncements on the church, on the schools, and on the improvement of the mind.

Perhaps Watts inclined to the Unitarian side of eighteenth-century theological controversy. Certainly Lardner thought he did, and he should have recognized a man of like principles.[45] Watts, although he stayed away from Salters Hall, quarreled with Bradbury and a bitterness crept into his remarks, rarely to be found in his other writings. The two men were probably antipathetic. Bradbury was dogmatic; Watts a convinced proponent of development in ideas. The dissenters of one age, he thought, were the orthodox of another. At all times there had been errors. Understanding was incomplete. If Christian history were studied carefully, variety in dogma would be discovered. Persecution was never justified. Christians should confine their testimony to a simple Scriptural rule of faith, leaving acceptance of different dogmas to the individual. The divergent practices of the honestly pious should never be criticized. Watts did not approve of an established church and thought that taxes imposed only for the benefit of one group were wrong. On the other hand, with his customary reasonableness, he admitted that tithe had been so long allowed for in the exchange of landed property that it was often not a legitimate subject for complaint. The ruler, Watts thought, was likely to choose officials from his own church and of like mind to himself. It was more important to emphasize men's knowledge and ability than their difference of opinion in the matter of faith. A civilian authority should not be in control of matters purely spiritual. Each church should do as it felt proper about restriction of membership and the discipline of its flock, but these actions should be purely spiritual; they in no way concerned the state. All penal and discriminatory laws were wrong. No one could force another into his own church;[46] all should be free to choose.

The great men of the seventeenth century had freed the intellect from the slavery of Aristotelian philosophy. Reason and experiment could now be used to discover the laws of nature. It was therefore a duty to improve the mind by observation, study, conversation. Teachers should encourage their students to make up their own minds and exercise their own judgment freely. The most important gift the teacher could make to his students was that of independence of himself and of other authorities. Doddridge's Academy followed methods very similar to those put forward by Watts, and drawn up in consultation with him. Besides Doddridge's lectures (for which plans and notes still exist), Watts's textbooks were also used. Some foreshadowings of their system can be seen in accounts of Rowe's school, but the Northampton instruction was even more experimental. All sides of a question were examined. References to varying authorities were given. Bibliographies for Doddridge's lectures would put to shame many a modern university syllabus. There was criticism by those who felt the teacher should at least guide his students towards the right view of the problem. Some undoubtedly did this. In any case the prejudices and beliefs of the instructor would appear, whatever his efforts at impartial presentation. The dissenters who received their education in such places were used to argument, to free enquiry about religion, politics, and philosophy. The place given science and modern languages in their schools[47] was likely to emphasize rationalism among the students.

Watts had a gift for clear exposition, whether of the Christian faith, or of logic or education. This probably accounted for the use of his works at English, American, and Scottish universities. In these widely read books liberal ideas derived from Locke and Hutcheson, as well as from dissenting forbears, were bound to affect those ready to learn from them. Watts not only wrote on what might be called the standard subjects of the curriculum; he also produced in *The Improvement of the Mind* one of the most sensible guides to self-education that has ever been written.

Visual, as well as oral instruction, should supplement the printed page. In a passage that has Newtonian echoes as well as a paraphrase of Horace, he wrote:

> Sounds which address the Ear are lost and die
> In one short Hour, but that which strikes the Eye
> Lives long upon the Mind; the faithful Sight
> Engraves the Knowledge with a Beam of Light.[48]

Advice was offered on the enlargement of the mind by reading. The readers, encountering a book for the first time, should look at the title page, the table of contents, and then skip through the whole book. Then they should go back and read more carefully, making their estimate of the whole at leisure. Readers should beware of exaggerating the merits of the strange and the new, and of discounting the familiar. Education could be carried on at any time, he felt, but older people should not waste too much time in trying, for example, to write if their early instruction had led them into bad habits. They would then be more profitably employed in enlarging their minds in another direction. At all stages both teacher and student should be careful to develop the capacity of the mind so that it could receive "new and strange ideas upon just evidence without great surprise or aversion."[49]

Like many others Watts wrote about the charity school movement. Unlike most, he displayed a real interest in the children's welfare. He did not feel that distinctions between rich and poor could be abolished or greatly altered. Nevertheless, there is interest in his answer to the familiar argument against the schools, that if the poor were educated there would be fewer servants and labourers to do the necessary work in the country. Watts felt that there could be worse evils than a servant shortage. Merchants and craftsmen, not the menial classes, brought wealth to the country. Ignorance could bring greater ills. Current difficulties might be due to the luxuries of the gentlefolk, rather than to the laziness of the poor, which some attributed to allowing them to learn to read and write. Surely an ignorant group was likely to be superstitious. This last was a much-used argument in favour of the schools which were fiercely Protestant. Watts raised a new question when he asked why a servant girl should not be taught to write a letter to her mother. Why should not everyone know how to write and read as well as speak? Learning could be abused. There were bad doctors, corrupt officials, self-indulgent gentlemen. Should they then be deprived of education? Literacy might increase the prosperity of the country rather than diminish the amount of work done. Finally, he reflected, have we any right to condemn to ignorance and drudgery the poor of the kingdom? God had not noticed class distinctions in his bestowal of talents. Poor boys might be as clever as rich boys. Ought they not all be led to use these gifts? The plea was modest and emphatic, but the reader was left with the feeling that Watts was by no means convinced that the maintenance of the social status quo was good. The way of advancement should be kept free. There should be no repression of whole categories of men.[50]

GROVE

Henry Grove (1684–1738) was Watts's first cousin and classmate at Rowe's Academy, and a teacher for many years of his life at Taunton where he had studied earlier in his life under Matthew Warren. He had also enjoyed the instruction of Eames of Moorfields. His nephew, Thomas Amory (1701–1774), was to carry on his work at Taunton until 1759. In that year he left the school for London, became a trustee of Dr. Williams' Library and a colleague of Price at Newington, and continued to support the cause of liberty for many years. Both uncle and nephew should be classed as rational dissenters. Taunton, under three generations of such men, was one of the centers of Commonwealth ideas in western England, with such students as: John Moore, tutor and parson of Bridgwater (d.1738); William Harris, the historian; and Nicholas Munckley, a medical friend of both George Benson and Hollis. Other west-country schools of a similar character and influence were at Exeter and Bristol (associated with the Rylands) and Tewkesbury, where Price as well as Secker and Butler studied.[51]

Grove seems to have shared the love of truth, the dislike of quarrels over difference of opinion, the search for "true principles of liberty," and the sympathy with advanced scientific and philosophical thought of the day that, at least up to the death of George II, characterized all these teachers and institutions. Much in Grove's writing—in his contributions to the *Spectator*, his tracts, sermons, and lectures on moral philosophy—reveals the similarity of his views with those of Watts and of their younger colleague, Doddridge.[52]

The contributions to the *Spectator* in the autumn of 1714 show the influence of Newton and of Cumberland on Grove, then a man of thirty. Man was both a sociable and a reasonable creature. Hobbes was wrong in considering him essentially on a level with the animals. His reason obliged him to pursue the general happiness of all. Self-love would lead inevitably to confusion. Man had a generous propensity for benevolence and this was serviceable to self. What could give more joy than the consciousness of virtue, of kindness to our fellows? Were self-love and benevolence inconsistent with each other? "No more than the diurnal rotation of the earth is opposed to the annual or its motion around its own centre, which may be improved as an illustration of self love to that which whirls it about the common centre of the world answering to universal benevolence." In the second essay he argued that although men appeared to differ very much, they were really the same, just as water, ice in winter, was the same as the fluid body of gentle streams. It was a property of the heart of man to be diffusive, but we should examine some of those checks which freeze its natural character. Bad habits were considered the result of worldly dispositions and discomforts, as well as of bodily defects. "Place the Mind in its right Posture," he said, and "it will immediately discover its innate Propension to Beneficence."

Grove's last *Spectator*, his fourth and the concluding essay in the periodical, was devoted to the glories of the Newtonian system. The third in the series better indicated the spirit which later animated his teaching. He stressed the love of novelty, unavoidable "growth of nature" and its advantages to learning and to our own contentment. Only novelty impressed us. Distinction of rank rested upon the difference it made to those unaccustomed to luxuries. Nature placed her children originally upon a level, and the strength of the fondness for

novelty which makes man out of conceit with all he has, preserved that
equality, in spite of all man's care to introduce artificial distinctions.[53]

A Philosophical Enquiry Concerning Human Liberty (1741) declared that
all actions were determined by causes preceding them. All sensations
arose from circumstances. Conscience restrained a man. The origin
of evil could be explained. Liberty was the self-determining power
of reason. He followed Shaftesbury in his association of beauty and
virtue and in his insistence on the fundamental benevolence of man.
Grove thought that to be virtuous required reason. Other animals presumably were not virtuous, even when they behaved in an innocuous
manner. In general, Grove was a philosopher in the same tradition as
Hutcheson, though his work lacks originality.[54]

Grove disliked controversy and disapproved of forcing subscriptions to articles and creeds. He emphasized the true principles of
liberty expounded powerfully by "the incomparable Mr. Locke, the excellent Bishop of Hereford (Hoadly) and other good hands." He criticized those independents who themselves persecuted others. God was
amiable and expected his servants to be benevolent. No one could
or should forget their natural and inherent right to liberty. He criticized "Cato" in the *London Journal* for attacking the Presbyterians in
June 1722, and for declaring that their "priests have Hawk's eyes at
Church preferment" and church dominion. He also denied the charge
of democratical ideas levelled at Presbyterians by Trenchard.[55]

In a further letter Grove described his view of his nonconforming
politics as follows:

> The principles of the *Dissenters* are the very same with those the
> *Revolution* was founded upon; they have had the sanction of *Acts
> of Parliament,* and the suffrage of the most august assembly in the
> world, in a late celebrated trial, the learned Counsel for the *Doctor*
> not excepted; to them, finally, we are obliged for our liberties, and
> the Protestant succession, the only security, under Providence, of
> all our blessings.

He considered that no one could, or should, forget his natural and inherent right to liberty. He opposed the celebration of the thirtieth of
January, the day that Charles I's head was cut off—an act for which the

whole nation was not responsible, and certainly not the descendants now living of the men who took part in the struggles of those days. Tolerance should be extended to all asserters of liberty, whether children of parliamentarians or royalists.

In considering the controversy about the origin and extent of civil power, it should be remembered that all power ultimately was vested in God. God allowed each man to protect himself, but no individual could pursue private interest except in such ways and by such action as were reconcilable with the general good of mankind. There was always a popular and a patriarchal argument. Civil society had full power to promote its own welfare; it had a divine right to do everything good and nothing more. Every three-half-penny author had his own schemes and these varied in merit. Ultimately political sovereignty came from God and the criterion it should use was the public welfare. A state of nature might be differently conceived. But more important than the solution of this much-disputed problem was the fact that only such developments as worked for the general good of all and for social tranquility were legitimate. Thus nothing could justify factions, mutiny, and rebellion except actions by a ruler which menaced public safety and right. At such times resistance might free the people. It might also be necessary to agree to laws whose principles ran counter to generally accepted principle, but again, only because of special danger. He referred to the Septennial Act which the Jacobite rebellion of 1715 made expedient.[56]

After Grove's death his nephew, Thomas Amory,[57] edited and completed his *Moral Philosophy* and published it in two volumes. The seventeenth chapter contained a summary of his uncle's teachings about government. Religious liberty was stressed, absolute toleration being the right of all. A mixed government maintaining a balance among its several parts was endorsed as the best form. The question of an established church was brought up and, although a hesitant and qualified assent was given to taxation for its maintenance, the discussion leaves less doubt about the dangers of clerical exactions than about the virtue of a state church. Such qualified statements reflected the nervousness of a minority. The absolute condemnation of tyranny supported by quotations from *An Account of Denmark* and the tenth *Freeholder* by Joseph Addison, however, could be made without apprehension, since all English were "Whigs in their Hearts" about the "Good Old Cause."

DODDRIDGE

The academy of Doddridge (1702–1751) at Northampton was more famous than Taunton or Bristol, because of the reputation of its chief instructor, who had been trained at the Kibworth School run by David Jennings. Doddridge carried out, in his school, the educational ideas of Isaac Watts, as well as the liberal traditions of earlier academies.[58] Doddridge's life was devoted to his students and his correspondents. He was said to have been a good preacher. He married a daughter of John Wright of Waltham Abbey. Students lived in their house, and the roll call is impressive: Benjamin Fawcett, later a minister at Taunton and Kidderminster; the puritanical Job Orton who wrote a life of his teacher; Andrew Kippis, the biographer of the dissenters; Hugh Farmer, a preacher at Salters Hall, and lecturer; John Aikin, who married a Jennings and produced two famous children and a literary granddaughter, and carried much of Doddridge's method into the Academy at Warrington—to name but a few. Doddridge had a gift for friendship and corresponded with Watts, the Lardners, some of the Anglican clergy, Fordyce, and the poet, Akenside.

Doddridge wrote, besides the famous *Rise and Progress of Religion* (which was read appreciatively by Wilberforce and Hannah More), a life of Colonel Gardiner (who was killed in the 'Forty-five), a moral story of a Christian soldier which achieved great popularity. His lectures were eventually published and went into several editions. Sam Sparrow sent the 1763 edition to Harvard, and many a student, trained as was usual in Rich's shorthand, had his own version among his papers at home. Doddridge suffered some persecution in 1732, from the archdeacon's court from which he was released by royal action, and from the rioters of 1737. His letters refer but rarely to politics. He once noted that his flock were far from political, nor were they even acquainted with the "depth of politics" though their common sense prevented their support of the Tories who were "united in thirsting for our ruin."[59]

Doddridge's educational methods were marked by the use of discussion already noticed. His students were given certain propositions the arguments about which would then be outlined and various authorities cited. Conclusions could be drawn. Differences were encouraged. He used English, as Scotch lecturers at Glasgow had done for some time, and as some other dissenting teachers had done as early as the days of the Charles Morton Academy described by Defoe in 1712. Like Morton, Doddridge encouraged the development of a good, clear style, and is said to have read the masters of English literature whilst shaving. He taught on the lines laid down by Watts. He was interested in a fairly wide choice of subjects including history, French, and some science, as well, of course, as much divinity and philosophy. He paid attention to elocution and deportment, emphasized wide reading and the acquisition of a good library. Favourites were Isaac Barrow, Archbishop Tillotson, Archbishop Leighton, Richard Baxter, and Fénelon, the pious author of *Télémaque*. The classical authors were recommended to the pupils: Cicero, Xenophon, Plato, Marcus Aurelius, Plutarch, and Seneca—the conventional list of contemporary favourites. They studied the continental legists: Grotius, Puffendorf; as time wore on, Burlamaqui and Vattel. They read the Cambridge Platonists and contemporary philosophers like Hutcheson, as well as Shaftesbury and Locke. Later editors of *The Lectures,* Andrew Kippis and Samuel Clark of Birmingham, added such names as those of David Hume, Adam Smith, Kames, Priestley, and Price. Polemical tracts and papers also appeared in these lists: Somer's *Judgment of Whole Kingdoms; Killing No Murder; The Occasional Papers; Cato's Letters;* and popular works like *The Preceptor.*[60]

Doddridge was attacked for encouraging the spirit of free enquiry. His own orthodoxy was questioned, though none doubted his genuine piety. He disliked the Methodists, though he admitted they were useful. He was friendly with churchmen, but found himself unable to conform. He believed that "nothing can tend more successfully to divide, than vigorously insisting upon an exact uniformity in things indifferent." He always emphasized the benevolence of the Almighty. The ethical criterion was the happiness of the whole. Moral sense provided a foundation for virtue. Rational creatures have just dispositions in the matter of the love of God and man. Doddridge's utilitarian philosophy was accompanied by a personal sense of religion. He seemed always to see Christ following after him with "a pardon in his hand." Doddridge combined much of the old puritanical sense of eternity and anxious examination of conscience with the new liberalism and tolerance of many of his contemporaries. He wished to reconcile the hearts of men to each other and wished to inspire men with his own passionate faith in God and in that eternity in which "heavenly luminaries burn with undying flame when sun and stars are gone out."[61]

This depth of religious feeling unexpected in a rational age, though to be found also in Law, Butler, and Blake, explains a part of Doddridge's influence on his students. His political ideas, revealed fairly clearly in his lectures, were Whig, derived from Locke and from Sidney. Society existed to provide security for life and property. To that end the compact was made. Tyranny might be resisted in certain cases where oppression was a greater evil than war. In the liberty secured to man he included freedom of conscience. Subscriptions, oaths, or qualifications might deter able and virtuous men from entering either the ministry or the government. Social ideas were rather less emphasized than by Foster, Hutcheson, or Watts, though in general Doddridge would seem to be of the Glasgow School. The labourer was born to freedom as well as were the richer classes. Slavery might be considered as a punishment or a penalty. Had he read Fletcher, one wonders? He was never as forthright in condemning slavery as Foster or Hutcheson. Reflecting upon the fruits of the earth and their distribution, he did not advocate an equality. On the other hand, something, he thought, should be appropriated for the relief of those who do not have a due proportion of goods. Primogeniture was against nature. Both extensive capital punishment and reckless warfare were deplored. The status of animals in the world was considered; he questioned the justification of meat-eating. Doddridge attracted good pupils and through these, who often became his assistants, the future academies of Daventry, Warrington, Hoxton, and Hackney were influenced. Aikin and Priestley were apostolic successors, both in their careers as teachers and as leaders of pedagogical experiment and theory. The importance of Doddridge and others like him can scarcely be exaggerated in any consideration of the history of the dissenting contribution to liberal thought.[62]

Poets, Publishers, Laymen

Strict nonconformists were excluded from active politics since they could not enter parliament without satisfying the requirements of the Test and Corporation Acts. The layman's share in the development of liberal ideas was neither large nor obvious. Men "bred among the dissenters" rose in church and state only as conformers. With increasing years their interest in their earlier associates and in the ideas they had studied grew less or vanished entirely. Secker never displayed any greater tolerance because of his upbringing at Tewkesbury, and one of Barrington's sons at least was definitely antidissenter. A few like Joseph Jekyll remembered their friends in their wills; Dudley Ryder seems to have lost interest as he grew older. Michael Foster, a more distinguished ornament of the legal bench, maintained an interest and was gratefully memorialized by his nephew, Dodson. In dissenting congregations in Liverpool, Birmingham, Norwich, Bristol, Taunton, Exeter, and Cambridge it is certain that there were men much interested in political affairs. How much the election of members like Jekyll, Hardinge, Rolle, Holden, and Grey Neville owed anything to dissenting supporters, is unknown. Small numbers of men genuinely interested in religious liberty might enter parliament through patronage but seldom through popular pressure. During the early part of the reign of George III, some members trained under liberal teachers were prepared to vote for toleration, and they attest the influence of mid-century Commonwealthmen. All political activity for and by dissenters was negligible. The dissenting politician was perforce a booklover, a subscriber to certain journals and societies favourable to his ideas. Industry and commerce could absorb their energies, and charitable foundations their largesse. William Coward (d.1738) and John Hopkins (d.1732) supported education in general and the work of some individuals.[63]

If the dissenters were prevented from being active politicians, nothing prevented them but lack of time or taste or talent from indulging in belles-lettres. No novel does for their clergymen, however, what Goldsmith achieved in his Vicar or Fielding in Parson Adams. There were a few poets of reputation and of some interest for the historian of ideas. Hughes and Elizabeth Singer, married into the famous

Rowe family, achieved a temporary fame, but their effusions were without social or political significance. Two others, James Thomson (1700–1748) and Mark Akenside (1721–1770), were passionately admired by all asserters of liberty. Thomson had early and while in Scotland developed a love for Milton, for English liberties, and for Shaftesbury's *Characteristics*. *The Seasons* paraphrased parts of the third earl's work. "Liberty" and the song, "Britannia Rules the Waves," from "The Masque of Alfred" revealed a combination of patriotism and Whig politics. Thomson deplored the evils of tyranny and detailed the blessings of liberty. His verses received far higher praise from Dr. Johnson than those of Akenside, though in the *Life* Thomson's friendship with Rundle, notorious freethinking clergyman through whom he obtained a position with Chancellor Talbot's son, and his enthusiasm were regretted. Thomson had a wider circle of readers than the "harbour spiders," who, according to Johnson, were the only panegyrists of liberty. He may be regarded as the laureate of the Commonwealthmen. Fat and silent, he was cheerful and beloved in his circle, and faithful to the friends of all stages of his brief career.

Mark Akenside, born twenty years later, was a north-country lad educated in Scotland who became a qualified doctor but lived throughout his life on the bounty of his friend Jeremiah Dyson. He too, was a disciple of Shaftesbury and became, during his very brief attempt at earning an independent livelihood, a friend of Doddridge. His *Pleasures of the Imagination,* written as a young man, gained him immediate recognition which Johnson at any rate felt he did little to maintain during the rest of his life. Johnson deplored his youthful warmth for liberty. It brought him early in the reign of George III the present from Thomas Hollis of the bed on which Milton died. Akenside never acknowledged the gift, being by then little interested in asserters of liberty. Both he and Dyson had become Tory courtiers and had renounced their old Whiggish principles. The poetry of both the Scot and the renegade, however, did something to popularize liberalism, though their poems were rather what Burke called "effusions which come from a general zeal for liberty," than statements of any considered program.[64]

Richard Baron was one of the most radical of dissenters in the eighteenth century before the reign of George III. He was, like so many others mentioned—Boyse, later of Dublin; Lindsey; Cappe—a native of Leeds in Yorkshire and attended the town's famous grammar school under Dr. Barnard, a Cambridge graduate. He ran away to be a soldier it was said, but afterwards attended Glasgow from October 1737 to May 1740 where he studied with Francis Hutcheson and Robert Simson, professor of mathematics. Hume and Smith must have attended classes while he was at the university, and he probably met there Thomas Brand of Essex, later the heir of Thomas Hollis. Both men at any rate conceived a tremendous admiration for Hutcheson and collected books he esteemed, portraits of him and notes about his advice. Some of these things found their way to Harvard later, some were lost sight of. Baron left Glasgow with a certificate, not only to his course of study in philosophy, mathematics, and languages, but to his virtue, probity, and high regard for what was honourable. He returned to Yorkshire and was for a while assistant to William Pendlebury in the meeting-house at Rotherham, closely associated with the Hollises. It is not quite certain when he left Yorkshire for London, since although he seems to have been a candidate for the ministry at Whites Alley, Moorfield, in the forties, he was not ordained until 1753 at Pinners Hall. He was most probably in Leeds when his edition of Milton appeared, since he described popular prejudice there against the defender of king-killing. By 1751 he was well launched on his editorial career, and published a Sidney, a Ludlow, two volumes of Milton's prose, some tracts by Abernethy and Trenchard, and two collections called *A Cordial for Low Spirits* and *Pillars of Priestcraft. Eikonoklastes* came out in 1756, and about that time he seems to have ministered to a chapel on Black-heath and to have been associated directly with Thomas Hollis of Lincoln's Inn. Thereafter, in spite of occasional outbursts of temper on the part of the choleric Baron, they worked together both in collecting Commonwealth works and in republishing them. Baron's last task before he died was the publication of Nedham's *Excellencie of a Free State* in 1767. He found rare books for Hollis and gave them to him or sent them to Harvard, and he left some annotations about relevant material on the items collected.[65]

Baron knew not only Thomas Hollis, but his cousin, Timothy; the historian, William Harris; Mrs. Macaulay, Alderman Sawbridge's sister; and Thomas Brand. He also talked to young Sylas Neville, a dissenting republican acquainted with Timothy. He knew Pitt well enough for the statesman to offer the always-indigent scholar some help. Thomas Bradbury has already been mentioned. Their tastes were the same, though their religious beliefs were probably very different. Baron was a republican. To him, as to Timothy Hollis, the Hanoverians were no better than the Stuarts. He despised titles and courts and was quick to be offended at haughtiness in a Cumberland, prince of the blood, or at Chatham, recently ennobled, whom he had earlier adored as the "scourge of impious ministers, their tools and sycophants."[66] Baron was also, as would be expected, an admirer of Anthony Collins and a whole succession of liberal or rational theologians and philosophers. Like his favourite professor, he believed (as Jeremy White, Cromwell's chaplain had written in *The Restoration of All Things*) that God would eventually unite all men in one great heavenly harmony.[67]

Specific remedies for England's problems remained ill-defined, and only one, Baron's plan for the reform of parliament, was clearly postulated. The solution to the problems of bribery and corruption in the Commons was the increase of members for the counties who were always more difficult to bribe than borough members. Hollis published the scheme twice in the London papers in 1765, even though his friend Blackburne thought the change not drastic enough. Blackburne believed that besides a place bill, severe penalties, even capital punishment for those taking bribes, would be necessary, as well as a thorough purifying of public religion.[68] Baron may have developed other proposals about the Lords, the throne, and about property, but little evidence remains save his character as it appears in records of the time and in the editions of the classical republicans and collections of Civil War tracts, to show the extent of his radical schemes. Thomas Hollis thought he had every sense but common sense, but gave no precise definition of his virtues.[69]

The only dissenting peers of the period were the Willoughbys of Parham, too poor to be of much consequence. Grafton, and possibly Shelburne were near-Unitarians but cannot be classed with dissenters. The sixth Hoghton (1728–1795) became a dissenter and married Elizabeth Ashurst, one of the Hollises of Essex. The Heathcotes were conformers in spite of strong ties with the sectaries; so were the Wards, though Mrs. Cappe, a grandniece of the alderman of Charles II's reign, became a Unitarian, and had inherited a liberal political tradition. The dissenters who made their mark and whose activity can be most fully traced were the ministers and teachers. Most prominent of nonconforming laymen were the Hollis family. Throughout the eighteenth century they maintained the traditions of the family and kept up associations with Pinners Hall, Rotherham, and Sheffield, as well as with New England. Their political views were regarded as downright republican. Their wealth gave them the opportunity for activity in almost any direction they chose. In their history, therefore, the secular nonconformist contribution is illustrated.

In the seventeenth century the Hollises were whitesmiths in Yorkshire. Thomas I, as it may be convenient to call him, lived in Rotherham, attended the dissenting meeting there, married Ellen Ramskar of Sheffield and then remarried after her death. He died in 1662–63. His eldest son, Thomas II (1634–1718), after an apprenticeship to an uncle in Sheffield, went to London and established a branch of the cutlery business in the Minories. He leased Pinners Hall for the dissenters and he founded the Hollis hospital in Sheffield. He married first Mary Whitby of Essex, and then Ann Thorner of Sheffield (1649–1729). The Thorner Trust and Hollis hospital have continued to be the care of the family down to modern times. He had a son, Thomas III (1659–1731), who had no family, but is still memorialized at Harvard in a hall and in the professorships he founded there. Increase Mather had interested him in the colonial college which, except for the gift of a Milton to Yale, seems to have remained his chief beneficiary in the New World. Benjamin Colman was another American friend. His circle in London included Isaac Watts who had briefly lived with his father; Barrington; Daniel Neal to whom he referred as "cousin"; and Jeremiah Hunt, the pastor of Pinners Hall. Hunt, like Neal, was a son-in-law of Nathaniel Lardner whose relatives included Listers and Jennings and so, if the Hollises be included, enjoyed a very wide connection with prominent dissenters.[70]

Nathaniel Hollis, who died in 1738, had one son, Thomas IV, who married a Scot of Wolverhampton and fathered Thomas V (1720–1774), generally known as Hollis of Lincoln's Inn and the last of the Thomas line. Thomas III and Nathaniel had another brother, John, who died in 1735 and was also a member of the New England Company. He had three sons: Isaac (d.1774) of High Wycombe; Samuel (1700–1724), whose son, John (1745–1824) was the last male Hollis of this family, but whose daughter's descendants, the Anthonys, are still among the trustees of the Hollis hospital; and Timothy who lived in the Minories, and died in 1790. One daughter, Anne, married Richard Solly; another, Elizabeth, married William Ashurst of Essex whose child married into the Hoghton family of Lancashire. Living descendants, all in the female line of this Hollis connection, are the Sollys, Anthonys, Listers, Mayers, Wicksteads, and Harrisons, most of whom have continued their connection with the Sheffield trusts.[71]

All the Hollises in the eighteenth century seem to have been interested in the American colonies. Thomas III constantly enquired in his letters about education at Harvard, and advised the adoption of liberal methods. Twelve heathen boys were to be trained at the college at Isaac Hollis's expense. Libraries like the collection of Joseph Hussey were reported as available, if proper steps were taken. News was sent overseas about members of parliament, like Grey Neville and Barrington, who had the right causes at heart. Timothy and his cousin once removed, Thomas V, were much excited about the Stamp Act, and always backed the colonists' side of any dispute. After Thomas's death in 1774 his heir, Thomas Brand Hollis, and Timothy exchanged news about Harvard and about the colonies throughout the war, in spite of the coolness felt by the family as a whole to the man who had received the fortune they felt was more properly theirs.[72]

A great deal of money had come to the last Thomas, fifth of the name, from his great uncle, his grandparents, and his parents, all of whom died before he was eighteen years old. John Hollister, Treasurer of Guy's Hospital, a Baptist foundation, was his guardian. Thomas was educated at Wolverhampton where his grandparents lived, at Newport in Shropshire, and at St. Albans. Thence he went to Amsterdam and acquired some of the languages he was to use in his reading later on and in his travels. He seems to have been proficient in Latin and Greek, French, Dutch, German, and Italian. On his return to London from Holland he lived with his cousin, Timothy, in the Minories. He studied with John Ward (1679–1758), a determined dissenter and lecturer at Gresham College, much respected in London intellectual circles and a member of several clubs for discussion of law and religion, among them the Spalding Society. Ward's works, *Lives of the Professors of Gresham College* (1743), and *A System of Oratory* (1759) brought him reputation, and he was recipient of a D.D. from Edinburgh bestowed by William Wishart, its Principal and his personal friend. He was vice president of the Royal Society, and one of the trustees of the British Museum. He lectured on a variety of subjects: law, divinity, geometry, and rhetoric. Hollis wrote to his old professor about his Italian travels, and continued to respect him throughout his life. He also profited from early association with Hunt and Foster of Pinners Hall, from whom, Blackburne later wrote, "he imbibed that ardent love of liberty and freedom of sentiment which so strongly marked his character through life." Another source of that enthusiasm was his study of Plutarch as a boy. Hollis also read and began to collect books whilst he was at Lincoln's Inn. His education was concluded in a formal sense by two successive tours on the continent in company with Thomas Brand in 1748–1753, probably postponed by the wars of the early forties and the rising of the 'Forty-five when Hollis bought himself a pair of pistols.[73]

On his return Hollis hoped to be useful to his country. He abandoned the idea of parliament, not apparently because of the tests required, but because of the bribery that was taken for granted. Instead he evolved a plan originally designed to occupy ten years, but which actually engrossed him for more than fifteen and affected both his health and his mental balance. This scheme was to disperse as widely as possible, over the world, books on liberty by the great English writers and by classical and European authors as well. Any history or essay which seemed to point the same moral was included. Sometimes republication was felt necessary and, with Baron's help or alone, this, too, was undertaken. Hollis had ample means and had inherited some of the family's business acumen. He carefully watched his own investments and his estates, chiefly the country place at Corscombe in Dorset, not far from Burton Pinsent where the Pitts had a farm, about whose management their friend advised them. Hollis kept a diary for a great part of his life, he kept copies of his letters, and he preserved commonplace books and newspaper cuttings all of which provide more about his character than can be learned about most of his contemporaries.

Hollis's acquaintance was large, though his intimates were few. His chief correspondents were two Americans, Jonathan Mayhew and Andrew Eliot; two Anglican clergymen, Archdeacon Blackburne and Theophilus Lindsey; and William Harris, a dissenting historian. He also wrote when away from home to his cousin Timothy. He distributed books and tracts to a long list of persons and institutions, often anonymous, and gave not only to Harvard, but to the Scottish universities, Trinity College, Cambridge, Berne, and some Italian libraries. He was on friendly terms with Arthur Onslow, the Speaker, with whom he discussed Cromwell, Milton, and other seventeenth-century heroes. He knew both dukes of Devonshire and admired Philip Carteret Webb, editor of *Doomsday Book,* and author of several other works. He esteemed as a "friend to liberty" John Gilbert Cooper. He met a wide variety of persons at the Society of Arts, the Royal Society, and the Antiquaries, and exchanged books and virtu with Walpole though they had no liking for each other. Cronies in London were, besides Thomas Brand when he was up from his Essex estate, ministers like Caleb Fleming and Nathaniel Lardner who lived in Hoxton Square. He also saw journalists like John Almon, printers like the young Nichols, and other persons connected with bookish things. He liked to drink tea and indulged himself with a cup of tea from time to time with Mrs. Winnock, Timothy's sister, with the famous Mrs. Macaulay whose history he admired, and with others.[74]

Hollis's most important friend was William Pitt, later earl of Chatham. He met him in the summer of 1756 at a country house in company with one other person and the conversation lasted for four hours "on the times and on the subject of government." Thereafter they met again and exchanged letters to the end of Hollis's life, becoming intimate friends. A great many letters survive including Pitt's praise of his friend to his wife and affectionate descriptions of his relations with the family in the country. Like Baron, Hollis was much upset by Pitt's acceptance of a title, but after some years' intermission, their friendship was renewed as a result of the determined overtures of the statesman. From 1770 to 1774 they were almost neighbours in the country, and saw each other frequently. They shared many tastes, for example an admiration for George Buchanan. Their political views were similar. Both deplored the Stamp Act and both worked in very different ways for its repeal. Both lamented the corruption of the times. Both endorsed reform of parliament as to duration and distribution of seats. They derived their radical political ideas from the great canon of English political thought. Molesworth's definition of a Real Whig was Hollis's creed, and he asked clergymen seeking the patronage his Dorset estate had brought him to endorse it before he considered their merits. The friendship of Hollis and Chatham confirms the idea that Chatham was fundamentally a Commonwealthman and shared most of their ideas, though he lacked the ability or opportunity to carry them out.[75]

The Hollis family had originally been Baptist, but it is obvious that as early as the days of Thomas III they belonged to the rational dissenters. They worshiped under men like Hunt, Foster, and Fleming at Pinners Hall. Thomas of Lincoln's Inn seldom attended, but made regular gifts to the clergyman, Fleming, and also contributed to the parish church of his country home in Corscombe. He studied the literature of the rational tradition. He esteemed all freethinkers. He was anxious to meet Jews and voted for Da Costa ("because a Jew," as he notes in his diary) as secretary to the Royal Society. His tolerance did not include papists. In this he and Priestley represented two stages of dissenting history, the one asking full freedom for all but papists and ready to include in that Jews and atheists; the other declaring that those of the Roman Church should enjoy inherent rights even if their own record had not always been one of tolerance.[76]

Hollis's "Plan," typical of the nonconformist contribution to liberal traditions, was well known to his contemporaries, and was blamed by Johnson for the American Revolution. Hollis thought that England had discovered liberty and that it should be shared with other people. After 1764 most of his attention was directed towards America. Harvard had a fire which destroyed her old library and the many gifts in it from the Hollis family. The Stamp Act controversy started a struggle between the government of George III and the colonists. These two factors determined Hollis to concentrate on providing the colonists with books of the right political principles. Up to this time he had spread his benefactions wider. Switzerland and Italy, Germany, Russia, Poland, and France, as well as some other lands, had received English books. These were carefully selected to show the advantages of Protestantism, the necessity for toleration and freedom of thought, the virtues of the parliamentary system, the horrors of tyranny, and the science of politics. He also sent grammars since English was the language of liberty.

He was a great collector. His own library contained many treasures from the Interregnum. He went to sales of old tracts. He bought manuscripts or secured their safe custody. Some of the Marvell correspondence included in Thompson's edition of 1776 was rescued by his efforts, and his care preserved the picture of Milton as a boy, now in the Morgan Library. Cambridge is indebted to him for portraits of Newton and of Cromwell. The list could be lengthened. Hollis collected what he called liberty coins and prints, books, and manuscripts. He was interested in any memento of a period of revolution and popular causes. Hollis's efforts induced Bute and George III to buy and present the Thomason tracts to the British Museum. It was in part due to him that Harris, and later Mrs. Macaulay, used the tracts of the Interregnum. With Baron and Hutcheson he probably did more to stimulate increased interest in the reforms of those days and to preserve their record than any other person or group in the period.

Hollis was not content merely to salvage old books. He brought about the publishing of new editions. In this he was helped by Baron, and to this he gave much of his own time and energy. Locke, Toland, Sidney, Neville, and Nedham were given new currency through his efforts. He took considerable trouble to see that their typography and the prints which illustrated them were in good taste. The title pages are a delight. Many copies were especially bound and decorated with stamps from tools cut for him by Cipriani. These bindings today are instantly recognizable and are charming, however eccentrically planned. He wished to induce people to read through curiosity. He tried to ensure correct interpretations. Many hundreds of his gifts to Harvard are inscribed, not only with a dedication from Hollis, "Englishman," but also with mottoes and quotations appropriate to the theme of the book. Conyers Middleton's reflections in his Cicero were often copied into histories. Passages from Harrington or Milton on liberty were also cited. A long list of these could be made. It would not differ very much from the reproduction of his commonplace book in the elaborate two-volume memoirs brought out at the instance of his friend and heir, Brand, and by the efforts of Archdeacon Blackburne, his correspondent and friend.

Hollis used his fortune to enlist the power of the press in behalf of the causes he favoured, whether religious liberty, reform of parliament, the freedom of the colonists, or the general propagation of what he felt to be the principles of a Real Whig, defined long ago to his satisfaction by Lord Molesworth and by Trenchard. He wrote to the London papers under a variety of names and reprinted in them favourite passages and mottoes. He induced Blackburne, Harris, Lindsey, and others to write, too. He rewarded helpful journalists, and continually admonished them to continue the good work. His letters went everywhere supporting his scheme. Works favourable to the American cause were reprinted by his request and often at his expense. These included tracts by colonial and English authors, as well as letters often written by his friends to the London press at his suggestion. When his gifts to Americans of his "liberty books" and his propaganda for them are considered, Dr. Johnson's attribution to Hollis of some share at least in the American Revolution seems hardly exaggerated. How far Hollis was representative of the politics of other dissenters cannot be stated with any certainty in the absence of evidence about men of like wealth and activity. But it can safely be assumed that, though his eccentricities were peculiarly his own, the general tenor of his politics and the character of his attack on contemporary conditions and politica—disgruntlement with parliament, reliance on press and library, hero worship and antiquarianism—were those of many of his dissenting fellows.[77]

None of the devices for parliamentary reform, either in the matter of distribution of seats, the franchise, the ballot, the exclusion of placemen, or frequency of meeting, were adopted in this century, and many of them never found a place in the reform of the next. Religious liberty eventually increased but the separation of church and state in England was never brought about. Educational methods and curriculum, in spite of the notoriety of Warrington and Hackney with respect to discipline and politics, found many imitators and influenced generations of teachers in Great Britain, though they were adopted very slowly. A respect for all sorts and conditions of men and recognition of the rights of poor men, of colonists, and of women, was certainly preached by dissenting groups. Of all these perhaps the most enduring and persistent was the doctrine of what is called anticolonialism today, which may trace its spiritual heritage to the Real Whigs of the schools of Molyneux, Trenchard, Hutcheson, and Dissent. In one sense Burke's attribution of responsibility for the troubled times to the rights-of-man proponents was correct. In another, of course, he did grave injustice to the moderate character of the Hackney Whigs, latest proponents of the dissenting tradition, who represented a wholesome element in public opinion. William Hazlitt, who had a long acquaintance with the Puritans, in a note to his essay *On Coffee-House Politicians* remarks half jestingly, half affectionately their intellectual political preoccupations:

> It is not very long ago that I saw two Dissenting Ministers (the *Ultima Thule* of the sanguine, visionary temperament in politics) stuffing their pipes with dried currant leaves, calling it radical tobacco . . . at every puff fancying that they undermined the Borough mongers . . .

He adjures them that,

> The world of Reform that you dote on, like Berkeley's material world, lives only in your own brain, and long may it live there! Those same dissenting Ministers throughout the country (I mean the descendants of the old Puritans) are to this hour a sort of Fifth-monarchy men; very turbulent fellows, in my opinion, altogether incorrigible, and according to the suggestions of others should be hanged out of the way without judge or jury for the safety of church and state. Narry, hang them! they may be left to die a natural death; the race is nearly extinct of itself, and can do little more good or harm! [78]

The dissenters carried on in the Whig party both the principles of the Sacheverell Trial so stressed by Burke himself, and those older and more experimental aspirations for better education, government, and law, which had flowered prematurely in the Interregnum and which, but for their continued study and temperate support, might have been altogether forgotten. The balance so beloved in the eighteenth century, between reaction and revolution, was in fact held by those moderate reformers: Foster, Watts, the Hollises. Without their reiterated reminders that law could be improved, that parliament could be reformed, that the way of advancement for all sorts of men should not be denied, the eighteenth-century politician might almost have forgotten that movement was possible or change ever desirable. The chief contribution of nonconformity of the age of George II was the raising-up of men like Priestley, Price, and Burgh, and the maintenance of connections and sympathy in the Atlantic community.

VIII

Staunch Whigs and Republicans of the Reign of George II (1727-1760)

Complacency and Politics

The notorious complacency and conservatism of politics in the reign of George II might seem to render futile any discussion of the maintenance and development of the revolutionary tradition in the England of that time. Among the dissenters already described, in Ireland, Scotland, and colonial America, circumstances and inheritance kept radical ideas and programs in mind. Similarly in France, social anomalies and constitutional restrictions strengthened a new egalitarianism evolving among the intellectuals, students also of English political writings. All important attention in England herself seemed in this period to be concentrated on transitory struggles for place and power and on a continuing and successful search for wealth and empire. Parliament might briefly discuss at long intervals increased toleration, the standing army, the desirability of more frequent elections, and the exclusion of still more officeholders from the Commons, but the debates lacked the force that either a coherent opposition or a settled government policy might have given to such controversies. Even the appearance in the political arena of a new reforming leader of great personality and integrity, William Pitt, later earl of Chatham, failed to achieve any success for the Real Whigs with whom he spiritually belonged.

Evidence about current theories may be derived from essays on government, political tracts, antiquarian studies, and historical treatises on the ancient and Gothic systems. Some of these were works of considerable scholarship. Few of them revealed the talent of a Moyle or a Trenchard, much less the genius of a Locke or a Harrington, but examination of their work reveals many of the preoccupations of politicians and students of the constitution, as well as of fashions of thinking. References to the contemporary world abounded in reflections upon the rise and fall of ancient republics or the manners of the early Germans. Moreover, among these academic scribblers will be found a number of Anglican clergymen, given over like their dissenting brethren, the Real Whigs, to polemics and pedagogy. By profession hortatory, they were critical of both church and constitution when such an attitude was rare. Their influence was felt in certain schools and at the University of Cambridge. It would indeed be a mistake to attribute more importance to Taunton, Northampton, and Warrington than to these Anglican centers. There were as many or more men trained in the latter, who led the Commonwealthmen in the reign of George III, as there were among those exposed to the better-known prejudices of dissenting academies.

What differentiates the long reign of George II from both preceding and succeeding reigns was the divorce between the realities of government and the campaigns of the scribblers. Reformers were not organized. They were not focused on any definite program. Issues of the sort that divided parties in the days of the American Revolution or in the days of Queen Anne were not to be found. Excise, Spanish policies towards English traders, Hanoverian troops, these things were not the kind of problems which much or specially concerned the Real Whigs.

Yet the reign was not deficient in important and significant works. During its course Englishmen could read among recent books Middleton's historical works; Law's translation of King's *Origin of Evil* with its famous "Preliminary Dissertation"; Law's own *Considerations on the Theory of Religion;* essays on study and education by John Clarke of Hull; Bishop Squire's *Essay on the English Constitution;* John Jones's *Free and Candid Disquisitions,* indispensable prelude to *The Confessional* and the Feathers Petition of the next reign; and more original, though not influential, Pownall's *Principles of Polity.* Two historical works reflected the gloom of the time, Brown's *Estimate* and Montagu's *Antient Republicks,* and brought sharply into focus the end of one phase of Georgian optimism and the beginning of a new climate of English opinion. None of these proposed a utopian or levelling scheme, but all have some importance in the history of liberalism.

Before estimating the nature of such parliamentary and literary manifestations as may be readily found, it would be well to pause and survey this much-talked-of complacency, this determined and in some ways un-English adherence to the status quo. The year 1727 may actually mark a period more distinctly than the year when Queen Anne died. Divisions, periods, and transitions are dangerous terms in history but an illustration may serve to make the point. In 1714, it was said on reasonably reliable evidence, that Stanhope and Richard Hampden (grandson of John, son of the Hampden involved in the Rye and member for Buckinghamshire and Wendover) plotted, or at least talked about, the assassination of the Tory ministers to save the Protestant Succession.[1] This sounds much more like the "Immortal Seven" of 1688, or the Council of Six in 1682, than like eighteenth-century England. Whether a man of violence or not, Stanhope was a reformer and he became chief minister with a policy at home and abroad of a liberal complexion. The Septennial Parliament ended shortly after his death and the scandals of the South Sea Bubble. The succession had again been threatened. But by the time that George II came to the throne the new dynasty had survived the Bubble and two rebellions. Moyle, Molesworth, and Trenchard were dead. The generation which had lived with Locke and Newton was nearly gone. Conduitt and Jekyll[2] were still in the House, the one representative of Newtonian science and heresy, the other of a certain bold independence. Walpole was in the office he had gained from the crises of 1721, and with only the briefest interruption continued his many services to England. But his role in the new order was more that of a Tammany boss than of a Pym, a Clarendon, or a Godolphin. His concern was the working out of parliamentary practice now that royal interference had so greatly diminished. He saw no need to alter or adjust the fabric of the constitution. The work was practical, his theories empirical. He studied public opinion and the decision to ignore the reformers may have reflected an exact reading of the nation's wishes. Instead he attempted party management. He experimented in taxation and finance.

Walpole provided a target for the opposition, both of discontented Whigs and of the Tories under their mentor, Bolingbroke. But this group lacked effective leadership and cohesive force. Its nature was never better revealed than when it became necessary at last to replace Walpole. These Whigs and Tories had uneasy relations. They lacked a focal point. They were a nonpartisan group, though men like Holden, Jekyll, Rolle, and Sandys might be referred to by similar terms—republican, discontented Whig, and flying squadron, and others.[3] The journal most powerfully and prominently against the government was *The Craftsman,* run by Nicholas Amhurst, the disgruntled Oxford Whig, and adorned by the effusions of Bolingbroke. Others, of course, appeared for special occasions like *The Old Whig, The Champion,* and the like. But the opposition, though vocal at all times, never seems to have been a large or coherent force, nor did it have decided leadership. Pulteney and Chesterfield were representatives of the out-of-office men who wanted power but did not pursue any discernible policy save criticism of the government. To some extent this was also true of the patriots whose leading ornament was to be William Pitt.

Pitt was claimed by the more radical politicians as their own, though he was by disposition slower to endorse new programs than he was ready to admire the heroics of past statesmen and writers. His letters reveal his reading and enjoyment of the works of Sidney, Ludlow, May, Rapin, and Buchanan, all Whig republican in tone, and he urged the same canon upon his young nephew, Thomas, later Lord Camelford, such learning being the inspiration of manly, honourable, and virtuous action. He was a defender rather than asserter of liberty, quick to sympathy with the oppressed and to criticism of the corrupt and cowardly, but there seems little indication in the record that Pitt had any definite scheme for preventing corruption or for making government really popular. He fought for habeas corpus when he thought it threatened. With his friend, Sir Charles Pratt, Lord Camden, he defended the rights of juries. He fought for the repeal of the Stamp Act and supported the Americans, less because he had any constructive ideas on colonial relations than because he shared the American admiration for the old classical pronouncements on the rights of Englishmen. As he had said on 26 February, 1755, he did not date his principles "of the liberty of this country from the Revolution; they are eternal rights; and when God said 'let justice be justice,' he made it independent."

Pitt believed in natural rights. He probably never understood the new complexity of government and the relation of policy to public opinion. Late in life, persuaded by his friend Thomas Hollis, he endorsed Baron's scheme for the reform of parliament "by counties," that is by an increase in county representation. But his own method may be summed up as oratory, appeals to the people, denunciations of evildoers and tyrants. These were his weapons. His speeches deviated, it was reported, into a thousand digressions—and "he seemed sometimes like the lion to lash himself with his tail to rouse his courage, which flashed in periods and astonished, rather than convinced by the steady light of reason." The immediate effectiveness of this eloquence in relation to his own reputation may have misled him as to its ultimate value and usefulness.

Yet Pitt had the heroic qualities of the great leader. John Gilbert Cooper (1723–1769) in his iambic ode, *The Genius of Britain,* addressed him as the great friend to liberty: "Oh Thou, ordained at length by pitying Fate To save from ruin a declining State . . . A friend to all mankind, but slave to none . . . From each low view of selfish faction free." Since Cooper despised "pensioned progeny," "Boroughmongers," and Newcastle's "reptile Wiles," and believed that Heaven created man for liberty—in short, since Cooper was a Real Whig and associated with Hollis and others of the band—his admiration for Pitt simply attested to the statesman's popularity, and the power which that might have given him.[4]

But neither the constitution as then devised, nor Pitt's own talent, made it possible for him to reform the body politic. The inspiration of this extraordinary man was heightened by emergency and controversy. He could condemn or protect, he could not construct. He had no idea of party give and take. He never distinguished between necessary concession and the surrender of principle to faction. He lacked the talents which had made Shaftesbury dangerous and Walpole powerful. A Churchill, rather than a Gladstone, his great achievements, the successes in the war, the repeal of the Stamp Act, the fight against general warrants, were all in response to clearly defined challenges from foreign foe or domestic bully. He dreamed dreams, but he was incapable of making them come true. At the period when the Real Whigs had a leader with popular as well as aristocratic support, they were no better off and their ideas no nearer fulfillment. Outside of the enlargement of the empire Pitt's achievement was negative and what he bequeathed to posterity a legend.

Leadership and organization were lacking. The complacency against which the Real Whigs fought had also infected them and weakened their force. The constitution was good. Parliament was powerful. The press was free. Not many people were persecuted. Some poor people drank too much. Some suffered from the Act of Settlement and faulty working of the old Poor Law. But the Real Whigs never seriously questioned the stratification of society or the existence of a privileged class. They were not insincere reformers. They continued to pay tribute to the equality of man, at least in a state of nature, and to the virtues of a fair distribution of property. But they lacked a sense of urgency. There was a lull in public affairs. And there was ample opportunity to argue about theology, about taxes, and about foreign policy.

What is more, the opening years of the reign of George II coincided with the flood tide of continental admiration for the English system; perhaps only the era of Scott, Byron, and Wellington produced as widespread adulation for all things English. Voltaire visited England and saw Newton interred as "though he had been a king who had made his people happy,"[5] and observed a happy land free from tyranny, poverty, and prejudice, where science and letters were honoured and where parliamentary institutions guarded the welfare of the nation. Locke, Bacon, and Newton were names to conjure with. On all counts, intellectual and political, England seemed preëminent. The descriptions by Muralt a little earlier; de Saussure, contemporary with Voltaire; Maffei, some ten years later—all supported this view. Ever since the days of the Revocation of Nantes, popery, France, and arbitrary government had been associated in Britain and echoed by her friends, continental authors of *Soupirs* and accounts of absolutism. In the eighteenth century men like Boulainvilliers, writing on the ancient parliaments of France, underlined for readers the fact that whilst others had declined, English Gothic estates had become more powerful than ever. Even in examining ancient Rome, Montesquieu was careful to point out the parallels and contrasts with British history. In the *Spirit of the Laws* the philosopher paid tribute to English thought, as D'Alembert had done in his introduction to the *Encyclopédie*. By mid-century admiration began to decline. D'Argenson and Le Blanc pointed out faults as well as virtues. An acid note crept into Frederick the Great's comments on English freedom. Jealousy, rivalry in war, and changing fashion were partially responsible, but as the fourth decade ended and the fifth began, there was a growing realization of something amiss in the English system.[6]

In mid-century the complacency in England herself was sharply declining. The 'Forty-five seemed to many to have revealed shocking decadence and weakness in the face of undisciplined and not very numerous invaders. The confusions that ensued after Walpole's fall, a failure to achieve any coherent policy and a ministry whose character might reflect dissatisfaction with his policies and methods, were disillusioning. Hollis told William Taylor Howe seven years afterwards (repeating the story he had poured out excitedly to Stanier Porten very soon after the event), about his memorable first meeting with Pitt at a friend's house in the country, the year of the loss of Minorca, 1756, when they revealed mutual anxieties as to the fate of kingdoms. Hollis, it may be remembered, had in 1754 decided that parliament was not for a Real Whig like himself. His chance of service lay in the implementation of his plan to distribute books.[7]

Nevertheless, throughout much of the reign satisfaction with the best of all constitutions militated against any vigorous propagation of reforms, even where these were thought by the Real Whigs to be necessary. They were more inclined to read about the heroic days of the seventeenth century in the calm retreat of their studies, than to conjure up means of creating an improvement for the present generation. The exiled Stuarts were quiet for a long while after Atterbury's exile, but they were there, they were reverenced publicly by Dr. William King and his like.[8] Praises of the Hanoverians made even the parliamentary Tories uneasy, but their striking power was a latent, not an overt, threat. The Stuarts' existence supported the government. No one wanted civil war. The argument was brought forward that any suggested change might overturn the present, excellent system. England was rich, peaceful, contented. Any suggestion that the contemporary mood produced stagnation could easily be contradicted by a glance at the controversies that kept the presses busy. De Saussure glancing with the impartiality of a foreigner at Whigs and Tories noticed that while some condemned party struggles, there were others that credited them with a stabilizing, balancing, moderating influence. Were the Tories altogether unopposed, absolutism might develop. Were the Commonwealthmen to gain sole ascendancy, a republic and anarchy might appear. So in the best of all possible worlds there was a constitution that needed no rectification, and an excuse for argument and discussion that kept its political balance steady whilst allowing to all free expression of opinion.[9]

Some difference in attitude in the three decades of the reign may be detected. The thirties saw parliamentary attempts at reform with all the old arguments about the dissenters and placemen. The forties were lived in a state of war and party confusion. There was no longer a Walpole at whom to tilt. There was less cause for self-congratulation. The Prime Minister could not be blamed for the ever-present corruption. The Act of 1729 against bribery, and the Act of 1742 disqualifying certain officers from the House made singularly little difference. The 'Forty-five was a shock to public morale and contentment, but its effect was not likely to make Commonwealth programs more attractive. All Whigs closed ranks against the popish pretender. The rebellion produced in England James Burgh's *Britain's Remembrancer,* pointing out the morals of the "times" but utterly lacking in the force and vision of Wallace's sermon on *Ignorance and Superstition* in Scotland. The preacher, but not the social or political reformer, had the chance of a hearing. The novelist and humorist could hint, probe, but not prescribe for social ills. In the fifties renewed war, unexpected dangers, earthquakes, and defeats threw the country into a fury of excitement over the militia once again and over the "times." Disunion, faction, luxury, vice, a loss of old courage and devotion to liberty, these afforded the moralist texts for many a sermon and tract. Complacency was gone. In spite of victory in war the stage was set for renewed revolutionary discussions in the turmoils of the next reign.

Parliamentmen, Historical, Constitutional, and Legal Commentators

Dr. Sam Peploe, a zealous Whig, politically connected with the liberal family of Hoghton in Lancashire, declared in one of his sermons that only the ghosts of Commonwealthmen and republicans could be found. He was not expressing regret, he was reassuring his audience against the forebodings of his colleague, Dr. Francis Hare, who feared subversion by such politics in church and state. Peploe was right so far as the parliament was concerned, whatever the writers of Utopian schemes might propose reminiscent of revolutionary ideas. There are fewer details on some debates in the Houses than exist about those of a hundred years before. It is easier to gain an impression of many a speaker in the Long Parliament, than to find a speech as it was delivered by William Pitt. Diaries like Egmont's, or memoirs like those of Hervey and Walpole, provide many a detail about persons and problems. They refer in speaking of such men as Henry Rolle, Samuel Sandys, and George Heathcote, to Staunch or Malcontent Whigs and republicans, but they seldom substantiate the opprobrious terms. Patriot was applied to Pitt's friends, but patriot could as Fielding, by no means unfriendly to reformers at any time, stated, mean only another name for a candidate for court favour. What seemed to remain throughout the whole reign, so far as parliamentary reformers were concerned, were occasional suggestions about the character of the government at certain times and on special issues.

But the issues themselves were pretty stale. Relief for dissent was brought up by the efforts of men like Samuel Holden, and supported by Heathcote, by William Plumer, and Jekyll. Walpole decided he did not wish the matter tested and brought all his guns to bear, even on such known friends to dissent as Speaker Onslow and Bishop Hoadly. The result was defeat in the House and less enthusiasm for their Whig friends than before amongst the sectaries. Motions for the repeal of the Septennial Act, supported by more or less the same group, or for place bills and bills against corruption, met the same fate as the efforts to repeal the Test. Such bills, passed in 1729 or 1742, or the more radical Jew Bill later in the reign, were put through by the government, and cannot be regarded as triumphs for liberalism. The Jew Bill was promoted by the Pelhams and written about by Philip Carteret Webb. Nicholas Hardinge spoke for it. William Pitt eventually spoke against it. Hardinge and Pitt held theories similar to those of the Real Whigs, but the course of government policy and public agitation divided them. Later, when Pitt was in a position of power, he was responsible for the extension of tenure to the Scottish judges, helped by Sir Charles Pratt, who was Nicholas Hardinge's brother-in-law. But during the whole thirty or more years of the reign there were no statutory triumphs and few parliamentary debates for liberals to look to for inspiration and guidance. An important act bearing the name of the heir to the Somers tradition, the Marriage Act of Lord Hardwicke was reactionary in character. Jekyll's reform of Mortmain and his bill against gin drinking were in no sense party measures.

Jekyll probably represented the best Whiggery of his time, like Sir George Savile (1726–1784) in the days of George III. He and his nephew, Lord Hardwicke, were of the old Somers connection. He supported every good cause, from the pleas of the Quakers about tithe to the efforts of Oglethorpe and his friends in behalf of Georgia. He was tolerant. In religion he was probably a freethinker like his friends Whiston, Clarke, and Onslow. He studied Interregnum history and helped Thomas Birch acquire Thurloe's papers for publication in 1742. His stand against Sacheverell in 1710 was remembered when as an old man he rose to address the House. Hervey thought him a double, balancing character, arguing on both sides and voting for neither. But Hervey detected perspicacity in the lawyer, and was forced to admit that in spite of the desire of appearing in the right more than the desire of being so, and a bias towards popularity, Jekyll was a speaker of greater weight than any other man in the Commons. Queen Caroline recognized his power and was always abusing, cajoling, hoping to manage the Master of the Rolls, but was as often disappointed in her efforts. Jekyll left money to the public and to his old friends, the dissenters. Perhaps he most resembled John Hampden or Andrew Marvell of the previous century.[10]

Three officers of the House of Commons also maintained ties with the great days of the Commonwealth. Nicholas Hardinge, already noticed for his support of the inherent right of the Jews to the privileges of Englishmen, was Clerk from 1731 until he retired in favour of Jeremiah Dyson, friend and benefactor of Akenside and at this time known for his radical views. Hardinge had a son, George. He was an adorer of Milton and commonly reputed a staunch Old Whig. He died in 1758.[11]

In spite of his reputation for republicanism, Dyson left very little to document this. Since he lived on into the next reign to become a Tory courtier, he may be ignored. Arthur Onslow (1691–1768), the Speaker, should be noticed in spite of his determined impartiality in office. He did much good service during his long tenure of the chair (1728–1761) and was revered and honoured by all parliamentmen. When he wrote his memoranda for his family, he dwelt on his own freedom from party and on the respectability of his family history. Yet, studying the record, it is hard not to credit him with being something to the left of the "Old Whig" doctrines to which only he claimed allegiance. In his office he drew even the praise of Hervey, though with the usual waspish qualifications. Hervey allowed him to be eloquent, warmly attached to the English constitution, and no favourer of either crown or church, but he also condemned Onslow as canting, fulsome and bombastic, passionate, coxcombical in gesture, and injudicious in conduct. Possibly the last referred to a moment, also remarked by Egmont, when the Speaker was said to be associating with Tories and malcontents. In general Onslow seems to have been grateful to Walpole, and friendly with the Pelhams. He had sat in parliament since 1720, had helped in the impeachment of Thomas Parker, Lord Macclesfield, and was known as an enemy to bribery and corruption in general. He supported frequent parliaments, but opposed the publication of parliamentary debates when the matter was debated in 1738. Only harm could come, he said in opposition to the Tory supporters of free publication, from spreading abroad the deliberations of the august assembly over which he presided.

No radicalism appears in this record, but Onslow's friends, both early and late in life, were in part at any rate among the liberal Whigs. In the reign of George I he had consorted, it must be remembered, with the heretical Whiston. He had corresponded with John Molesworth and shared his politics. Onslow was also a friend of the printer, William Bowyer, and through him met James Burgh, author of the *Political Disquisitions* as well as of *Britain's Remembrancer*. Dedications to the Speaker were frequent; among them Middleton's *Senate*. Franklin dedicated a history of Pennsylvania to him and Richard Jackson, M.P. for Weymouth (1762), who probably wrote the history under Franklin's direction, was his friend. John Jones, whose projects will be described later in this chapter, also hoped to interest Onslow in them. Late in the reign of George II the eccentric, Thomas Hollis, waited on him with the Italian artist, Cipriani, in order to obtain a copy of a picture of John Milton. Five hours of conversation ensued, and the two Whigs found much in common. Both passionately admired Milton, both looked back to the martyred Sidney, whom the Speaker thought "barbarously murdered." Both condemned Charles I's actions and the tyrannical maxims of the Stuarts. Both collected and marked books of the great period of revolutionary thought. Both supported toleration, and perhaps Onslow was more ready than Hollis to ameliorate the lot of Catholics. He disliked oaths which "tortured the mind but never influenced the actions" of those forced to take them. He was devoted to an ideal of parliamentary service stemming from the best English traditions. At no time was he ever connected with projects of reform or with anything that could have justified calling him a Commonwealthman, but possibly he came as near it as circumstances and period allowed.[12]

A self-styled Real Whig, William Talbot (1710–1782), was in parliament as member for Glamorgan (1734–37), during the early years of Onslow's speakership. He was raised to the peerage and became a Tory courtier later during the reign of George III. He therefore belongs with the renegades like Dyson. Nevertheless his views as stated in a letter written to a friend, Sir John Dutton, during the elections of 1734, are interesting and serve to define what men like Talbot and probably Thomas Rundle, later bishop of Derry, and others believed their philosophy to be. Talbot had been educated at Eton and at Oxford. He was later to cause considerable scandal by his liaison with Elizabeth Pitt, sister of Chatham. He was a bitter opponent of Walpole, but neither during that long period, nor later, does he seem to have played any considerable role in politics. His definition of Whiggery survives in a volume of his friend Rundle's correspondence and in a letter dated Barrington, 1734:

> The principles of a Real Whig, in my sense of the term are these, that government is an original compact between the governors and governed, instituted for the good of the whole community; that in a limited monarchy, or more properly legal commonwealth, the majesty is in the people and tho' the person on the throne is superior

to any individual, he is the servant of the nation;—that the only title
to the crown is the election of the people; that the laws are equally
obligatory to the Prince and people; that as the constitution of England is formed of three legislative branches, the balance between
each must be preserved, to prevent the destruction of the whole;—
that elections ought to be free, the elected independent;—that a
Parliamentary influence by places and pensions is inconsistent with
the interest of the public; and that a Minister who endeavours to
govern by corruption, is guilty of the vilest attempt to subvert the
constitution;—that a standing mercenary army in time of peace is
contrary to the laws, dangerous to the liberties, and oppressive to
the subjects of *Great Britain;*

He goes on to deal with further considerations:

> . . . that our posterity depends on trade, which it is our interest to
> encourage, our duty to protect;—that our colonies are the founda-
> tion of a very beneficial commerce; that honour, justice, and policy
> oblige us to defend them; that our navigation is not to be inter-
> rupted, or our merchants plundered with impunity to those who in-
> sult us;—that all unappropriated subsidies and votes of confidence
> are dangerous precedents, and always to be opposed; unless so ap-
> parent exigencies of affairs evidently and absolutely require such
> extraordinary and unconstitutional measures;—that the freedom of
> the press is the bulwark of religious and civil liberty; that as religion
> is of the utmost importance to every man, no person ought to suf-
> fer civil hardships for his religious persuasion, unless the tenets of
> his religion lead him to endeavour at the subversion of the estab-
> lishment in Church or State.

If this definition be compared with Molesworth's definition published in his Preface to the *Franco-Gallia,* it will be seen to have none
of the reforming character of the earlier statement. Only in his expressions about religious liberty, which may in a friend of Rundle's be
taken to mean all they say, did he in any way extend the doctrine to
which a Bolingbroke, a Newcastle, or a Walpole might have subscribed.
The passages might almost come from the *Dissertation on Parties* where

the Revolution was termed "a new Magna Carta." Nearly all effusions for dissent, against the standing army, on faction, on excise, on foreign relations, assumed such principles.[13]

The commentators outside of parliament on old or current political problems suggest almost as little revolutionary zeal as Talbot. They incorporated a certain amount of Whig history about the early Germans with some Harringtonian ideas and a tribute or two to natural law, but only very fragmentary suggestions about reform emerge from a study of these works. St. Amand had written against the Peerage Bill of Stanhope. Somewhat later he wrote an *Essay on the Legislative Power* (1725) without more than a glance at contemporary politics, but with deep admiration for "our ancestors in Germany," a free people with the right to assent or dissent to all laws, which might seem appropriate to Jefferson during the revolutionary years, but hardly affected English politics in the twenties. William Hay, whose support of a state-endowed church has already been noticed, was less of a historian and more of a politician than St. Amand. He was an advocate of a reform of the Poor Laws, a consolidation of financial and administrative units to level out the costs of relief, and a reform of the criminal law. He did not approve of that extensive use of capital punishment for which England was famous. Law was also the subject of similar suggestions in *An Essay Concerning the Original of Society* published shortly after these works by Hay and St. Amand. This essay was faintly reminiscent of Cumberland, though its author denied any "wild pursuit of nature." Government, the author felt, should be secular—the tone throughout is anticlerical—and should promote education and virtue.[14]

The thirties were not fertile in Whig essays, except for such periodicals as the dissenting *Old Whig* and the pseudo-Whig *Craftsman*. In the forties another crop of tracts and treatises was produced. *Harmony without Uniformity* (attributed to Henry Lord Paget), together with *Some Reflections on the Administration* (1740) possibly by the same author, shows signs of Shaftesbury's continuing influence in an insistence upon the connection of liberty and virtue and the slavery of mind that degenerate priests might promote. People of the lower rank, less biased by privilege, did for the most part pursue more steadily the interest of the country. Moreover, in distribution of talent, equality was not to be found, nor any relation between genius and wealth. Levelling principles were not sensible, since differences in rank, like seasons in the climate, were necessary.[15]

An Essay on Civil Government in Two Parts (1743) was longer than these tracts and was full of suggestions about remedies for the abuses in the constitution. The advantage of militia over standing army and of a free press over censorship were stressed. Toleration, even for Jews and atheists, was urged, together with a general encouragement of religion and honour. Locke's statement of the necessary limits of civil power was endorsed. Parliament should be triennial. The electors should guard against corruption and should choose men who were independent, both financially and spiritually—not "yea and nay men" of any minister. Faction should be avoided. Officers should be changed frequently. The welfare of the whole should outweigh the interest of any part of the body politic. Too numerous a nobility should be guarded against. The industrious and laborious part of the nation created its wealth. Their freedom should be secured. The author denied any desire to give the "rabble" power, but nonetheless emphasized the importance of many below the aristocracy. Good laws were necessary. England's laws badly needed revision and clarification. The writer was not, he remarked, a lawyer,[16] but was obviously a gentleman of some independence, a supporter of resistance rights, and of reforming ideas.

This author never went as far as *Liberty and Right,* the tract already mentioned, demanding abolition of primogeniture, redistribution of seats, voting by ballot, payment of members, annual parliaments, and a national militia, but this was probably written by a Scot and not by an English Whig. In the *Essay* of 1743 with all its suggestions there is very little of the republicanism that Perceval, later second earl of Egmont noticed as prevalent in his *Faction Detected* (1743) in the same year. He admitted that the people were still able to remove—or cause to be removed—a poor minister, and force a change of measure on a government. But he saw more danger in the decline of royal authority than in any encroachment on popular power. He pointed out that the country was wealthier and more populous than at the Revolution. The crown had lost its feudal dues and other revenues. Was not the balance of the constitution more likely to be disturbed by too much power in one part of its three bodies and the absence of royal authority? Placemen in parliament represented one way of righting that balance. Impossible schemes and utopian pretension should be avoided.[17]

Another fling at the evils of current parliamentary practice was taken by a friend of Franklin, James Ralph (1705–1762) in his *Use and Abuse of Parliaments* (1744). This was a curious work incorporating an essay by Thomas Rymer on parliament (which Ralph attributed to Sidney), and some lengthy reflections by Ralph himself which do little more than condemn bribery, the Septennial, and the "deafness" of parliaments to the cries of the people. Burghley's prophecy that parliament alone could undo parliament was all too likely, he thought, to be fulfilled, but the work prescribed no remedy to avert the coming catastrophe. Ralph's *History* (1744–46) was a better job. It was strongly Whig in tone, but presented a pretty fair account of the events of the last hundred years and was as scholarly as any of the histories of the time.

Ralph was associated in the early forties with Henry Fielding (1707–1754), the novelist, in a periodical called *The Champion*. Fielding had for some time been among the critics of Walpole's administration, and had been in a good deal of trouble in the thirties because of his satirical plays. In *The Champion,* in his novels and later works, a keen political and social conscience may be seen. In many ways Fielding is of all these Whigs the one most drastic in attacks on the evils of the times. When he became a stipendary magistrate, he made his peace with the government of the Pelhams, and was even to write a tribute to Walpole's virtues. But the inconsistency was not that of a Dyson or a Talbot. It sprang in part from the novelist's need for work, in part from his anxiety to be useful in the reformations that could be effected by the law as it then stood. No one can follow Fielding's work without realizing how soaked he was in the great classical tradition, in the works of Shaftesbury, and the political essays of English writers. Fielding was a friend of the third earl's nephew, James Harris, author of *Hermes*. If the use of the pseudonym, Lilbourne, had any significance in *The Champion*—and such names usually did—maybe both the partners in that venture were also steeped in the literature and the history of the Interregnum.

The Champion chiefly berated the government about a place bill, about fewer taxes, about sound foreign relations based on naval power —conventional opposition cries common to all Whigs, and even some Tories, around 1740. But much more than usual was made in it of the instruction of cities like Bristol, London, Edinburgh, and York to their representatives about the reforms demanded. The weight of the people was mentioned and, it was suggested, might if it were ever fully exerted, resolve current discontents. *The Champion* disliked the doctrine of "ubiquitarianism"—that is, whatever is, is right. And Fielding recurred to this in the second chapter of *Amelia* (1751). Persistent faults in administration revealed defects in the constitution itself. In spite of the "great lord Coke," who thought the English constitution unequaled and perfect, Fielding maintained that it needed reform.

The novelist laughed at the fourth estate, the "mobility," in the *Covent Garden Journal*, and outlined the achievements of Cade, Kett, and Tyler with no particularly favourable pen. He recognized the mob's power and, too, the necessities of the poor. He felt responsible for them. He feared them. Only poor relief kept them from overturning everything. He was equally keen sighted about the great whom he bitterly attacked for "power, pride, insolence and doing mischief to mankind." Every man, even if he had "sprung up out of the dunghill," was entitled to credit for his virtues. "Would it not be hard," he wrote in *Joseph Andrews* (1742) "that a man that hath no ancestors should therefore be rendered incapable of acquiring honour; when we see so many who have no virtue enjoying the honour of their forefathers?"[18] Fielding in such passages was the most radical of the Whigs of George II's reign.

By the middle of the eighteenth century the Whig saints and martyrs were less sharply defined. Sidney had become almost respectable. Harrington was endorsed by Jacobite and by oligarchical Whig alike, and was regarded a supporter of the Establishment by Anthony Ellys, and of property and the status quo by Bishop Squire. The Bishop's work represents a curious example of the use of Whig canonical writers.

The *English Constitution* and *An Essay on the Balance of Civil Power in England* (published together in 1753, but dating back to the late forties) revealed once again the impression made by Harrington upon all sections of Whig thought, and produced a spirited defense of the dependence of the Commons upon ministry and king through pensions and places. Squire's parentage was relatively humble. He received a good education and went to St. John's College, Cambridge, where his charming aunt's husband, John Newcome, was master 1734–1765. Newcome was an ardent Whig and tried to infect the college with his politics. He was friendly with Archbishop Herring, a "friend to mankind and liberty." Squire became Newcastle's chaplain and private secretary and was thus directly involved with the politics of the ruling oligarchy rather than with its critics. Other Cambridge friends were Middleton and William Bowyer, the printer.[19]

In his book Squire dissociated himself from any utopian or levelling schemes. Nevertheless, like Moses Lowman, whose *Dissertation on the Civil Government of the Hebrews* often was quoted throughout the book, he was deeply saturated with Harrington's work. The history was Whig. The perfection of the old German constitution had suffered no diminution when the Saxons brought it with them to Britain. Troubles, it was true, nearly overthrew the early English. The Danes ravaged the country. The Normans imposed wardship and other burdens. The folk assembly remained a vital tradition. To it went all landowners for whose ancestors there had been a distribution of land, and whose presence was a right, not a privilege, bestowed by the king. True, the dregs of the people, the vulgar herd, did not come, but throughout England's history Squire saw principles of equality and right in the ancient constitution. Since the civil wars of the seventeenth century, which he treated in Whiggish fashion, he saw a vast growth of the power of the Commons. What he feared in England was such a preponderance that the balance would be disturbed. He pointed to the troubles of Poland and Sweden as a lesson for those who argued that royal power and the size of the civil list were to be feared.

No one who has studied the eighteenth-century parliament can deny the element of truth in his contentions. Squire attacked the republicans for striking at the constitution, and for pulling down the throne itself, though in his historical account of the struggles of the seventeenth century he paid a tribute to their deep thought, moral character, and extensive reading. He then proceeded to prove the impossibility (as things were) of the king subverting the constitution. Squire realized that times and wisdom changed. "The maxims and measures of government must not only vary with the manners and circumstances of our own people; but must be adapted likewise in some degree to the changes which happen in the neighbouring nations," and therefore a standing army should now be kept. Squire denied utterly that the ministry had acted against the public interest and moreover asserted that should that be the case, neither places nor pensions would prevent courtiers from voting against the king and administration. Will, he asked the republicans of his own day, an exclusive place bill really lessen bribery and corruption? Will it not augment the value of the commodity? He quoted Harrington and Vertot on the dangers of an undisciplined integrated commonalty in Germany and Sweden, and suggested that the republicans would find the establishment of a commonwealth difficult in modern England—a vicious and corrupt people was incapable of bearing the agrarian that would be necessary. Squire thought that a true and consistent Whig was a balancer, a mediator, always against violence and against encroachment; a countryman under Henry VII, Charles, or James, a courtier under William or George, but still a friend to law, truth, justice, and the Establishment.[20]

History in England was always the stuff of which controversy was made, Petyt, Prynne, and Spelman wrote under the impetus of contemporary discussion under the Stuarts. In the eighteenth century there was an acceleration of interest in the authentic records of history, in the *Foedera* and the statutes, in the state papers of Thurloe, in the parliamentary histories, in the *Doomsday*. The tracts collected by Somers and Harley were published in the forties, among them some of the levelling Civil War pamphlets, as well as the familiar pieces of the reign of William III. Sales catalogues of eighteenth-century libraries often list boxes of tracts. Some, like that of the Anthony Collins' Library, list the pieces; others most tantalizingly do not. Ralph collected; Bridges collected; so did Devonshire. The shelves of Longleat were stuffed with pamphlets. Hollis picked up an astonishing number and either left them to his friends or gave them away to Harvard, to Dr. Williams' Library, to Switzerland. He had civil war tracts bound with his characteristic tooling, some of which are preserved in the Rothschild collection at Cambridge. Occasionally a reference was made to an attic full of old tracts. Blackburne read in such a one as a boy. The Thomason tracts had been hidden away, lost sight of, when Hollis's attention was drawn to them. In other words, the explosive material produced during the Civil War lay ready to hand and was, now that bitterness was past, circulating more freely. This interest and the exchange of old diaries and documents was on the part of many, men like Ducarel, simply antiquarian. For others, however—the Barons, Onslows, and Macaulays—it strengthened political sympathies and historical interpretations.[21]

Thomas Birch was of Quaker descent, but, conforming, he entered the church and took orders as early as 1728. He lost his wife after a year of marriage and devoted himself to his studies, becoming a member of the Royal Society of Antiquaries and a trustee of the British Museum, to which he left his estate. He published editions of Bayle, Milton, Thurloe, *An Inquiry into the Share Which Charles I Had* (1747), and many others. His interests may have been affected by his politics, but his politics appeared only in the mildest of forms. He was a Whig, but a trimming Whig. Commonwealth history owed much to him, but his introductions and memoirs lacked the vigour of Toland or Baron.[22] John Jortin (1698–1770), a Cambridge classmate of Blackburne, was also a clergyman of the church of England who devoted his life to scholarly pursuits. He loved liberty and his *Life of Erasmus* (1758) had sufficient interest to induce John Disney, Blackburne's son-in-law and a radical of the reign of George III, to write a memoir. Disney obviously regarded Jortin as a Unitarian not sufficiently clear-sighted to realize the anomaly of his position in the church. Whatever his views on the nature of certain Christian doctrines, his character was such that he received the enthusiastic patronage of Herring and Hardwicke. He was a poet, divine, philosopher, and musician. His *Erasmus* was long a standard work, among those who saw in it confirmation of their Unitarianism, and among scholars all over Europe.[23]

Conyers Middleton (1683–1750) was a Yorkshire man by birth and was educated at Trinity College, Cambridge, of which he was elected fellow in 1706. His extensive studies were said to have been stimulated in the first place by a contemptuous comment of Richard Bentley who dubbed him a "fiddler."[24] Whatever the cause, he became very learned and devoted his life to writing about ancient Rome, with digressions on the character of modern Romanism. He married three times. His last wife had lived with Mrs. Thomas Gordon, the former Mrs. Trenchard, before her marriage. Middleton was well-to-do and traveled. He was contentious, as his notorious dispute with Bentley showed, but was also a man with a number of friends and a list of those may throw some light on his political affiliations, although he never took any direct part in the disputes of his day. Sykes, Blackburne, and Jones whose ideas will be discussed later in this chapter, all men who were unorthodox and anxious to improve the Established Church, liked him. He was intimate with Coulson Fellowes, Member for Huntington, 1741–1761, "a hearty friend to religious and civil liberty" as well as a well-wisher to the improvement of agriculture, arts, and sciences.[25] Jones evidently regarded Fellowes as one of his disciples, and in general the evidence would place him among the discontented or republican Whigs of the day. Middleton, though widely regarded as almost an atheist, retained his tie with the Anglican church and devoted his pen to antiquarian pursuits and the safe hobby of antipapistical writing. He discovered an astonishing similarity between ancient heathen superstition and those of contemporary Christian Rome, using this for an effective but indirect attack on all orthodoxy. To him all priestcraft, all ceremony, and all miracles, Christian, Jewish, Roman, or Egyptian, were a part of the same family of outmoded and unreasonable ideas used to tyrannize over the minds and actions of men.[26]

Middleton was said to be hard to read. Although progress through his chapters is thoroughly impeded by quotations, he is still worth the effort, and in his own time attracted many readers. He admired the popular elements in ancient Rome, and citizens like Cicero, and was a worthy successor to Moyle and to the seventeenth-century translators and commentators. In the Roman Senate he found an absence of hereditary distinctions, a way open for the advancement of merit and the infusion of new blood. The Abbé Vertot—one of the most popular writers of the first half of the eighteenth century and author of books on revolutions in Rome, Portugal, and Sweden, among others—was consulted by Stanhope at the time of the drafting of his Peerage Bill about the method of recruitment for the Roman Senate. Middleton wrote later on the same theme but emphasized much more strongly the popular elements in the Roman system and criticized Vertot's suggestions which were published at the end of a late edition of his book, *Revolutions of the Roman Republic.* According to the English writer, the

Roman people took a much more vigorous part in the government. They were a court of ultimate appeal. There were party struggles, of course, necessary effects of freedom, but on the whole so long as the republic lasted, the people's role in it was a source of strength and a defense against tyranny. The Senate might act without them, but they were the dernier ressort.[27]

Middleton's arguments about Catholicism need not concern us here, but his aversion to it was grounded not only on a dislike of pagan superstition and idolatry in its liturgy and creeds, but in its calculated support of despotic power, and its intolerance. Like Hoadly, Middleton believed passionately that "truth was never known to be on the persecuting side."[28] Modern Italy provided a moral for his countrymen. Once upon a time the Romans had written of the barbarousness and misery of England, and as one reads, he said,

> One cannot help reflecting on the surprising fate and revolutions of Kingdoms; how *Rome,* once the mistress of the world, the seat of arts, empire and glory, now lies sunk in sloth, ignorance and poverty; enslaved to the most cruel, as well as the most contemptible of Tyrants, *Superstition and religious Imposture:* while this remote Country, anciently the jest and contempt of *the polite Romans,* is become the happy seat of liberty, plenty and letters; florishing in all the arts and refinements of civil life; yet running perhaps the same course, which *Rome* itself had run before it; from virtuous industry to wealth; from wealth to luxury; from luxury to impatience of discipline and corruption of morals; till by a total degeneracy and loss of virtue, being grown ripe for destruction, it falls, prey at last to some hardy oppressor, and, with the loss of liberty, losing everything else, that is valuable, sinks gradually again into it's original barbarism.

Middleton distinguished between revolutions which brought about decline and fall, and those which were "restoration to a primitive state of virtue" where true merit received its reward and freedom, though not equality, was enjoyed by all.[29]

The emphasis on continuity and recurrence in history was not original with Middleton, but it was made more popular by him. He did much to draw English attention to the parallel between England and Rome on which Edward Wortley Montagu (1713–1776) was to draw in his *Reflections on the Rise and Fall of the Antient Republicks Adapted to the Present State of Great Britain* (1759). Montagu, one of the more extraordinary of eighteenth-century eccentrics, was not as serious a student as Middleton, but in this volume he wrote with some learning and liveliness. It has been suggested that Montagu could not have produced this work, and that credit should go to his tutor, the Reverend John Forster, who claimed it after his pupil's death. Since Montagu's name appeared in the four English and two continental editions of the *Antient Republicks,* it may, without prejudice to other claimants, be used here. Montagu was Member of Bossiney at the time of the debates on Pitt's Militia Bill, which in part, at any rate, suggested the theme of the book and the role of militia and standing army respectively in the rise and decline of states. The dangers of corruption in Athens and Rome were described and the effects of a standing army in Denmark in more recent times pointed out. A national interest in military matters was essential or England, like Carthage, might fall a victim to her own wealth and luxury. He pointed to the 'Forty-five as a horrible foretaste of what would happen if a militia along the lines suggested by Pitt and supported by such men as Charles Sackville, duke of Dorset, were not seriously adopted. This militia should be not from the dregs of the people, but from the gentry. The landed interest of Rome had flourished when it had a general naturalization of foreigners and a strong national army, before it attained undue wealth.

Middleton and Montagu stressed the evils of faction, but in spite of a comment on Solon's law against neutrality in public concerns, Montagu never seems to have been as aware as Middleton and Edward Spelman, a contemporary classical scholar, of the inevitability of party in a free state. He suggested disunion and faction, the bane of stability, as the chief reason for the decline of Carthage,[30] though mercenary troops and the pursuit of wealth through commerce played a part in this also. Spelman who, like Middleton, entered the lists against Vertot's denial of the popular element in the renewal of the Roman Senate, was a proponent of annual parliaments and equal representation and tucked these recommendations into his introduction to a *Fragment Out of the Sixth Book of Polybius* (1743), as well as in a short review of Nathaniel Hooke's *Observations on the Answers to Vertot* in 1758. Throughout the classical commentators of the time, Gordon, Middleton, Spelman, Chapman, and Montagu, to name no more, runs this thread of moralizing. The opportunity was too good to miss. Rebuttals like Hooke's were regarded as further challenge, and a whole philosophy about contemporary conditions may be discovered in these classical studies.[31]

Lawyers of this period were protectors of tradition and contributed little to the development of liberalism in any way. Blackstone occasionally surprises with a phrase—the game laws as a "bastard slip" of the old laws of the forest—but unlike his seventeenth-century predecessors, seldom or never interpreted the constitution in a popular way. Hardwicke and Mansfield were great judges. The former inherited the integrity of the Somers connection, but none of its creative political inspiration. Mansfield's Somerset decision was striking and dramatized the belief of every Englishman in his personal freedom on English soil, but in all other respects Mansfield was an enemy to reform and could even be described as reactionary in his attitude toward the habeas corpus debates of the fifties. Three lawyers of the period—Jekyll, Ryder, and Foster—came out of the dissenting tradition. The first certainly remained a consistent Whig. Ryder became a good government official. Foster, Recorder of Bristol, and Justice of King's Bench in 1745, was as close an inheritor of the tradition of Hale and of Coke. He never failed to support his sectarian friends. His remarks about the matter of indefeasible right were a good treatment of the subject and were remarkably free from the exaggerations and misconceptions of popular Whig treatises. He opposed the creation of new crimes by legal decision. On the other hand, he supported the legality of impressment of mariners, and utterly ignored any possibility of infringement of natural rights and individual liberties in connection with arguments about it.

The law of the period worked against liberty rather than for it. In the hands of the country justices the game laws, which reached their apogee in the reign of George I, became an expression of class privilege much more distinctly than any earlier English custom. There were some protests about these laws. *An Alarm* in 1757, and half a dozen other tracts, noticed the cruelty of the system. Pownall, as will be noticed, remarked on the absence of any such regulations in the New World as amongst its advantages, but on the whole lawyers and laymen alike ignored the question, except to provide useful handbooks to the statutory regulations and to notice that the gentry had taken over from the monarch's control of the wild life of the kingdom.[32]

Anglican Innovators and Reformers — The Hoadlyites

There can be no question that the clergy of the eighteenth century contributed more to the development of the radical tradition than the lawyers and constitutional writers, and their work affords a great contrast to that of the legal luminaries. Much abuse has been heaped on the church of the period, while its many creditable achievements are often forgotten. Lacking a Laud, an Andrews, a Sheldon, a Tillotson, it produced a Butler, Berkeley, Hoadly, Watson, and Law. In the intellectual activity of the time these had their part. The theological controversies of the age, whether dissenting or Anglican, concerned much the same matter. The innovators in religion inclined toward liberal political theories. There were anomalies in England, as on the continent, where a pope, Benedict XIV, was among the philosophers. Not all Latitudinarians were inclined towards political reform. Bolingbroke was a freethinker and a Tory, albeit one who could put Scripture to his own uses and cite the canonical Whig writers in defense of his own devious ways. Nevertheless, among the Anglicans the active and questioning debaters were generally the supporters of revolution politics of civil and religious liberty.

Since the government included and supported their church, the conformers looked on themselves as an integral part of the constitution. They did not suggest a retreat from their privileged position. Their efforts, looked at from the political point of view, were of at least three different kinds. Whigs in the church endorsed the Revolution, the Toleration Act, the Union, and in general the Hanoverian system against Tory detractors, but were, like their lay associates, unwilling to change or develop any part of the Settlement. These were vastly in the majority. There was a second group, of whom Hoadly and his disciples are representative, who were prepared to concede vastly greater toleration to all outside their church. Differences were slighter than the common bounds of Protestantism or, as time went on, of common recognition of the religion of nature-reason or what you will. Some of the tracts written by these men went so far in favour of concession to dissent, for example, and spoke so eloquently of the heavenly kingdom of Christ where all believers would live in peace, that it is sometimes difficult to see why they at the same time remained in the Establishment.

A further group, not entirely the same though obviously nearer the Hoadlyites than the orthodox, favoured a reform of the Church itself. This idea can be traced back to Tillotson and the talk of a comprehension. It gathered force from the examples of men like Dr. Samuel Clarke who preferred not to reiterate assent to certain parts of the liturgy, and from a literature of which Jones's *Free and Candid Disquisitions* is a good example, and contains suggestions for considerable and quite radical changes. The well-known Feathers Petition for modification of discipline and dogma grew out of this, and its failure caused an exodus from the church of some important characters of the latter half of the century. Lindsey, Disney, Frend, and others left the church, and the Unitarians of a conforming background made common cause with those from the old sects. Among this group there was actually no move to break the bond between church and state. In this sense they may be said to be nearer the position of the Puritans who wished to mold the church to their own pattern in the days of the struggle with Charles, rather than with those Independents who advocated a divorce between matters spiritual and temporal. Times had changed. In 1774, when the Essex Street congregation was formed, its motives were respected, if deplored, and the illegality of its position led to no government recriminations. Burke was later to abuse them and to associate their independence in matters of discipline with their libertarianism in politics and to frustrate, because of this evil association, attempts to legitimatize their dissent. So once more the connection of Commonwealthmen with the spiritual nonconformist must be examined.

To do this it will not be necessary to describe the debates about the Trinity, about the Athanasian Creed, or about some of the Thirty-Nine Articles. These have been amply discussed. Here a few clergymen will be mentioned and a brief indication given of their role in movements regarded as leading to greater freedom in church and state. In a concluding chapter the Unitarian group of the reign of George III will be dealt with in relation to current reform movements. Only a few of the mid-century figures will be described, in relation to two of the groups specified. A fourth category of clergymen, the teachers, will be illustrated by reference to two men, John Clarke of Hull and Edmund Law (later Bishop of Carlisle) of Cambridge.

Most of these clergymen were educated at Cambridge in the days when Samuel Clarke and Isaac Newton were its most famous representatives in England and abroad. Anthony Ashley Sykes (1684–1756) was a student at Benet College under the famous Charles Kidman (B.D., 1694), one of the first to introduce the reading of Locke's essay at the university. Sykes embraced Locke's philosophy. He was vehemently antipapistical and wrote a violent tract, reprinted twice in the century, against popery. He defended Whiston and pled the cause of the Quakers. Government was a trust for the general good of the public. Sykes was a sincere believer in the truth of the Christian religion and wrote against the heresies of Collins and later of Hume. Though he was a protagonist of Samuel Clarke, of Hoadly, of Rundle whose suspected lack of orthodoxy resulted in exile to an Irish bishopric rather than the English see of Gloucester, he was to be reproached late in the century by his memorialist, Disney, with a lack of liberality in his theology. Disney, in short, would have had him declare his Unitarianism, but made some allowance for the times in which Sykes lived.[33]

Sykes was an advocate of charity; no schism was so damnable as a sinful life, no heresy so destructive as wicked actions. He supported the repeal of the Schism and Occasional Conformity Acts in 1718 and continued his efforts into the thirties when Stanhope was dead, and almost no one in government office was friendly to the dissenters. Disney reported that he favoured the Septennial Act, and commented that Sykes thus revealed ignorance about the nature of representation. Sykes's political activity was chiefly directed towards increased toleration and it was on this that he wrote most interestingly.

He pointed out the weakness of dissent and the low social status of most dissenters, with scarcely a peer or even a gentleman among them. He brushed aside arguments about fundamental law and the Union. That is, he disagreed with those who regarded any change in church and state as a departure from the Settlement after the Revolution. Sykes regarded the Union with Scotland as an act or treaty made to secure the Kingdom from civil war. He did not conceive of it as preventing an extension of religious liberty. He pointed out that the Test, for whose repeal dissent was asking in the thirties, was originally passed not against them, but against papists. He believed every Englishman had a right both to his own opinion and to the service of his country, were he fitted to perform it in a political capacity. Popery, because of its old associations, was in a different category from Protestantism. Keeping the dissenters out of office was wrong. Episcopacy would not be endangered if dissenters were relieved from the penal laws. He combined practical arguments—repeal would in fact make no difference—with an insistence on natural right. If physical deformities like squints didn't disqualify, why should mental quirks like erroneous beliefs? Sykes was a vigorous Whig. His chief friend, an Essex neighbour who shared his politics, to whom he left his estate, was Robert Bristow (1712–1776) M. P. Winchelsea 1738–1741, and 1747–1761.[34]

Other Cambridge men who supported Hoadly were less prominent, like Thomas Pyle (1674–1756) and Thomas Herne (d. 1722).[35] John Jackson (1686–1763) of Rossington was as much read as Sykes. He was a Yorkshireman and a protégé of Samuel Clarke, whom he succeeded at Wigston's Hospital. This job required no further subscription to the Articles and was thus attractive to men like Jackson and Clarke, and in an earlier time to Chillingworth. In his contribution to *The Old Whig* (according to Nichols), Jackson indeed advocated the abolition of all impositions and subscriptions. Like his colleagues on that paper, he was a strenuous asserter of his own rights and a zealous advocate of those of others. He resented all inquisitions. The Scripture should be the rule of faith. It was plain and easy to follow in all things essential. Society demanded the sacrifice of freedom to prevent injury to life and property. All might read, or play as preferred. Any difference should be tolerated except Toryism and Catholicism.[36]

The state, maintained Jackson's book, *The Grounds of Civil and Ecclesiastical Government,* should abide by natural law as well as by those laws passed by its legislature. Natural rights should not be ignored. Public welfare was the supreme test. Civil law was relative. Time and circumstance altered many things. There could be no divine right in government. No oath should be conceived that would bind anyone to accept destruction passively. The obligations of civil law ceased when the ruler ruled badly. Government then dissolved. In such a situation the major part of the legislative body must decide what to do. Religious behaviour was a matter for the individual. Though episcopacy seemed to Jackson the best form of church government, he did not think it essential. Presbyterian baptism must be regarded as valid. All sects had a right to toleration and should be independent of the civil government in their establishments. Atheists and papists presented a somewhat different problem—in this Jackson was not ahead of his age. But in criticizing William Law's rebuttal of Hoadly he did admit that if absurd tenets, like those of a Muggleton ranter or Quaker could be sincerely held, so might the beliefs of Turks, Deists, Fifth Monarchy men, and others. Since men were equal in nature and rights and those rights included civil liberty, property, and religious freedom—all should be free to do anything that did not endanger the state. The state should rest on consent and the representation of all who lived under it.

Jackson thus supported a full measure of toleration and was very much the disciple of Dr. Clarke. Like him, he insisted that moral freedom lay not in the power of doing contrary actions with the same indifference, but in being endowed with reason, the perception between good and evil, and the power to choose good or bad deeds. Cato (Trenchard), Mandeville, and Collins would make the difference between a virtue and vice itself precarious.[37]

William Hopkins (1706–1786) was in many ways a younger Jackson, but his life was uneventful and the tone of his tracts less violent. He was an Oxford graduate and became Vicar of Bolney and master of Cuckfield School. His chief works were *Appeal to the Common Sense of all Christian People* (1754), *Serious and Free Thoughts* (1755), and *The Trinitarian Controversy Reviewed* (1760). He emphasized the right of all to judge for themselves, the privilege of rational creation. He supported John Jones's *Free and Candid Disquisitions,* and was later to sign the Feathers Petition. He was almost a Unitarian. His review of the controversy about the Trinity was a moderate plea for some modification of the *Book of Common Prayer.* He brought up all the authorities of the period as support for his views from Newton through Clarke, Hoadly, Taylor, Sykes, to Edmund Law. He never, however, left the Church.[38]

John Jones of Alconbury (1700–1770), a Welshman, was the most vigorous of the reforming group before Blackburne. He took his degree at Oxford in about 1721 and left the university about 1727. It is possible he knew Hopkins, though younger than himself, at college. Not only a would-be reformer of the church, he was also an antiquarian and collector of memorials of his contemporaries, a number of which were printed by Nichols, and many others which may be traced in the British Museum and in extracts printed in such places as *The Gentleman's Magazine.* He was a friend of Birch, and much of this material appeared in a series of letters to him which centered on his own plans and works, but which provide a good deal of material about other notables of the day. He thought Speaker Onslow, Lord Lonsdale, Edmund Law, James West of Lincoln's Inn, and Coulson Fellowes would be interested in his book. In fact, though some of these may have read it sympathetically, his *Disquisitions* stirred up little discussion and attention, and it was his admirer, a Cambridge contemporary, Blackburne, who really publicized his views in the next reign.

The plan was to attract into the church as many persons as possible. Times had changed; a new translation of the Bible was desirable; a new and shorter liturgy should be drawn up. The Athanasian creed should be omitted and certain services shortened for special occasions. Jones questioned the value of ecclesiastical courts. He advocated a discipline which "inflicts no fines, obliges to no suit, requires no cost, deprives of no civil liberty, nor is attended with any corporal punishment." Jones did not think the reformation of the church had ever been brought to perfection. Alterations might be necessary as allowed under the constitution. He felt strict uniformity was not essential, but a greater degree might well be achieved by dispensing with contentious ceremonies. Jones seems to have been optimistic at first that his ideas would meet with approval. He was encouraged by his correspondence with Birch and his conversations with Fellowes. His own sincerity in his design of advancing true Christianity upon a Scriptural, i.e., a "rational bottom," is manifest. The *Monthly Review* supported him and expressed the hope that his schemes would receive favourable attention. But he made no impression on those important enough to help his cause, though it would be legitimate to regard the signatories of the Feathers Petition in 1772 as his spiritual disciples.[39]

Another Oxford and Whiggish clergyman was Edward Bentham (1707–1776), author of the mediocre *Moral Philosophy* which revealed an acquaintance with some of the literature of revolution politics, but which was largely hortatory. Bentham preached to the House of Commons on the hundredth anniversary of Charles I's martyrdom, and the sermon was printed subsequently. Here his Whiggery was more pronounced, and he pointed out that the kind of exorbitant claims made by a Charles or a Cromwell were always fatal to their governments. The wise magistrate did not encroach on liberty. Christianity was not concerned with forms.[40]

Unfortunately for the student of ideas, the teaching of many of the schoolmasters and professors of the eighteenth century was poorly recorded. One famous master, John Clarke (1687–1734) of Hull, wrote *An Essay upon Study* which recommended as many Commonwealth ideas as any of the lectures in dissenting academies. Clarke was born in Yorkshire and his father was said to have been an innkeeper. He studied at St. John's College, Cambridge, took his M.A. in 1710, and became a firm disciple of Locke and Newton. Clarke had many ideas on education in general, and as many specific recommendations on reading. He did not consider all men equal in ability but felt that differences between them were due only to their education. Many blunders had been made in this. He listed them. Teachers should be better paid and selected more carefully for their virtues, for their acquaintance with English geography, philosophy, and Latin. Their services were valuable. Learning should be more widely diffused. The gentry needed to study to enable them to help those poorer than themselves. Ladies should study history—Echard, Molesworth, Rapin, as well as *Don Quixote, Télémaque,* Dryden, and Pope. All should beware of reading without thinking. The well-to-do should read all kinds of books, orthodox and heterodox, Anglican and dissenting. Certain authors should be read for their style—Tillotson, *The Spectator,* and the like. As the essays of the Hull teacher are read, it becomes a little difficult to decide on the age group to which Clarke was mainly directing his attention. He thought usually in terms of the boys of his own school, wandering off into generalization about study in general as the spirit moved him.

The recommended reading was interesting. Renaissance science and philosophy should be studied as well as Reformation history. Locke, Newton, Descartes, Clarke, and Hutcheson were required. He endorsed Locke, Puffendorf, Buchanan, Mariana, and Tyrrell on government. Students were to study the rise of popery, the downfall of liberty, and the decay of arts and sciences with their subsequent renewal after Protestantism. They were to read modern history, modern philosophy, and its discussions of liberty and virtue. Clarke preferred small private boarding schools to others. He obviously intended the course to fit his students for life and for those problems of morality and politics which they would encounter as they grew up.[41]

Another school outside of London, the free school at Leeds, was run by Thomas Barnard (1712–50). Two sermons by this headmaster, funeral orations for Lady Elizabeth Hastings (1742), and for Henry Lodge (1718) reveal nothing about Barnard's character or work. Baron, Lindsey, and possibly Lee, may have picked up their ideas in their native Yorkshire, outside the school, or at Glasgow and Cambridge respectively. But the connection of Yorkshire and the Commonwealthmen of the eighteenth century is strong, and has never been entirely explained.[42]

Hackney, nearer London, was famous for at least two teaching institutions in this century. The later Unitarian dissenting academy need not be described. An earlier school there was run by Benjamin Morland of Jesus College, Cambridge, whose daughter married Henry Newcome (1689–1756), son of a Tory parson at Hastings, and himself at Emmanuel College, Cambridge, in 1706 and father of Peter (Queens, 1731). These two Newcomes ran the school from 1714 onwards; yet a third generation continued the connection until 1803. Henry Newcome's will wrote of him as a doctor of laws and mentioned property in the parish which would go to the son who carried on the school. The most famous student of Hackney was the dramatist, John Hoadly, and this association has led to frequent errors about Bishop Benjamin's connection with the school. A Reverend Peter Newcome was educated under his relative, according to Nichols. So was John Luther of Essex. So far, at least, I see no reason to suppose these Newcomes to have been anything but rather conventional teachers and citizens, but the connection might be worth pursuing.[43]

Cambridge in the eighteenth century obviously contained many teachers and scholars whose influence was likely to be progressive. Men of the Newton connection, like Samuel Clarke, Roger Cotes, Whiston, and Smith (Cote's cousin who was master of Trinity in mid-century) were unlikely to be convinced that all that was, was right. They were trained to observe and to consider new as well as old facts and ideas. The early teachers of Locke, such as Kidman; R. Laughton, the "Pupilmonger" of Clare,[44] and their successors, made Cambridge far more than his own alma mater, Oxford, the home of the Lockians. Formal instruction is less easy to classify at Cambridge than at Glasgow or other Scotch institutions. The tutors' work was not susceptible to documentation, and most of the teaching at the university was given by them. There is no doubt, however, that the radicalism of the reign of George III at Cambridge was not purely coincidental. Blackburne, Clarkson, Jones, Grafton, Savile, Watson, Jebb, Disney, Capel Lofft, and Baynes, to note only a few, were all educated there, and not only came under the general influence of Whig ideas and the effects of Newtonian and Lockian philosophies, but also were in colleges where some teacher, tutor, or master seems to have talked and thought about political matters.

Edmund Law and John Brown

Much the most important of the Cambridge Anglicans and because of his writings outside of the university, was Edmund Law (1703–1787) who, through the influence of his pupil, Augustus Fitzroy, duke of Grafton (1735–1811), was created Bishop of Carlisle, 1768. Law was born in Cartmel in Lancashire. His father was a clergyman and sent his son to St. John's College, Cambridge, in 1720. Edmund was later elected fellow of Christ's College. His thesis was thought to have been Socinian, but Archbishop Herring, always liberal and appreciative of good Christians, secured the degree for him. In 1737 Law obtained a living in Cumberland and there married Mary Christian. Her ancestor had taught the great Archbishop of Dublin, William King, whose *Origin of Evil* had already been translated by Law, a work which brought him instant recognition. Law became Archdeacon of Carlisle in 1743. In 1745 he published *Considerations on the State of the World with Regard to the Theory of Religion* (1745) which, altered and enlarged, went into eight editions in English and another one in German. In 1754 Law returned to Cambridge and stayed there until his death in 1787. He wrote and published a dissertation, *Upon the Sleep of the Soul*. He was master of Peterhouse and University Librarian. He became a bishop in 1768. He edited Locke's works in 1777, reprinted in 1794 and 1801, and he wrote various briefer tracts. Among his students and disciples were Jebb, Disney, Paley, Wilson (1741–1793), and James Adair. He was much beloved by his family and numerous friends amongst whom must be included Jortin; Taylor, the translator of Demosthenes; David Hartley, another Lockian; and Archdeacon Blackburne. We are told that he was a small man but well formed. He had gentle manners, and a mild and tranquil disposition. His voice was never raised. He had an utter dislike of mixed companies:

> Next to his books, his chief satisfaction was in the serious conversation of a literary companion, or in the company of a few friends. In this sort of society he would open his mind with great unreservedness, and with a peculiar turn and sprightliness of expression.

Jones testified that he was modest, free, open, and devoid of ceremony.

> No man formed his own conclusions with more freedom, or treated those of others with greater candour and equity. He never quarrelled with any person for differing with him . . . he was zealously attached to religious liberty because he thought that it leads to truth; yet from his heart he loved peace.

Such a man was likely to have much influence without becoming a center of controversy. Even after his elevation to the See of Carlisle, he continued to spend all but the summer in the university. His personality won adherents to his views and his writings enjoyed a much larger audience.[45]

He believed in the necessity for reviewing ancient customs and constitutions. He refused to live altogether in the past and by its laws. That could be a disease. All should consider the present, and children should be brought up to enquire freely into all questions whilst avoiding judgment on those who differed from them.[46]

Law early adopted the rational theology of Samuel Clarke and the profound optimism of Archbishop King. He leaned definitely towards the Socinian or Unitarian side of orthodoxy. He also held a belief in the "sleep of the soul," as he termed it, which was peculiarly his own. Christ would at his second coming restore the dead of the human species by an act of power to life and consciousness; without this miracle they would remain forever insensible in the death brought on mankind by Adam's sin. Religion was important. Happiness depended upon it. Law's translation of King's book on the difficult problem of evil and of sin was one attempt to justify the ways of God to man by clearing away misconceptions, and to present a system built upon "such principles as are perfectly consistent with Revelation." Argument merely *ad ignorantiam* would not convince an infidel. For that a true notion of human liberty must be substituted for the false. King had found that equality of perfection in creation was neither possible nor desirable. Sensation could not be all of a kind—thus all could not be agreeable. Happiness depended on the due exercise of the faculties given man by God. There should be some competition between superior and inferior by which these would be brought nearer than if everything were entirely determined by fate and necessity. Pain and sin thus had a place in the natural order. There was no need to assume the existence of an evil principle in the world. A mixture of nonexistence would take its place. God gave existence to man, but did not give more than possible in the general state of the universe. Diversity brought different conveniences. Mankind had a choice of action. He could choose aims, and could degrade himself by his own deeds. No one should grumble since he could maintain a good and improve a less agreeable position. Law saw in the contest of good and evil something for the benefit of the universe, which was thus better ordered than if all were fixed by fate and necessity.[47]

What Law's share in the "Dissertation" written by John Gay (1699–1745) was cannot be precisely determined, but he certainly shared its views. Gay had entered Sidney Sussex in the year he came to St. John's. He was ordained and became parson of a west-country living. Very little else is known of him but this one important work. Priestley regarded his observations on the association of ideas as little more than conjectures. Nevertheless he placed him between Locke and David Hartley in the development of that theory. Gay deduced all passions and affections from association, but he separated from this the workings in human nature of a love of happiness. Hutcheson had seen a moral sense directing the choice of mankind; Gay saw nature, reason, truth, the common good, and the will of God all working together. What was the secret of choice? Virtue must be approved and there should be some criterion of conduct which might guide that selection. Self-interest might prove to be the determining factor. All man desired happiness and might by association find that happiness and virtue for one and for all were closely knit into a golden chain. There must be a rule of life directing the actions of all rational creatures with respect to their own and each other's happiness. Virtue thus implied obligation and approbation. Men were naturally inclined to some things. With others reward and punishment might form association, and habit signposts to good conduct.[48] Hartley, considering Gay's work, eventually came to believe that all intellectual pleasures and pains, all phenomena of memory, imagination, volition, reasoning, and all other mental operations were only different modes or cases of the association of ideas—a single property admitting of great variety. Judgment became perception of universal concurrence of ideas. Priestley made Hartley's ideas intelligible.[49]

The impression made by Law's notes in the edition of King's book, and by his later writings, is that he was less concerned with necessity and free will than with a doctrine of gradualness in all things. He had an optimism which overcame all apparent consistencies and defects, and a conviction of the wide variety apparent in all creation. Revelation had been vouchsafed gradually, more to some nations and to a greater extent in some ages than in others. Christianity had not yet reached "its mature state" and its fullest perfection. No church had a monopoly of truth, though one might be better than another. Nevertheless we should always be "cautious to guard against implicit prejudice of every kind." All persons were equally part of creation, and they had equal natural rights and equally desired happiness.

> The great offence which in all nations and in all ages had hindered the propagation of the gospel of truth, has been a hypocritical zeal to secure by force a fictitious uniformity of opinion, which is indeed impossible in nature.

Law was prepared to find disagreement with his views, and to make allowances for very wide divergence. A decent uniformity might be desirable at certain times, but could not be expected of savages. They could not become Christian before becoming rational and civilized.[50]

Although truth appeared but slowly, progress was being made. The world was improving. "Say not thou," he preached, "what is the cause that former days were better than these or thou dost not enquire wisely concerning this." There was talk of bad times, but the arts, sciences, even the governments had made great strides. The intellectual world had been vastly extended with the work of Bacon, Locke, Newton, and Hartley. The more that was known of the universe, the more its beauty and symmetry appeared. There were more people in the world and modern governments were better calculated for the good of the governed. People were more public-spirited, more liberal, and less warlike. Progress meant change and this must continue. Institutions must be reviewed for possible solecisms. This would mean variety, but Law was continually emphasizing "the grand principles of human liberty which renders it morally impossible for anything relating to the mind or circumstance of mankind to remain long in a state of perfect uniformity."[51]

Law seemed to have gathered in himself the moderation of the Platonists, the scientific philosophy of Newton, and the ideals of Locke, and to have formed from them a body of liberal and optimistic reflections which stimulated and inspired his circle. His chaplain, John Disney, became one of a large band of Unitarians and reformers in the reign of George III. Peterhouse, of which he was master, was also the alma mater of men like Liddell, Cavendish, Lowther, Meredith, Tierney, and Lofft. Paley's tribute to Law revealed the affection which his personality aroused and, explained the liberality of at least a section of Cambridge in the half century after his return to it in the fifties.

Yet another Cantabrigian, John Brown (1715–1765),[52] must be noticed. Since he considered the education at both the universities poor, perhaps it would be unfair to stress his connection with one of them. Oxford concentrated too much on classics. Cambridge paid too little attention to style and belles-lettres. Brown was born in Northumberland in 1715. His father was a clergyman of Scotch ancestry. He was at St. John's College 1732–1735, obtained his M.A. in 1739 and his D.D. in 1755. Brown was ordained and held first a minor canonry at Carlisle, and then moved to Westmorland and wrote *An Essay on Satire* (1745) commemorating the recently deceased Alexander Pope. Warburton, favourably mentioned in the poem, sought out its author and became his patron and adviser, although Brown was later to be disappointed at the result of his suggestions. *Essays on the Characteristics* (1757), refuting Shaftesbury's idea that ridicule was the test of truth and stating that virtue was the conformity of private and public affections, made some reputation for its author who, as we read the work, seemed to be hardly less utilitarian than his subject.

After making the acquaintance of David Garrick, Brown wrote two plays which were produced: *Barbarossa* (1755) and *Athelstan* (1756). He obtained the living of Great Horksley in Essex, and a few years later became Vicar of Newcastle-on-Tyne. There he committed suicide shortly after refusing a tempting offer to journey into Russia and advise Catherine II about education. A very qualified appreciation of Brown by Thomas Hollis was published in the *St. James Chronicle.* Brown is chiefly known for his *Estimate,* first published in 1757 at the time when the war was going very badly, and reprinted at least ten times in the next year with rather bewildering changes of publishers and format. This *Estimate,* heavily annotated by the donor, was given to Harvard by Hollis, who endorsed the gloomy tone of criticism in the book but held somewhat different views about the proposed remedies.[53]

The manners and principles of countries were, Brown thought, more important than their laws. A country with poor laws but good principles was in a better position than one in the contrary state. France had a bad constitution, unlike Britain, which enjoyed a good one, but she had retained her military spirit and therefore constituted a real threat to the effete, luxurious British. Brown examined the parlous state of his country in 1757 in order to point out ways of remedying the trouble. England had virtues, of course, some induced by soil and climate. The English system of justice was excellent. Hardwicke was a good chancellor. There were many foundations for charity. Englishmen were humane and strong for liberty. Nevertheless, the ancient virtues were more than offset by present servility, luxury, effeminacy, and lack of valour. The youth of the nation trifled away their time and neglected serious study. Military spirit was dead. The progress of industry and commerce which had at first induced frugality and diligence had now brought wealth, avarice, and over-refinement of living.

Luxury had corrupted the nation. The gentry who had profited almost without effort were become effeminate. Religion had declined and public morals had sharply deteriorated. The country was disunited. It was torn by factional strife. Brown distinguished between good and bad parties. Difference of opinion could be of value where the subject was only truth and the public welfare, but factional seeking after place and pension could only be condemned.

Parliament since the Revolution had been in a situation of great power. No tyranny threatened and public spirit had declined. Power had brought with it the disposal of lucrative offices. This in turn led to strife and corruption. Brown's remedy seemed to be a self-denying ordinance about strong liquor and gaming, and a new resolution for public service. Hollis, in the copy he sent to Harvard, suggested a reform of the constitution—Parliament by Counties—as a necessary cure. Brown showed common sense in his remarks about Walpole. He admitted his use of corruption but pointed out that he did not start it, nor could he have corrupted an upright people. Walpole was a peace minister without a very heroic conception of his country's role. The times in 1757 needed a great man who would lead the country into new ways. Brown suggested that the commonalty was not to blame, but those who led them, and it was to those who should be the leaders that he addressed his exhortations.

Like Adam Ferguson, Brown was convinced that reformation was possible. He did not agree with "the trite and hackneyed comparison between the life of man, and of states in which it is pretended that they both proceed in the same irrevocable manner from infancy to maturity, from maturity to death, a comparison perhaps as groundless as it is common." The human body had in it the seeds of dissolution, but society had no inevitable tendency to decay, though accident, disease, or external violence might weaken or destroy it. Englishmen should examine the effects of too much wealth. They should control and check the vices that had become obvious. Some expedients, like the establishment of police in London, might help, but Brown put his chief faith in a spiritual revival, perhaps stimulated by his book and, most important, led and directed by a great minister. Brown's philosophy of history and his analysis of principles, his freedom from complacency about the workings of the old constitution are interesting.

His economic reflections were worthless. His politics were those of the pulpit and the soap box. He reflected the change in the mood of eighteenth-century England—perhaps marked the end of the Augustan calm.[54]

Thomas Pownall's Principles of Polity

In many ways the most interesting of eighteenth-century republicans was Thomas Pownall (1722–1805), civil servant, colonial administrator, and writer. He was born in Lincolnshire and educated first at the Lincoln grammar school and then at Trinity College, Cambridge, where he must have been a student as the mastership of Richard Bentley, the famous scholar and controversialist ended and Robert Smith's began. Smith was a cousin of Roger Cotes, the Newtonian, and himself professor of astronomy and experimental philosophy and author of a system of opticks and a book on the philosophy of musical sounds, *Harmonicks* (1760). Throughout Pownall's work, from *Principles of Polity* (1752) to his *Study of Antiquities* (1782), can be seen, not only the Lockian philosophy, but the influence of Newtonian science. After he took his degree, Pownall seems to have worked at the Board of Trade where his brother, John, was also employed.

In 1753 he crossed to America. He attended the Albany Congress. Pownall traveled widely and became very well informed about problems of colonial administration. He memorialized Lord Halifax. He drew up *Considerations Towards a General Plan of Measures for the English Provinces,* and *Proposals for Securing the Friendship of the Five Nations,* both published, though without his knowledge, at New York in 1756. Lewis Evans dedicated his map to him. The Penns asked him to be governor of Pennsylvania. He was made lieutenant governor of New Jersey in 1755, captain-general and governor of Massachusetts in 1757, and was generally known as "Governor" thereafter. He returned to England in 1761, having made several crossings during his American stay, and went to Germany 1762–63. After 1765 he never held any government office, although he sat in parliament 1767–1780, first for Tregony and then for Minehead. During the stormy period of George III's reign he published in successively enlarged versions *The Administration of the*

Colonies, 1764–1774, and works on economics, the East India Company, and antiquity.[55]

Pownall's colonial activities have been carefully studied. His parliamentary pleas for a new policy have been analyzed. He was the friend of Franklin and of John Almon. He was twice happily married. He was known to be independent, moderate, and well educated. His political theories have been neglected. If he had had a good literary style he might have attracted more readers, but his vocabulary was formidable and his phraseology ponderous. Yet his ideas show more originality than those of almost any of his contemporaries. A republican and an innovator, at the same time he surveyed the past with a certain calm detachment that was very rare.

Pownall's philosophy of history was outlined in his *Study of Antiquities.* He was interested in discovering the internal capabilities, happiness, wealth, and the power of external exertion of any country. History, generally only the recital of the "brutal part" of man, should be "experimental knowledge," should through an analytic description of progress, — expansion and decay of the civil community — explain the vicissitudes of nations. This analytic history revealed to him a natural system of attraction which, when properly understood (as by Alexander the Great), was used to achieve universal empire — and the foundation of Alexandria in the center of his world. Alexander was the first to combine interest in commerce with the operations of polity. Pownall was deeply interested in the economic development of states, in the relation of freedom and military service in the division of the community into labourers and administrators. He wished antiquarians to dissipate some of the fogs of history and discover relation of causes and effects. Remarks on fable and its lessons were sound. The springs and principles which affect human affairs must be studied as well as the facts; there must be learning as distinguished from knowledge.[56]

The Newtonian system was constantly in Pownall's mind. It provided the main theme of his earliest, and in some ways most important book, *Principles of Polity.* He described his motives in writing it in a letter to Harvard when he sent them a copy in 1764.

To the President, Fellow and Students of Harvard College in Cambridge New-England. As it is the most perfect State of Society, wherein a People enjoy their Rights with Liberty and their property in Peace, under the Blessings of an enlarg'd Communion: So it is the true End of all Government to protect the Unity of this Communion, in the several conspiring Orders and Powers. Those, therefore, who by their Station have a Share in the lead of, or by their Appointment may be set apart to teach the People, cannot more essentially serve Mankind, than by promoting this *great Truth*. To promote this Truth as arising from Nature and leading to Peace, in Opposition to those erroneous Theories, which arising from Artificial Invention, lead to Faction, was the following Treatise written and publish'd; and is now put into the hands of the Students of Harvard College recommending to them to point out all their Studies and all their labors to the Peace of Mankind, as founded in the Universal Law of Nature, and in the positive Command of the Author of Nature. T.P.

In order to avoid presenting final conclusions, *Principles of Polity* was written, in conscious imitation of Shaftesbury, in the form of three dialogues which take place about 1746 in a country house adorned with arms and armour, "monitors of liberty" and reminders of England's past. Lucius Crassus, Pownall himself, and Scaevola discuss politics. In the first dialogue they argue about the original contract; in the second, the revolutions brought about by changing balance between property and power; in the third and last, the matter of allegiance, though this has also been stressed in the first.[57]

As his letter shows, he wished to correct the idea of the original contract. It was not an alliance or a treaty between two separate groups, the governors and the governed: it was a union—a "concatenation" of the different groups whose communion and dependency upon each other made up government. The natural state of man was social and political. Isolation was impossible. All were connected with others; labour should be for the common interest. Existence was a golden chain and polity was the care of this necessary communion of mankind.[58]

In his letter of 1776 to Adam Smith, Pownall was to claim that in this early work he had analyzed those laws of motion which caused and directed the labour of man and the "intercommuning" of mutual supplies that created government. Reciprocity of wants caused division of labour and an inequality of accumulation of property led to barter. Early in the *Principles* Crassus pointed out of the window to a lovely farm, apparently containing everything necessary to sustain and adorn life. However, he drew attention to a point in the distance where a mine was busy producing tools and materials without which the farm could not have operated, and he used this picture to illustrate the moral for his doctrine of community or union in which all was necessary to each. All parts of the country depended on each other—the mine, the farm, the river which transported materials to city and manufacturer—all formed a part of the whole. There could be no distinction between the interest of one and the other parts of the country.[59]

Pownall discussed the balance, source of so much conflict in European affairs as well as of endless domestic strife. It was sometimes represented as a scale in which the steadiness of the connecting rod, on which the sides were balanced, alone maintained equilibrium. Or it might be shown to be a contest among different parts of the society, each balancing the other, or some other device to justify the power of the "ingenious few" over the "servile many." This principle of opposing parts lay at the root of all party strife and factional disputes. Boasted principles of liberty contained seeds of contention, civil war, decay, and ruin. Country had been played off against court, landed interest against manufacturer. A wise ruler hoped to keep the balance, but how often had he been successful?[60]

There was a natural balance in the state, the balance of property and power. This was long talked of without any real understanding, even by Sir Thomas More, until the days of the great Harrington. Natural balance was determined by "the scite and circumstance" of country and people. It could be rectified if the changes brought about by unequal accumulation, especially in a commercial state, had put it awry. Revolutions and changes in government were due to a changed relation of wealth and power. Much care must be devoted to studying the reasons for this and to understanding of the necessary connections between different parts of the whole.[61]

Pownall thought that people, after early experiment, were likely to settle round a natural center. In England he saw the early kingdoms as the outcome of settlement. Then he saw the formation of the nation.

The friends in *Principles* asked why this union should not be extended to all mankind who could be thought to have a necessary connection between all of them, not merely those of one country. Pownall replied that for the present he was considering these natural areas of union. In his later work on the colonies and in his *Memorials,* 1780–1784, he returned to the possibility of wider associations. He there endorsed Adam Smith's ideas on freedom of trade. He urged Europe to unite in a congress for certain aspects of her mutual concerns. He had advocated a federal union of colonies and England. He very early apparently made up his mind that the natural center of union and attraction was in America rather than in England and expected independence to be the outcome of the struggle between the two countries. He hoped, since so much could still unite them, for a "family compact."[62]

Government arose out of circumstance and out of mutual necessities. Pownall did not much stress the guarding of individual rights, but emphasized mutual obligations to serve in the militia and to perform duties according to function. He thought a good deal about allegiance and in *Principles* was disinclined to allow that Irish who had left Ireland and served in France could actually have forsworn their allegiance. Loyalty was demanding. At any rate the Irish who had left would have no right to return. He stated that England had ruled the colonies as sovereign and had taxed them. What he fully recognized was the change in circumstances which led them to dislike the continuance of this practice and a reaffirmation of an old right.[63]

Pownall early noticed a change in American opinion as well as in the English attitude to the colonies. There ought, he thought in 1764, to be a new plan of administration to meet new needs and new interests. What he proposed was a "grand marine dominion" of all possessions bordering the Atlantic, united in one empire, one center. This would need new government planning, either by the old Board of Trade and Plantations or by the creation of some new secretariat. But all should have one center and direction. All affairs should be unified that in any way concerned this empire. Organization should reflect current conditions and needs. His own attitude, as the conflict he feared developed, changed. He hoped for a federal union, he hoped for a family compact; eventually he could only hope for friendly relations after independence had been recognized. He persisted in attempts to explain and conciliate. He never dwelt on metaphysical considerations, but on the facts. In the past England had indeed acted as sovereign, had taxed and regulated colonial affairs. In his own time he was not concerned with rights, but with possibilities and with difficulties. One difficulty in the way of conciliation was less obvious at the beginning, even to Pownall. He was later to say the colonies had "hardened into republics" as long ago as the Restoration, but his earlier impression was of their loyalty and determination to remain in the British orbit. He had seen, even at Albany, a Newtonian law of attraction uniting the societies of the eastern American seaboard. He saw a force working for union in the north. Later he saw this as immensely more powerful in the struggle for independence than centripetal ties among South American colonies. Though these appeared to have certain material advantages, he rightly prophesied an earlier maturity for the northern Americans.[64]

Pownall recognized certain cohesive forces, compulsions, and perceived the sea change that manners, habits, and opinions had undergone. America was peculiarly fortunate in natural resources, in absence of dominion, in her freedom from many ancient European institutions. America had no game laws, no sordid marriage customs, and an equality for which there were few advocates and little hope in old Europe. He esteemed the liberty of conscience enjoyed and the possibilities of reward for individual efforts offered by the wilderness. He admired the natural beauties of the continent, the "flaunting blush of spring," and he published six views of the scenery on his return to London. He knew America as very few visiting Englishmen did at the time, and he had during his stay managed to achieve a perceptive understanding of the colonial mind. He liked American ways and planned to make a career there. Later he might have lived overseas, if marriage had not kept him at home. America would attract settlers from Europe and would be an asylum, as Brand Hollis told Franklin later, for the oppressed.[65]

Pownall's ideas on government concentrated on the free working of natural laws—Newtonian laws. America, he thought, should become a free port for the whole world. Pownall enthusiastically endorsed Smith as the author of a *Principia* of social science, and he urged Americans to follow his precepts. Natural laws were immortal in that they reflected changes in the society as its character developed. They united amidst the "flux of mortality," by which he meant that the principles of action remained constant though manifested in divers form. For example, in 1783 Pownall discussed the Articles of Confederation, and suggested that now monarchy was abolished, Americans should restore that strong executive power without which government could not effectively unite communities. Had England realized this natural law when Charles I was overthrown and established a governor or consul, Cromwell would never have been able to set up his military dictatorship and then perhaps the Restoration might never have taken place. The multitude was by its nature incapable of administration. They must be encouraged to think freely and properly, but they must be led by the executive power.[66]

Pownall distrusted infringements on sovereignty of all kinds. He disliked the idea of the East India Company collecting taxes and treating with Nabobs. Merchants had a function but should not be allowed the rights of state. Those belonged inalienably to the government of which they were subjects. Their duty was to the English government and in turn they could expect protection and assistance, charters of incorporation with privileges, but not the extraordinary powers they had exercised of late. And in America the Union would fall apart if more care were not given, as he suggested, to the executive branch of government.[67]

Natural laws working in society implied more duties than privileges in Pownall's definitions. He said almost nothing of rights of the individual. Children were born subjects of immortal laws and members of a family and a community. They were not born equal and adult. They might because of their birth and function be the governed rather than governors, but they were safe if the government was run in accordance with law and utility. Pownall suggested that rotation in power was desirable in a state. He endorsed freedom of opinion and of religion. He disliked European restrictions on labour. He liked the absence in America of an established church. He hoped to see the slaves freed and supplying the need for labour. Pownall suggested possible limitations of their capacity to hold land except as leaseholders, but he obviously felt the problem should be solved in a free world. Opportunity to Pownall was more important than an equality of status.

He had always denied any levelling plans, but he admired the liberty of the New World and hoped it would set up a standard to nations everywhere. Moreover, he had the interests of all parts of the society or community in mind. When he wrote to Adam Smith, he reminded him that though rising prices and wealth would in the long run increase the prosperity of the nation, the process might bear hardly both on landowners and on labourers, whose wages seldom rose as fast. This was an intelligent and humanitarian comment.[68]

Pownall's theories were put forward over a long period of time, and many of them after the limits of this chapter. They serve as a bridge to a discussion of the ideas of the age of the American Revolution. He was a disciple of Harrington, of Locke, and of Newton. He fully appreciated and understood the situation and character of the Americans. A man of unusual insight, he was less thought of by his English contemporaries than by men like Franklin.[69] Yet his scheme, based on his earliest political philosophy, was progressive in the best sense of that word, and could well have been adopted by imperialists of his own time and of the next century. Neither he nor Pitt, whose conception of empire possibly came nearest to his, were able to realize their vision of a great Atlantic community. The most severe criticism of the Whigs of the reign of George III might be evoked by their failure to profit by the talents of either Pitt or Pownall, as well as of the galaxy of reformers and Real Whigs who wrote during the emergencies that developed so soon after the Peace of Paris. The men and the hour were there for a restoration or a reformation of the ancient fabric of the constitution whose shortcomings were responsible, in part at least, as Fielding had pointed out, for defects in administration. The old institutions were as yet unadjusted to new demands. The ruling oligarchy failed to understand the needs of the situation. England's extraordinary line of politicians of integrity and vision had not really come to an end, but eighteenth-century circumstance always prevented the implementation of the most practical suggestions, like Pownall's dominion status or Walpole's excise. It may not be inappropriate to recall, in ending a discussion of this Georgian period, Pownall's last tribute to Walpole and his administrative genius. No one was better fitted to realize the skill of the Prime Minister, and no one less likely to resent his failures than he. Pownall believed in good government, and by stressing its union and its concatenations in his curious phraseology, he rightly diagnosed the difficult problem of management in the new days of parliamentary supremacy.[70]

Pensioners and placemen were the distressing manifestations of the crucial problem of administration. The achievement of a popular, a powerful, and an efficient governmental machinery which would neither fall into a Polish or Swedish anarchy, nor into a Prussian despotism was desirable. A study of the more thoughtful among these Staunch Whigs and political commentators will show that this most difficult of puzzles was slowly appreciated, and its solution was to be found not only in the natural rights theories of the past, in the humanitarianism of the present, and in the capacities or ambitions of the bureaucracy and the ruling caste, but in some sort of fusion which in spite of differences, in "scite and circumstance," as Pownall would put it, was to be as successful in the English future as in the great republic rising overseas.

IX

Honest Whigs Under George III, 1761-1789

Character of Radicalism in the Period

Revolution politics, which had seemed to be dying in England, achieved a new vigour in the first half of the reign of George III. Prominent and talented men in church and state professed their adherence to the great tradition and devoted themselves to the protection of the liberty of the individual even against parliamentary encroachment, to the reform of the parliamentary system, to amelioration of the law and to the achievement of an unlimited toleration. They announced their sympathy with demands for the full rights of Englishmen overseas in Ireland, in the colonies, and, as the period ended, for Frenchmen. There was activity in the Commons. There were meetings and associations outside its walls. Much more was written. A real attempt was made to disseminate tracts as well as the works of the Whig canon or portions of them. Political controversy flourished. In fact, however, the achievement of the Real Whigs was as slight as that of their predecessors. Their history was one of failure and frustration. A few lived on through the French Revolution. The radicalism that began to manifest itself in the early nineteenth century, though indisputably connected with earlier movements, was strongly coloured by newly defined utilitarianism, by continental theories, and by the changed balance of town and country, of industry and agriculture. The terror of the Gordon riots, the failure of Wyvill's associations, the outcry about the speeches and sermons which celebrated in short succession the anniversary of the English Revolution and the birth of a new order in France, marked the end of the Commonwealthmen.

The great theorists of the seventeenth and eighteenth centuries discussed political freedom within the framework of a Gothic system transformed by the intellectualism of the Renaissance and Reformation. They realized the changed balance of society. They entirely failed to foresee anything remotely resembling modern economic development and the changes in class structure that have accompanied it. The weight of the people meant something so entirely different to them that it has been difficult, often impossible, for twentieth-century students to understand what sort of world they were writing about. Their determination to obtain liberty for individuals to think, talk, write, and worship freely and to be tried for their social sins only by fair and legal means, was admirable, and they deserve the gratitude of all free peoples today. But their formulae, in a world of a growing industrial population, were not easy to apply, and it may be doubted whether this problem of the rights and liberties of numbers has yet been solved by philosophers. Even the success of the Founding Fathers of the United States, themselves profoundly convinced of the validity of the creed of Real Whigs, was very largely due to the fact that for over a century the agrarian population of the New World, settled or nomadic, so much outweighed the urban.

The failure of the Honest Whigs under George III hardly needs explanation here. Recent and brilliant studies of the politics of that reign have shown the confusions of administration, and even of theory, amongst the ruling class and their monarch, though the ideas of George III at least seem more comprehensible. In spite of Burke's often-quoted phrases, the party system without which popular parliamentary government cannot work was not accepted in any modern sense of the term by many within the political English community. Its discipline would have been irking; its theory, though implicit in some discussions and in many arrangements, was yet to be absorbed into any important sector of public opinion. Americans, framing their new republic, guarded against anything like party. Real Whigs often started their works as Montagu had done with pious endorsement of Solon's law about neutrality as a crime in matters concerning the welfare of the state. They realized, as Toland had long ago, the value of difference of opinion and debate. They were aware that organization could be a legitimate weapon in political campaigns. But on the whole the reformers, utopians, and philanthropists relied on old-fashioned petitioning and the patronage and activity of considerable persons in English society.[1]

Chatham, Wilkes, and Fox were believers in what might be described as highclass rabble-rousing—but this, after all, was what Pym and Shaftesbury had indulged in and it had not made a lasting contribution to sober political progress. In all the discussions of an extended franchise there was almost no debate about what the new voters would do, except to follow their benefactors into better world policies. When the course of events in France showed once again that popular revolutions might get out of control, the cause of the men to be discussed in this chapter received a check from which it never recovered.

Despairing efforts might be seen in the weekly penny numbers, already referred to, of *Pig's Meat, or, Lessons for the Swinish Multitude* (a reference to Burke's jibe) put out by Thomas Spence at the "Hive of Liberty, High Holborn" (1793–95), consisting of extracts to promote among the labouring men proper ideas of their importance and rights, and to convince them that their forlorn condition had not been entirely overlooked and forgotten, nor their cause unpleaded "by the best and most enlightened men of all ages." The selections were taken from writers like Milton, Sidney, and Harrington (whose agrarian had been enforced and transformed by Spence's earlier Newcastle Lecture, 1775), Fletcher and Trenchard, Swift and Berkeley, as well as by recent tractarians like Erskine, Cappe, and Spence himself. Henry Yorke, in a letter to John Frost (1750–1842), was ready to prove that, even in the celebrated writings of Thomas Paine, there is not a political maxim which is not to be found in the writings of Sidney, Harrington, Milton, and Buchanan. Not many Real Whigs or Commonwealthmen had troubled about the dregs of society, but it is worth noticing that the exponent of a new egalitarianism looked not to levelling tracts, but to the great Whig canon for support. This was the very slender connecting link between this generation, the practical beliefs, causes, and philosophies of radicals including Thomas Paine (who will be ignored here), and older Commonwealthmen.[2]

Superficially, circumstances had seemed propitious as opinion was stimulated by the sins of a favourite, the troubles of a rake, the much more serious problems of colonial management. Considerable apathy persisted and, added to the confusion of public life and political theory, made the success of the various causes of the Real Whigs of the period impossible from the start. Had a leader of sufficient talent and determination appeared among the politicians, had Shelburne or Chatham in their different ways been able to exert the influence they undoubtedly enjoyed in certain circles and at certain times, the story might have been different. Some reforms like modifications of penal laws of various kinds, some concessions about unrepresented towns might have been pushed through the old House of Commons, even if other suggestions were premature or seemed unsuitable.

The reformers were hopelessly divided at the lowest as well as the highest levels. The Commonwealthmen had by now adopted a good many so-called levelling ideas, but these in turn were being transformed by contrary and novel developments among philosophic radicals and continental doctrinaires. Society itself was also changing in England, and they were fortunate in seeing so much of their program taking shape overseas, even at the cost of their own beloved country. On the higher levels the only achievements of any kind seem to have been the work of the less liberal Rockinghams, rather than the more liberal Chatham-Shelburne groups. Burke did not appreciate the natural rights and popular theories of the colonists, but in spite of his shortcomings in this respect, his speeches probably did more to make friends overseas than anything put forward by Grafton or Chatham or Shelburne. His "economical reform," even if it has been shown to have been almost unnecessary at that time, was at least as satisfactory as Dunning's motion about the crown. He worked to ameliorate conditions of Irishmen; he defended the cause of justice in India. Ancient and Christian precepts were held sacred by him, but he distrusted the ideologies of the Commonwealthmen and they distrusted him, even when circumstance brought them into the same camp. Burke believed in working from moment to moment and "in the closet" silently. The theorists he so often denounced proposed a staggering variety of plans for the colonies, for the government, for forms of propaganda, but their very fertility defeated them.[3]

Details of political activity in and out of parliament and as it affected humanitarian and reforming movements will be neglected. Attention will be focused on a number of liberal Anglicans, some were to form a Unitarian congregation, and some stayed in the church, but all were associated with Archdeacon Blackburne and those matters in which he and his connection interested themselves. The dissenters must once again be mentioned, this time chiefly through works by Priestley and Price revealing the development of ideas and a reinterpretation of traditions and ambitions. Avowed republicans of the period must be briefly examined and also two important political treatises, *An Historical Essay,* and Burgh's *Political Disquisitions,* whose precepts were extended and in general carried on by the Jebb-Cartwright connection and the Society for Constitutional Information. All these in one way or another looked back to seventeenth-century theories of both revolutionary periods and restated their doctrines in the light of contemporary conditions. The Society for Constitutional Information was disseminating, with some additions from the pens of their own members, very much the same Whig canon which had formed the core of Thomas Hollis's plan devised over twenty years before. Jebb and Cartwright tried to use committees and associations to press not only the first objective of the Yorkshire group led by Wyvill, economical reform, but their own program of drastic changes in the representative system. Only the briefest commentary on their objectives will be given here as illustrating the final concerted effort of the Real Whigs, before they lost their identity in the radicalism of a new age.

The Blackburne Connection, "An Amiable Band of Well Wishers to the Religious and Civil Rights of Mankind"

The violent theological controversies of the first thirty years of the eighteenth century had consumed a great quantity of paper and print, but not, after 1719, very much parliamentary time and effort. With the publication of Archdeacon Blackburne's *Confessional* in 1766, a vigorous movement developed at first among certain churchmen only, then among some other citizens and members of parliament, which was directed towards statutory modification of the Articles and of the subscriptions required of clergymen and of students at the universities. This was in turn to inspire the dissenters to try again for repeal of the Test and Corporation Acts and the efforts of the Old Sects continued to the end of the century. No appreciable success was achieved by either group. During their campaigns some prominent publicists appeared and the Unitarian secession from the Establishment, which followed the failure of the Feathers Petition of 1772, in turn brought about associations of rational Protestants of both dissenting and Episcopalian ancestry. These supporters of undogmatical Christianity increasingly and continually participated in all crusades for reform and for greater civil and religious liberty. Blackburne was important, not only because his book quickly achieved three editions and some measure of success, but also because he formed a large connection of able men who met at his hospitable house in Richmond, corresponded with him and with each other, and combined in cooperative ventures to further the causes in which the Archdeacon was interested.

Blackburne was born at Richmond in Yorkshire in 1705. After his father's death his mother, the former Alice Comber, daughter of a well-known dean of Durham, remarried Onesiphorus Paul of Gloucester. Francis loved foxhunting in his youth and his companion was often Edward Thompson, member for York 1722–1742. He developed an interest in reading, and when he visited his uncle, Thomas Comber, in East Newton, he browsed in a library of old tracts collected by his ancestor, William Thornton, an Oliverian Justice. Comber had been conservative in religion and politics, Thornton inclined to dissent and to the parliamentary side. When Blackburne went up to St. Catherine Hall at Cambridge he met an old gentleman who admonished him to let the first book he read there be *Locke Upon Government*. Whether the tracts or Locke must be held responsible cannot be determined, but the liberality of Blackburne's philosophy as formed by all sorts of influences early barred his advance to a college fellowship.[4] He continued to follow what might be termed the avant garde in literature of his times and was early an admirer of David Hartley (1705–1757) and his philosophy about the association of ideas. He was a friend and defender in print of Edmund Law. He settled down as a country parson in Yorkshire. By 1749 he was already in touch with John Jones whose *Free and Candid Disquisitions* he endorsed publicly.

In 1752 he published *A Candid Address to the Jews* in which, like Nicholas Hardinge in the Commons, he professed himself utterly unable to find any defensible ground for the exclusion of Jews from citizenship. Christians should neither persecute, nor should they deny the natural rights of anyone. Persecution was wicked and moreover seldom beneficial to its perpetrators. Blackburne consistently practised the toleration he professed, whilst steadily maintaining his own right to disagree, both with the orthodox of his own communion and with dissenters from it. He was more courageous in his defense of nonconformists than his friend Edmund Law. Since he was certain that the American colonists would not welcome a colonial episcopacy at a time when this was being mooted, he opposed the plan and bolstered his argument with the authority of Burghley, Milton, Harrington, Sidney, Marvell, Locke, Molesworth, Trenchard, "and their like." His friends were to be found among all sorts of sectaries and churchmen. So well were his liberal views known to his contemporaries that he was asked to become minister at Old Jewry Meeting on the death of Dr. Samuel Chandler.[5]

Scruples about subscription effectively prevented Blackburne's advancement beyond the rank of archdeacon in the Church of England. Yet he wrote a tract on why he was not a Socinian. He entirely disavowed the Unitarianism of the husbands of his stepdaughter, daughter, and grandchild—Lindsey, Disney, and Frend. Had he believed as they did—he wrote to the Reverend John Wiche of Maidstone, a freethinking, dissenting parson also associated with Lardner and Priestley—he would not have considered himself entitled to be called a Christian.[6] He himself was anxious for considerable modification in the Establishment of the kind suggested long before by another Cambridge alumnus, Dr. Samuel Clarke, and by John Jones. His ideas resembled those of Brian Herport (d.1768), whose *Essay on Truths of Importance to the Happiness of Mankind* (tr. 1768) was published just after his own *Confessional,* and as a result of the same influence with the printers Bowyer and Millar—that of Thomas Hollis, a friend and correspondent. The Scripture should be a sufficient rule of faith. Acknowledgment of this fact should be all that was necessary for the clergy or students of universities. Blackburne wished to omit from the service the Athanasian Creed, to simplify certain traditional ceremonies and purge from the prayer book certain repetitions that seemed meaningless. The Reformation had brought about changes in the church in England and elsewhere. These could not be regarded as final. Further rectifications were necessary and even more might be needed. Men like Law and William Paley (1743–1805) agreed on the whole with these suggestions. Like Blackburne, and unlike his sons-in-law, they did not feel obliged to leave the Church after the failure of the Feathers Petition.[7]

That petition, called after the tavern where meetings to draft it were held, was largely organized by Theophilus Lindsey (1723–1808). It was presented to parliament by Sir William Meredith (1725–1790), member for Liverpool and acquainted with the Blackburne connection. In the Lords only Camden and Law of Carlisle supported it, but in the Commons, in spite of opposition by Burke, Cooper, Fox (still unallied with liberal elements among Whigs), Newdigate, Stanley, and Fitzmaurice, a fairly substantial number spoke in its behalf. Many of these were, like the petitioners Blackburne and Lindsey, from Cambridge; one or two were educated at Glasgow and at Warrington Academy, 1758–1786. There were some differences in the lists of supporters of dissenting attempts a little later, but not very many. These efforts were to no effect.[8] The rejection of the Petition resulted in some resignations from the church over the next twenty years or so. Lindsey now followed Robertson's example and was in turn followed by Jebb, a Cambridge contemporary and friend, by his brother-in-law, Disney; Gilbert Wakefield, William Frend, and Thomas Tyrwhitt.

Blackburne remained in the church and continued his activities and his friendships. *The Confessional* was perhaps his most important literary work. His collected opera fill seven volumes and these do not include the two large quartos of *Memoirs of Thomas Hollis,* some scattered sermons, and his contributions to the press which, with others inspired by him and written by his friends 1764–1770, appeared in three volumes in 1774 as *A Collection of Letters and Essays in Favour of Public Liberty.* The *Hollis Memoirs* provide almost as much information about the politics and activities of Blackburne himself (though he remained anonymous throughout) as about the eccentric of Lincoln's Inn. The *Letters* were written by Jebb, John Luther (c.1739–1786), Caleb Fleming of Pinners Hall, and Lindsey, and opposed the Stamp Act as well as the sending of bishops to America. Blackburne introduced Priestley and Lindsey to each other, and this friendship continued throughout their lives. He corresponded with Americans, mostly those also in touch with Hollis. And Hollis recommended the letters of Harris (the historian) and Lindsey to Strahan and Kearsley for the London press. Blackburne was a friend of Wyvill, and a supporter of the more radical band of reformers led by Jebb. He seems always to have retained the affection and respect of these as well as others of his Cambridge acquaintance like Law.

The founder of the Essex Street Chapel and organizer of the Feathers Petition, Lindsey,[9] once he had established himself in London, was rather less occupied by purely political or literary pursuits than his stepfather-in-law. Jebb was active at the hustings and in committee. Lindsey concentrated on his letter writing, on his clerical duties, on conversation with his friends, and visits to those who were in distress. His sympathies and his beliefs were well known. His charm was widely felt and his influence was exerted through the force of his personality rather than by the weight of literary accomplishment or the impact of platform oratory.

Lindsey's father was a mercer of Scotch ancestry and his mother was distantly connected with the Spencer-Marlborough family. He was educated at Leeds and then at Cambridge. He was ordained by Bishop Gibson and held a curacy at Kirkwood for three years. He became vicar of Piddleton, not far from the estates of Thomas Hollis in Dorset in 1756. He went thence to Catterick where Mrs. Cappe's father, Jeremiah Harrison, had preceded him. He and his wife, Hannah, once more took part in the society around her stepfather. While in Dorset, Lindsey had heard about Unitarian William Robertson's scruples and pondered them. Robertson had long before been a pupil of Hutcheson in Dublin and had then attended Glasgow. After some years he felt obliged to resign. A good many years elapsed before Lindsey brought himself to do likewise.

With the failure of the Petition, Lindsey made up his mind. He and his wife being agreed, they began in December, 1773, to move slowly toward London with very little money and no particular prospects. They stayed on the way with William Mason, the poet (1724–1797), and with John Disney, their brother-in-law. They left behind many Yorkshire friends as well as the Archdeacon, the Cappes, and the Turners. In London another Yorkshireman, a Rockingham Whig, John Lee (1733–1793), was ready to help them. He had been educated at Leeds (possibly the school attended by Baron and Lindsey), had become a friend of Priestley's while the latter was preaching in that city, and had introduced Priestley to Edmund Burke. In London he was one of the Honest Whigs with whom Franklin consorted at the London coffee house, among whom were Kippis, Price, and Burgh. Lee lived in Lincoln's Inn and had, at the time his friend moved south, been engaged with Serjeant Glynn (1722–1779) in the defense of Wilkes, and had seconded Dunning's efforts on behalf of the colony 19 January, 1774, though he "spoke but feebly," it was reported by Priestley. He was to be Solicitor General in 1782 in the Rockingham administration, and resigned when Rockingham died. Lee was consulted by Price when he wrote his reflections, *On Civil Liberty,* and he met regularly on Sunday nights in his chambers with Lindsey and Priestley to talk, conversations Priestley later recalled nostalgically. Here he also talked with Timothy Hollis, Hollis's cousin, Brand Hollis, and others about the Americans. Lee was beloved by a very wide circle including not only his Unitarian friends, whose church he supported until the end of his life, but also such men as Rockingham and Eden, Lord Auckland.[10]

"Amidst the bustle of politics" Lee always preserved "his attachment to theology" and "the cause of truth," and it was he who persuaded Lindsey not to worry about the absence of a license for the chapel he opened in Essex Street not very long after his arrival in London. In fact, though technically illegal, the chapel was countenanced by many of the carriage trade, and even the list of those known to have attended is very impressive—including eccentric noblemen, rational dissenters, wealthy women, and professional men—and attests to its having become an accepted part of London life. Lindsey's sermons were admired and so were those of friends who preached for him. Disney joined him as assistant some eight years later and continued his work. With the closing of Pinners Hall, some of those Unitarian dissenters, like Timothy Hollis, transferred their moral and financial support to Lindsey's work. Sir George Savile helped and occasionally attended services. Richard Price, though he was Arian and not Unitarian in his faith, occasionally preached. Many of the group around Lindsey assisted in the foundation of Hackney College, Burke's "hotbed of sedition," and preached or taught there during its brief span as a dissenting university. In short, Lindsey's chapel, like his father-in-law's house, was a place where tolerance was acted upon and where all shades of liberal opinion thrived.[11]

Lindsey's letters, both published and unpublished, reveal his politics. He was intensely interested in the cause of the American colonists and eagerly sought news of their opinions and their activities. As the war developed, communication was more difficult, but some sort of link was maintained and soon after the war was over Lindsey with the rest of his circle was able to welcome Adams and Jefferson to London. Brand Hollis, John Jebb, and the Lindseys seem to have seen a great deal of the Adamses during their embassy. John Disney printed some of the correspondence between Hollis and Adams after the latter's return to America.

Lindsey also supported Cartwright and Jebb's suggestions for parliamentary reform. He was interested, like Jebb, in law reform and in the antislavery movement which Granville Sharp and Wakefield were developing. During the French Revolution he attended the celebrations held by the Revolution Club, and he visited the martyrs of renewed intolerance, William Winterbotham and T. Fyshe Palmer when they were imprisoned. He welcomed Thomas Paine's *Rights of Man* in which Brand Hollis had had a share, to the extent of helping it through the press, though not to the degree of collaboration of which he was often accused. Lindsey belonged to the left wing of the Whigs and made no secret of his beliefs. His public activity continued to be chiefly in connection with his ministry.[12]

Lindsey's brother-in-law, John Disney (1746–1816), was educated at Wakefield under John Lark and at Cambridge. He became chaplain to Edmund Law about 1772 and married Jane Blackburne about two years later. The Disneys were a Nottinghamshire family that had once been dissenters. The Cartwrights were first cousins. John Disney, after deciding to leave the church, joined Lindsey at Essex Street. They shared their friends and their principles. Disney's chief service to the cause was the writing of many biographical studies of men important in the development of the group. Works on Sykes, Jortin, and Hopkins have already been referred to. He also wrote a long memoir as a preface to an edition of the works of John Jebb (1786) in three volumes, and a charmingly illustrated memoir of his friend, Brand Hollis, from whom he inherited the Hyde and the fortune both of

Brand and of Thomas Hollis of Lincoln's Inn on the former's death in 1804.[13]

The Newcome Cappes were members of the Blackburne-Lindsey circle. Catharine Harrison was born in 1744 in Yorkshire and as a girl knew the Archdeacon and became friendly with the Lindseys when they were at Catterwick. Her father, who had preceded Lindsey in that church, had taught her not to despise dissenters. She received some of her education from an aunt who was a niece of Sir Patience Ward, London Alderman and associate of the Whig martyrs, Russell and Sidney. She learned French by reading Fénelon's *Télémaque*. The Wyvills, the poet Mason, and Priestley were among her acquaintance. In 1788 she married Newcome Cappe, a widower with seven children by a daughter of William Turner (1714–1794), a Glasgow-trained minister of liberal views at Wakefield and member of the Priestley-Blackburne coterie.

Cappe was born in 1733. His father had been a dissenting minister at Mill Hill, Leeds, at the chapel later served by Priestley. His son was named Newcome for his mother's family and was educated at Kibworth with John Aikin (later a teacher at Warrington), under Doddridge, and at Glasgow under Leechman, Adam Smith, and James Moore. In the seventies Cappe was one of a literary circle which met on Wednesdays at York to discuss politics and religion. He was friendly with Savile and Lee, the Shores of Sheffield, Kippis, Dodson, and Toulmin of London dissenting circles. His second wife, Catharine, was a charming writer. From her accounts of the Yorkshire circle, as well as of the Lindseys, much information may be gained about the role of Unitarians at this time. The Cappes were typical in their union of Anglican and dissenting families, traditions, and politics of the mixture which these pro-American liberal reformers represented. They combined the Commonwealth and the aristocratic Whig legends in their own family history. The congregation at Essex Street, at Cappe's chapel in York, the groups at Archdeacon Blackburne's hospital house at Richmond, or the Manchester philosophical group meeting in the eighties to discuss science and politics, were all leavened by this rational Protestantism and represent a small Whig world within the old vanishing world of the great families or the small dissenting communions.[14]

Another Cambridge alumnus who left the church for activities at Warrington and Hackney, as well as literary and political work, was Gilbert Wakefield (1756–1801). He was born in Nottingham and studied at Peterhouse in Cambridge. He attributed his religious and political heresies, not to Jebb who was teaching Newtonian mathematics at the time, but to the influence of a university where Bacon, Newton, Milton, Clarke, and Whiston had lived and where others he admired like Jortin, Jackson of Rossington, and David Hartley, the philosopher, had also studied. Wakefield admitted the effect of a sermon delivered by Bishop Law in 1773 on the fifth of November showing that popery was not alone in exercising spiritual tyranny. In spite of all these influences, Wakefield was ordained and always reproached himself thereafter for not being more scrupulous. He blamed men like Paley whom he felt had continued to avoid the issue raised by subscription. Wakefield himself soon made his ideas known. At Liverpool he, like Thomas Wren of Plymouth and James Freeman of Sheffield, visited prisoners of war and tried to alleviate their distress. He taught briefly at Warrington and at Hackney. He was not an easy person to live with and was intolerant of those more dogmatical than himself. He may not have made many converts to the good causes he supported at such considerable cost to himself of time and comfort.[15]

There were professors and clergy who, like Blackburne, stayed in the church but became prominent for liberal views not always as clear cut as the archdeacon's but of some importance. Others, for example, Thomas Rutherford, whose *Institutes* repay reading by students of eighteenth-century ideas, must be neglected. Dean Tucker has already been mentioned as a foe to the Lockians, but his Toryism was neither diehard nor reactionary. John Hinchliffe (1731–1794), Bishop of Peterborough and master of Trinity Cambridge after some years, was one of Grafton's bishops, and was said by Nichols to have endeared his name to Britons by "having constantly and uniformly given his vote on every bill brought before the House in a way that reflected honour on the liberality of his sentiments." He was very much less consistent than Jonathan Shipley, another churchman elevated by Grafton in 1769, or Watson whose advance came later through Shelburne's efforts.[16]

Shipley (1714–1788) was educated at Oxford, was a chaplain at Fontenoy, and married into the Mordaunt family where he had briefly been a tutor. He was patronized by Hoadly and became a canon of Christ Church in 1748. He supported the Feathers Petition and the efforts of the dissenters for repeal of Test and Corporation Acts. He opposed changes he thought inimical to colonial liberty, such as the Stamp Act, and alteration of the Massachusetts Charter, and was constantly unhappy about the developing American struggle. Intimate with Franklin, he was and was one of the Honest Whigs that met at the London Tavern. With most of these he looked increasingly to America as the only remaining nursery of free men. Shipley's bent was thoughtful. He was convinced of the importance of time and the slow working of natural forces in the development of government. He was sure that there was a law of public happiness which should be recognized by reforms, for example, of the penal code whose severity he condemned, and promoted by the provision of education, even for the poor. All dissidents should be tolerated. "The men I am afraid of," he said in 1770, "are the men who believe everything and subscribe everything." Had his wise and moderate counsels been followed both with regard to certain domestic reforms and to American demands, much trouble might have been averted.[17]

Richard Watson was slightly junior to Hinchliffe at Cambridge. There he early knew Wilson (1741–1793), Paley's tutor, and Edmund Law, intimacy with whom he always regarded as the fortunate event of his life. Other friends were John Luther, one of Blackburne's "band," and Henry Strachey (1736–1810), as well as Grafton who had been educated like Luther and Benjamin Vaughan at Newcome's academy at Hackney. Watson supported Jebb's schemes for university reform and enjoyed a wide acquaintance with dissenters like Percival of Warrington and Liverpool. He claimed that his politics were those of Locke, Somers, Hooker, and Sir George Savile, another Cambridge alumnus and the most respected of Yorkshire reformers. He supported toleration and conciliation of the Americans, but did not endorse the writings of Paine, and this caused Wakefield to regard him as a renegade to reform. Watson was not as liberal as Jebb, but he was not as cautious about the whole matter of natural rights as his colleague, William Paley. Both were tolerant, but on different grounds. Both remained within the church.[18]

Paley was also a disciple of Law, to whom he dedicated his *Moral*

Philosophy (1785). Its analysis in it of the English constitution is perhaps the most subtle and thoughtful of this period. The interpretation was Whig, but not of the Commonwealth variety. He defended the old unreformed Commons, though he did not deny that change might sometime become necessary. Paley had more sense and less sentiment than Burke. Remarks on religious establishments show most clearly the influence of Law and explain his popularity among many who did not endorse his politics. The church did not form a fundamental part of the state, but a parochial clergy was sufficiently useful to justify the Establishment. Much simpler tests of orthodoxy should be used, and all citizens, whatever their faith, should enjoy civil rights. This textbook was deservedly popular in both Britain and America for many years, and its influence must always have been on the side of liberty if not on that of the political reformers.[19]

The Blackburne and Law connections achieved no program. The Feathers Petition failed and instead of promoting continued effort it resulted in an exodus of some good men from the church. The associations then formed pointed the way to other societies and organizations, and they brought together men interested in liberal ideas and movements of all denominations. In the history of liberty Blackburne's "amiable band" must be recognized as significant.

Price, Priestley, and Some Other Dissenters

The contribution of the dissenters in this period is still of significance in connection with the development of the Commonwealth tradition. Two writers at least achieved some reputation and produced work which remains interesting to read. Price and Priestley both attracted much attention from their contemporaries in England and in America at certain moments of their lives. They both incurred the wrath of Edmund Burke, yet they both, to the end of their lives, protested their devotion to English tradition and to English liberty.

Richard Price (1723–1791) had much charm and many talents. His fellow dissenters in England and Scotland admired him. He was urged by Washington to become an American. Yale bestowed an honorary degree upon him in 1789. He was proud of his dissenting connection.

He had been educated by Samuel Jones at Pentwyn in his native Wales, by Vavasor Griffiths at Talgarth, and by John Eames in London. His uncle Samuel had been associated with Isaac Watts; his father, Rees, was a minister and a teacher of the old academy of Carmarthen, ancestor of all university education in the Principality. He acted for thirteen years as chaplain to George Streatfield (d.1756) of Stoke Newington, one of the Abney family and assisted Samuel Chandler at Old Jewry. He was a minister at Newington Green and then taught at Hackney, a college which came to an untimely end shortly after his death. His wife, Sarah Blundell, had a little money and a house left from the wreck of her father's fortunes in the Bubble. They were married in 1757, but she was always sickly and predeceased her husband, having borne no children.

Price had many friends. Chief among these, perhaps, were the Lindseys; Brand Hollis; his neighbour, James Burgh (1714–1775); Andrew Kippis, the dissenters' biographer; the Vaughans, London merchants; and John Horne Tooke. More surprising, perhaps, was his acquaintance with Lady Elizabeth Montagu to whose salon he went until differences over the American situation separated them. Through her he met Shelburne to whom he in turn introduced Priestley. Most famous of his coteries was that of the Honest Whigs meeting fortnightly at the London Tavern near St. Paul's and refreshing themselves with apple puffs, rarebits and punch, wine and beer. Members of the group whose views to their American member, Benjamin Franklin, best represented Old English Whiggery, were Jonathan Shipley, already mentioned; John Canton, a member of the Royal Society; Fothergill, the Quaker; James Parsons, the philologist; Boswell, at this time known chiefly for his liberal *Corsica;* William Rose, a schoolteacher and coeditor of the *Monthly Review;* and some doctors—besides Kippis, Burgh, Priestley, Price, Lindsey, and Lee. This group was predominantly dissenting, and dissenters, Price was to write Lindsey in 1789, had always distinguished themselves in the cause of liberty. With Priestley he represented the best of that group in the reign of George III.[20]

Most of Price's political ideas may be found in his *Observations on The Nature of Civil Liberty, The Principles of Government and The Justice and Policy of the War with America* (1776). He began by the statement that the North Americans were now determined to risk and suffer everything under the persuasion that Great Britain was attempting to rob them of the liberty which was their natural and inalienable right. It was therefore necessary to examine the nature of liberty and form a correct idea of its nature, limits, and principles. He accordingly devoted the first part to an examination of the general nature of liberty, to civil liberty and the principles of government, and to the authority of one country over another. In the second part of the *Observations,* published after considerable pamphlet controversy over the first, he supplemented these remarks by some additional statements on the essentials of a free government and its excellency in which he endeavoured to clarify his position. The second part of the *Observations* is devoted to discussion of the American problem as such. This and the third part of the *Observations* extended the learned appendix to the first on the economic state of the nation, of its adversaries, particularly France, and on the probable effect of the war on public finance.[21]

Price considered liberty under four heads—physical, moral, religious, and civil (civil actually comprising all other kinds). Physical liberty meant self-preservation, our own control over our own actions. Moral liberty was the power of following our sense of right and wrong. Religious liberty, he said, "signifies the power of exercising, without molestation, that mode of religion which we think best . . . civil liberty is the power of a *civil society* or *state* to govern itself by its own discretion; or by laws of its own making, without being subject to any foreign discretion, or to the impositions of any extraneous will or power."

One idea ran through all different kinds of liberty, the idea of self-direction or of self-government. There was a force which stood opposed to the agent's own will which, as far as it operated, produced servitude. In the case of civil liberty any will "distinct from that of the majority of the community which claims a power of making laws for it and disposing of its property" was, if it won the contest, tyrannical. In other words, any cause coming in to restrain the power of self-government might introduce slavery.

To be free was to be able to act, or to forbear acting, as thought best, and in the case of a composite person or state, the freedom of the whole through the suffrage of all the members composing it, or by their representatives, to express the general will. Price distinguished between a free government and a government under which freedom

was enjoyed. One ensured civil liberty, the other provided only "an indulgence of a precarious nature and may, indeed, produce a species of
slavery." The mark of the free state was that in it every man was his own
legislator, all taxes were free gifts, all laws were established by common consent, all magistrates were trustees. A government by laws and
not by men was not necessarily a definition of liberty. Laws could be
made by one or by a junta. Government by them would not differ from
slavery. Price pointed out that in its most perfect form, civil liberty
could only be enjoyed in a small state. In the largest, proper regulations about representation might produce peace, order, and liberty.

The existence of a great number of independent kingdoms as in
Europe often resulted in war. Should one state become supreme, this
would only establish ignominious slavery for the rest. Price therefore
suggested, what he protested was a purely theoretical plan of his devising, the following scheme:

> Let every state, with respect to all its internal concerns, be con-
> tinued independent of all the rest; and let a general confederacy
> be formed by the appointment of a SENATE consisting of Repre-
> sentatives from all the different states. Let this SENATE possess the
> power of managing all the *common* concerns of the united states, and
> of judging and deciding between them, as a common *Arbiter* or *Um-
> pire,* in all disputes; having, at the same time, under its direction, the
> common force of the states to support its decisions. — In these cir-
> cumstances, each separate state . . . would be secure against all op-
> pression and insult from every neighbouring state. — Thus might the
> scattered force and abilities of a whole continent be gathered into
> one point; all litigations settled as they rose; universal peace pre-
> served; and nation prevented *from any more lifting up a sword against
> nation.*[22]

Europe was not to profit by Price's utopian federation, but in the New
World his ideas were studied carefully.

All civil governments were either governments of the whole by the
whole, or by a power extraneous to it, or of a part, and only the first
provided civil liberty. Government by representation alone was free,
but all such governments did not fulfill the intention of freedom. Price
did not oppose an hereditary council of men of the first rank, nor a

supreme executive whose office could also be hereditary, but he insisted on a fair representation of the people in the legislative part of the government. Were that not provided for, the essentials of liberty would not be preserved. Whilst admitting the dangers to freedom from a king, grandees, or other despotic rulers, as well as from a lawless mob, Price maintained that there is less danger from such a mob and its licentiousness than from the despotism of the others. A people were rarely so organized that they could maintain tumultuous rule for long. "Despotism wearing the form of government and being armed with its force, is an evil not to be conquered without dreadful struggles . . . in a state habituated to a despotism, all is still and torpid. A dark and savage tyranny stifles every effort of genius; and the mind loses all its spirit and dignity."[23]

Government, by its very nature a trust, might be abused and defeat its own end. Parliament would forfeit its authority by perpetuating itself, even prolonging its duration, accepting bribes, or subjecting itself to sovereign influence. Parliaments should possess no power beyond the limits of the trust by which they were formed. Parliament's delegated power is subordinate and limited. Omnipotence could only lie where all legislative authority originated, that is, in the people. In other words, government, "does not infringe liberty, but establishes it. It does not take away the rights of mankind but protects and confirms them." Free government gave scope to the exertion of the powers of men, it afforded them scope for self improvement.

> The subjects of free states have, in all ages, been most distinguished for genius and knowledge. Liberty is the soil where the arts and sciences have flourished; and the more free a state has been, the more have the powers of the human mind been drawn forth into action, and the greater number of brave men has it produced.[24]

A government might be free and yet lose its original character. There was nothing that required more to be watched than power. Price feared that the "fair inheritance of liberty left us by our ancestors" was threatened by banality, dissipation, and extravagance. "A standing army, the danger of the public funds and the all-corrupting influence of the Treasury," were likely to produce servility in the people at large. The best form of government united wisdom, union, dispatch, secrecy, and vigour. The wisest of men could render no more valuable service than in contriving plans to make such government possible. Flaws in the constitution could result in violent internal contests with which free governments are often reproached. Price pointed out that such tumults were the effect of health and vigour and the quiet which prevailed under slavish government proceeded from stagnation of human faculties. Price condemned the inequalities and inadequacies of the contemporary English representative system. Corruption he reckoned the worst enemy of liberty. It poisons the fountains of legislation. It excludes the best men. A nation so governed was indeed unfortunate. The principle of representation might vary as to the number of voters and the delegates proposed, but these must be free from corrupt influence, independent, and subject to very frequent change, that is to say, short parliaments.[25]

Price saw in England three classes of people—a gentry, a yeomanry, a peasantry. Overseas in America he saw a one-class society consisting of independent yeomen. He knew of the existence of Negro slaves, but believed that the colonists freed from the demands of the British Negro traders would soon abolish slavery.[26] Price's remarks on the natural equality of mankind were less optimistic than his observations on colonial slavery. He devoted a most interesting paragraph of his *Additional Observations* to a discussion of equality. He suggested that equality is the independence of each of every other. No man could be ruled without his consent, or taxed, or abridged of his liberty. Distinctions of rank would arise within and without a state of nature in all forms of civil government, in families, between clever and stupid, strong and weak men. But where a person had let out his labour to another or put himself under the direction of superior talent—he should still have it always in his power to quit the chosen service or servitude. No one was born with an inherent right of dominion. God had endowed no man with divine right. No government had any right to impose its rule over persons other than those who chose it. The people were the spring of all civil power; they had a right to modify it as they pleased. Whenever it betrayed its genuine intention, that is the maintenance of fundamental equality or independence by defending it against the encroachments of tyranny. Magistrates did not govern the state; the state governed them. They were the servants of the public. Yet, of course, civil governors unfortunately thought of themselves as masters, of their stations as their right, the people their property. Price quoted from Hutcheson's *Moral Philosophy,*

> Mankind have been generally a great deal too tractable; and hence so many wretched forms of power have always enslaved nine tenths of the nations of the world, where they have the fullest right to make all efforts for a change.[27]

It followed from what has been said about civil liberty that "no one community can have any power over the property or legislation of another community, that is not incorporated with it by a just and adequate representation." The subjection of one country to another produced an extraordinarily virulent form of rapacity, cruelty, and injustice. Roman provinces remote from the capital city suffered at a distance which made it nearly impossible for them to obtain by personal petition any redress from the government. Not only was such slavery or dependence one of the worst fates that can befall a country, it was also completely unjustifiable. One state might be subjected to another by conquest, contract, or obligation conferred, but none of this could possibly give a rightful title. Price quoted with approval Molyneux's famous passage in *The Case of Ireland* and suggested that Locke inspired Molyneux's view. No compact of subjection made by the tameness and folly of their ancestors could subject a people to arbitrary power, nor could obligation confer rights. How much, said Price, had been done by England for Hanover, but that gave her no right to tax or make laws for that kingdom.

Price returned in the *Additional Observations* to the justice of dominion or empire, and in a long footnote quoted at length Hutcheson's discussion of when colonies have a right to be released from the parent state. "The insisting of old claims and tacit conventions to extend civil power over distant nations and form grand unwieldy empires without regard to the obvious maxims of humanity has been one great source of human misery." Hutcheson concluded his examination of colonial rights with the statement that they might secede from the parent state "whenever they are so increased in numbers and in strength as to be sufficient by themselves for all the good ends of a political union." Price endorsed this "wise man's" opinion.[28]

Price concluded that an empire was a collection of states or communities united by some common bond or tie.

> If these states have each of them free constitutions of government, and, with respect to taxation and internal legislation, are independent of the other states, but united by contracts or alliances . . . in these circumstances the empire will be an Empire of Freemen . . . if . . . none of the states possess any independent legislative authority; but all are subject to an absolute monarch, whose will is their law; then is the Empire an Empire of Slaves.

He went on to say that if the governing state (rather than an absolute monarch) were free itself, the condition of the subject states was thereby worse, since despots might die, but bodies of men "continue the same and have generally proved the most unrelenting of all tyrants."[29]

Having defined liberty with respect to government and empire, Price proceeded to an examination of the justice of the war with America, whether it were justified by the principles of its constitution, by dictates of wise policy, by the honour of the nation, and by the probability of success. The claims made by Britain were irreconcilable with the principles of true liberty and liberalism of government. In spite of the English prejudice or belief that the colonies were naturally subject to them, such sentiments were unreasonable. Price pointed out that his argument rested on his discussion of general principles and not on the practice of former times nor the charters granted to the colonies.[30] He suggested that the war with America was not just; that the claim in the Declaratory Act that Britain had the power to make laws and statutes to bind the colonies in all cases whatever, that is logically a claim to complete supremacy, could not be justified by right reason; that the assertion that legislative right "must be lodged somewhere 'in order to preserve the unity of the British Empire'" was a fallacy. Such claims used by the Pope, for example, to preserve Christian unity, had produced nothing but discord. He dismissed the idea that the British were superior. If the arguments of supremacy were based on wealth, he denied its dignity; if on population, knowledge, and virtue, he protested that the colonists would soon exceed the English. Moreover "the magic words which have fascinated and misled us," the parent state, meant nothing. Did the Germans have a right to tax the English because the English came from Germany? Far from their being in the debt of Britain, Britain may be considered to owe much of her prosperity to them. Nor was the claim that the land they lived in was ceded to Britain and that they held by charters of one kind and another, capable of being defended logically since they had cultivated it and "without any help from us converted a wilderness into fruitful and pleasant fields."

Price was apparently most indignant over the argument that the defective state of English representative institutions proved a right to tax America—"we submit to a Parliament that does not represent us and therefore they ought." The statement, moreover, was misleading, since in Britain freeholders and burgesses did have representatives and granted aids proportionately paid by themselves and made laws which they must themselves observe. But the Americans had no representative. Their taxes would be paid to someone else; their laws would be made by other people. Price drew a very gloomy picture of an extension of the claim to supremacy now made over a vast variety of states all equal or superior to England. Britain might herself find that her excellent constitution was subverted, that she would be greedy to draw revenue from every distant province when the influence of the crown would have increased, when a general election would be nothing but an auction and parliament a body of sycophants. Should, then, he asked, the colonists be bound to unconditional submission? Price saw in the Quebec Act an extension of the royal authority over Canada, and in the Act about Massachusetts an attempt to do the same thing there.

The fundamental principle of the English government was the right, whether always properly exercised or not, to give and grant money. Civil wars were fought in the past to protect this English right. No war to enforce taxation without representation in America could be justified. Moreover the war was impolitic, since it seemed to be a war to impose our will on others. Ministers had declared that they wanted no money and regarded the trade with America as of no consequence compared with the principle of the Declaratory Act. What a horrible war it was "to sheathe our swords in the bowels of our brethren and spread misery and ruin among a happy people, for no other end than to oblige them to acknowledge our supremacy."[31] Price confessed himself astonished at public feeling against the colonies who had neither rebelled nor invaded England, nor stolen from her. What is more, had we not provoked the contest by pushing the principle of authority so far, by the duties on tea imposed less than a year after the repeal of the Stamp Act, and had we not stationed troops at Boston to enforce obedience to the unpopular Acts, the chances were that the current conflict would not have broken out. Then, he said, a state of war existed in which the colonies were likely to win and were likely, when successful, to resent and abhor England. Trade would be interrupted, the empire dismembered, and many thousands killed. What is more, property would have been destroyed and public credit shaken. An unfavourable balance of trade would exist and our revenue would be deficient. He concluded: "A KINGDOM ON AN EDGE SO PERILOUS, SHOULD THINK OF NOTHING BUT A RETREAT."[32]

Price could see no reason which could be argued against receding from the war. He quoted Chatham: "rectitude is dignity, oppression only is meanness and justice honour." Furthermore, prudence required retraction. Sympathy for the colonists was rising, Englishmen should feel the sympathy they felt for the brave Corsicans in their struggle and should recall that Holland was once subject to Spain and the Sicilians to Athens. Was it not strange, he asked, "that the people who cry out most vehemently for liberty for themselves are the most unwilling to grant it to others. One of the most violent enemies of the colonists has pronounced them 'all Mr. Locke's disciples' — Glorious title! — How shameful is it to make war against them for that reason?"[33]

The *Observations* concluded with a brief listing of small states which, fighting to preserve or acquire liberty, defeated larger and apparently more powerful people. Englishmen were now execrated on both sides of the globe, in India as well as in America. Price quoted at considerable length the scheme outlined to the House of Lords by the earl of Shelburne for conciliation. Shelburne (1737–1805) had urged the repeal of the Acts which immediately distressed America, even whilst the regulation of trade for the common good of the empire was maintained as a fundamental right of Great Britain. He had further suggested some attempts to raise revenue with the consent of the Americans, with full security that such aids should be inalienably appropriated to the discharge of debts. Remarks by the earl had concluded with the reflection that if force were persisted in, "it only remains to apply what has been so often remarked of unhappy periods,—Quos deus vult. . . ."[34] In the *Additional Observations,* Price sadly annotated his earlier conclusion by saying that while Shelburne's plans were being considered in Congress, there was news of another severe act of parliament passed in Britain which brought about the abandonment of further negotiations.

Shelburne had earlier emphasized the determination of Americans to find a solution to their difficulties within the empire. He stated on the authority of letters from America that in 1775 even Hancock and Adams were averse to independence so long as freedom from oppression could be secured. Americans were loyal subjects and were suffering very much from the present conflict. However, the rejection of the petition from Congress which Governor Penn brought over, the last Prohibitionary Bill, the employment of foreign troops to subdue them, and the rejection of the March, 1776, Petition of the City of London had now converted Congress and the colonies to independence. Price reflected that it was easy to see that James II might have gained all he wished if he had been more patient, that William might have been refused as a foreigner at the head of an army, had he not waited for an invitation to deliver England. Ireland had been corrupted by slow and insidious use of prerogative; America might also have been. The empire, once united and happy, was falling, a sacrifice to violence and blindness. A Franco-American alliance, rumoured as he wrote, would end all hope of reconciliation. As the conflict eventually ended, Price refused all suggestions of leaving England. The constitution might still be the best in the world if it were to return to those principles upon which it had been founded and to maintain them. An honest parliament, even if not ideally constituted, could rule well.

The passionate anger of the *Reflections on the French Revolution* was provoked by a most moderate Commonwealthman. The fundamental difference between Burke and Price must be found in the denial of natural rights by one and in the assumption by the other, by Price, of the right of resistance exercised at least twice by Englishmen in the previous century. Both the *Sermon* of 1789 and the *Observations* proclaimed the justice of the cause of reformation in government if dissatisfaction with it prevailed among its subjects. Price once wrote for

Shelburne an elaborate plan for overhauling the English financial system. Though his ideas on matters economic were taken very seriously at the time by Americans, by Shelburne, and by the younger Pitt, they seem impracticable now. In this scheme he emphasized the point that drastic revision of the basis of taxation would make it possible to establish a free port and dispense with the whole army of customs officials then maintained to collect dues. This in turn would deprive the crown of a vast amount of patronage. Such a scheme, he admitted, could only be hoped for "after a convulsion that shall overturn all government, destroy artificial wealth and the means of corruption, reduce the kingdom to poverty and simplicity and set it upon new and free ground." Should such an event occur, Price would be found, as he was when the French Revolution started, eager to take advantage of the opportunities offered, but it is impossible to imagine him either desiring such an upheaval in England or taking practical steps to bring it about.[35]

The circle around Shelburne at Bowood to which Price and, more briefly, Priestley belonged, included many Commonwealthmen. The earl prided himself not only on his indifference to popular clamour, but on his friendships, and showed great discrimination in forming them. Thomas Jervis, Disney's son-in-law, was tutor to his son. Franklin frequented the house. Shelburne wished to advance Jonathan Shipley to Canterbury. Mirabeau and Romilly were his guests. Isaac Barré (1726–1802), Glynn, Adair, and John Dunning were connected with the group to which Bentham and Charles Grey later belonged. Through Shelburne's efforts Sir William Jones was advanced to an Indian judgeship. Shelburne was never devoted to Chatham, although friendly with Camden, but he loyally supported Chatham's policies and may be said to have inherited a part of his political mantle. Yet he only briefly assumed the responsibilities of leadership, and failed to hold the position among the reformers which birth, talents, and policies might have given him.

Shelburne entered politics under the patronage of Bute, but soon dissociated himself from the Scotsman and allied with those supporting Wilkes, opposing the Stamp Act, and critical of the Quebec Act. This last measure Shelburne thought was designed to intimidate New England rather than to administer Canada wisely. Molyneux, Molesworth, and Lucas were his mentors in the matter of economic poli-

cies toward Ireland. Later support of the younger Pitt's Union was undoubtedly induced by hopes that it would, whatever its deficiencies,
remedy many grievances and ills. Curious about scientific and philosophic movements of the day, Shelburne was a freethinker, almost an
anticleric, and was tolerant of nearly all but the papists. Constitutional
liberty consists, he wrote, "in the right of exercising freely every faculty
of mind or body which can be exercised without preventing another
man from doing the like." Efforts should be made, if not toward an
equality, at least toward the improvement of conditions and education
among the lower orders of society.[36]

Ill fortune dogged the reformers in the characters of the men who
might have led them to some measure of success. Savile was too independent, too cautious, too little of a practical politician. Shelburne
lacked the taste and determination for prolonged political activity.
Chatham was wrecked by eccentricities and ill health. Among all the
assorted noble proponents of American and religious liberties, none
had the necessary qualities and patience for the tasks their projects
involved.

Joseph Priestley (1733–1804) only entered Shelburne's household
after much heart-searching and consultation with Price and other
friends. When he did so it was quite frankly from financial motives.
Though there was never any open quarrel, the arrangement was not
a success, or at least so Priestley felt, and he left Bowood with relief.
Shelburne sought him out after Dunning's death, but though Priestley
seems to have had a gift for friendship, he never seems to have developed any warmth of feeling for the earl. Yet, any account of Priestley's life must include some survey of acquaintances, for wherever he
went he formed lasting ties — at Warrington with a brilliant group of tutors; in Leeds when he served the Mill Hill Chapel; in London with his
cronies, the Honest Whigs at the London Tavern; the Essex Street connection; the Hackney professors; at Birmingham, the Lunar Society
with Small and Erasmus Darwin, his brothers-in-law (the Wilkinsons),
and others. He became friendly with Franklin and met Quincy, Adams,
and Jefferson over a period of years. Men like the Vaughans, connected with more than one period of his English life, continued their
acquaintance in America. Tutor, minister, scientist, and writer, Priestley had contacts with all circles of the Honest Whigs of his time in York-

shire, Lancashire, Warwickshire, and in western towns like Exeter and Taunton, as well as the metropolis. He met at Shelburne's many of the French philosophers. His studies of the Scripture, in a society which lasted over a decade, brought him into direct touch with Edmund Law as well as old friends amongst rational dissenters like Dodson and Tayleur (1713–1796) of Shrewsbury.[37]

His relations with a famous contemporary, Edmund Burke, were related by Priestley only five days before he died in 1804. They had met through John Lee's good offices while Priestley was at Leeds and seemed to have no differences of opinion on matters political except that Burke looked to the great Whig families to check the crown and Priestley to a more equal representation of the Commons. In 1770 the appearance of *Thoughts on the Present Discontents* revealed aristocratical principles of which both Lee, himself a Rockingham Whig, and Priestley disapproved. However, a mutual interest in the conciliation of the colonies, on which Priestley had written as early in 1769 in *The Present State of Liberty,* seemed to unite them for a while longer. They met often while Priestley was with Shelburne, between 1772 and 1778, and after Priestley moved to Birmingham in 1780, Burke called on him for a long afternoon visit. On Burke's joining the coalition soon after the intimacy ceased, and in his *Reflections* in 1791, he not only attacked Price but also misrepresented Priestley who felt that a reply was necessary. Thereafter Burke seemed only to rejoice at the misfortunes of his erstwhile companion.[38]

Priestley started his education at home and continued it at Daventry and during work on his lectures at Warrington. Even the most cursory glance at his works shows the vast extent of his reading and the width of his interests. He was first and foremost, perhaps, a dissenter by training and by lifelong disposition. His theological presuppositions underwent a drastic transformation from early Calvinism to Unitarianism. He spent much time, as already noted, in study of the Scriptures. Much of his published work consists of Bible commentary. It is worth emphasizing this in view of the confusion, real or feigned, in the minds of contemporaries between men like Priestley and the continental freethinkers and atheists. But of course his interest spread far outside of matters theological, and he wrote on history, education, and science as well as government and politics. He acknowledged his own indebtedness to scholars of all kinds, but above all to Locke, Newton, Clarke, the towering genius of Hutcheson, and the philosophy of David Hartley whose work he edited and popularized. Jebb was reported by young Sylas Neville as referring to the "Divine Priestley," and there does seem to have been something singularly engaging and yet impressive in his character and personality, which the range of his friendships reveals.[39]

When Priestley wrote on religious liberty and the problems of the sectaries he was always careful to state that he spoke only for himself, and excluded from his consideration the Quakers, not because he had no acquaintance with them—Fothergill was his old associate in many ventures—but because he recognized a difference in their approach to politics. Even so, he was not always approved of by his fellow dissenters. He was one of a minority among them, the rational Protestants or Unitarians, as he pointed out himself, and exchanged friendly arguments, even with Richard Price who never ceased to be an Arian and to deny the determinism Priestley recognized. Nevertheless in his *Letter to Pitt* and his *View* and other works, Priestley summed up certain attitudes and emphasized the virtues amongst the nonconformists.[40]

The unthinking part of a community normally attended the services of the Establishment. So did sectaries when they lost interest in their doctrinal heritage. Priestley believed that difference of opinion in religion was healthy in any society. He hoped that there would never be fewer dissenters in England. He saw no danger to any one from them. They were mostly found among the middling and lower ranks of society. They had lost much of their old bigotry and less desirably, perhaps, their zeal. They were not fond of undue prerogative, yet had until very recently almost always supported the Hanoverian court interest. He entirely disagreed with William Blackstone's published remarks to the effect that the spirit, doctrine, and practice of the dissenters were not likely to make them good subjects. On principle Priestley disliked any claim by anyone to dictate in matters of religious dogma or discipline. He himself was much interested as he studied the history of his coreligionists to discover the changes that had occurred in their attitudes and convictions. He abandoned the old prejudice against papists, and exchanged rather sharp notes with Thomas Hollis about the latter's more traditional nonconforming intolerance. Blackburne's change of heart concerning papists was undoubtedly due to Priestley's influence, and he seems to have worked on all his friends about their prejudices and fears.⁴¹

Priestley taught at Warrington, and was interested in all aspects of his profession. He was extraordinarily anxious that no state should attempt the education of its subjects. If government took control, the dangers of uniformity would be increased. The attempt of Oxford to discourage the reading of Locke's *Essay on Human Understanding* was the sort of danger to which the population would be exposed under a state system. Religious, moral, and political principles would be inculcated in infant minds by state-endowed teachers. The chief glory of human nature, the operation of reason in a variety of ways and with diversified results would be lost. Every man should educate his children in his own manner to preserve the balance which existed among the several religious and political parties in Great Britain. If any one group was responsible for the whole, that one would soon be in the ascendancy. Youth must be inspired with a love of truth, and a sense of virtue and public spirit. They must be encouraged in the method of free enquiry. Priestley had original ideas about the curriculum, particularly the study of history for which he provided a most detailed scheme. Both natural science and chemistry should be included in the curriculum. He was inclined to restrict the study of classics to those designed for the church and to stress English composition.⁴²

In his preface to *An Essay on the First Principles of Government* (1771) Priestley disclaimed originality except in so far as he was able to set things "in a new or clearer point of light." Indeed, he continued,

> Whenever the interests of truth and liberty are attacked, it is to be wished that some would stand up in their defence, whether they acquit themselves better than their predecessors in the same *good old Cause,* or not. *New books* in defence of any principles whatever, will be read by many persons, who will not look into *old books,* for the proper answers to them.⁴³

He was not occupied by utopian speculation. He wanted to preserve liberty—political, or the power to vote; civil, or the power reserved to oneself; religious, or the right to freedom of thought. Man's natural powers and his capacity for improvement by education enabled him to consider past, present, and future. Governments might be imperfect, but when a proper attention was given to the problems of society, its improvement seemed likely. Man was possessed of a much greater power to be and to make happy than persons of the same age and country some centuries ago. There is no reason to doubt that centuries hence persons would be much superior to the present generation.

The great instrument of the progress of the species toward perfection was, to Priestley, government. He foresaw a great extension of knowledge by a commodious subdivision of the labours towards its attainment. The contemplation of the glorious and paradisaical future always made him happy. The form of government which most favoured progress towards the happiness of mankind must be approved, the general welfare being, of course, the criterion by which it must be judged.[44]

The origins of society were much less important than discussion about its validity in terms of general happiness. Representation must follow inevitably on the natural discovery of the inconveniences of independent living. In large countries the representative body must be understood to voice the sentiments and aspirations of the population. Rousseau's reservations were brushed aside most casually. Priestley was sure the deputies must be guided by reason and conscience and judged by their constituents. Every individual might attempt to convince others of his own opinions and thereby control them. Political liberty meant to him the right of being eligible for office, and of having a voice in the nominations of those who achieved it. This was the compensation that small sacrifice of civil liberty, power over all one's own actions which must be made to establish government.

Officers should always remember they are servants of the public and may be deposed and punished if failing in their duty. It need not, however, be supposed that much danger to place and security existed from the admission of this right. How long, for example, had the Norman kings reigned before the revolts of the age of John and Henry III brought redress and Magna Carta? How long before the tyrannies of Charles I caused the civil wars of the seventeenth century? Nevertheless abuse of power by members of parliament—such as, for example, the passing of law excepting themselves from taxation, or the misuse of riches, of rights of whatever kind—should bring criticism and in the last resort armed resistance. No one who was taxed should be unable to criticize and thus influence the collection and the expenditure of public funds. Property was founded upon a regard for the general good, nothing being a man's own but what general rules for the general good gave to him. Without overt acts the governors may never be awed by the voice of the people.[45]

The form and the extent of power in governments must, Priestley maintained, be carefully distinguished. Administration should be uniform and certain. It must secure the greatest possible number of the natural rights of the people. Laws should be fixed.

> [Laws] are defective when they leave an individual destitute of that assistance which they could procure for him, and they are burdensome and oppressive; i.e., injurious to the natural rights and civil liberties of mankind, when they lay a man under unnecessary restrictions, by controlling his conduct, and preventing him from serving himself, with respect to those things, in which they can yield him no real assistance, and in providing for which he is in no danger of injuring others.[46]

It was not easy to circumscribe exactly the limit of civil government. People might, it was true, subject themselves to whatever restrictions they pleased, but it was worth taking thought which restrictions and laws would be wisest. The spirit of the times restrained despots from certain actions for a while. If England, like Denmark, were to surrender her liberties, some time would still elapse before trial by jury, and habeas corpus would fail to safeguard certain individuals. Similarly, the House of Commons—though only elected septennially, and often corruptly—still faced the countryside at intervals and were presumably somewhat restrained by this. But they were probably, because they never conversed with them, less troubled by the complaints of the poor than by the criticisms of their rich neighbours.

Old forms of government were likely to persist. Habit of mind often disposed men against change. Europe was thus unlikely to develop republican forms; America, on the other hand, must be naturally against the monarchical. Other factors might preserve liberty. The division of power was essential. The legislative should be separate from the judicial bodies. All legislators should be under the same law as the rest of the community. They, like the magistrates, should regard themselves

as the servants of the public. The just limits of government were difficult to establish. Experiment would reveal them, but a wise rule might
be for government not to be exercised "by the mere tendencies of
things." Only manifest and urgent necessity could justify extension of
authority. All must be designed to encourage a spirit of liberty, security, and independence without which no great improvements would
ever be made.[47]

The study of history was absolutely necessary for all who wished to
be good citizens and to travel.[48] Women might discover by it that men
were by no means always guided by gentler emotions. Everyone may
find out the vast number of different governments there were in the
world and the advantages of one over the others in meeting specific
dangers. Republics should guard against the emergence of a Medici
class and also the undue accumulation of wealth. Perhaps a limitation of inheritance might be necessary. The Chinese had extraordinary
security in property. In despotisms it was the poor, on the whole, so
long as they aspired to no more than the bread won by their labours,
who were the most safe. Wealth seemed likeliest to come from cities
rather than despotisms. The enslaved were more poor, according to
Beccaria, than the free; their passions were unrestrained by the uncer-
tainty of everything.[49]

Priestley deplored the English game laws which conflicted with the
natural rights of men. He observed the progress of wealth and luxury,
but he also noticed that the well-fed had greater courage and spirit
than the half-starved with little for which to fight. High living might
corrupt the body, but idleness and barbarity were unlikely to profit
society. In the long run riches might bring knowledge, power, and
progress. All schemes of improvement should be designed not only
for the present, but for the future extension of happiness. Indubitably
there had been progress and "let us not doubt that every generation
in posterity will be as much superior to us in political, and in all kinds
of knowledge, and that they will be able to improve upon the best civil
and religious institutions that we can prescribe for them . . . let us
make this great and desirable work easier to them than it has been
to us."[50]

The roster of students of Warrington and other academies suggests
many lines of investigation, but these cannot be followed here. Nor can

the membership of many local societies, nor of occupational groups—like the London publishers, printers, and journalists—be dealt with. The circle in which, for example, one of Bishop Watson's correspondents, Thomas Percival (1740–1804), moved would certainly reveal the existence of many Real Whigs of liberal politics. Percival himself was one of John Seddon's first students at Warrington (1757). He then attended the University of Edinburgh and met Hume and Robertson —in whose sister's house he lived—as well as a man who became a life-long friend. Thomas Butterworth Bayley (1744–1802) of Hope, a Cheshire baronet, later became a much-respected magistrate keenly interested in the welfare of the poor, the condition of penitentiaries, in public health, and in education. He was hot-tempered, versatile, tolerant, and a "Whig of the old school." Other friends included Dr. Haygarth of Bath, Dr. Falconer, Dr. Aikin (separately mentioned) and Sir Lucas Pepys. He corresponded with Franklin, Bishop Watson, Priestley, and William Magee of Dublin. He was a busy doctor, a member of a conversation club at Manchester, and was elected to the American Philosophical Society in 1787. He was also the author of works on a variety of subjects which, when published in 1807, filled two volumes.

Percival believed in "calm investigation" of constitutional principles. He worked for repeal of the Test and Corporation Acts, and in the antislavery movement. *An Inquiry into the Principles and Limits of Taxation* reveals his belief that man had natural rights to liberty and property and that liberty was essential to the perfection of reason. He obviously had studied history and strongly reprobated the compensation voted Charles II for the abolition of the Court of Wards in 1660, which fell on the labouring poor. Hewers of wood, he felt, should be encouraged; and with Raynal, he opposed taxing the less privileged and cited Molesworth's *Denmark* on the evils that followed when the rich refused to bear their fair share of public burden. He also supported the idea of making wages high and taxes on necessities low. America was prosperous. Percival seems to have profited by a study of the best in the literature of his generation and to have used his talents for the public welfare.[51]

One of Priestley's Warrington associates and Percival's friend was John Aikin (1747–1822) who had been educated at the school, at Glasgow and had studied medicine at Edinburgh. His parents were the son of a tutor at the academy and the daughter, Jane Jennings, of another tutor. He practised in Manchester, Yarmouth, and finally in Stoke Newington where he died. He was a friend not only of the chemist, but of Thomas Percival and Thomas Butterworth Bayley; the geographer, Thomas Pennant; Gilbert Wakefield; John Haygarth; Dr. James Currie; Erasmus Darwin; John Howard; and Southey. He was a member of the Revolution Society, and defended Price against Burke and the Socinians against everybody. Though a student of Rousseau, he early concluded that some inequality was inevitable. Happiness could come from a restraint of disparity. Wretchedness would be avoided if the levelling principle implicit in nearly every government involved security of equal laws, rights, and opportunity. He had a daughter, Lucy, who memorialized her father, and her aunt edited the latter's works and wrote about the courts of the early Stuarts. She had been adopted out of a large family by the childless Anne Barbauld, who begged her brother to spare one of his numerous brood for herself and her husband.[52]

Mrs. Barbauld (1743–1825) was a gifted children's teacher. She had a catholic taste in literature, and wrote hymns and miscellaneous pieces. The daughter of a teacher, as well as one herself, she was well informed in the literature of the subject of education from the Greeks to Mrs. Macaulay. She minimized the share which direct precept should have in the educational process and maintained that people, adult and children alike, as well as nations, were educated by circumstances. Circumstances produced different customs and principles. She was keenly aware of changing opinion, and noticed that where the English formerly despised the French for being slaves, they then censored them for daring to be free and equal.

She took some part in the campaign to secure repeal of the Test and Corporation Acts in 1790, and wrote a very interesting tract on dissenters. She listed their virtues, their sobriety, their contributions to commerce and industry. They did not seek public positions, nor overthrow of the government, nor anything but the inalienable rights of the human race. There were, she thought, three periods in the history of sects. In the first the sectaries may be less attractive, but their faith will be strong and the sacrifices they make and the persecutions they endure will inspire their devotion. In the second they may engage in controversy and become more worldly. Finally they may conform. The nonconformists with the growth of tolerance may lose some eccentricities. They may also lose some of their virtue "for it may be of advantage to bear what yet it is unjustifiable in others to inflict."[53]

Rather different stages in dissenting history may be illustrated by the career of another friend of Franklin, Price, Priestley, and the rational dissenters. William Hazlitt (1737–1820), father of the more celebrated essayist of the same name, was born of Presbyterian parents in Tipperary. He was educated at Glasgow between 1756 and 1761 and became a Unitarian. He first ministered to a congregation at Wisbech in Cambridgeshire, also known as the birthplace of William Godwin. He then moved to Gloucestershire, and in 1770 to Maidstone in Kent where his son, William, was born. Here he knew John Wiche, a Baptist minister widely acquainted with the Blackburne-Priestley coterie, and here he was able to see Franklin, Price, and Caleb Fleming. In 1780 Hazlitt moved back to Ireland and befriended American prisoners at Kinsdale. As soon as the war was over he visited New York, Philadelphia, and Boston before returning in 1786 to settle for the rest of his life at Wem in Shropshire. He sent his son to study in Liverpool where he stayed with the Railtons, friends of the family, and then to Hackney College, where Joseph Fawcett (d.1804) taught him. Both William and his brother John, a painter, were radicals and remained so throughout their lives when others of their early friends had grown more conservative. William the younger often laughed at his dissenting forbears, but he had absorbed from his father a deep love of liberty and respect for the traditions of the sectaries. The elder Hazlitt and his colleagues served as the model for the essayist's sketch of clerical character in 1818. "They set up an image in their own minds—it was truth; they worshipped an idol there—it was justice."[54]

Political Disquisitions, Societies, and Associations

Blackburne and his friends worked for religious liberty, but were also involved in the propagation of other liberal causes. Priestley and Price were both ministers, Bible students, and one of them devoted time to science and the other to economics, besides the attention that both gave to politics throughout their lives. The bonds between rational Protestants of all sorts brought them together in many activities. The tradition of the Commonwealth Whigs manifested itself in connection with some specific issues of the reign of George III which may be illustrated in discussion of a few well-known republicans and the supporters of the Bill of Rights, in two important works, *An Historical Essay* and Burgh's *Political Disquisitions,* and in the crusades led by Cartwright and Jebb and other members of the Society for Constitutional Information. These last were involved in the organizations stemming from Christopher Wyvill's Yorkshire association which should be given some credit for the passage in the Commons of Dunning's famous motion against crown influence, and Burke's equally well-known economical reform. But Jebb and Cartwright had hoped for much more drastic statutes or even, if support were forthcoming, more vigorous action through these committees. They were not satisfied with the Rockingham achievement, were disgruntled with Fox and with the younger Pitt. With their program and its failure the tradition traced here may be said to end, even though some survivors among their associates lived on to welcome the French Revolution and to work with the newer generation of reformers and the early radicals of the nineteenth century.

Almost as soon as the Peace of Paris ended the Seven Years' War, signs of discontent, in spite of the victory it marked for English arms all over the world, may be found. Straws in the wind suggest the direction of later movements. *Political Disquisitions Proper for Publick Consideration* (1763) wanted a change in representation in favour of mercantile interests. Hollis and Baron, as already described, wanted more county members and advertised their program. Edward King, a lawyer, wanted to disenfranchise some boroughs and to raise property qualifications in the counties. He was not radical in his suggestions in his *Essay* (1767), but he thought the times ripe for a new government to appear. "There is not," he declared, "a greater solecism in politicks than that common one of continuing customs after the reasons for them cease."[55] Numbers of tracts and letters in the newspapers discussed the issues raised by the Stamp Act and by the twofold attack on Wilkes, legal and parliamentary.

Few of these publications betrayed any antimonarchical sentiment, but a handful of outright republicans may be discovered in the first twenty years of George III's reign. Some of these were listed by Horace Walpole, though he ignored a couple known to us by their works and a few others whose names chance has preserved. Benjamin Rush (1746–1813), later a signer of the Declaration of Independence, a famous Philadelphia doctor and a treasurer of the United States Mint, arrived in Liverpool in October 1766, on his way to study medicine at Edinburgh. His landlady gave him an introduction to her nephew, John Bostock (1740–1774), then a student at that university. The two young men became friends, and Bostock, a rapturous admirer of Sidney and an ardent republican, converted the American to his own way of thinking.

Spence, whose penny numbers have been referred to more than once, was the son of a Scotsman from Aberdeen. In 1775 he delivered what was to become his famous Newcastle lecture advocating redistribution of land, parish by parish, and thus anticipated Ogilvie by some five or six years. His theories made life difficult for him in his native city and he made his way south to London to engage in various republican activities during the French Revolution. The lecture was reprinted before the end of the century and was to influence Owen later. Among his contemporaries perhaps Catherine Macaulay most nearly resembled him in the works she studied and admired and in her emphasis upon decentralization.[56]

Walpole named only four republicans—Mrs. Macaulay; her brother, Alderman John Sawbridge (1732–1795); Sawbridge's brother-in-law, John Stevenson (1710–1794), another city politician and an East India Company merchant; Thomas Hollis. Another, known now by the diary he kept from 1767–1788, was Sylas Neville (1741–1840). From the record he kept some names may be added to this list, like those of Timothy Hollis, cousin of Thomas; Richard Baron; Thomas Brand; and a friend in the customs called Thomas Deverson. Before analyzing the nature of the politics professed by Mrs. Macaulay and Neville, the career of Sawbridge may be summarized.[57]

The Sawbridges were a well-to-do Kentish family of decidedly Whig politics. John was thought to be less clever than his sister, but he had the advantage of sex and served as Member for Hythe, as Sheriff of Middlesex, and as an alderman of the city of London. He became prominent as a supporter of Wilkes, but he continued activity in parliament supporting the Americans, the cause of shorter parliaments, and reform of the representative system. He had supported Chatham in the tradition of William Beckford (1709–1770) and he also supported Shelburne. He was one of the founders of the Society for Constitutional Information. Perhaps his chief title to fame was his share in founding the Society for the Supporters of the Bill of Rights in 1769, prototype of this and so many other societies. Others who helped him were three fellow aldermen, Oliver, Townshend, and Wilkes; John Glynn, James Adair, and Robert Morris, lawyers; the rector of St. Stephen Walbroke, Dr. Thomas Wilson (1703–1784), Mrs. Macaulay's admirer; Sir John Barnard; Sir Francis Delaval, a friend of John Lee; William Tooke; the Reverend John Horne, who afterwards resigned from the church and adopted Tooke's name as his own. These men met at the London Tavern to help all whose rights had been violated, in particular Mr. Wilkes. Before the Society had put out its eleven-part program, however, Tooke and Wilkes had parted company. Most, though not all of these men, were involved in the controversy over freedom to publish parliament debates in which Brass Crosby and the printer, John Miller, were victims. Indeed, there seems to have been less of republican spirit than of city recalcitrance in the activity of Sawbridge.[58]

Catharine, his sister, inherited the same disdain for titles, their father having followed Pulteney till he was ennobled, as his children admired Pitt until he became Chatham. Catharine was beautiful. She married first Dr. Thomas Macaulay, and then William Graham, many years her junior. She was also admired by Dr. Thomas Wilson who commissioned a statue of her as Dame Thucydides (now at Warrington) and left her his fortune. Later in life her appearance was striking and this has been made familiar by many caricatures. Thomas Hollis as long as he lived enjoyed both her work and her company, though he was annoyed at gossip about their friendship. Catharine made many American friends and stayed at Mount Vernon with Washington and in New England with the Warrens, amongst others, in a visit of some length.

Her reputation was made with the first volume of the *History* which appeared in 1763, though the sixth and last was almost despaired of before it came out in 1781. She wrote on a variety of other subjects in the course of her lifetime. She defended religion against what she felt were the heresies of William King's *Origin of Evil.* Although she associated with persons professing a variety of beliefs—Hollis, a free-thinker; Caleb Fleming, a rational dissenter; Wilson, Anglican parson; and William Harris, the west country dissenting clergyman and historian—she seems to have been entirely conventional in her own religion, and quite willing to defend her position. Most of her work was written on political or social topics: against Hobbes; on education; on copyright; against Burke, both in 1770 and in 1791; on a constitution for Corsica. Lecky regarded Mrs. Macaulay as the ablest writer of the radical school and there can be no doubt that her tracts as well as her *History* impressed contemporaries even when they did not entirely agree with her. The *History* owed a part of its immediate success to the fact that it provided a Whig counterpart to the history Hume had recently published and to the revelations of John Dalrymple, based on Barillon's correspondence. Hume's bias was Tory; Dalrymple's point, acceptable to Tories, was that many a Whig hero of the last days of the Stuarts had taken money from Louis XIV and that they were therefore no purer than the court they had condemned. Both men were also North Britons. Mrs. Macaulay pleased those who disliked Scots, whose unpopularity was great during Bute's period of influence, and soothed Whig sentiments, even though she had been carried away by sympathy with the fate of Charles I.

Mrs. Macaulay was thirty when she started work in 1761. She was already soaked in Whig traditions, but on the publication of her first volume she attracted Hollis's attention. He introduced her to many Civil War tracts and pamphlets, and her later work shows that she had read them. She did a great deal more research than her rival, Hume, and she made good use of the recently published debates and state papers. Sympathetic towards the experimenters of the Interregnum, her politics were of the Commonwealth, republican kind, in spite of sympathy for the royal martyr. She supported an agrarian and rotation in office, and advocated annual parliaments, equal electoral districts, and manhood suffrage. She discussed with Washington a love for simple clothes and living, and a dislike of luxury and ostentation, although her own record in this respect was hardly unblemished. Comments to Mercy

Warren about American politics show her distrust of too great centralization in the new constitution, though she had apparently earlier felt that Congress had had too little power. Catharine's republicanism was manifest in the days when young Sylas Neville first met her and noticed her intimacy with Richard Baron, who called her by her given name, and it remained consistent throughout her life. It was linked with earlier republican traditions in England, and was connected, but without violent partisanship, with the republicans in America and in France. There was a certain detachment and independence in her commentary that entitles Mrs. Macaulay to more serious study than she normally provokes.[59]

Nothing could be further from detachment than the politics expressed in his diary (1767–1788) by Sylas Neville. Though he was nearly fifty as it ended, his entries still seem naive and immature. If he lacked judgment, he had brains, and he had a large acquaintance which entitled him to some serious consideration as representative of republican politics. Neville's ancestry is unknown, but he seems to have been brought up in London of dissenting parents. At the time his diary commences he was involved, not only in a variety of amorous adventures with which only a Boswell could compete, but was also already a determined republican. He was a frequent of Pinners Hall in London during Caleb Fleming's ministry and of the churches of men like George Walker (1734–1807), Samuel Bourn (1714–1796), and other rational Protestants in the provinces. Wherever he was, he celebrated the thirtieth of January, anniversary of the execution of Charles I, with calves head dinners and toasts to the "deserved death" of the King. Wherever he was, in London, Norfolk, or Edinburgh, he at once became known to men of like principles.

When in London he sat in Timothy Hollis's pew in Pinners Hall, and seems to have had tea with the old gentleman quite frequently, to have talked freely with him and to have been introduced by him to Baron and to Mrs. Macaulay. Neville immensely admired Timothy's cousin, Thomas, but never met him, nor does he seem to have met Thomas Brand, though the diary speaks of him as a republican. At Timothy's request Neville waited on Wilkes about the time of the election in 1769 to pass on certain warnings to him. Wilkes, like his admirer, Hollis, was of London dissenting stock and education. Fleming is reported to have said that the Society of the Bill of Rights, formed at this time for the support of Wilkes, was for the greater part composed of true friends of liberty, but that there were "Judas's among them." In the provinces Neville made friends with Thomas Deverson, already mentioned as a republican. In Scotland, where he went to study medicine, his greatest friend was Thomas Blackburne, son of the Archdeacon, about whom he had heard from old Timothy shortly after the publication of *The Confessional.* He had been astonished that an Anglican clergyman could produce such a book. Through another friend John Wilson, he met Sir George Savile and reported of the fifty-eight-year-old member for Yorkshire that "the old patriot is a very sensible entertaining man." Sir George gained the universal respect of his contemporaries—whatever their particular political connection—by support of religious liberty, of moderate reform, and by his sturdy independent integrity. Neville met friends of John Jebb about the time of the campaign against subscription in 1771–72.[60]

Of course Neville's politics were antimonarchical. No one could be a friend to liberty who was not a republican, both he and Timothy Hollis agreed. He distrusted all kings and aristocrats. Even as liberal a peer as David Erskine, eleventh earl of Buchan, only received a reluctant tribute from him. He endorsed the politics of Tom Paine's *Common Sense* (1776), and thought it treated George III "as the dog deserves." What kind of government he would have substituted for the English does not appear in the *Diary.* Throughout the period he supported the American stand and he welcomed their eventual victory. He thought of emigrating, but was dissuaded by Caleb Fleming, perhaps because the old minister thought England needed men of his politics, or perhaps because he realized that Neville had not the stamina necessary for colonial ventures. Neville sought out Americans at Edinburgh when he was studying medicine. At Deptford in 1783 he paused to admire the pennants of the new republic's ships stationed there, flying in the breeze, white on blue ground, some bearing thirteen stripes, others thirteen stars, and he reflected that the Americans could consider themselves as "stars of no mean brightness." Their triumph had secured glorious principles which the power of oppression could never shake.

The diary throws some light on the social ideas of this small group. Timothy and his young friend discussed politics very frankly. "Mobs,"

Hollis thought were the "Dernier résort of the People and have ever been productive of the best revolutions and (even when in the wrong) are to be tenderly used." The two men agreed that there ought to be no hereditary honours, and that there should be but two orders in the state; presumably the rulers and the ruled. Neville was surprised after this to find that Timothy would have denied the lower kind of people any education. He thought that unless people could read and write, they could hardly understand either their temporal rights or the means of salvation. Poor laws, of course, encouraged sloth.[61] Neither Hollis nor Neville seems to have indulged in the nauseating, though well-meant, sentimentalizing about the lower classes that can be found in Thomas Day's *Sandford and Merton,* nor to have adopted its rather woolly kind of egalitarianism.

Two works which appeared before the outbreak of hostilities were both stimulated by the controversy already raging between England and the colonies, and may be said to represent expressions of the Commonwealth tradition. Both influenced greatly the theories and the activities of the Jebb-Cartwright connection and both were absorbed by the Society for Constitutional Information into their canon of Real Whig writings. These books were *An Historical Essay on the English Constitution* (1771), and *The Political Disquisitions* by James Burgh, which appeared in 1774. The earlier essay was anonymous. It has been carelessly attributed to Allan Ramsay the Tory and anti-American court painter, but the *Gentleman's Magazine* in 1791 noticed the death of Obadiah Hulme of Charterhouse Square and identified him as the author of this specifically mentioned work and some other unnamed tracts. Elsewhere Hulme was reported to be the brother of a well-known doctor, physician to the Charterhouse and of Yorkshire extraction. The significance of the *Essay* depends upon its interpretation of history and upon certain suggestions in it which greatly influenced Burgh and then both Jebb and Wyvill. Moreover Jefferson was to owe to careful study of the *Essay* at least some part of his obsession with the Saxon Myth and of his knowledge of the faults in the English system which had resulted from a lack of "constant Watchfullness."[62]

English liberty, in the *Essay,* as well as in a host of other earlier works based on equally unsound historical folklore, had come to England with the Saxon invaders and had been fostered by Alfred. The lessons

Robert Brady and others had long ago sought to teach were ignored, but some very important remarks were made about the contemporary parliament and about the colonies. The *Essay* was anticlerical in tone and spoke of the "baneful influence of the clergy," regretting that all church lands had not been permanently confiscated at the time of the Interregnum. Hulme pointed out the degeneration of parliamentary liberty after 1660. The evil game laws were due to the victory of a propertied class after the Qualification Act of 1711. Another mistake was made when the Septennial Act was passed. Both acts, Hulme thought, should be repealed. Parliament should be freed, too, of officers and ministers. Annual elections would purge the constitution of the evils of the long extension of sessions. The country constituencies should be reformed on the basis of tithing or hundred, in a scheme not unlike that of Richard Baron. If parliament would not consent to these changes, it should be possible to form country associations and constitutional societies which could carry them through. Hulme made observations about the tax system, and condemned the bounty on corn and taxes on malt and soap. A tax on land or rent should be the same for York and Boston, and all property, fixed or movable, should be assessed and taxed all over the empire, though necessities should never be amerced. The colonists would not mind this if all English also endured the same system. Evils like the Stamp Act came from corrupt parliaments, and a reform of the parliamentary organization, affected, if necessary, by an extra-parliamentary convention, would probably be necessary before the financial changes could be made.[63]

This essay was read by James Burgh (1714–1775) to whom "history was an inexhaustible mine out of which political knowledge is to be brought up." A Scot, a cousin of the historian, William Robertson, he was educated at St. Andrew's. Ill health cut short his course, and he seems to have engaged briefly in very unprofitable business activities. He then went south to London and helped correct proof for William Bowyer, the printer. Nichols says he met Arthur Onslow, "whom he not infrequently attended with the proof sheet of the Votes" of the Commons to which Bowyer was printer. He taught in the free grammar school in Marlow and wrote *Britain's Remembrancer* in 1746, a much-reprinted tract which pointed out the moral of the Rebellion. In 1747, after one other job, he opened his own school at Stoke Newington and

began to write on education and philosophy. He was enormously industrious. When at Newington Green, to which he had moved, he married Mrs. Hannah Harding. He retired in 1771 to Islington. Probably
he then gave up attendance at the club of "Honest Whigs." In spite of
illness, Burgh managed to write the three volumes of his best-known
work, *Political Disquisitions,* before his death in 1775. Nichols asserted,
on the basis of long personal acquaintance, that he was communicative and agreeable as well as benevolent and pious.[64]

The *Disquisitions* dealt with the problems of the day: parliamentary
corruption, a standing army, and the nature of colonial government.
It is perhaps the most important political treatise which appeared in
England in the first half of the reign of George III. Burgh attributed
all the troubles of the period to the absence of an independent parliament. He foresaw a fearful and horrid prospect ahead if steps were
not taken to remedy the constitution.

> Pursuing those gloomy ideas I see—how shall I write it?—I see
> my wretched country in the same condition as *France* is now. Instead
> of the rich and thriving farmers, who now fill, or who lately filled,
> the country with agriculture, yielding plenty for man and beast, I
> see the lands neglected, the villages and farms in ruins, with here
> and there a starveling in wooden shoes, driving his plough consist-
> ing of an old goat, a high-backed bullock and an ass, value in all
> forty shillings. I see the once rich and populous cities of *England* in
> the same condition with those of *Spain;* whole streets lying in rub-
> bish and the grass peeping up between the stones in those which
> continue still inhabited. I see the harbours empty, the warehouses
> shut up and the shopkeepers playing at draughts, for want of cus-
> tomers.[65]

What is more he prophesied in the near future a standing army of
200,000, and the end of Magna Carta, Habeas Corpus, the Bill of
Rights, and trial by jury.

The whole of the first volume, as well as the first book of the second
volume, described the unrepresentative character of the English parliament and the corrupt system by which it was chosen and managed.
He calculated that 800 men ruled England. These were elected by less
than 50,000 out of the 5,000,000 inhabitants. He based his figures

on the population as reckoned by his incomparable friend and neighbour for many years at Newington Green, Dr. Price. No member of the House of Commons should, he felt, be elected by less than 800 people, 401 representing a majority for the winning member. This represented a minimum. Burgh believed that all able-bodied males not in receipt of alms should vote. Parliaments should meet much more frequently than the Septennial Bill allowed. Precedents were listed for annual parliaments, familiar stories of Stuart shortcomings were retailed, and the vicissitudes of the Triennial Act described at tedious length. He believed that no crisis could really have justified the passage of the Septennial Act of 1716.

Corruption could be cured, only if membership in parliament were changed often—a rotation, in fact—if all voting were by ballot, and all debates were public. Brass Crosby (1725–1793), Lord Mayor in 1770 and himself a member; John Wilkes; and their colleague, Richard Oliver (1735–1784), had just made a stand on public debates in the case of John Miller, printer of the *London Evening Post,* as Burgh was writing, and he may not have thought the results assured. Pensions and places should be abolished and with them the dependence of members on ministers. He quoted with approbation a resolution passed in Pennsylvania in 1683, "that no person appointed by the Governor to receive his fines, forfeitures, or revenues whatsoever, shall sit in judgment in any court of judicature when a fine may accrue to the Governor."[66]

If redress could not be obtained in a parliamentary way, he proposed the establishment of a grand national association for restoring the constitution into which all propertied men, all friends of liberty should be drawn. Every parish must be included and a grand committee elected in every county, even in America. The response to this would show how great was the desire for reform. The associations would reveal public opinion, present petitions, and might even, though he never directly said so, be used for the nucleus of military organization for resistance to the apathy of the government, if other means failed. This was to be copied by Cartwright in *Take Your Choice!,* by Wyvill, and by Jebb.[67]

Burgh's work was chiefly occupied by his consideration of parliamentary abuses and of contemporary colonial problems. He also displayed enormous interest in the militia question, that is, in voluntary service of all citizens as contrasted with the mercenary troops paid and deployed by the government and representing a potential menace to free institutions. Writers used to buttress his arguments were Trenchard, Fletcher, Moyle, and also Charles Davenant, whose collected works had recently been reprinted by Charles Whitworth, kin of an ambassador to Russia in the reign of Anne. He drew on Molesworth's account of Danish slavery, on Gordon, on Sidney's justification of rebellion by the oppressed. Davenant had in his *Essay on Private Men's Duty in the Administration of Public Affairs* stressed the ruin that was bound to come when purely party interest was followed, when public funds were squandered, when statesmen were vainglorious, and when a standing army was in existence. The people should be vigilant about Whigs who preached liberty, but did not practice it. Burgh was himself following Davenant's advice in his warnings to his countrymen. *The Disquisitions* was full of reflections on such things as undue severity of punishment, the shortcomings of the poor laws, manners, and education (on which he had written a treatise). In a note he deplored the failure of the Feathers Petition and seemed to suggest that his father was a clergyman of the Establishment. No reformation of any kind could be expected until parliament was reformed.[68]

Book two of the second volume dealt with taxing the colonies. Burgh knew Benjamin Franklin well and profited by the friendship. He read Davenant on plantations, republished in the same year, 1775, as his own third and last volume.[69] He had studied, as shown not only here but in every other part of his work, parliamentary debates wherever he could find them. He quoted Governor Pownall and Pitt. He compared the events at Boston in March, 1774, with those in Edinburgh, February, 1737, with very unfavourable reflections on the justice of the English procedure in America.[70] Burgh denied the necessity for taxing Americans at this time. He suggested that Americans had paid their way during the Seven Years' War by their fighting, and at all times by their indirect taxes and their share in the increase of trade. The colonies had been an advantage, not a liability, and deserved better treatment.

Burgh quoted Beccaria, *Crimes and Punishments,* that every authority of one man, or a body of men, over another for which there was no absolute necessity, was tyrannical. There were many actions that were by no means necessary, nor were they profitable. Even if the colonists were obliged to submit England might lose all advantage from them. Surely cordiality should be promoted. Taxation without representation was wrong, Burgh wrote, and the economic discrimination was such that Americans were probably worse off than the Scottish, Irish, or Welsh. Violence, like the Tea Party riots, was deplored, but many of the grievances which lay behind it were entirely justified. He quoted Franklin to the effect that burdens were best borne by the people when they had some share in the direction of public affairs, and that when measures were distasteful, the wheels of government were likely to move more slowly. Burgh also quoted tributes to the courage and nobility of the settlers of the New World facing serpents, Indians, and savage beasts. These men would only rebel if they were made desperate by arbitrary government and by the refusal to them of the rights of Englishmen.[71]

Other pro-Americans of the war period were articulate and have often been described. They began to combine their demands for conciliation or recognition with increasingly emphatic cries for parliamentary reform. One example may suffice. Charles Stanhope (1753–1816), afterwards the third earl, but known till 1788 as Lord Mahon, came back from a sojourn in Geneva in 1773, and at once became involved in politics. He married Lady Hester Pitt, Chatham's daughter. He became acquainted with Franklin, and scientific interests cemented friendship. Under the aegis of Wilkes, he fought the Westminster election of 1774 on a platform of conciliation, repeal of the Quebec Act, and more frequent parliaments. He continued political work, even after defeat, and joined with Cartwright, Jebb, and the rest in the societies and associations of 1779–80. Sympathetic toward the French Revolution, he was generally thought a republican and was referred to as "Citizen Stanhope" by his enemies. By 1805, when his old comrade, Cartwright, was once more attempting to stir up petitions, he wrote, "I must confess I have seen too much not to be thoroughly sick of the old dull meetings of freeholders convened by the aristocracy. If the people be true to themselves they will inquire of the candidates for high offices, what it is they will solemnly pledge themselves to do for the people in case they should come into place. Everything else is firing at Sparrows."[72]

Major John Cartwright, with whom he had a friendly rivalry for the title of first proponent of American independence, was a native of Nottinghamshire and a cousin of John Disney, Blackburne's son-in-law and Lindsey's associate in the Essex Street Unitarian Chapel. In his youth he was filled with apprehensions about parliament by his old uncle, Lord Tyrconnel, who very early had announced that nothing but a miracle could save parliamentary government in England. Cartwright served in the Navy from 1758 until 1773, and produced a good plan for more efficiently supplying it with timber. On his return home he at once began to interest himself in the American cause and dedicated *American Independence* (1774) to Sir George Savile. In the following year, although he was a major in the county militia, he refused to fight the Americans. In *Take Your Choice!* (1776) he combined an appeal to end what he feared would prove a disastrous war with a plan to reform parliament. He had studied *An Historical Essay* and the *Political Disquisitions*. He was friendly with his cousin Disney's close friends, John Jebb and Theophilus Lindsey, and he knew the nobles Richmond, Shelburne, and Effingham. He was intimate with Granville Sharp (1735–1813), already writing on political reform and against slavery. With all these he was associated in the formation of the Society for Constitutional Information, and in the agitation for parliamentary reform following the setting up of the Yorkshire Association. In the latter he was ranged with Jebb and the more radical reformers against Wyvill and the less ambitious among them. He was to welcome the French Revolution, but Paine's republicanism was not acceptable to Cartwright who believed with Machiavelli that transformations in ancient constitutions should be achieved under the shadow of old forms.[73]

To Cartwright corruption in parliament and court, discontent in the colonies, antiquated and over-severe penal laws at home, and an overload of debts all threatened English security. In *Take Your Choice!* he noticed the prevalence of vice and the numbers of unemployed. Time was bound to bring about some artificial distinctions, but all should be able to vote and should be equally free regardless of wealth. The capacity for labour and personality were valuable assets all could claim. Cartwright recommended annual parliaments, voting by ballot, manhood suffrage, and equal electoral districts. The diagram in his book illustrated its theme. Each 3360 people should be represented by one member. There would therefore on his calculation be 558 members in the lower chamber and 230 hereditary members in an upper. A crown was at the top of his pyramid and at the base the national liberties of people. He believed in payment of members. He wanted, since he was desperate about George III's parliament, a grand national convention on the lines already laid down by the *Essay* and by Burgh, which would reform the constitution. Jebb maintained that such a convention might settle the franchise whereas it might have difficulty in intervening in American affairs. Cartwright was essentially a joiner. He threw himself into the Society for Constitutional Information with Brand Hollis, Horne Tooke, and others. He worked on the county meetings organized by Wyvill. Even when efforts failed he always hoped for another chance and joined clubs like the Friends of the People and later the Hampden Society.[74]

Cartwright and John Jebb (1736–1786) were influenced by the same traditions and shared most of their ideas and aspirations, although one had spent his early life in active service and the other in the duties of a clergyman and teacher at Cambridge. Jebb was the son of a former Dean of Cashel who was a friend of David Hartley, the philosopher (1705–1757). After attending school in Chesterfield and college in Dublin, the younger Jebb went to Peterhouse, just before Dr. Law became Master, and studied under Daniel Longmire (who later supported his reform schemes), and William Oldham. He took his degree in 1757 and began to take pupils as he completed his studies. In 1762 he was ordained and in the same year served with Richard Watson as Moderator for the sophs. He taught mathematics and published a small work on Newton's system in collaboration with Robert Thorpe and George Wollaston. To him the Newtonian system was the strongest and only rational demonstration of the existence of God. He married Ann Torkington, daughter of a Huntingtonshire rector and later a writer of considerable sprightliness under the name of Priscilla.

Education interested Jebb and he evolved a scheme for university reform, supported by Dr. Law, Watson, and Paley, among others, which roused considerable controversy. It failed to gain sufficient endorsement and was abandoned when he left the university in 1776 after resigning his livings in 1775 for the same reasons which moved his friend Lindsey to leave a Yorkshire living in the previous year. Unlike his associate in the Feathers Petition, however, he did not resume pastoral duties but began to study medicine in London and Scotland. He eventually published on medical as well as educational, religious, and political subjects. He was versatile and although he made some enemies, he impressed those who met him, as a vigorous controversialist. Two of his students at Cambridge, John Baynes and Capel Lofft, became his devoted disciples. Baynes (1758–1787), it may be recalled, recommended Wilberforce to the electors of Hull and left his law library to Samuel Romilly (1757–1818). Lofft (1751–1824) entered wholeheartedly into the reforming movements of his time. Both men helped Disney with the *Memoirs* of their teacher published in the year after he died; Lofft spoke the funeral oration in Bunhill Fields on 9 March, 1786.[75]

Jebb was a thorough-going supporter of the American cause which he had followed through all its stages. He read John Dickinson's tract with approval, and was surprised that Chandler in his *Free Examination* supported Archbishop Secker's plan to send bishops to the colonies. Like Hollis and Blackburne, he deplored the Quebec Act. By 1775 he began to despair of accommodation being effected. Middleton's melancholy remarks in his *Cicero* on the fall of Rome were recalled. He was in touch with Archdeacon Blackburne (with whom he spent a happy day just before he resigned his livings) and with Brand Hollis who undoubtedly shared colonial newsletters with him. In London he moved with a group that discussed America all the time. Lindsey's letters were full of the matter. By the time Jebb settled down to medicine, books by Cartwright, Price, and Priestley, as well as speeches and letters by Stanhope and Richmond, were voicing the opinions he himself held. At the end of the war he sent congratulations to Franklin in Paris through a mutual friend saying that he had never held any other hope but that "Victory and Honour might rest on that cause, which, in an especial manner, was the cause of justice and freedom." Locke had taught him that the Americans were right, his own countrymen wrong.

As early as 1776 he was also involved in the matter of parliamentary reform and had talked with Sir George Savile about it. In 1779 and 1780 he came before the public eye with an address to James Townshend (1737–87) and a speech at the Westminster meeting of 2 February, 1780. At the meeting a petition for economical reform was voted, Fox was asked to present it, and Jebb urged Fox to present himself as a candidate for parliament. On 6 April he again supported him and Fox was elected in due course. Later, after Fox entered the coalition, Jebb pushed the candidacy of Sir Cecil Wray in his place. About the same time he became involved in the Society for Constitutional Information. His own views were on the extreme left of the reformers and were more liberal than Wyvill's. Equal constituencies, universal manhood suffrage, and sessional parliaments—these alone were worthy of an Englishman's regard and were also advocated by Brand Hollis, Sawbridge, Cartwright, and others of his coterie. Jebb had no fears of a divorce of property and franchise, but recognized the rising power of the people and hoped it would rectify the deficiencies of the contemporary parliamentary system.[76]

Jebb worked for a reform of the legal system and the prisons of the country. He infected others with his ideas. Capel Lofft published at his suggestion a list of penal statutes. Sir William Meredith, who had presented the Feathers Petition, also brought before the House arguments against the increase of penal laws. Franklin was interested in Jebb's activities. John Howard (1726–1790), author of *The State of the Prisons*, owed much to both Jebb and Price. Another matter that much concerned his last years were the efforts to obtain reforms in Ireland. Jebb corresponded with the volunteers in 1783, and hoped that reform in that country would in turn improve English affairs. In Lofft's funeral oration on his friend he credited him with a universal patriotism, a desire for the protection of the rights of mankind against fraud and force, in Ireland, India, and America. Jebb hoped to see unrestricted liberty in the exercise of the rights of citizenship, guaranteed trial by jury, true representation in parliament, and entire religious freedom.[77]

Lofft's life was almost entirely devoted to the same causes as those promoted by his teacher. He wrote many tracts. He opposed the American war, the slave trade, the claim that any prince had an inherent right to regency (that being a matter for parliament to decide), all disqualifications for religious opinions. He worked for legal and parliamentary reform. In the present writer's possession is a volume of Algernon Sidney's works, edited by Law's cousin, Robertson, and based on Hollis's text and notes of 1763. This belonged to Lofft, and was annotated by him, probably after he bought it in 1777 when he left Peterhouse for the Inns of Court. He greatly admired Sidney, though in marginal notes he denied the doctrine that conquest confers any lasting rights or that the best governments are those most successful in war. He endorsed the emphasis on reason and nature, and fulminations against divine right in the ninth section of chapter two. The virtuous cannot endure tyranny. He noted agreement with Price on the stability of virtue and wisdom and, as Sidney discussed the vicissitudes of state, Lofft expressed his own hopes that his country would not prove the truth of the adage, "whom the gods would destroy, they first make mad." He was apprehensive of the betrayal of the country by parliament and magistrate. He agreed that the revolt of a whole people could not be a rebellion. This commentary affords interesting evidence about eighteenth-century interpretations of Sidney.[78]

Another member of the Society for Constitutional Information, acquainted with Priestley's friends, the Lunar circle at Birmingham, as well as with Jebb, was Thomas Day (1748–1789), author of the *Dying Negro* (1773) and *Sandford and Merton* (1783–1789). Day was the son of a customs officer who spent his early years at Stoke Newington where his mother imbued him with a love of reading. He attended Oxford and there formed a lifelong friendship with Richard Lovell Edgeworth (1744–1817). Through him he made the acquaintance of Dr. Small and was persuaded by the good doctor to abate his enthusiasm for Rousseau and study law. He went to Ireland with Edgeworth and no doubt shared his liberal views about that country. *Reflections,* published in 1782, reveal Day's fears for the future of England, and his belief that neither justice, reason, nor nature has given to a few individuals the right of judging for all the rest. He engaged in politics and Jebb urged him to run for parliament. He did not become prominent politically, but probably achieved more for the liberal cause, by his poem against slavery, and the somewhat sentimental egalitarianism of his widely read novel, the writing of which occupied most of the rest of his short life.[79]

Brand Hollis was one of the Jebb circle and had been a great friend of Thomas Hollis of Lincoln's Inn. He worshiped at Essex Street, was one of Lindsey's financial backers, and also contributed liberally to Hackney, 1786–1796. He continued his friend's benefaction to Harvard and other American libraries. He became acquainted with Jebb about 1766, and in 1804 he left his fortune and that of his friend to John Disney. Born in Essex of wealthy dissenting parentage, he was educated at Glasgow under Hutcheson at the time that Richard Baron and the earl of Selkirk went there. He became a passionate admirer of his teacher. He was strongly pro-American and, after his friend Hollis's death, in the early part of 1774, decided to run for parliament and engaged the services of an unscrupulous man to secure his election. His liberal politics were well known; the election was disputed, and he served a term in prison for bribery. His friends remained loyal. The offense was no worse than that of many of his contemporaries, but it gained a certain notoriety since it was committed by the heir of so famous a critic of parliamentary corruption. In 1779 he was associated in the formation of the Society for Constitutional Information, and by 1780 was prominent both in the association meetings and in the Westminster meeting, which passed resolutions advocating equal electoral districts, manhood suffrage, the ballot, and annual parliaments. As steward of the Friends of Constitutional Liberty, on 4 November, 1788, he was to rehearse the rights of Englishmen. He was a friend of Paine who gave him the key of the Bastille to forward to Washington. Not a man of great talent, he was a consistent and determined proponent of what he felt were the rights of Englishmen.[80]

Another associate in the Society for Constitutional Information was William Jones (1746–1794), educated by parents of learning and originality, son-in-law of Jonathan Shipley, and a friend of Dunning. His father was a Newtonian mathematician, his mother a woman of lowly birth who educated her son on her own system of "read and thou shalt learn." William more than justified her methods, becoming a lawyer of distinction, an Indian judge, and a famous Oriental scholar. He was a Wilkesite, a pro-American, and a parliamentary reformer like Jebb and Cartwright. His speech at the London Tavern in 1782 reveals clearly the quality of his mind. He distinguished between the form and spirit of a constitution of long standing. The spirit might remain, but the form must be altered to suit changing circumstance. Feudalism warred with commerce. This was a commercial age and the old property qualifications were anachronistic. The English revolution was unfinished. Virtual representation was in fact no representation at all. While those in receipt of alms should not vote, all others should. The old differences between landed and trading interests should be abolished. Jones supported many other reforms of law and of national service. His contributions to the Society for Constitutional Information were numerous and apposite. Perhaps his humour deserted him when he refuted Fielding's statement that the English constitution was as variable as the weather, seeing in it anarchical tendencies which his orderly and concrete imagination rejected with horror, and he proceeded to analyze that whole majestic body of public law and to see in the body of people at large, and in their petitions a high court of appeal to preserve the spirit of the constitution.[81]

The Society reprinted many tracts and published others for the first time, among them those by Jones, Brand Hollis, and Lofft. In the list of works they put out may be found, in part or in whole, the long succession of treatises adored by the Real Whigs of the Commonwealth tradition. They go back to Poynet in the sixteenth century; to Nedham, Milton, and Locke in the seventeenth, as well as to Trenchard, Molesworth, Fletcher, Fordyce, and others of the eighteenth century, including Wilkes's speech in 1776 on a just and equal representation, as well as passages from Burgh and *An Historical Essay.*[82]

This Whig canon was spread about just as the county associations supporting the Yorkshire petition for economical reform were being formed. The public response to the efforts, not only of the Cartwright-Jebb connection, but to those of Wyvill and Rockingham, was considerable. Reform was in the air. Motions were brought to purge parliament of certain sinecures. Hope was expressed everywhere for greater parliamentary reform. Fox was elected at Westminster by electors who thought he would further their cause. Once more, before five years had elapsed, these expectations were disappointed. The Rockinghams were only prepared for the mildest of measures against officeholders. Fox preferred office to principle. Shelburne could not command the respect and support of the followers of Rockingham. William Pitt the younger, whom Wyvill hoped would bring about some of the desired changes, was discouraged by his first very moderate sally and dropped the whole matter. Christopher Wyvill himself had never endorsed the wholehearted radicalism of Jebb and his friends. He saw the need for some change in representation, but feared too drastic and too sud-

den a change. He shared the Unitarian faith of Jebb and Disney, but
not their political ambitions. He preferred to trust in Pitt and when he
failed, to have recourse once more to petitioning. When Brand Hollis
suggested, in the days following the French Revolution, that moderate courses would no longer suffice, Wyvill was horrified. Nevertheless
he continued to support reform as long as he lived, though the differences between himself and the left wing Jebb connection had done
much to weaken their cause at the moment when its prospects seemed
strongest.[83]

Once more the party of movement had failed to achieve a united
and popular program and to forward it in parliament. The division of
Chatham and Rockingham had proved fatal to formation of sound imperial policy; the differences between Jebb and Wyvill at a lower political level, but organized as radicals had not been organized before,
together with the general apathy, proved fatal to any reform of parliamentary representation worthy of the name or of the efforts that had
been made. As the anniversary of the centenary of the English Revolution came around, though bold words were spoken, there seemed
less chance than ever of completing its work or of implementing the
ambitions of the Commonwealthmen. The French Revolution in the
next year seemed to offer much more occasion for rejoicing. Dr. Price,
preaching in 1789, *A Discourse on the Love of Our Country,* felt obliged
to warn his fellows of his concern for the future and the urgent need
for patriotic services. The freedom of America reflected in France,
encouraged all engaged in the cause of public liberty. Perhaps our
labours, he said, have not been in vain; the light struck has warmed
and illuminated Europe. "Restore to mankind their rights; and consent to correction of abuses, before they and you are destroyed together." As he spoke he could hardly forsee that the Revolution he
welcomed instead postponed for his own country redress of grievances
for more than a quarter of a century.[84]

X

Conclusion

No simple answer can be given to the question of what happened
between 1660 and 1780 to the progressive or seminal ideas of the English seventeenth century. That there were a number of persons dis-
satisfied with contemporary conditions in society and in government
throughout the period has been demonstrated. That some humanitari-
ans like Firmin, Bellers, Oglethorpe, and Fothergill may be omitted
from a consideration of political theorists seems obvious. Among the
others may be discovered a wide variety of persons diversely motivated
and holding by no means uniform philosophies, who cannot be elimi-
nated from any study of eighteenth-century liberalism. Of these some
looked back to the Interregnum and adapted the revolutionary theories of a whole century to the circumstances of their own times. Others,
associated with them by later readers, if not by contemporaries, were
led by special conditions and problems to suggest remedies and modifications of established policies. There were men of liberal presuppositions whose inspiration came, as so often in England, from the Bible,
from the classics, from constitutional pronouncements, and from such
writers as Sir Thomas More. Burke's attempt to separate the sheep
from the goats among those calling themselves Whigs developed from
his personal dilemma and preferences, but the results he presented
cannot be sustained by detailed study of early English radicalism. A
vast difference separated the innovators of the Interregnum and the
wise men of the Glorious Revolution, but the revolutionary potential
of Locke was as fertile in the eighteenth century as were the utopian
chimeras of the Levellers.

The stream of political invention did not entirely dry up between the English and American revolutions, but it ran slowly and partially underground. The Interregnum was immensely stimulating to all sorts of persons, but its own excesses and the anarchy they generated did much to discourage similar speculations thereafter. Moreover, in spite of the new outpouring of polemical literature between 1680 and 1714, the situation created by the flight of James II was such as to deter Englishmen from seeking to achieve any further visible change in the body politic. Criticisms of church and state by Leveller, sectary, Jacobite, or divine righter, alarmed a country apprehensive both of renewed anarchy and of foreign intervention. This familiar situation explains in part the long existence of the Augustan calm. English self-satisfaction was bolstered by two generations of continental visitors heaping praise and adulation upon the system which allowed enjoyment of so many liberties. Parliament, an almost unique example of the lost Gothic systems of the past, had won survival after a century of conflict with the prevailing European absolutism. Its independent, restless members might form connections without end, but they were almost indifferent to criticism. Redress of grievance was much more difficult to wrest from the entrenched oligarchy than from the Stuarts, and signs of disillusionment with Parliament may be discovered among Real Whigs. Public opinion was apathetic or more success by the reformers might have been achieved. England was prosperous; Scotland was becoming richer. Success abroad and expansion overseas enforced the belief that Great Britain was indeed most fortunate. Economic developments and population pressures had not before 1760 really dislocated society; they had only shifted the balance from aristocracy to gentry. The mob was not sufficiently self-conscious or confident to make its wishes known except in relatively minor outbursts of popular prejudice of little political significance. Religion no longer drove men into fanatical defense of the rights of conscience.

Separation of those liberal thinkers who may be properly thought to derive from seventeenth-century origins, from those whose inspiration was otherwise, cannot be precise. The attempt is justified by the composite nature of eighteenth-century liberalism. Cumberland and King, as well as scientists like Newton, owed relatively little to the republican ideologies of the Interregnum but much to growing optimism about man and the universe. Berkeley and Swift, a generation later, were stimulated by the situation of Ireland, by Christian charity —combined in the complex personality of the Dean with a most unchristian sense of grievance—to preach reform. Swift at once acknowledged some debt to the Commonwealthmen. Both claimed to be Tory, but they chiefly influenced men of radical inclinations to endorsement of liberal programs. Another Anglo-Irishman made extraordinary contributions to the literature of politics, but the violence of Burke's diatribes against Commonwealthmen and their natural rights doctrines affords sufficient justification for his exclusion from a book about his enemies. Edmund Law and David Hartley mingled little with politicians and indulged in few political speculations, but their disciples were for the most part found amongst the innovators. The greatest British philosopher of the eighteenth century was also a Tory, but David Hume, too, must be numbered among the prophets. Some stirring of intellectual waters must be expected at any time when men of genius emerge. In the examination of liberal ideas in a conservative age these churchmen and philosophers cannot be ignored.

Furthermore, they lived and worked in the same circumstances that produced confessedly liberal ideas among the Whigs. Hume was a Scot, Berkeley an Irishman. In both countries society presented problems which stimulated the investigations of thoughtful men whatever their prejudices about contemporary politics might be. It is immensely significant that the most fertile ideas in politics and in economics are to be found in eighteenth-century Ireland and Scotland. Men and theories moved from one to the other. Certain conceptions developed about the rights of colonies and plantations in connection with the inherent rights of all mankind, about the obligations of society to its poorer members, about the advantages of a general widely diffused well-being and standard of living for the whole—all these and some others were developed in these parts of the British Isles. In Ireland and Scotland may be found the most radical thinkers—Molyneux, Hutcheson, Wallace, Millar, and Ogilvie. Such intellectual giants as Smith and Hume may be regarded as exceptional in any period.

In England seventeenth-century traditions remained strong among the nonconformists. Demands for civil and religious liberty were continued. Seventeenth-century struggles were studied and written about. In schools and academies a liberal pedagogical method enforced the liberal politics and theology thought. Contacts between English dissent and their colleagues in Ireland and in Scotland were frequent. Congregations were small, schools ephemeral. Yet in Wales, in west-country centers like Bristol, Taunton, and Exeter, as well as in the great belt of chapels stretching from Liverpool through Yorkshire, Nottinghamshire, down through East Anglia to London, intellectual interest in speculative politics persisted.

Though all varieties of dissenters were committed to support of at least some of the liberties claimed by their ancestors, activity was most noticeable among the rational Protestants. Friendships amongst them crossed denominational lines. Blackburne, Law, Watson, and Shipley in the Established Church; the Episcopal Unitarians, Lindsey and Disney; dissenters like Watts, Foster, Price, Priestley, and Hazlitt all consorted in Christian fellowship and with considerable agreement in matters political. All shared a passionate concern for reform, for liberty, and most were connected in coteries and in clubs. Only rarely a man like Thomas Pownall studied Harrington and Newton, and apparently developed his highly original philosophy in a semi-vacuum, though a member of the large Franklin circle. For the most part the Real Whigs, the liberals, seem to have been associated in certain areas and institutions around a few persuasive men. They were related by a bewildering series of marriages. A more detailed investigation of the Molesworth connection during the first quarter of the eighteenth century or the groups of Newington of the last half of the period might be profitable. So might a study of the relationships of Henrys, Heywoods, Rowes, Lardners, Hollises, Blacketts, Blackburnes, and Turners, to name no more.

Some characteristics of those claiming to be Real Whigs must be emphasized. They were not in any sense of the word an organized opposition. They were not until after the death of George II closely connected with parliamentary politics and politicians. Nor were they to be found in those often surprising combinations of persons—out-of-office Whigs, Jacobites, city and country representatives, and other interests—who briefly allied at certain moments to embarrass the government and to press for or against some specific measures. The liberals or Real Whigs could always be relied on to agitate for shorter parliaments, fewer placemen, a national militia, and greater religious liberty; but, unlike many who occasionally roused themselves to the support of any one or all of these reforms, the Commonwealthmen continued to write and talk about them in and out of season. They relied on conversation, on letters among themselves or occasionally in the public press, on the dissemination of the printed word. Indicative of their mixed feelings about the parliamentary system as it then existed is the fact that in the last phase of their activity in 1780, it was through extra-parliamentary associations that they hoped to rouse an apathetic public to bring pressure upon the unreformed houses of parliament.

Organization came late. Then the chasm which divided the Rockingham Whigs and radicals like Cartwright, even when they seemed to be acting in unison, was sufficiently deep and wide to render entirely futile the aspirations of the reformers of the reign of George III. The associations and committees in the third decade of his reign achieved nothing of importance. Throughout the whole period the inexperience and detachment of the reformers from practical politics hampered them. When statesmen like Stanhope, Chatham, or Shelburne seemed sympathetic to their cause, the shortcomings and the lack of political know-how in these great men prevented effective intervention. Without leaders and organization the reformers failed. When they achieved these they still failed to attract sufficient public support and interest.

A part of their failure to organize must be attributed to their detestation of party. None had the faintest conception of what was necessary and what was wrong, what was legitimate and what was unprincipled in the compromises and adjustments inevitably imposed upon groups anxious to implement reforming programs. Neutrality, it is true, was often equated with cowardice; nonetheless, independence was universally esteemed, even when it meant refusal to endure even the smallest adaptation to the prejudices and beliefs of associates. Public opinion was infinitely confused by the freedom of speech and press advocated by the Whigs for so long, yet the development of some sort of organized program out of this babel was seldom suggested. Bolingbroke, well acquainted with the facts of political life, continued to condemn party. The Real Whigs of this study were so much outside of practical politics that they were unaware of the pressure to unite, with which experience might have made them familiar. Instead they followed a hit-and-miss method, consistent only in their determined faith in the printed tracts and treatises continually produced by them.

The Real Whigs were not a coherent party. They professed almost as many creeds in politics as in religion. But they were not revolutionaries. Not even the most extreme advocated the overthrow of the government by force or the implementation of their wishes by active resistance. Jebb said that the unrepresented might be obliged to act to induce parliament to cleanse its Augean stables, but it seems unlikely that he was thinking of the barricades, or that, had he indeed erected them, he would have been joined by Priestley or by Price. Endorsement of the events of 1688, nostalgia for the experiments of the Interregnum, admiration for the Americans and even for the French—none of these things implied a wish to disturb the English "trinity" of King, Lords, Commons. But they believed in progress and in the possibility and desirability of reform. They hoped for a government that would respond to enlightened public opinion. They emphasized the popular element. They believed in the natural rights of everyone everywhere. They found much food for thought in copies of the Agreement of the People—reprinted in mid-century in the *Harleian Miscellany*—in books by early law reformers and social critics, in the histories of ancient republics, civil wars, and revolutions. Sidney, Milton, Locke, and Harrington were continually studied. They believed in a mixed government and they sought to preserve it by halting developments, like cabinet and party, which seemed inimicable to its balance. The advantages of parliamentary government must be preserved by the separation of powers, by an enforced rotation, by an awakened and strengthened electorate. Checks and balances must be maintained rather than that growing emphasis on legislative sovereignty which threatened to overshadow an older constitutional equilibrium. They hoped to extend education and thus make possible the improvement of vast numbers whose inequality of opportunity they regretted. They were increasingly tolerant of all sorts of religious belief. Popery was no longer thought to exercise the sole monopoly of spiritual tyranny. They became more consistent but less effective. Since they no longer regarded everyone but themselves as wrong, they lacked the force that fanaticism gave the

Civil War sectaries. Nor were circumstances propitious for the establishment of the rule of the saints.

Revolution politics as professed in the eighteenth century were not of a very drastic kind. Berkeley made some radical suggestions and Hutcheson, Wallace, and Millar were concerned more than most Whigs about the poorer members of society. Mrs. Macaulay believed in property limitations. Fielding considered compassionately the social status of the "dregs." The Real Whig was not much concerned with the mob as a political factor, though he was prepared to grant a certain respect to the rights of those composing it. Nor did the eighteenth-century rabble favour the so-called revolutionaries. When there were popular riots they were against papists, Jews, and dissenters. Sacheverell and Wilkes were briefly heroes to the London crowds. Specific grievances might provoke disturbances. Game laws were resented and no doubt as always poor people envied the rich. But the impression left on domestic observers like Defoe, as well as on the continental traveler, was of a fair standard of living and of considerable pride in English liberties. Whatever discontent there may have been in any class, it found expression chiefly in the works of the Real Whigs or Commonwealthmen. These were articulate and generally from the middle classes of society.

These liberals were very academic in character, though beginning to influence the industrial bourgeoisie who were to be so important in the future of liberalism in England. But in this period their most notable achievements were at places like Glasgow under Hutcheson, Smith, and Millar; Cambridge in the days of Law and Jebb; Warrington when Seddon and Priestley taught. It was in such centers as these that the eighteenth century formed its own revolutionary amalgam of the scientific and political ideas of their ancestors. The famous plan of Thomas Hollis of Lincoln's Inn was itself a microcosm of the activities of all his liberal contemporaries. Those books, pictures, medals, and manuscripts he began to collect as a young man in the reign of George II represented to him and to his friends the great tradition of English liberty. He wanted to spread knowledge of this sacred canon around the world. As he saw in the policies of George III and his ministers a threat to all he most valued in his dear, native land, he concentrated his efforts to send overseas to his American friends as much of the heritage as could be confined in print and portrait. The New World would provide an asylum for the freedom his ancestors had fought for in the old.

Hollis was right. In America the academic ideas of the Whigs of the British Isles were fruitful and found practical expression. Americans opposing English policies made claims which could be contradicted from past experience and practice, but in using the natural rights doctrines they were appealing to a tradition still lively among their English sympathizers in spite of long confinement to the printed page. Party must be prevented in the new order. Church and state must be separated. A balance between its various parts would prevent undue power in any organ of government. Further security could be achieved by rotation in office and in various electoral devices. A supreme court would protect that law which embodied the necessary checks on the natural rights of the people and which stood above all ministers and legislators. As the new state structure was builded, Real Whigs in England watched attentively. Brand Hollis speculated about jury rights. Mrs. Macaulay was troubled about conflicts of state and federal powers. Priestley feared possible reelection of presidents and he condemned the oaths Americans already demanded of citizens and visitors. This anxiety reveals their interest in the fulfillment of so many of their ideals.

In England the evolution of a constitution no less careful of liberty and the rights of man was slow and its virtues were not to be visible to the Real Whigs. What they saw of its transformation from the old Gothic system astonished and alarmed them. They could not foresee the future nor the changed demands of an industrialized society. Of all those men mentioned in these pages only Pownall seems to have been even faintly aware of the advantages of the developing executive in England and the necessities of imperial organization.

The service of the Commonwealthmen was twofold. For over a century they kept alive political ideas which proved suitable and useful for a great new republic. The American Founding Fathers were influenced by the whole body of this tradition; Harrington and Sidney through Molesworth, Molyneux, Moyle, and Trenchard, as well as Hutcheson and the Scottish School, and gained as much from the moderators and commentators as from the Whig classics themselves. In England the Real Whigs did not achieve rectification of the constitution along Harringtonian lines. They were unable to stop the progress of the developing cabinet. They never shortened parliaments nor introduced a rota. The extended franchise came so much later as to acknowledge as much debt to continental example as to domestic tradition. The Commonwealthmen were asserters of liberty. Hazlitt, one of their sons, averred, "the creed they professed neither suffered nor exalted domination, but preached self-dominion. Their sympathy was with the oppressed. They cherished in their thoughts and wished to transmit to their posterity those rights and privileges for which their ancestors had died on the scaffold or had pined in dungeons or in foreign climes. This covenant they kept—this principle they stuck by—as it sticks by them to the last. It grew with their growth. It does not wither in their decay." The eccentric, the utopian, the fifth monarchy man— men whom Bishop Watson said esteemed the Revolution which saved us all—these rescued England from uniformity and intolerance even in a period of conservatism and indifference. Constant restatement of concepts of liberty by the Commonwealthman preserved a great tradition even in the rapidly changing conditions of the next century. In the troubled twentieth century, recollection and consideration of their passionate refusal to restrict human speculation must still command respect.

Bibliographical
Commentary

Bibliographical Commentary

No complete catalogue of works referred to nor of authorities consulted is given here. It has seemed wiser in a work covering so long a period of intellectual history to document quotations and references to little-known sources in the appropriate place, to suggest certain overall obligations to biographical and monographic materials in their context (though the many debts of the author to standard histories must be obvious, even where these are not cited), and finally to make some general bibliographical commentary upon the fortunes of certain authors and their works. The general reader will find among other valuable aids that the *Bibliography of British History . . . 1714–1789* (eds. Stanley Pargellis and D. J. Medley, Oxford, 1951) and *English Literature, 1660–1800* (ed. Louis A. Landa, Princeton, 1950–1952) provide excellent guides to books and periodicals.

MANUSCRIPT COLLECTIONS

Manuscript collections which yielded significant data only have been listed, though any reader familiar with even a part of the history of the period will realize how greatly this list could have been extended.

United States
Harvard University Library, Cambridge, Massachusetts.
Massachusetts Historical Society, Boston, Massachusetts.
Presbyterian Historical Society Library, Philadelphia, Pennsylvania.
Rosenbach Foundation Library, Philadelphia, Pennsylvania.
Sterling Memorial Library, Yale University, New Haven, Connecticut.
University of Pennsylvania Library and Archives, Philadelphia, Pennsylvania.
William L. Clements Library, University of Michigan, Ann Arbor, Michigan.
    Manuscript Division.

England
Bodleian Library, Oxford.
British Museum Library, London.
Cambridge University Library, Cambridge.
Dr. Williams's Library, London.
Longleat House Library, Wiltshire. Coventry Papers.
Manchester College Library, Oxford.
Unitarian College Library, Manchester.

Public Records Office, London. Shaftesbury and Chatham Collections; State Papers, Ireland.

Somerset House Records, London. Probate Registry.

Ireland

Marsh's Library, Dublin.

National Library of Ireland, Dublin.

Trinity College Library, Dublin.

Presbyterian Historical Society, Belfast.

Scotland

Glasgow University Library, Glasgow.

The National Library of Scotland, Edinburgh.

A note on material for studying the dissemination of Commonwealthmen's ideas:

Only a fraction of authors and their works which this study has used can be commented on here, and this note is intended only to suggest certain lines of bibliographical investigation which could be pursued indefinitely but which may be more profitably limited to a few examples. In the days when a few pounds would cover publication costs, the appearance of a tract, sermon, or treatise need have had little significance save for its begetters. Reissue, however, suggests a demand or conscious purpose or both by the agents. Today, for example, it would be safe to guess that very few people have read either Molesworth's *Account of Denmark,* or his once-famous preface to Hotoman's *Franco-Gallia.* Yet a glance at the greatly condensed list below should afford ample evidence of the popularity and even authority the Irishman's work once enjoyed. Similarly among the great "classical republicans" of the seventeenth century, neither Neville nor Sidney has attracted modern readers to any great extent, though Harrington and Ludlow, not to mention Milton and Locke, have received some scholarly attention. A brief résumé of Neville's literary fortunes and a selected list of tracts stimulated by his *Plato,* when it appeared, are therefore given here, with a brief reference to editions of Harrington (since he and Neville so often appeared together), and the major editions and translations of Sidney's *Discourses* follow. Some account of the editions of certain works by Cumberland and Law reveal an interest in them by eighteenth-century students which could hardly be deduced from the brief respectful tributes they receive in histories of the Utilitarians.

Though this book has attempted to throw some further light on the political interest and contributions of Scotland, the Scottish thinkers of the age are readily available and considerable research has been done upon their works. On the other hand, in spite of his fame, Molyneux's *Case,* some of the literature stirred up by it, and the situation out of which it derived, have never received any adequate bibliographical attention. The notes here offered may reveal something of the abundance of Irish polemical tracts before the days of Grattan and Flood.

Sermons have been noticed only in notes to the text—it would take more courage than I have to attempt even a superficial survey of the many orations by parsons of the different sects and persuasions of a day when even a minor Irish preacher could publish four volumes of his efforts and hope for a second or third edition to be in demand. A Hoadly, of course, could stir up hundreds of replies to a single harangue and rival the public enjoyed today by the modern paperback.

A great deal of time and energy was spent on the study of eighteenth-century notebooks and on book catalogues of which Harvard has a superb collection. These have nowhere been listed. I decided that the influence of teachers like Doddridge and Hutcheson could be amply documented without the further support student notebooks from academy and college could give. I furthermore decided, perhaps too arbitrarily, that the references of the catalogues to, for example, seventeenth-century tracts, were on the whole unsatisfactory. Not all libraries were catalogued; to guess at the percentage later sold, to calculate the total sum of any category of tract or pamphlet, was impossible. The existing material is simply not susceptible to reliable statistical analysis. Tracts were often noticed, even in the lists we have, by box or bundle. Even where their character was suggested, there was nothing to show that their position on the shelves of a great house, or the library of a small manse signified anything but a chance heritage from some ancestor or idle curiosity. Catalogues like those of White Kennett or Anthony Collins, or lists which can be made of the Hollis gifts, as well as the famous Hollis, Brand Hollis, and Disney Library, sold in 1817, are exceptional in showing the tastes and interests of the collectors who have also left additional evidence of their political preferences. As time passed naturally more and more antiquarian attention was directed to the period of the Interregnum and other troubled eras of controversy, but long before the Thomason Tracts were respectably housed in the British Museum for the benefit of scholars, innumerable pamphlets survived in libraries all over the British Isles and colonial America. But we may only guess at their readers.

Collections of tracts reprinted from earlier issues were available. The State Tracts of the later Stuarts began to be reissued by Darby and other printers as soon as the Revolution Settlement was secured. In mid-eighteenth century republications from the Somers and Harleian collections were made, though the editions commonly used now date from the early nineteenth century. By the eighties the Society for Constitutional Information was keeping, by means of reprinted extracts, the names of most of our Commonwealthmen, as well as other writers whose writing could be drafted for the purposes of the society, before the public. The members wrote themselves but utilized appropriate passages from famous men as well as obscurer polemicists to swell their pamphlet output. A study of the tract collections of the century serves to confirm the impression that Commonwealthmen continued to make available works of the political canon they esteemed. Their efforts were not essential to the continued renown of major writers, but without them it would be hard to account for the popularity enjoyed by Neville, Sidney, Trenchard, and Moyle.

There are certain categories of eighteenth-century publication which almost seem to defy the would-be bibliographer—that is, the pamphlet that was the joint product of several men, and the republication of these works usually catalogued under a couple or more names. Sometimes these appear in series, "Occasional Papers," sent to a journal and then reprinted under a separate title. Of the earlier kind must be noticed the welter of tracts like *An Argument* (against a standing army) and *A History of Standing Armies* continued to appear throughout at least a century after their appearance and were attributed to any or all of the members of the club, though undoubtedly Trenchard and Moyle were the dominant partners. Fletcher's contribution, owing nearly everything but his specifically Scottish reflections to the club, appeared several times separately and found a place in his collected works, which enjoyed four editions during the eighteenth century. Tindal and Toland, both famed for other polemical efforts, also produced tracts which were reissued in collections of their tracts and in more miscellaneous publications. Moyle, Trenchard's chief and closest associate, was given credit for *An Argument* in the edition of his *Works* in 1726 and in the two editions of *A Select Collection of Tracts* by Walter Moyle, brought out in Dublin in 1728 and in Glasgow in 1750. It appeared *A Choice Collection of Papers* (London, 1703), *A Collection of State Tracts*, II (London, 1705), and *A Collection of Tracts*, advertised to be by Trenchard and Gordon in 1751 (vol. I). And this represents but a fraction of reissues. Trenchard always received sole credit for *A Short History of Standing Armies* (London, 1698), which appeared nearly a dozen times before mid-century and was abridged and put out by the Society for Constitutional Information as well as by the compilers of penny numbers and weeklies of other kinds during the French Revolution. Walter Moyle's famous essays upon Greek and Roman governments have not escaped the general confusion attending authorship but were both published under his name in editions and translations up to 1801 at least.

The most famous of occasional papers were of course *Cato's Letters* and the *Independent Whig*, of which much has been said in text and notes here. It may suffice to add that at least six editions of *Cato* appeared before 1754, and seven of the *Independent Whig*, not counting a Philadelphia edition in 1740 and a French translation printed at Amsterdam in 1767, the work of Baron P. H. D. von Holbach.

Besides these collected reissues, supervised until the fourth or fifth, at least, by Thomas Gordon, Trenchard's collaborator and amanuensis, selections from them appeared constantly in press and in collections of one kind and another. Gordon, as has been seen, devoted himself to translations of Tacitus (London, 1727–1729 and 1737) and Sallust (London, n.d.) after the death of Trenchard and his marriage to Trenchard's widow. He also prepared parts of three collections which contain a large proportion of tracts extracted from the *Independent Whig* and *Cato* but did not live to see them through the press. This task fell to the lot of Richard Baron, like John Toland one of the most industrious editors of Commonwealthmen.

A category of publications which may be regarded as insignificant in the present context is the American reprint. Americans received books from England in remarkably short space of time after their publication. Many of these early Atlantic voyagers may still be seen in older libraries like Harvard and the Library Company of Philadelphia. Reprints of English books by American presses seems to have been largely restricted to manuals of a moral or technical character. Even apparent exceptions to this cannot be emphasized. There are not enough to prove any interest or purpose. A fair number of puritan and dissenting works were put out by presses in Newport, Providence, Boston, and Philadelphia.

Very few English political tracts or treatises came off the American presses before the reign of George III, in spite of occasional flurries of both native and imported controversy. Even the appearance twice in the century at least of *English Liberties* (Boston, 1721; Providence, 1774) means no more than that Americans, like Englishmen, cherished Magna Charta, the jury system, and the Bill of Rights. During the last forty years of the century, of course, the printers in a good many towns hurried to reproduce the works not only of native polemicists but of English sympathizers with the American cause like Burgh, Cartwright, Price, Priestley, Shipley, and others. This is a well-known tale. Americans had already been influenced by the writings of the men this book has discussed, but this must be deduced from writings and constitutional achievements rather than from the products of the early presses.

The lists which follow are intended to illustrate typical bibliographical reflections of the persistence and currency of the ideas of the Commonwealthmen. They could be vastly multiplied, but the examination of these and others in the text should suffice to explain the thesis of this book.

ROBERT MOLESWORTH (1656–1725)

The best account of Molesworth's work and reputation is in Christian H. Brasch, *Om Robert Molesworth's Skrift,* "*An Account of Denmark as it was in the year 1692,*" Copenhagen, 1879. Brasch examines the replies to *An Account,* lists editions, translations, and describes some of those continental writers like L. Holberg, E. Pontoppidan, and J. B. Desroches, who used it with or without acknowledgment. P. H. Mallet, *Histoire de Dannemarc,* 3rd ed., vol. 9, Geneva 1788, p. 11, also considers Molesworth. *An Account,* London, 1694 (in print by December, 1693), went into five English editions before 1696, the last bearing Molesworth's name. A so-called fourth edition, revised with other works, was published in London in 1738. Two Glasgow editions appeared in 1745 and 1752. Parts of the book, most commonly the preface or chapter vii, were continually reprinted, for example in 1713—when Molesworth was quarrelling with Tory churchmen in Ireland— *Mr. Molesworth's Preface . . . With Historical and Political Remarks, to which is Added, A True State of his Case, with Respect to the Irish Convocation,* London, 1713. His seventh chapter was reprinted with *The Royal Law of Denmark,* London, 1731; much the same material was printed in the *Scots Magazine,* 7 March, 1741 (Edinburgh); J. Harris, *Navigantium Atque Itinerantium Bibliotheca* vol. 2, London, 1744; Oliver Goldsmith and Samuel Johnson, eds., *The World Displayed,* vol. 20, London, 1778, pp. 54–73; *Somers Tracts,* XI, London, 1814.

Translations. Brasch, p. 168, refers to a German translation in 1694 (The Library of Congress lists 1695 for a German translation). A Dutch translation *De Vrye Staats Regering geschetst in een besschryvinge van Denemark,* zoo als't war in den jare 1692, Rotterdam, 1694. French translations too numerous to list in detail were either of the whole, *Memoires,* or *Extrait,* that is, parts: Nancy, 1694, 1695; Paris, 1697, 1705, 1715, 1790; Amsterdam, 1695.

Answers to *An Account* included: S.s., *The Commonwealths-Man Unmasqu'd or a Just Rebuke to the Author of the Account of Denmark,* London, 1694; J. Crull, *Denmark Vindicated: Being an Answer to An Account,* etc., London, 1694. [Wm. King] *Animadversions on a Pretended Account of Denmark,* London, 1694; translated into French with additions by the translator, de la Fouleresse, Cologne, 1696.

Some Considerations for the Promoting of Agriculture and Employing the Poor, Dublin, 1723. Answered by *Considerations upon Considerations,* Dublin, 1723.
A Short Narrative of the Life and Death of John Rhinholdt Count Patkul . . . , By L.M. (Lord Molesworth), London, 1717.
Observations upon a Pamphlet (probably by the same), London, 1717, reprinted in 1738 edition of *An Account* as such.
A preface by Lord Molesworth to his daughter, the Hon. M. Monck's *Marinda. Poems and Translations Upon Several Occasions,* London, 1716.
A preface to a translation of Francis Hotoman's *Franco-Gallia,* first published in 1711 without the preface but reissued with the preface in 1721 (London) and attributed to Molesworth as early as 1726 by John Ker, who used it in his *Memoirs.* Also London, 1775.

Wrongly attributed to Molesworth, *A Letter from a Member of the House of Commons . . . Relating to the Bill of Peerage lately Brought into the House of Lords,* London, 1719 (Probably by Robert Walpole).

HENRY NEVILLE (1620–1694)

Plato Redivivus: or, a Dialogue Concerning Government. London, 1681; two slightly different editions, both marked 2nd ed., London, 1681; 3rd ed., with title, *Discourses Concerning Government by Way of Dialogues,* probably ed. by John Toland,

London, 1698; 3rd fol. ed., repr. of 2nd ed., with *Oceana* and life by Toland, Dublin, 1737; another ed., with *Oceana* and life, Dublin, 1758; 4th ed. with account of Neville by ed. T. Hollis, London, 1763 (misprint for 1765).

Answers to *Plato Redivivus: The Apostate Protestant, a Letter to a Friend*, 1681 (2nd ed., 1685, attributed to E. Pelling); *Oceana and Britannia*, 1681 (repr. as Marvell's in A. B. Grosart, *The Complete Works . . . of Andrew Marvell*, 4 vols., 1872–1875); *Impartial Trimmer*, 1682; *An Address to Freemen and Freeholders*, 1682; W.W., *Antidotum Britannicum, or A Counter-Pest Against the Destructive Principles of Plato Redivivus*, London, 1681, and William Atwood, *Reflections on Antidotum; Coleman's Ghost, an Answer to Henry Neville*, 1681; Thomas Goddard, *Plato's Demon: Or, the State-Physician Unmaskt*, London, 1684; *The Head of Nile: or the Turnings and Windings of the Factious Since Sixty in a Dialogue Between Whigg and Barnaby*, London, 1681; (Edward Pettit), *The Visions of Government*, London, 1684; John Northleigh, *Tryumph of Our Monarchy*, London, 1685; (George Savile, 1st Marquis of Halifax?), *A Seasonable Address . . .* , in *Somer's Tracts*, London, 1813; Thomas Otway, *Venice Preserved, or a Plot Discovered*, 1682.

The Works of N. Machiavel, translated into English, by H.N., London, 1675; 1680; 1694; 1720; a fragment only reprinted in Richard Baron's *Pillars of Priestcraft and Orthodoxy Shaken*, 2nd ed., vol. II, London, 1768.

JAMES HARRINGTON (1611–1677)

The Commonwealth of Oceana, London, 1656. *The Oceana of James Harrington and His Other Works*, with his life, by J. Toland, London, 1700; ed. with appendix containing all of the political tracts omitted in Toland's ed., London, 1737, 1747, 1771. Other eds., with Neville's *Plato Redivivus*, Dublin, 1737, 1758. *Oeuvres Politiques . . . précédées de l'Histoire de sa Vie*, par J. Toland, trad. par P. F. Henry, 3 vols., Paris, 1795. Ed. of *Oceana* with introduction by H. Morley, London, 1883; ed. by Liljegren, London and Heidelberg, 1924 and 1929.

ALGERNON SIDNEY (1622–1683)

The present whereabouts of the manuscript of the *Discourses* is unknown and all printed versions lack a part of the text; these missing portions may possibly be those passages partially reproduced in printed accounts of his trial, which were cited as evidence of his treasonable motives.

Discourses Concerning Government, published from the original MS. of the author, London, 1698. *Discours Sur le Gouvernement, Traduits De L'Anglois, par P. A. Samson*, La Haye, 1702, 3 vols.; reissued in 4 vols. duodecimo, La Haye, 1755; a new ed., 3 vols., Paris, 1794. *Discourses*, 2nd ed., London, 1704; another ed., with author's life and an index, 2 vols. Edinburgh, 1750;

Richard Baron's so-called 3rd ed., London, 1751; Thomas Hollis's ed., *With His Letters Trial Apology and Some Memoirs of His Life,* London, 1763; this was reissued with few apparent changes by the Rev. J. Robertson as—

The Works of Algernon Sidney, London, 1772; a German translation following Robertson, *Algernon Sidney's Betrachtungen uber die regierungsformen . . .* Leipzig, 1793. A further German Sidney appeared at Hamburg, 1795— according to Heinsius.

The Essence of Algernon Sidney's Work on Government to which is Annexed his Essay on Love, by a student of the Inner Temple (and dedicated to Stanhope), London, 1795; 2nd ed., London, 1797.

Editions of the *Discourses* appeared in Philadelphia and New York in 1805.

Sidney Redivivus, London, 1689, and *The Dying Speeches of Several Excellent Persons,* London, 1689 (no. III, being Sidney), revived Sidney orations of 1683. Reprints of the trial and speeches are too numerous to list here.

RICHARD CUMBERLAND, BISHOP OF PETERBOROUGH (1631–1718)

De Legibus Naturae Disquisitio Philosophica, London, 1672. Third ed., Lübeck and Frankfurt, 1694.

A Treatise of the Laws of Nature, translation by John Maxwell, London and Dublin, 1727.

A Philosophical Enquiry into the Laws of Nature . . . , translation, with notes and appendix by the Rev. John Towers, Dublin, 1750.

Traité Philosophique des Loix Naturelles, translation from Latin by Barbeyrac, with notes of translator and those of English translation, *A Brief Account of the Life of Richard Cumberland* by S. Payne, Amsterdam, 1744; reissue, Leyden, 1757.

A Brief Disquisition of the Law of Nature, abridged and translated by James Tyrrell with additions by translator, London, 1692. Second ed., corrected and somewhat enlarged, London, 1701.

Cumberlandius Illustratus, sive, Disquisitio Philosophica de Lege Naturae, Ulm, 1693 (adaptation by Daniel Ringmacher).

EDMUND LAW, BISHOP OF CARLISLE (1703–1787)

Considerations on the Propriety of Requiring a Subscription to Articles of Faith, London, 1774.

Considerations on the State of the World with Regard to the Theory of Religion, Cambridge, 1745. Eight editions in English with some variations of title. 2nd ed., enlarged, and including discourse on the life of Christ, Cambridge, 1749; 3rd ed., Cambridge, 1755; 5th ed., Cambridge, 1765; 6th ed., enlarged, Cambridge, 1774; 7th ed., enlarged, etc., Carlisle, 1784; 8th ed., *Considerations* with a life of the author by W. Paley, ed. by G. H. Law, London, 1820.

A Defence of Mr. Locke's Opinion Concerning Personal Identity [By E. L.], London, 1769.

Translation of William King, Archbishop of Dublin's *Origin of Evil,* with notes, etc., London, 1731, 1732; Cambridge, 1739; London, 1758, 1781.

Works of J. Locke, with life, ed. by Edmund Law, London, 1777. Other ed's, London, 1794, 1801.

WILLIAM MOLYNEUX (1656–1698)

The Case of Ireland's Being Bound by Acts of Parliament in England Stated. Orig. autograph ms. in Trinity College, Dublin, No. 890 in Abbott's Cat., Trinity MSS. J. 4, 16., 1st ed., (Dublin, 1698) and another ed. (London, 1698) have prefaces signed 1697–8. Other editions: Dublin, 1706; Dublin?, 1719; London, 1720; with J. Barry's *Case of Tenures,* Dublin, 1725; Dublin, 1749; with new preface by John Almon, London, 1770; with protests, ed. Milliken, Dublin, 1773; Belfast, 1776; with Owen Roe O'Nial (O'Neill), *Letters to the Men of Ireland,* Dublin, 1782; Belfast, 1796; two modern reprints in Dublin, 1892 and 1897.

Selected tracts relevant to *The Case of Ireland* controversy: *A Discourse Concerning Ireland and the Different Interests Thereof,* London, 1697–1698; *The Substance of the Arguments For and Against the Woollen Bill . . . With Some Remarks . . .* London, 1698; Richard Cox, *Some Thought on a Bill for Prohibiting Woollens,* and an answer, *Remarks Upon a Book Entitled Some Thoughts,* 1698; *A Discourse of the Woollen Manufactures in Ireland,* Dublin, 1698; *The Protestant Case Who are of the Woollen Manufacturers in Ireland,* Dublin, 1698; *A Letter from a Gentleman in the Country with Reference to the Votes 14 December, 1697 Relating to the Trade of Ireland, by Sir F. B.,* Dublin, 1698, and *An Answer to a Letter,* 1698; John Cary, *An Answer to Mr. Molyneux,* London, 1698; *Considerations of Importance to Ireland,* December 1698; *The Interest of England as It Stands with Relation to the Trade of Ireland,* London, 1698; (Phillips), *The Interest of England in the Preservation of Ireland,* 1698; William Atwood, *The History and Reasons of the Dependency of Ireland Upon the Imperial Crown of the Kingdom of England; Rectifying Mr. Molineux's State of "The Case of Ireland's Being Bound . . . ,"* London, 1698; *A Brief Account of the Woollen Manufacturer,* 1707 and 1708; J.T., Esq., *An Act for the Better Securing the Dependency of Ireland . . .* (should nor pass), 1720; *A Letter from a Member of the House of Commons in Ireland . . . ,* 1720; Richard Cox, *Some Observations on the Present State of Ireland, Particularly The Woollen Manufacture,* 1731; *Some Remarks on the Conduct of the Parliament of England,* 1731; *The State of Woollen Manufactures Considered,* B. Ward, London, 1731; *An Enquiry into Some of the Causes of the Ill Situation of Ireland,* 1731; Thomas Sheridan, *A History and the Relation, or A Discovery of the True Cause of Why Ireland Was Never Entirely Subdued,* (new version of Davies), Dublin, 1733; *Argument Upon Woollen Manufactures,* 1735; *The Golden Fleece, or the Trade Interest and Well Being of Great Britain Considered,* London, 1737; *A Scheme to Prevent the Running of Irish Wool,* 1744; [J. Leland] *The Case Fairly Stated,* 1754.

HARLEIAN MISCELLANY

*Harleian Miscellany: or, a Collection of Scarce, Curious, and Entertaining Pamphlets
and Tracts, as Well in Manuscript as in Print, Found in the Late Earl of Oxford's
Library,* ed. by William Oldys, with an introduction by Samuel Johnson,
8 vols., London, 1744–1746. Second ed. made up of 1st ed. with new Vol. I,
London, 1753. Another ed., interspersed with historical and critical
annotations by W. Oldys and add. notes by Th. Park, 10 vols., London,
1808–1813. Ed. by J. Malham, 12 vols., London, 1808–1811.
*A Selection from the Harleian Miscellany of Tracts Which Principally Regard the English
History* . . . London, 1793.
*A Compleat and Exact Catalogue of All the Pamphlets Contained in the VIII Volumes of
the Harleian Miscellany* [by W. Oldys], London, 1746.
*Historische Nachrichten ueber Verschiedene Merkwuerdige Revolutionen und
Vershwoerungen in England und deren Urheber.* Aus der *Harleyischen Sammlung
von Memoires* . . . Altona, 1796.

SOMERS TRACTS

*A Collection of Scarce and Valuable Tracts on the Most Interesting and Entertaining
Subjects* . . . *Selected from* . . . *Public, as Well as Private Libraries, Particularly That
of the Late Lord Somers,* 16 vols., London, 1748–1752; 2nd ed., with slightly
different title, revised, augmented and arranged by Sir Walter Scott, 13 vols.,
London, 1809–1815.

THE PUBLICATIONS OF THE SOCIETY FOR CONSTITUTIONAL INFORMATION

The Society printed, and often distributed gratis, tracts by its members and other
contemporaries, as well as works, or extracts from them, by earlier writers going
as far back as Bracton, Fortescue, and Bishop Poynet which seemed likely to per-
suade the public of the respectability and importance of the reforms advocated.
Parts of important constitutional documents were reproduced and speeches by
Queen Elizabeth and St. John Aubyn. Carefully chosen passages from Swift and
Bolingbroke appear in the lists but the great majority of selections published
were from Whigs like Somers, Fletcher, Molesworth, Trenchard, Gordon, James
Thomson, David Fordyce, James Burgh, and the author of *An Historical Essay.*
The records of the proceedings of the Society may not itemize every one of its
tracts. For a select bibliography as well as a study of the Constitutional Society
an unpublished dissertation by Dr. Eugene Black in the Harvard Archives may
be consulted.

Acknowledgments

Only a few of the many obligations incurred over several years can here be mentioned. Henry Allen Moe and James Matthias of the Simon L. Guggenheim Foundation encouraged me enormously by personal interest and kindness on all sorts of occasions, and the Foundation most generously assisted me with subventions towards the costs of travel, study abroad, and publication. The American Philosophical Society has twice granted me welcome aid towards the ever-mounting expense of secretarial and bibliographical help. Bryn Mawr College allowed me a sabbatical year when I was awarded a Guggenheim Fellowship and has once allowed me to take a partial leave for work on this book. Without the time thus obtained this book could never have been written, since the activities of small liberal arts colleges seldom permit adequate and continuous time for private research on lengthy subjects. Douglass Adair and Carl Bridenbaugh, then of the Institute of Early American History at Williamsburg, assisted me in all kinds of ways as my work was first taking form and gave me permission to use parts of material originally published in the *William and Mary Quarterly*. Dr. John M. Coleman gave permission to use material originally published in *Pennsylvania History*. Mr. Thomas Wilson has taken a kindly interest in my subject and I am thankful to him and the editorial department of the Harvard press for much help and patience.

At different stages, Mary Terrien, Winifred Allen, and Helen Maggs Fede have struggled with problems created by my handwriting, typing, and voluminous references. To them is due much of the accuracy of this volume and none of its mistakes. I can never thank them enough for effort and sympathy.

Librarians on both sides of the Atlantic have dealt painstakingly with all sorts of problems: Pamela Reilly and Mrs. Cornelius Whetstone of Bryn Mawr; Dr. Charles W. David, recently of the University of Pennsylvania, Edwin Wolf II and Barney Chiswick of the Library Company, Dr. Guy Klett of the Presbyterian Historical Society, and William

McCarthy of the Rosenbach Foundation, all of Philadelphia; Professor Howard Peckham of the William L. Clements Library, Ann Arbor, Michigan, and Dr. Louis B. Wright of the Folger, Washington, D.C.

Abroad, the custodian of the collections of manuscripts listed have been considerate and helpful. I should like to thank Dr. R. J. Hayes of the National Library of Ireland for much more help than any reader has a right to expect. Dr. H. W. Parke, librarian and vice-provost, and the Board graciously allowed me access to and permission to quote from the King Manuscripts in the collections of Trinity College, Dublin. In Dublin, also, Mrs. Harold Leask and Dr. Barbara Bradfield Taft gave me valuable assistance with my Irish researches. Dr. Raymond V. Holt, then of the Unitarian College, Manchester, gave me invaluable and generous aid. Mrs. Onslow allowed me to borrow some Hollis letters. R. M. Anthony, Esq., has most generously allowed me to use his valuable material about his Hollis ancestors.

William A. Jackson graciously allowed quotation from manuscripts in the Houghton Library at Harvard University. Without many hours in both the Widener and Houghton libraries, and the ready advice and comfort always forthcoming from Robert H. Haynes and Carolyn Jakeman this book, which concerns so many of the works on their shelves and not a few of the university's earlier benefactors, would have been vastly more difficult to write. I hope that the kindly spirits of past readers, authors, and benefactors of this greatest of American collections will be pleased with a study of the Commonwealthmen's traditions in which they too shared.

Many friends have given me criticism and advice — my colleagues, Felix Gilbert and Milton C. Nahm; Professors Jacob Viner of Princeton, and Verner W. Crane of Michigan; Professor Norman Sykes, Professor Herbert Butterfield, Dr. J. H. Plumb, and Dr. Peter Laslett of Cambridge. Sir Lewis Namier, an inspiration and a stimulus to all would-be students of the eighteenth century, has been ever kind and learnedly helpful to me. There is no space to list the many others, though the kindly help of Carol Biba must be noted.

Dr. John H. Powell generously read my typescript and made many valuable suggestions about certain parts of it. In this as in so many of my activities throughout my life my greatest obligations are to the kindest of fathers, Rowland R. Robbins, and to my brother, Lionel Robbins.

Notes

List of Abbreviations

Publications and sources frequently mentioned are referred to in the notes by the following code letters. These abbreviations follow for the most part, as do the notes, the rules of the *MLA Style Sheet;* proper names follow, where possible, the *Dictionary of National Biography,* and spelling, with some minor exceptions, has conformed to Webster.

APT—American Philosophical Society Transactions
BIHR—Bulletin of the Institute of Historical Research
BJS—British Journal of Sociology
CHJ—Cambridge Historical Journal
CSPD—Calendar of State Papers, Domestic
CSPV—Calendar of State Papers, Venetian
GEC—Cokayne's *Complete Peerage*
GM—Gentleman's Magazine
HLB—Harvard Library Bulletin
H.M.C.—Historical Manuscripts Commission
JHI—Journal of the History of Ideas
JNH—Journal of Negro History
Mo.R—Monthly Review
MP—Modern Philology
MR—Monthly Repository
NEQ—New England Quarterly
PAPS—Proceedings of the American Philosophical Society
PDM—Protestant Dissenters' Magazine
PMHB—Pennsylvania Magazine of History and Biography
PQ—Philological Quarterly
P.R.O.—Public Records Office, London
RPSGP—Royal Philosophical Society of Glasgow Proceedings
SAR—Scots Arts Revue
SM—Scots Magazine
WMQ—William and Mary Quarterly

Notes

CHAPTER I. Introduction

1. Molesworth's preface to Francis Hotoman's *Franco-Gallia, or An Account of the Ancient Free State of France* (1721), p. viii (not in 1711 edition). This was reprinted as *The Principles of a Real Whig; Contained in a Preface to the Famous Hotoman's Franco-Gallia, Written by the Late Lord-Viscount Molesworth; and now Reprinted at the Request of the London Association* (London, 1775). An earlier reprint of a part of the preface may be found in John Ker, *Memoirs* (London, 1726), II, Part III, 191–221. The Society for Constitutional Information reprinted a part also in 1786. Molesworth uses "real" and "true" interchangeably.

2. *A Brief Reply to the History of Standing Armies in England* (London, 1698), preface; pp. 3, 15, 24, 25. This tract is attributed to Daniel Defoe but references to dissent seem to make this unlikely. The author comments at length on the publication in years since the Revolution of works by Socinians and politicians, and on the role of the Grecian in the appearance of Ludlow's *Memoirs,* Sidney's *Discourses,* Milton's works, as well as tracts by the clubmen themselves.

3. In spite of his earlier Jacobitism, Godolphin was enthusiastically admired by the Molesworth-Shaftesbury circle, as a letter in the Shaftesbury papers in 1709 attests (P.R.O. 30, GD–24, Bdl. XXI, 180).

4. Élie Halévy, *The Growth of Philosophic Radicalism,* Eng. tr. (London, 1952), p. 261.

5. Roger L'Estrange, *The Observator,* I, no. 445 (28 November, 1683).

6. See Chap. VII below for further discussion of dissenting education. Also see J. W. Ashley Smith, *The Birth of Modern Education* (London, 1954), for much information about teachers and their students, lists of whom were printed in various years of *The Monthly Repository* (London, 1806–1837).

7. Simonds D'Ewes, *Journal,* ed. W. Notestein (New Haven, 1923), p. 43. Uncalendared MSS. at Longleat, Coventry Papers, VIII, fol. 294, ca.1677. Anchitell Grey, *Debates* (London, 1763), IX, 21–22 (28 January, 1688–89).

8. Joseph Priestley, *An Essay on the First Principles of Government and on the Nature of Political, Civil and Religious Liberty* (London, 1769; here 2d ed., 1771), dedicated to David, earl of Buchan, Sec. 4, "Effects of a Code of Education," p. 91.

CHAPTER II. Some Seventeenth-Century Commonwealthmen

1. *Calendar of State Papers Venetian,* 1659–1675, ed. Allen G. Hinds (London, 1931–1938); XXXVI, no. 193, p. 180 (18 April, 1670); no. 221, p. 202 (6 June, 1670); no. 235, p. 216 (27 June, 1670); no. 369, p. 310 (12 December, 1670); Andrew Marvell, *Letters,* ed. H. M. Margoliouth (Oxford, 1927), p. 102 (26 March, 1670); p. 302 (21 March, 1670). G. Burnet, *History of My Own Times,* ed. O. Airy, 2 vols. (Oxford, 1897), I, 487.

2. See P. Laslett, "The English Revolution and Locke's Two Treatises," *CHJ,* 12, no. 1: 40–55, for the dating of Locke's works.

3. On the Rye, see *Calendar of State Papers Domestic,* eds. F. H. B. Daniell and F. Bickley (London, 1933–34) for the years 1683–84, *passim;* and, *inter alia,* Thomas Sprat, *True Account and Declaration of the Horrid Conspiracy against the Late King, his Present Majesty, and the Government* (London, 1685), 2nd ed. (London, 1685) where many of the depositions are printed. On Abraham Holmes (d.1685), see *DNB* and *The Western Martyrology or Bloody Assizes* (London, 1705), pp. 170–173. On Monmouth, see *Western Martyrology, passim;* T. B. Macaulay, *History of England* (London, 1934), chap. v; M. Ashley, *John Wildman* (London, 1947); and others.

4. Anonymous tract, "Now is the Time; a Scheme for a Commonwealth," followed by "Good Advice Before it be too Late," from *A Collection of Scarce and Valuable Tracts,* ed. Walter Scott (London, 1813), X, 197–202; hereafter referred to as *Somers's Tracts.* For an eighteenth-century list of the "Canon," see F. Blackburne, *Memoirs of Thomas Hollis,* Esq., 2 vols. (London, 1780), II, 554*n,* 659–660; hereafter referred to as *Hollis Memoirs.*

5. For the Rota, see John Aubrey, *Brief Lives,* ed. A. Clark (Oxford, 1898), I, 288–295, under James Harrington (1611/2–1677). For Nonsuch House, see Ashley, p. 142 and *passim.*

6. For Neville's life, see *DNB* and authorities cited. Also Marvell, *Letters* (11 February, 1658), p. 294; (25 November, 1669), p. 91. Ashley, pp. 217–218. L. Magalotti, *The Travels of Cosmo of Tuscany* (1669; tr. London, 1821), pp. 159–160, 194, 199, 277–279, 281, 301, 312, 347, 370, 462. Also H.M.C., *Portland MSS.* VI (London, 1901), 16, letter of 15 July, 1726, from Henry Grey: "I send you a few letters from the Duke of Tuscany who was pleased to honour my great uncle Harry Neville with his correspondence." Neville's will is at Somerset House, P.C.C., Box Irby, 174. His heirs were nephews and nieces. For his religion, see *England's Confusion* (London, 1659), p. 10. His activities in Richard's Parliament may be found in Thomas Burton, *Diary,* 4 vols. (London, 1828); *Journals of the House of Commons,* VII, 1651–1659 (London, 1813). See G. Kitchin, *Sir Roger L'Estrange* (London, 1913), p. 334, for a report about Neville in 1684.

7. *Plato Redivivus,* 2nd ed. (London, 1681) cited throughout, publisher to the reader (unpaged), *passim;* reference to the Parliament of 1680, p. 253. Compare

pp. 214–225 of this edition with the earlier one of 1680, p. 207, to see omitted passage.

8. Walter Moyle, *The Whole Works, to Which is Prefaced Some Account of his Life and Writings by Anthony Hammond, Esq.* (London, 1727), pp. 75–76, 22–27 (Hammond to Moyle). For the Grecian, where Moyle wrote that Neville talked in his old age, see George W. Thornbury and E. Walford, *Old and New London* (London, n.d.), III, 65.

9. *Plato,* p. 237 to end.

10. *Ibid.,* p. 35; jury, p. 135.

11. *Ibid.,* pp. 140–142.

12. *Ibid.,* pp. 237–240.

13. *Ibid.,* pp. 50–51.

14. See Bibliographical Commentary for a list of replies to Neville and for later editions of his work, of which the last by R. Baron and T. Hollis (London, 1763) contained a prefatory memoir which should be used with caution.

15. William Petyt (1636–1707), *Antient Right of the Commons* (London, 1680). William Atwood (d.1705), later Chief Justice of New York, *Jus Anglorum* (London, 1681). *Plato,* p. 110.

16. For all Sidney material and references, see Caroline Robbins, "Algernon Sidney's Discourses," in *WMQ,* 3rd ser., 4, no. 3: 267–296 (July 1947).

17. I have Capel Lofft's copy of the 1772 edition of Sidney's *Works,* copiously annotated by him.

18. Algernon Sidney, *Dying Speech,* reprinted at the Revolution, 1689, and thereafter a part of Whig legend.

19. Sylas Neville, *Diary,* ed. B. Cozens-Hardy (London, 1950), p. 13; a story about Baron's talk with Chatham about republicanism, p. 19.

20. E. Ludlow, *Memoirs,* ed. C. H. Firth (Oxford, 1894), II, 99, 172–173. The notes contain suggestions that seem anticipatory of American practice. Firth's introduction gives a useful bibliographical history, vii.

21. See below, Chap. IV.

22. Marchamont Nedham, *The Excellencie of a Free State,* ed. R. Baron (London, 1767; repr. Amsterdam, 1774), pp. 47–49 and *passim.* On Nedham, see *DNB;* G. P. Gooch and H. Laski, *English Democratic Ideas* (London, 1927), pp. 159–162. Marchamont Nedham may have quieted down politically after 1660, but he continued to support freedom in his own way. *Medela Medicinae* (London, 1665) was a plea for free inquiry in science, to rescue man from old tyranny of disease, and an endorsement of the new methods and advances of the century. See John Adams, *Works* (1851) VI, 3–220.

23. For excellent treatment of the much-discussed writers, Marvell and Milton, see amongst others, P. Legouis, *André Marvell, Poète, Puritain, Patriote* (Oxford, 1928), and Z. Fink, *The Classical Republicans* (Evanston, 1945), *passim,* for useful bibliographical and biographical material.

24. A. Browning, *Life of Danby* (Glasgow, 1951), III, no. I, pp. 2–3.

25. Roger L'Estrange, *Observator,* I, no. 259 (16 December, 1682).

CHAPTER III. The Whigs of the Revolution and of the Sacheverell Trial

1. William Temple, "On Government," in *Works* (London, 1750), I, 95–108; "On the United Provinces," 7–77; "Popular Discontents," 255–271. The latter is very interesting on difficulties and diseases of government. See also section on retirement, in *Works* (London, 1757), II, 537. George Savile, Marquis of Halifax, *Works,* ed. W. Raleigh (Oxford, 1912), p. 211.

2. H. R. Fox Bourne, *The Life of John Locke,* 2 vols. (London, 1876), is my authority for most biographical details. J. W. Gough, *Locke's Political Philosophy* (Oxford, 1954), chap. vi on Locke in '88.

3. See Laslett, "English Revolution," *CHJ,* 12, no. 1.

4. *The Correspondence of Locke and Clarke,* ed. B. Rand (Cambridge, Mass., 1927), p. 289. Lady Mordaunt's letter (8 February, 1689), quoted above, is in Laslett, p. 40.

5. Fox Bourne, II, 155. See reference to Occasional Bill in *Locke-Clarke Correspondence,* p. 595.

6. Fox Bourne, II, chap. xiii.

7. *Ibid.* For William's favour, see p. 397.

8. Josiah Tucker, *A Selection from his Economic and Political Writings,* ed. R. L. Schuyler (New York, 1931), on Locke, pp. 403–553; quotation, p. 421. Tucker's fears would have been doubly enforced by such tracts as Henry Yorke's *The Spirit of John Locke,* published in Sheffield in 1794.

9. Tucker, p. 465. See also Benjamin Turner's letter (15 November, 1819), J. Nichols, *Illustrations of the Literary History of the Eighteenth Century* VI (London, 1831), 167–168.

10. J. Locke, *Two Treatises of Government,* ed. T. I. Cook (New York, 1947, cited throughout), par. 79, p. 61.

11. Locke, *Second Treatise,* chap. v, "Of Property."

12. *Ibid.,* pars. 157, 158, 222. I shall not annotate every sentence, but only suggest such paragraphs as may illustrate familiar but less obvious phases of Locke's thought.

13. Locke, *Letters Concerning Toleration,* ed. Hollis (London, 1765), p. 61; and *Second Treatise,* pars. 203–204, 226, 243, etc.

14. Locke, *Second Treatise,* par. 223.

15. *Ibid.,* par. 224.

16. *Ibid.,* pars. 176, 177.

17. *Ibid.,* par. 192.

18. Most biographical details may be found in any general work of reference. For comment on the new light thrown on Newton by study of the MSS. acquired from the Portsmouth Collection for Cambridge, see J. M. Keynes, *Essays*

in Biography, new ed. only (London, 1953), pp. 310–323. I. B. Cohen, *Franklin and Newton* (Philadelphia, 1956), is valuable, in the present context especially chap. iii.

19. The most recent work on Newton in parliament may be found in M. Rex, *University Representation in England* (London, 1954), chap. xii, pp. 296–325, and authorities there cited.

20. Sir John Craig, *Newton at the Mint* (Cambridge, 1946). Craig does not credit Newton with any responsibility for the rather dubious reform of the currency.

21. John Conduitt (1688–1737), M.P. for Whitchurch, 1715–1734; S'Hampton Borough, 1735–1737. See also *DNB.*

22. H. Pemberton, ed., of 3rd ed., of *Principia* (1726), Preface to *A View of Sir Isaac Newton's Philosophy* (London, 1728).

23. W. Whiston, *Memoirs of Dr. Samuel Clarke* (London, 1730), *passim.* See p. 96 for Onslow's chairmanship of this group during 1716. For Onslow's remarks on Newton, see *Diary of John Perceval, 1st Earl of Egmont, 1730–47,* in H.M.C., *Egmont MSS.* (London, 1920–1924), I, 112–113; hereafter referred to as *Egmont Diary.* On Newton's religion, see two works by H. McLachlan, *The Religious Opinions of Milton, Locke and Newton* (Manchester, 1941), and *Newton's Theological Manuscripts* (Liverpool, 1950), and in the latter Hopton Hayes is quoted as calling Peter King and Joseph Jekyll others of a Unitarian way of thought, p. 6. Newton's mathematical piety is well illustrated in "Letters to Bentley," for which see R. Bentley, *Works,* ed. Alexander Dyce (London, 1838), III, 201–215. A new edition of the *Clarke-Leibnitz Correspondence* in defense of Newton recently appeared, edited by H. G. Alexander (Manchester, 1956). An amusing popularization of Newton was published in London in 1761 by an author using the pseudonym of "Telescope Tom," *The Newtonian System Adapted to the Capacities of Young Ladies.*

24. Sir Isaac Newton, *Mathematical Principles of Natural Philosophy,* tr. by Andrew Motte, rev. and ed. by F. Cajori (Berkeley, 1954), xvii; hereafter referred to as *Principia.*

25. *Principia,* Cotes's introduction to 2nd ed., xxi.

26. *Ibid.,* p. 669.

27. *Ibid.,* p. 544.

28. Colin Maclaurin, *An Account of Sir Isaac Newton's Philosophical Discoveries* (London, 1748), p. 6.

29. *Principia,* pp. 398–400.

30. Maclaurin, pp. 17–18.

31. *Ibid.,* p. 23.

32. *Principia,* appendix, pp. 633, 668–669, 671–676; Pemberton, p. 22.

33. For Tyrrell's life, see *DNB.* There is no critical study. Besides works mentioned in the text, he wrote *A History of England,* 3 vols., to the death of Richard II (London, 1696–1704).

34. *Bibliotheca Politica,* 2nd ed. cited throughout, Dialogues III and V.

35. *Ibid.,* pp. 456, 503.

36. *Ibid.,* pp. 505–511.

37. *Ibid.,* p. 576, and throughout, Dialogues X and XI.

38. *Ibid.,* p. 118.

39. *Ibid.,* p. 672.

40. *Ibid.,* pp. 25, 33; about family life, p. 36.

41. *Ibid.,* p. 132.

42. *Ibid.,* pp. 209–210, 277, 278.

43. See arguments, for example, in works by John Withers: *Whigs Vindicated,* 4th ed. (1715), at Oxford, Bart. Pamph. 326 (28), pp. 20–22; or *Revolution Principles Fairly Represented and Defended* (1714), at Oxford, Godwin Pamph. 1893 (3), *passim,* but especially pp. 7, 12–13. For Withers's historical defenses see *MR,* 4:250–275 (1809).

44. For Cumberland, see *DNB* and Bibliographical Commentary for editions of his work.

45. Richard Cumberland, *A Treatise of the Laws of Nature,* tr. by John Maxwell (London and Dublin, 1727), chaps. i, v, ix. See also pp. 136–137 for Hobbes on human nature; mutual benevolence, pp. 159–160; limitations of government, pp. 350–351. For Maxwell, see Chap. V below.

46. On Somers there is very little good material. See *DNB;* also John Lord Campbell, *Lives of the Lord Chancellors,* 10 vols. (Boston, 1874), IV, 457–502; V, 1–119, for fullest but inaccurate treatment. There is no bibliographical study. Some Somers material is in P. Yorke, Earl Hardwicke, ed., *Miscellaneous State Papers,* 2 vols. (London, 1778), II, no. 7 (The Somers Papers), which contain valuable notes on the Convention by Somers. See also Somers's *Memoir* (London, 1716); Richard Cooksey, *Essay on the Life and Character of John Lord Somers* (Worcester, 1791).

47. *The Judgment of Whole Kingdoms and Nations Concerning the Rights, Power and Prerogative of Kings and the Rights, Privileges and Properties of the People* (London, 1710); eleven editions by 1717, "the tenth ed. corrected," 1771; a Philadelphia ed., 1773.

48. Somers, *The Judgment,* 10th ed. (London, 1771), pars. 85–100; quotation, p. 73.

49. Somers, *The Judgment,* par. 46, p. 39.

50. *Baldwin's State Tracts* (London, 1689), I, 383–400, 397; More and Fisher, p. 400.

51. Somers, *The Security of Englishmen's Lives* (London, 1681), pp. 17–20, 45–46 and *passim.*

52. For the best account of this, see A. T. Scudi, *The Sacheverell Affair* (New York, 1939), and *The Tryal of Dr. Henry Sacheverell* (London, 1710, folio, cited throughout).

53. Lechmere's speech, *Tryal,* begins p. 20; this quotation, pp. 22–23. Edmund Burke, *An Appeal from the New to the Old Whigs* (London, 1791), here cited

from *Works* (London, 1887), III, 1–115; pp. 45–66 are specifically on the Trial, quoting long excerpts from it.

54. Burke, pp. 59–60, 64.

55. On Hoadly, see N. Sykes, in *Some Thinkers of the Augustan Age,* ed. F. J. G. Hearnshaw (London, 1923; reprinted New York, 1950), pp. 112–155. G. Every, *The High Church Party, 1688–1718* (London, 1956), pp. 156–157, 160–167; and Chap. IV below. What is usually known as "Hoadly on Government" appeared in London, 1710: *The Original and Institution of Civil Government Discuss'd,* the second half of which is *A Defense of Mr. Hooker's Judgment.* . . .

56. Hoadly, *On Government,* appendix, p. 201.

57. John Adams, *Works,* ed. C. F. Adams (Boston, 1850–1856), VI, 4. J. Mayhew, *The Snare Broken* (Boston, 1766), p. 32. See also Chap. IV below.

58. *Tryal,* pp. 71–77.

59. *Ibid.,* p. 77.

60. Compare Locke's *Treatises* to Somers, *The Judgment,* par. 187, p. 155. See also par. 186 above where Somers, like Locke, stresses the reluctance of the people to take up arms and resist. And note Stanhope on remedy and resistance, *Tryal,* p. 73.

61. Burke: against innovators, p. 114; against "pretended" rights of man, p. 11; and opposition to reform of parliament, p. 27; diatribe against the idea that the *people* retain a continuing right, pp. 76–77; definition of "people" as the "wiser" sort, p. 85.

CHAPTER IV. Robert Molesworth and His Friends in England, 1693–1727

1. For example, S.S., *The Commonwealthsman Unmasqu'd, or, a Just Rebuke to the Author of the Account of Denmark* (London, 1694).

2. James Arbuckle, et al., *Hibernicus's Letters* (London and Dublin, 1729), I, 187; II, 426.

3. The best account of Molesworth in English is in G. E. Cokayne, *Complete Peerage,* rev. ed. (London, 1936), IX, 31–32. The most useful is in Christian H. Brasch, *Om Robert Molesworth's Skrift, an Account of Denmark* (Copenhagen, 1879). There are many letters of the Molesworths in H.M.C., *Various Collections,* VIII (London, 1913), 214–397. Molesworth-Toland letters in J. Toland, *Miscellaneous Works,* 2 vols. (London, 1726), II, 461–495, *passim.* Many letters from Denmark in State Papers Foreign, Denmark, P.R.O., London. See Chap. V below for Molesworth-King letters.

4. See Toland, *Misc. Works,* II, 493, for Westminster plans.

5. See letters from Scots in H.M.C., *Var. Coll.,* VIII, *passim.* See Chap. V below for Swift and Molesworth. For *Cato's Letters,* see below, n. 55. C. B. Realey, "*London Journal* and its Authors, 1720–23," *University of Kansas Humanistic Studies,* V, no. 3 (Lawrence, Kansas, 1935). Letters in H.M.C., *Var. Coll.,* VIII, 326, 347–349. H.M.C., *Carlisle MSS.,* in *App. VI to Fifteenth Report* (London, 1897), p. 33; and

Bath MSS., 3 vols. (London, 1904–1908), III, 499. B.M.Add. MSS. 4282, no. 40, Anthony Collins to Desmaiseaux.

6. Brasch has a good list of rejoinders. See Bibliographical Commentary.

7. For Locke and Molesworth, see below, n. 19. Brasch, p. 171, quotes *Bayle. CSPD, Wm. and Mary,* ed. W. J. Hardy, V, 1694–1695 (London, 1906), p. 181, and VII, 1697 (London, 1927), p. 259.

8. See letters in Toland, *Misc. Works,* cited in n. 3 above. In these works may also be traced the disillusionment of Toland with Harley. Molesworth's attempts to secure a job through Harley may be studied in H.M.C., *Portland MSS.,* IV (London, 1897), 489, 612–613, 637; Shaftesbury and Harley, 697–698. See *The Letters of Lord Shaftesbury to Molesworth,* ed. J. Toland (London, 1721) for friendships; hereafter referred to as *Letters.*

9. C. Davenant, *Works,* coll. by Whitworth (London, 1771), IV, quotation, 152; 157–158. *Letters,* p. 13, for Jacobites.

10. *Letters,* for friends, *passim;* for Halifax, pp. 9–10. For Molesworth's letter about Godolphin, see Shaftesbury Papers, P.R.O., London, 30, GD–24, Bdl. XXI, nos. 180–181; for Junto, *ibid.,* Bdl. XX, no. 137 (18 December, 1707).

11. H.M.C., *Var. Coll.,* VIII, 258–260, about Godolphin and about Tindal's visit, mentioned below.

12. Matthew Tindal (1653?–1733), *Reasons Against Restricting the Press* appeared in 1704, reprinted in R. Baron's *Pillars of Priestcraft* (London, 1768), IV, 279–299 and note on p. 281; Baron owned Anthony Collins's copy. Tindal was educated at Exeter and Oxford, frequented the Grecian, was a friend of Toland and Asgill, opposed Walpole and the Highchurchmen, and used John Silk as amanuensis. See *The Religious, Rational and Moral Conduct of Matthew Tindal* (London, 1735) for biographical details; for Grecian, pp. 8, 119. T. Hearne, *Remarks and Collections,* Oxford Hist. Soc., eds. C. E. Doble, D. W. Rannie and H. Salter, 11 vols. (Oxford, 1885–1918), VI (1902), 251, 256–257.

13. John Asgill (1659–1738), b. in Worcestershire; student at Middle Temple, 1686–1692. *Journal of the House of Commons of the Kingdom of Ireland* (11 October, 1703), II (Dublin, 1796), 333–334. See also *DNB.*

14. See *GEC* for Sunderland; also John Macky (d.1726), *Memoirs of Secret Service* (London, 1733), p. 69; H.M.C., *Var. Coll.,* VIII, 281–282, 287, 299, 305, 308, 339, and Countess Judith, 280, 295; J. Evelyn, *Diary,* ed. E. S. de Beer (Oxford, 1955), IV, 595. See *Bibliotheca Sunderlandiana* (Sale-catalogue), 1881–1883; for books sold from Blenheim in London; see Evelyn, V, 322, n. 2.

15. H.M.C., *Var. Coll.,* VIII, 300, 308. *Life, Unpublished Letters and Philosophical Regimen of Anthony, earl of Shaftesbury,* ed. B. Rand (London, 1900); hereafter *Life, Letters:* letters to John Molesworth, pp. 444–445, 452; Molesworth's father, 461; encomium on Stanhope, p. 480. For perfunctory references to Stanhope, see H.M.C., *Var. Coll.,* VIII, 248–250 and 299.

16. See *A Collection of State Tracts Published During the Reign of William III,* 3 vols. (London, 1705–1707), *passim,* for Johnson's and Hampden's tracts, and many

others, including the most important on the Standing Army controversy of 1697–99.

17. See Brasch throughout. For other works on Danish Revolution and Molesworth, see Franz von Jessen, *En Slesvigsk Statsmand*, 2 vols. (Copenhagen, 1930), I, chap. v, 141–190. *Letters* (1721), p. 26.

18. The preface to *An Account* is not paged in the first three reprints or editions, but is numbered in the edition of 1738. See Bibliographical Commentary for separate reprints. The quotation opens it; what follows is from the remainder.

19. J. Locke, *Works*, IX, 435, 449. The preface to *An Account* contains Molesworth's theory of education, but chap. xvi also reflects sharply on the Lutheran clergy and their role in Denmark on education and on other matters. Brinck, a Lutheran in London, helped William King with his rebuttal, noticed above, n. 6.

20. See below, Chap. V, for Turnbull and Fordyce. Also Toland, *Misc. Works*, II, "A Letter Concerning the Roman Education." M. Tindal, *Four Discourses* (London, 1709), p. 235, in "An Essay Concerning the Power of the Magistrate" (1697). W. Moyle, *Whole Works*, "An Essay on the Lacedaemonian Government," pp. 61–62; Moyle, *Works*, ed. Thomas Sergeant, 2 vols. (London, 1726), I, 87, "An Essay on the Roman Government"; John Trenchard, *Cato's Letters* (London, 1721), 3rd ed. quoted here (London, 1733), I, 139–140; IV, 236.

21. B. Williams, *Stanhope; a Study in Eighteenth-Century War and Diplomacy* (Oxford, 1932). Toland, *The State Anatomy of Great Britain* (London, 1717), chap. xii, 69–81. T. Hearne, for endorsement of some criticism, VI, 23, 198, 242. *An Account*, pp. 268–269. Moyle, *Whole Works*, p. 173.

22. *An Account* (1694), pp. 46, 73; chap. vi on form of old government; chap. vii on events of 1660.

23. On the Peerage Bill, see E. H. Turner, *EHR*, 28:243–259 (1913). Turner attributes *The Patrician* to Molesworth. Division lists in Cobbett, *Parl. Hist.*, VII (London, 1811), 624–627. Toland, *State Anatomy*, chap. viii, pp. 39–40. T. Gordon, *Septennial Parliament* (1722), pub. in *A Collection of Tracts* by J. Trenchard and T. Gordon, 2 vols. (London, 1751), II, 31–82. The continuing interest in the peerage may be seen not only in the publication in London of *A Memorial Sent . . . by the Late Earl Stanhope to the Abbé Vertot* . . . (1721), but in a rather elaborate collection in 1758 of reflections upon Vertot's answer about the method of appointment to the Roman Senate by Edward Spelman, Conyers Middleton, and Thomas Chapman with a rather more elaborate commentary on each by the compiler, Nathaniel Hooke (d.1763), as in Chap. VIII below, n. 27.

24. *An Account of Denmark*, chap. vi; preface to *Franco-Gallia*, xxv–xxxi. Cobbett, *Parl. Hist.*, VII, 536–537.

25. On the literature of the standing army controversy, see an unpublished dissertation by Lois Schwoerer, Bryn Mawr College Library. For the Grecian in Devereux Court off Essex Street near Temple Bar, see above, Chap. II, n. 8. See also A. Fletcher, *Political Works* (London, 1737), *A Discourse of Government with Relation to Militia* (London, 1697; Edinburgh, 1698), pp. 6–10. Also see C. Robbins,

"Causes of the Renaissance," *HINL,* I, no. 2:7–10 (March 1955). *An Argument Against a Standing Army* (London, 1697) by Trenchard and Moyle is here quoted from Moyle, *Whole Works,* pp. 161, 163–164, 173.

26. Moyle, *Whole Works,* p. 168. Fletcher, *Pol. Works,* quotation, p. 9.

27. See below, Chap. VI.

28. Moyle died in 1721. His unpublished *Works* were published in 1726 in two volumes by Thomas Sergeant; those already in print were collected with a prefatory note and some letters between Moyle and Anthony Hammond in 1727. Hammond corrected Sergeant's statement about the date of composition of "The Roman Government" and said it was the work of his twenty-seventh year. This essay was reprinted by John Thelwall, the radical, as *Democracy Vindicated* (London, 1795). *An Apology for the Writings of Walter Moyle, Esq.* (London, 1727), pp. 21–22, praised his zeal for the liberty of his country and his wit, good sense, and learning. A modern account of Moyle is in Z. Fink, *The Classical Republican* (Evanston, 1945), pp. 170–174.

29. Trenchard and Gordon, *A Coll. of Tracts,* I, 57–62, in reprint of *A Short History of Standing Armies* (1698).

30. Moyle, *Whole Works,* p. 63.

31. *Ibid.,* pp. 59–62.

32. Moyle, *Works,* I, 1–148, "An Essay Upon the Roman Government"; methods of preserving liberty, 73–75, 84–98; Roman religion, pp. 12–50; "served for naught," p. 49; naturalization, p. 89; Harrington, p. 113.

33. *Ibid., passim* and p. 81; ballot, pp. 96–98; rotation, pp. 94–95.

34. *Ibid.,* the second essay, pp. 99–148. See also *Cato's Letters,* I, no. 2.

35. Moyle, *Whole Works,* pp. 75–77; *Works,* I, 112, 148.

36. Preface to *Franco-Gallia,* xxxiii, x; *Cato's Letters,* I, no. 12; *An Account,* pp. 164, 250–251, 246, 239.

37. *Ibid.,* chap. vi, p. 45.

38. Preface to *Franco-Gallia,* xvii. Samuel Johnson (1649–1703), *An Essay Concerning Parliaments, or, the Kalends of May* (1693), reprinted in *The Works of the Late Rev. Mr. Samuel Johnson* (London, 1710), pp. 279–293.

39. William Coxe, *Memoirs of Sir Robert Walpole,* 3 vols. (London, 1798), II, 62–63, Moyle to Horace Walpole. Gordon, *Septennial Parliament* (1722), in *A Collection of Tracts* (1751), II, 31; B. Williams, *Stanhope,* Appendix E.

40. Molesworth's *Considerations,* pp. 43–44. Preface to *Franco-Gallia,* xxiv. Compare with J. Toland, *The Art of Governing by Partys* . . . (London, 1701), pp. 75–77.

41. *Cato's Letters,* II, no. 61, pp. 239–240.

42. J. Trenchard, Preface to *A History of Standing Armies* (1698), in *A Coll. of Tracts* (1751), I, 57–62. William Stephens, *A Letter to King William,* in *A Coll. of State Tracts,* II, 631–637. On Scipio Maffei's account of England (ca.1737), see Luigi Rossi, *Opera* (Milan, 1941), *Un Precursore di Montesquieu,* pp. 43, 71.

43. See below, Chap. V.

44. *Reflections and Resolutions Proper for the Gentlemen of Ireland* (Dublin, 1738, repr. 1816), p. 99. Trenchard's report in *A. Coll. of State Tracts*, II, 709–722, 723–788, with other material about the commissioners. See also Cobbett, *Parl. Hist.*, V (1809), 1202–1217 (March 1700).

45. Preface to *Franco-Gallia*, xx–xxi.

46. *Cato's Letters*, IV, no. 106, 3–12.

47. Preface to *Franco-Gallia*, xxxiv; C. Davenant, *Works*, II, 1–76. *Characteristics*, 4th ed. (1727), "An Essay on the Freedom of Wit and Humour," I, Sec. 2, 64. *Cato's Letters*, I, no. 10, 51.

48. Preface to *Franco-Gallia*, and *Considerations, passim.*

49. *A True Way to Render Ireland Happy and Secure, or a Discourse Wherein 'Tis the Interest both of England and Ireland to Encourage Foreign Protestants to Plant in Ireland— in a Letter to . . . R. Molesworth* (Dublin, 1697); preface to *Franco-Gallia*, xxiv.

50. *An Account*, chap. viii, pp. 86ff.; preface to *Franco-Gallia*, xxii; Johnson, *Works*, p. 335; Moyle, *Works*, I, 88–89; Tindal, *Four Discourses*, p. 261. Toland, *State Anatomy*, chap. x, 53–58; Toland, *Reasons for Naturalizing the Jews* (London, 1713). Shaftesbury, in *Life, Letters*, p. 377.

51. *An Account*, chap. viii; preface to *Franco-Gallia*, xxiv.

52. See below, n. 54.

53. Journals of the Irish Parliaments full of this for December 1713. Nicholas Tindal, *Continuation of Rapin's History* (London, 1751), II, 331–332. And see [J. Swift], *Examiner*, V, no. 10, 28 December—January 1713 (December 1713); no. 14 (January 1713); no. 16 (January 1713); and R. Steele, *The Englishman*, no. 46 (January 19, 1713–14). Molesworth's preface to *An Account*, and *A True State of His Case* was published (London, 1713–14) to justify his behaviour.

54. Preface to *Franco-Gallia*, x–xvi; Cobbett, *Parl. Hist.*, VII, 584–589. David Bogue and J. Bennett, *History of the Dissenters from the Revolution in 1688 to the Year 1808*, 1st ed. (London, 1808–1812), III, 127–128 (26 March, 1717).

55. *Two Independent Whigs* (London, 1721); J. Bulloch, *Bibliography of Thomas Gordon* (Aberdeen, 1918). See also Archdeacon Blackburne, *Hollis Memoirs*, II, 569–573, and Gordon's introduction to *Cato's Letters*. H.M.C., *A. C. Stuart MSS., App. I to Eighth Report* (London, 1881), pp. 311a, 314b, 315a. Harvard, Houghton Library, MSS. Engl., 592F, a Trenchard MS. with note by R. Baron.

56. G. Every, *The High Church Party*, chap. viii, 147–168.

57. W. Stephens (1647–1718), Rector of Sutton, Sermon on 30 January, 1700 (n.s.). Baron said that Trenchard wrote its shining conclusions, *Pillars of Priestcraft* (London, 1768), II, 256–257, n. p. 262.

58. Abbey lands. Of many references, see T. Burton, *Diary* (of Cromwell's Parliaments), III, notes, pp. 201–203; A. Grey, *Debates*, VII, 400–401; T. Sprat, p. 21; W. Coventry, *A Letter Written to Dr. Burnet* (1685); and a host of others during the eighties. Eighteenth-century references were numerous, e.g., *Some Useful Remarks*

(London, 1683), p. 35. *Cato's Letters*, IV, no. 130, 213; *The Freeholder's Alarm* (London, 1734), p. 130; [Attributed to H. Fielding], *A Serious Address* (1745), p. 43; [Attributed to E. Weston or A. Tucker], *A Country Gentleman's Advice to His Son* (1755), p. 35; or M. Tindal, *The Defection Considered* (1717), p. 14.

59. *Independent Whig*, no. 50 (1720), pp. 404ff., abbey lands, xxvii–xxviii.

60. *Ibid.*, no. 16, p. 116; no. 3, p. 15f.

61. *Ibid.*, no. 34, pp. 264–265. See *Tacitus* (London, 1728), I, Ninth Discourse, Cromwell, p. 105.

62. *A Coll. of Tracts* (1751), I, 311.

63. *Cato's Letters*, III, no. 96, pp. 258–259.

64. *Ibid.*, II, no. 37, p. 28.

65. *Tacitus* (London, 1731), II, 93. *Cato's Letters*, II, no. 43.

66. *Ibid.*, no. 50, p. 120.

67. *Tacitus*, II, 95–100.

68. *Tacitus*, II, Discourses IX–XI, rabble, p. 109. *Cato's Letters*, II, no. 42, p. 70; no. 43, pp. 71–76; no. 45, p. 90.

69. *Cato's Letters*, II, no. 43, p. 75; also II, no. 38, p. 34 and no. 45, *passim*. See Chap. III above, Locke and Somers on slowness of people to rebel; also Gordon, *Sallust* (London, n.d.), Discourse IX, p. 159.

70. *Cato's Letters*, II, no. 38, 42; I, no. 33, 260; III, changes in government, 154; on judgment of people, I, no. 22, 153; on education, III, no. 102, 3; III, no. 71. *Tacitus*, II, Discourse XII, 117–145.

71. *Cato's Letters*, II, no. 59, 217–225.

72. *Ibid.*, no. 59, 225.

73. *Ibid.*, I, no. 26 on Sidney; no. 28 on "Defense of Cato"; II, nos. 36, 55; no. 54, 163–164.

74. *Ibid.*, II, 216–217.

75. *Ibid.*, II, no. 62, 253.

76. *Ibid.*, III, no. 85, 160.

77. *Ibid.*, I, no. 15, 96; and II, no. 67, 303ff.

78. Two good studies are: F. H. Heineman, *John Toland and the Age of Enlightenment* (Oxford, 1944); Albert Lantoine, *John Toland* (Paris, 1927). He was commonly regarded as one of those at the Grecian responsible for a number of publications new and old. See above nn. 12 and 25, and *A Brief Reply* (1698). His Milton and Harrington alone, however, suffice to show his interests, and his *Militia Reformed* (London, 1698) reflects his association with the anti-army coterie of which Trenchard was chief.

79. The British Museum now has the copy of Martin's *Description of the Western Islands of Scotland* (London, 1716), annotated by the friends, C. 45 c.l.

80. For Toland's life, see Desmaizeaux, introduction to Toland, *Misc. Works* (1726); *Modesty Mistaken or a Letter to Mr. Toland* . . . (1702). Anthony Collins supplied Desmaizeaux with some of his facts, see below, n. 81. T. Hearne, *Remarks*

and Collections, VII (Oxford, 1906), "died that impious wretch, John Toland, author of a great many horrid books," p. 343. E. Curll, *Historical Account* (London, 1722).

81. See above, n. 80. Add. MSS. 4282, no. 46, 190 (5 March, 1721 and 17 April, 1722), Collins to Desmaizeaux.

82. See Toland, *Misc. Works,* "Memoirs," *passim,* and II, 226–231 for an excellent statement of his politics; also Toland, *Vindicius Liberius* (London, 1830), p. 113.

83. See *State Anatomy, passim.*

84. For Shaftesbury I have relied on *Life, Letters* (B. Rand, already cited); on *Second Characters* (Cambridge, 1914); on his *Letters to Molesworth;* and on some unpublished material in the Shaftesbury Papers, for which see n. 10 above. Also on A. O. Aldridge, "Shaftesbury and the Deist Manifesto," in *APT,* new ser., 41, Part 2 (June 1951).

85. *Letters of Shaftesbury to Molesworth,* p. 13. T. Forster, *Original Letters of Locke, Algernon Sidney, and Anthony, Lord Shaftesbury* (London, 1830), p. 113.

86. Forster, pp. 171–175 (27 February, 1702). D. Ogg, *England in the Reigns of James II and William III* (Oxford, 1955), pp. 462–464.

87. Forster, p. 270; *Life, Letters,* p. 424.

88. Forster, p. 105; *Life, Letters,* "truly monarchical," p. 481.

89. *Characteristics,* II, "laborious hinds," p. 282.

90. *Ibid.,* I, in "Of Wit and Humour," 110–115; "to cantonize," 113; "Patria," in "Miscellaneous Reflections," III, 149.

91. *Ibid.,* III, 150–151.

92. *Life, Letters,* p. 485.

93. Besides Shaftesbury's letters to his friends and such protégés as Michael Ainsworth, and his writing in general on freedom of thought, see Anthony Collins, *Discourse of Free-Thinking* (London, 1713), *passim.* On the title page he quotes from *Characteristics* on attempts to confuse license and liberty. Margaret L. Wiley, *The Subtle Knot* (London, 1952), p. 235, regrets that Collins's honest free-thinking was little regarded in the eighteenth century, but perhaps rather underestimates the skeptical tradition of that period.

94. *Characteristics,* II, *The Moralists* Part 2, Sec. 3, 258–280.

95. Shaftesbury's *Second Characters,* ed. B. Rand (Cambridge, 1914), pp. 22–23.

96. On party see Rapin in A. Browning, *English Historical Documents* (London, 1953), pp. 259–269. César de Saussure, *A Foreign View of England in the Reigns of George I and George II,* tr. Van Muyden (London, 1902), Letter XV. Toland, *State Anatomy,* preface. On Jacobites and unity, see E. Fitzmaurice, *Life of William, Earl of Shelburne* (London, 1875), I, 21.

97. *Life, Letters,* reference to Shaftesbury's friendship with Trenchard, p. 309; on fluctuations in government and on lessons of history, see, *inter alia, Cato's Let-*

ters, III, 153–154; *Characteristics,* III, 148–150; on Denmark, 171; I, 107–108, 212, 216, 239, and many other references.

CHAPTER V. The Case of Ireland

1. *The Case of Ireland's Being Bound by Acts of Parliament in England Stated* appeared in 1698 in Dublin and London; in 1706, in Dublin, 1719, 1720, 1725, 1749, 1770; Dublin, 1773 used here; Belfast ed., 1776; Dublin, 1782, 1892, 1897. See Bibliographical Commentary.

2. Art. Molyneux, *DNB.* Gisborne Molineux, *Memoirs of the Molyneux Family* (London, 1892), IV, 83–87; and Molyneux, Sir Capel, *An Account of the Family and Descendants of Sir Thomas Molyneux* (Evesham, 1820).

3. MSS., Marsh's Library, Dublin, Z.3.2.5, on Derry and Molyneux, pp. 301–304. C. S. King, *A Great Archbishop of Dublin* (London, 1906), n. to p. 175.

4. *The Case.* For Molyneux-Locke letters, see Locke, *Works,* IX, 289–458; ref. to *Case* and *Treatise* (19 April, 1698), 455.

5. C. H. McIlwain, *The American Revolution* (New York, 1923), chap. ii, "Realm and the Dominion."

6. John Davies, *A Discoverie of the True Causes Why Ireland Was Never Entirely Subdued* (London, 1612, 1664, 1666, 1705, 1747, 1761, etc.). H. Reilly, *Ireland's Case* (1695 and 1720), preface.

7. T. C. Dublin MSS., J.4.16.

8. T. Hearne, *Remarks and Collections,* IV, ed. D. W. Rannie (Oxford, 1898), 110–111; *Diary,* 1731–1735, in Hearne, XI (Oxford, 1918), 394–395.

9. *The Case, passim.*

10. See Bibliographical Commentary for tracts on wool.

11. William Atwood, *The History and Reasons of the Dependency of Ireland* (London, 1698), pp. 28–29, 197–198. John Cary, *An Answer to Mr. Molyneux* (London, 1698), p. 11; *A Letter to an M.P. at London* (Dublin, 1741), p. 6.

12. G. Berkeley, *The Querist,* nos. 90, 93, in *The Works of George Berkeley, Bishop of Cloyne,* ed. A. A. Luce and T. E. Jessop (London, 1953), VI; hereafter referred to as *Works,* VI.

13. *De Origine Mali* (London, 1702; tr. E. M. Law, London, 1731). See Bibliography. For criticism by a contemporary, see G. W. Leibnitz, *Theodicy,* ed. A. Farrar (London, 1952), pp. 405–442.

14. C. S. King, *Great Archbishop,* prints brief autobiographical notes. For the correction of a friend, see King Papers, T. C. Dublin MSS. (14 December, 1714), letter to Molesworth, N.2.24, pp. 144–147.

15. William King, *State of the Protestants of Ireland* (1691; 3rd ed., 1692), defense of Protestant and Revolution principles. For controversy with J. Boyse, see *A Discourse Concerning the Inventions of Man in the Worship of God* (London, 1694), frequently reprinted; and *An Admonition to the Dissenting Inhabitants of the Diocese of Derry* (London, 1694); *A Second Admonition* (London, 1695).

16. On Toland, see King Papers, T. C. Dublin MS. N.3.6, pp. 117–119, 124–125 (10 and 29 September, 1720), letters to Molesworth, the second quoted here.

17. King was a voluminous correspondent and very few of his letters have been published. In addition to the collections and transcripts at Trinity College, Dublin, there are letters from King in the Wake MSS. at Christ Church, Oxford. Transcripts of letters from Ireland may also be found at the Pearse St. Library in Dublin, and in B.M. Add. MSS. 6116–7. These contain, for example, letters from both King and Nicholson to Wake, the selection being at the discretion of the compilers. The P.R.O. State Papers for George I contain other letters from King, a critical study of whom is long overdue. Photostats of the King-Molesworth correspondence at Trinity have been used here, but the collection has been searched, as have those at Pearse St. and Marsh's Libraries, and the Irish volumes at Christ Church (cited as Wake MSS.). Citations here refer to Archbishop King's correspondence in nine folio volumes at T. C. Dublin (cited as King Papers), and if so stated, to three folio volumes, 1699–1725 (known as Fisher's Transcripts).

18. C. Leslie, *An Answer to a Book Intituled The State of the Protestants of Ireland* (London, 1692), pp. 2, 5, 7–8. See King, *State of the Protestants*, p. 24.

19. King Papers, T. C. Dublin MS. N.3.7, pp. 60–64 (2 January, 1721), letter to Robert Molesworth.

20. Marsh's Library, Z.3.25, 312, no. 79.

21. King to Edward Southwell (4 July, 1724), in Fisher's Transcripts III, T. C. Dublin MS. N.1.9, pp. 115–116.

22. Letters to Molesworth in King Papers (23 February, 1719, and 16 April, 1720). N.3.6, pp. 22–24, 61–62.

23. King Papers, T. C. Dublin MSS. (1699–1703), letter of 14 November, 1699, to Robert Southwell; Fisher's Transcripts N.1.7, pp. 89–91, I (4 February, 1699), and see letter to Molesworth (13 February, 1719/20) in King Papers N.3.6, pp. 29–31.

24. For Henry Maxwell (1680–1729), see Wm. Hamilton in *Hamilton MSS.* (Belfast, 1867), pp. 76 and lxxix. MP Bangor, 1698, 1703; Killybangs, 1713; Donegal, 1715. Died 1729–30, in Dublin. Married (a) Jane Maxwell, sister of John, Lord Farnham; (b) Dorothy, daughter of Edward Bruce. Maxwell and Molesworth associated in the Irish Commons, for which see *Journals of the Irish House of Commons*, II, 5 October, 1692–24 December, 1713 (Dublin, 1796); 8 September, 1697, p. 189; 1 October, 1703, p. 325. On John Maxwell and Molyneux, see Nicholson to Wake (1 September, 1719), B.M. Add. MSS., 6116, no. 115; and Wake Papers, Christ Church, Epistles 13, ccxlvi (30 December, 1720), Meath to Wake, p. 217; and ref. to John whose brother was a leading man in the Commons (12 January, 1721), p. 224. See P.R.O. State Papers, 1716, Ireland, Bdl. 374, for some Maxwell letters.

25. William Petty, *Tracts* (Dublin, 1769), pp. 322–325.

26. Other essays, *inter alia*, are: *A Union Between England and Scotland . . . Preju-*

dicial to England Except Also that Ireland is Included (1706); *Some Thoughts Humbly Offered Towards an Union Betwixt England and Ireland* (1708); or for later examples, *Policy and Justice,* attributed to Edward Synge (London, 1755); and *Proposal for Uniting* (1751).

27. *An Essay Towards an Union* (Dublin, 1703); my copy has slightly different title (London, 1703), *passim.* T. C. Dublin MSS., Fleetwood on Courts, G.4.13, contains Thomas Talbot on Welsh Union. Fletcher, *Pol. Works,* p. 413f.; on Ireland and Wales, pp. 409–410.

28. Mr. Desmond Clarke, Esq. of the Royal Dublin Society, who has done so much research on Dobbs, kindly helped with material about him. "A Short History to Show the Expediency, if not Political Necessity of a Union," in P.R.O., N.I., Dobbs Papers, D.O.D. 1–162, p. 54. See also Desmond Clarke on *Thomas Prior . . .* (Dublin, 1951) for information on founding of the Royal Society, and *Arthur Dobbs, Esq., 1689–1765* (Chapel Hill, 1957).

29. A. Dobbs, *An Essay Upon the Trade of Ireland,* in two parts (Dublin, 1729–31), Part I, quotation, p. 1; also see p. 74.

30. *Ibid.,* Part 2, pp. 98, 124.

31. *Ibid.,* Part 2, pp. 92–93, on toleration and redress of tithe to both papist and Protestant, if well affected.

32. Mr. Desmond Clarke kindly lent me a typed copy of the Scheme, of which a précis is given here.

33. J. Swift, *The Drapier's Letters to the People of Ireland,* ed. H. Davis (Oxford, 1935), pp. 79, 108, and *passim.*

34. Henry Yorke (1772–1813), *Thoughts on Civil Government* (London, 1794), quotations from Swift's *Gulliver,* pp. 25–26, 66–67. T. Spence, *Pig's Meat, or, Lessons for the Swinish Multitude* (London, n.d.), II, 44–46, 159–161.

35. Charles Lucas (1713–1771). See *DNB,* and *The Political Constitution of Great Britain and Ireland Asserted and Vindicated* (London, 1751), I, 114, 120, and *passim.* See W. E. H. Lecky, *A History of Ireland in the Eighteenth Century* (London, 1913), I, 211, 461; II, 205–206. McIlwain, p. 36.

36. *Northern Revolutions* (Dublin, 1757), *passim;* Trenchard and Molesworth, pp. iv, v, 100.

37. *Some Considerations for the Promoting of Agriculture and Employing the Poor* (Dublin, 1723), p. 29 and *passim;* and note acid account of it by Nicholson (19 October, 1723), Gilbert MSS. 327, no. 160 (Pearse St. Library, Dublin), and Wake MSS. Oxford XXXLVII, fol. 104. An immediate answer to Molesworth's suggestions appeared on 3 November, 1723, *Considerations Upon Considerations,* printed by George Ewing of Dublin, and generally speaking opposing his suggestions. Almost immediately, however, Swift dedicated the fifth of his Drapier's Letters to the Viscount with commendatory remarks in it, and, therefore, most references are favourable, e.g., *Further Considerations for the Tillage in Ireland* (Dublin, 1728), speaks of that true patriot, Lord Molesworth; see also *A Treatise on Tillage* (Dublin, 1737); and *Some Thoughts on the Tillage of Ireland* (1738).

38. S. Madden, *Reflections and Resolutions,* preface, pp. vii–xxi; on education, pp. 52–61; quotation, p. 56.

39. *Ibid.,* Resolutions XVII–XXI, XXIX, XXX, XXXI.

40. *Ibid.,* pp. 82–83.

41. *Ibid.,* on union, Resolution, XVI; amphibious, pp. 95–96; on Trenchard, p. 99; and see J. G. Simms, *The Williamite Confiscation in Ireland, 1690–1703* (London, 1956), chaps. x–xi, *passim.*

42. See above, n. 28.

43. Berkeley, *Works,* VI, 17–46, and see editor's introduction, 3–11.

44. *Discourse to Magistrates* (1738), in *Works,* VI, 201–222; "asserter," 211.

45. *Essay Towards Preventing the Ruin of Great Britain* (1721), in *Works,* VI, 69–85.

46. *Works,* VI, 96.

47. *The Querist,* in *Works,* VI, no. 167.

48. There are useful remarks on Berkeley's economic theories by Joseph Johnson in *Hermathena* (Dublin, 1939; 1940; 1942). On Catholic industry, *A Word to the Wise* (1749), in *Works,* VI, 247. Molesworth had suggested that too many holy days explained poor production.

49. On Irish banks, see F. G. Hall, *The Bank of Ireland, 1763–1946* (Dublin, 1949), pp. 14–29; for the abortive project of 1719, p. 21. See Berkeley, *Works,* VI, for *A Letter on the Project of a National Bank* (1737), pp. 185–187. Many tracts by Maxwell and Hercules Rowley, his uncle. King to Molesworth (17 November, 1721), a long letter about the debates, in King MSS.

50. *The Querist,* in *Works,* VI: incentive, no. 567; wants, nos. 20, 62, 63, 112, 123, 577; criminals, nos. 53, 54; an equal distribution, no. 214.

51. *Ibid.,* wants, no. 168; mart of literature, no. 186.

52. J. Ramsay of Ochertyre, *Scotland and Scotsmen,* 2 vols. (Edinburgh, 1888), I, 238.

53. T. Spence, *Pigs' Meat,* II, 72–74, extracts from *The Querist* for legislators to ponder; see n. 34 above.

54. On Rundle, see memoir prefaced to *Letters . . . to Mrs. Barbara Sandys* (Gloucester, 1789).

55. See art., R. Clayton, *DNB;* also Leslie Stephen, *English Thought in the Eighteenth Century,* 2 vols. (New York, 1949), I, chap. viii, 53, 421–422. His speech was reprinted in Baron's 3rd ed. of Thomas Gordon, *A Cordial for Low Spirits* (London, 1763), III, no. 8.

56. See art., Edward Synge, *DNB.* For his connection with Molesworth, Berkeley, and Hutcheson, see W. R. Scott, *Francis Hutcheson, His Life, Teaching and Position in the History of Philosophy* (Cambridge, 1900), *passim.*

57. *The Case of Toleration* (London, 1726), preached 23 October, 1725. For suggestion about Catholics, see Dobbs, *Essay on Trade,* II, 91–93, and n. 48 above.

58. *An Axe Laid to the Root* (Dublin, 1749), pp. 7, 13–14, and *passim.*

59. Henry Brooke, *The Fool of Quality* (London, 1906), with a biographical

preface by Charles Kingsley, and a new life by E. A. Baker. Chap. xvi contains, besides a typical story of Harry and a poor woman, a long conversation on the subject of the constitution, pp. 257–284, most interesting, perhaps on intestine commotions; party, a kind of yeast, p. 265.

60. J. S. Reid, *History of the Presbyterian Church in Ireland,* 3 vols., 2d ed. (London, 1853), III, 409. Law died in 1810.

61. Nicholas, Lord Taaffe, *Observations on Affairs in Ireland . . . ,* 3rd ed. (Dublin, 1767), p. 28.

62. H.M.C., *Var. Coll.,* VIII, letters to Molesworth from Arbuckle, Wishart, Turnbull. Scott, *Hutcheson, passim.*

63. P.R.O., N.I., D.O.D. 531, Arbuckle to Drennen (n.d.). On Turnbull, see James McCosh, *The Scottish Philosophy* (New York, 1874), pp. 95–106. Also Birch Correspondence, B.M. Add. MSS. 4319, 321. H.M.C., Var. Coll., VIII, letter to Molesworth.

64. P.R.O., N.I., T1072, 1–2, p. 130, Bruce to Drennen (13 January, 1738).

65. Transcript of wills, P.R.O., N.I., T403, pp. 1, 15, 39, 49, 50, 76.

66. William Drennen, *Fugitive Pieces* (London, 1815), character of Alexander Haliday, pp. 155–159; on father, pp. 192–193; also poem, p. 121. See n. 77, below.

67. See below, Chap. VI, for Hutcheson.

68. See above, n. 66, and Reid, III, 134–135, and n. 32; 173, 185–186.

69. For Abernethy, life by James Duchal prefaced to *Sermons* 2 vols. (London, 1748–1751), I; F. J. Bigger, *The Two Abernethyes* (Belfast, 1919). *Scarce and Valuable Tracts and Sermons,* reprinted by R. Baron (London, 1751).

70. H.M.C., *Var. Coll.,* VIII, 351, 354; and Scott, *Hutcheson, passim.*

71. W. R. Scott, in *Mind,* new ser., 8:194–215 (London, 1899), but Scott is probably mistaken in the date of Arbuckle's death. Transcript of will in P.R.O., N.I., T403, probate granted 1747. Molesworth left Arbuckle ten pounds in his will, 1725 (dated 30 April, 1725; proved November, 1726), P.C.C., Somerset House.

72. Debt to Lord Molesworth and his work, *Hibernicus's Letters,* I, iii–vii, 187; II, 385.

73. Hutcheson contributed six numbers to the collection: nos. 11, 12, 13, 45, 46, 47. General philosophy of the Letters stated best in nos. 1, 2, 73, 83; Ireland discussed, I, 297, 301. Among authors cited, see Montaigne, II, 16–17; Temple, II, 301; Locke II, 237; Milton, I, 149; Machiavelli, I, 237. The London edition of 1734 has an index to each volume.

74. Arbuckle to Drennen, P.R.O., N.I., D531 (18 April, 1737), for reference to Swift; and see also Bruce's will, above n. 71.

75. For Bruce, see Reid, III, n. 12 on p. 323; and n. 36 on p. 270. Alexander Gordon, *Sketches* (Belfast, 1902). *An Essay on the Character of the Late Mr. William Bruce,* dedicated to Alexander Stewart and published by J. Smith, the dedication by J. Duchal, the essay probably by Gabriel Cornwall of Antrim (Dublin, 1755). See, too, *Mo.R.,* 13:253–267 (London, 1755). F. J. Bigger, *William Bruce* (London,

1843). *Mo.R.*, 14:351–356 (1756), "Monody." Bruce letters, P.R.O., N.I. T1072, *passim*.

76. J. Duchal, life by James Wodrow, prefaced to 2nd ed. of *Sermons,* 3 vols. (London, 1765), II; and Duchal-Drennen letters, Belfast Presbyterian Historical Society MSS. Reid, III, n. 14, pp. 257–258.

77. T. Drennen, see tribute above, n. 66; and D. A. Chart, *The Drennen Letters* (Belfast, 1931); James Mackay (d.1781), funeral sermon on the death of Thom (28 February, 1768). Hutcheson's letters to Thom are printed in Scott, *Hutcheson.*

78. R. Jacob, *Rise of the United Irishmen* (London, 1937), p. 225, and *passim,* on dissenters and Irish Catholics. Also R. R. Madden, *United Irishmen* (London, 1842–1860).

CHAPTER VI. The Interest of Scotland

1. Dugald Stewart, "Progress of Metaphysical, Ethical and Political Philosophy," in *Works* (Cambridge, 1829), VI, 57–58.

2. George Buchanan, *The Powers of the Crown in Scotland,* tr. C. F. Arrowood (Austin, Texas, 1949), pp. 131–132.

3. A. Fletcher, *Political Works* (ed. used, London, 1737; others, London, 1732; Glasgow, 1749; and London, 1797, with preface by R. Watson). Notes by Buchan in *Essays on Lives and Writings of Fletcher of Saltoun and the Poet Thomson* (London, 1792), *passim*.

4. *A Discourse of Government with Relation to Militia's* (Edinburgh, 1698), in *Pol. Works,* pp. 6–10.

5. *Ibid.,* p. 10.

6. *Ibid.,* pp. 11–13.

7. *Ibid.,* pp. 13–20; quotation, p. 15.

8. *Pol. Works,* pp. 281–288.

9. Preface to *Franco-Gallia* (1721), xx.

10. Fletcher, *Pol. Works,* Wales and Ireland, pp. 402–410. See H. Maxwell, *Essay Towards An Union* (London, 1703). Fletcher, pp. 399, 398 (last quotation).

11. *Pol. Works,* "Second Discourse on Affairs of Scotland," pp. 121–175; ref. to Edinburgh, p. 172.

12. Robert Wodrow, *Correspondence,* ed. T. M'Crie (Edinburgh, 1842–43), III, 482–483; and *Analecta,* 4 vols. (Edinburgh, 1842–43), IV, 186–187 (3 November, 1730). Scott, *Hutcheson, passim,* for biographical details.

13. Scott, *Hutcheson,* pp. 113–114; and see Frederick Tolles, *Meeting House and Counting House* (North Carolina, 1948), 177; and in *PMHB,* 65, no. 3:316–317 (July 1941). See C. Robbins, "When it is that Colonies May turn Independent," *WMQ,* 3rd ser., 11, no. 2:214–251 (April 1954). For full bibliography of works, Scott, *Hutcheson,* pp. 143–145, to which should be added two Glasgow reprints, 1770 and 1774, of *Considerations on Patronage* (Glasgow, 1735); a brief preface by Hutcheson to Foulis's ed. (Glasgow, 1743) of Henry More (1614–1687) *Divine*

Dialogues; A System (see n. 16) was translated by Lessing (Leipzig, 1756); The popular latin text, *Philosophiae Moralis Institutio Compendiaria* (Glasgow, 1742; 2nd ed., altered and amended, Glasgow, 1745) translated Glasgow, 1747; 2nd ed., Glasgow, 1753 (used here) as *A Short Introduction to Moral Philosophy in Three Books, Containing the Elements of Ethics and the Law of Nature;* hereafter referred to as *Compend;* 5th ed., Philadelphia, 1788.

14. J. Disney, *Memoirs of Thomas Brand Hollis* (London, 1808), p. 27; and A. Mc-Claren Young, "A Portrait by Allen Ramsay," *SAR,* 3, no. 4:11–13 (1951).

15. Scott, *Hutcheson,* chap. iv, *passim;* Hutcheson on Foulis, p. 81.

16. Francis Hutcheson, *A System of Moral Philosophy, in Three Books,* 2 vols. (London, 1755), I, 300ff.; hereafter referred to as *System.* Also W. Sypher, "Hutcheson and the Classical Theory of Slavery," *JNH,* 24, no. 3:263–280 (July 1939). *Compend,* pp. iv–viii. *System,* II, Book III, chaps. vii–viii.

17. *System,* II, Book III, chaps. i–iii, 149–212.

18. *An Inquiry Concerning Moral Good and Evil* (London, 1738), pp. 204–205; *System,* II, Book III, 222.

19. *System,* II, Book III, 279, 308–309; and see all Book III, *passim.*

20. *System,* II, Book III, chap. vii. *Massachusetts Spy,* no. 50 (Thursday, 13 February, 1772).

21. *System,* II, 276, 308–309.

22. *Ibid.,* chap. vi, 240–266; n. on Harrington, 264–266.

23. Scott, *Hutcheson,* pp. 230–243 on Hutcheson and Smith. See *Compend,* 2d ed. (Glasgow, 1753), chap. xii, pp. 199–203. "On Value," *System,* I, 318, and chaps. vii and viii.

24. *System,* II, Book III, chap. vi, 248. Robert Wallace, *Ignorance and Superstition* (Edinburgh, 1746), pp. 23–24, *passim; Various Prospects of Mankind, Nature and Providence* (London, 1761), pp. 49ff., and Prospect III, *passim.*

25. *Compend,* p. 288; *System,* II, Book III, 260–266.

26. *System,* II, Book III, 260. *Liberty and Right* (1747), *passim.* For Baron, see below, Chap. VII.

27. *System,* II, 316–317. *Compend,* pp. 304–306. And see Wodrow, *Analecta,* IV, on Hutcheson's religion, 99, 190–191.

28. *System,* II, 322–324; all chap. ix, *passim.* And see James Burgh, *Political Disquisitions,* 3 vols. (London, 1774), II, Book III, 341–389.

29. Algernon Sidney, *Discourses Concerning Government,* 2d ed. (London, 1704), p. 337. R. Molesworth, *An Account,* chap. xv. *System,* II, Book III, chap. ix. See Scott, *Hutcheson,* pp. 273–274 on Beccaria.

30. *System,* II, Book III, chaps. viii and x. See also *Compend,* Book IV, pp. 302, 303.

31. Hutcheson, *An Inquiry,* reminiscent of Cicero, p. 165.

32. Adam Smith, *An Inquiry into the Nature and Causes of the Wealth of Nations,* ed., E. Cannan (New York, 1937), pp. 78–79.

33. *Ibid.,* p. 98.

34. *Ibid.*, p. 141.

35. *Ibid.*, all Art. 2, pp. 716ff., "Education of Youth." See also *Lectures on Justice, Police, Revenue and Arms, Influence of Commerce on Manners*, in *Moral and Political Philosophy of Adam Smith*, Hafner ed. (New York, 1948), pp. 319–321.

36. Smith, *Wealth of Nations*, pp. 81, 83, 134–143, etc.

37. *Ibid.*, Book IV, chap. vii.

38. Adam Ferguson (1723–1816). J. Snell, "The Political Thought of Adam Ferguson," in University Studies, no. 21 (Wichita, Kansas, May 1950). R. L. Meek, "The Scottish Contribution to Marxist Sociology," in *Democracy and the Labour Movement; Essays in Honour of Dana Torr* (London, 1954). On Ferguson, see Alexander Carlyle, *Autobiography* (Edinburgh, 1910), *passim;* J. Small, *Memoir* (London, 1864); *DNB;* Lois Whitney, *Primitivism and the Idea of Progress* (Baltimore, 1934), pp. 145–154; W. C. Lehmann, *Adam Ferguson and the Beginnings of Modern Sociology* (New York, 1930). H. Cockburn, *Memorials of His Time* (Edinburgh, 1910), I, 40–44.

39. From Ferguson, *Remarks Upon a Pamphlet . . . by Dr. Price . . .* (London, 1776), pp. 29–31, and *passim.* D. Fagerstrom, "Scottish Opinion and the American Revolution," *WMQ*, 3d ser., 11, no. 2:252–275 (April 1954). See D. Hume, always anti-imperial, in, e.g., "That Politics May be Reduced to a Science," *passim;* see n. 75 below.

40. This paragraph is from *Institutes of Moral Philosophy* (Edinburgh, 1769), Part VII, pp. 262–319. *Civil Society*, II, Sec. 3, and p. 61. Also *Roman Republic,* 3 vols. (Edinburgh, 1783), III, 367; II, 238–239; and on party in Monarchy, *Institutes*, p. 313. *Principles of Moral and Political Science*, 2 vols. (Edinburgh, 1792), I, 111; II, chap. vi, Sec. 4.

41. *Essay on the History of Civil Society* (Edinburgh, 1767), pp. 236–256, 282–287. *Roman Republic*, I, 3, 11, 67, 146; II, chaps. ii, iii, iv; and III, 552.

42. *Roman Republic*, I, Book II, chap. ii, 274–307; *Civil Society*, Part V, Sec. 1, quotation pp. 363–364; *Roman Republic*, I, 283 and Book II, chap. ii as before.

43. *Civil Society*, p. 430; *Roman Republic*, III, 574.

44. John Ramsay of *Scotland and Scotsmen*, I, 8n, 8–10. A. F. Tytler, Lord Woodhouselee, *Life of Henry Home of Kames*, 3 vols. (Edinburgh, 1814), III, 75–77, appendix 8; and see Wodrow, *Analecta*, and *Correspondence, passim*, for Wishart.

45. Wodrow, *Analecta*, III, 167–168, 239; IV, 125, 129. Ramsay, *Scotland*, I, 7.

46. On Wallace (1696/7–1771), see Ramsay, *Scotland*, I, 238–247; *SM*, 33: 340–344 (1771), and 591–594 (1809). *MR*, 2:517–520 (1807). See also E. Mossner, *The Forgotten Hume* (New York, 1943), pp. 105–131; Mossner and Klibansky, *New Letters* (Oxford, 1954), nos. 11–19.

47. Wallace's works included: sermon on behalf of charity schools, *Ignorance and Superstition* (1746), which with *Doctrine of Passive Obedience and Non-resistance Considered*, Edinburgh (1746), and *The Regard Due to Divine Revelation . . . a Sermon . . . with a Preface Containing . . . Remarks on a Book* (by M. Tindal) *Entitled "Christianity as Old as the Creation"* (London, 1731; 2nd ed., London, 1733), he

gave to Harvard; *A Dissertation on the Numbers of Mankind* (1753); *Characteristics of the Present Political State of Great Britain* (1758); *Various Prospects of Mankind, Nature and Providence* (1761); *A View of the Internal Policy* (1764). According to Ramsay of Ochtertyre (I, 244), he attempted to write about dancing after he had passed his seventieth year. There may be other writings in manuscript collections. *The Reveur* (Edinburgh, 18 November, 1737—26 May, 1738) may be his.

48. The sermon is at Harvard, presented by Wallace (Tract 43); on knowledge, pp. 7–8; on Mandeville, pp. 17–18, 20; utopia, pp. 20, 21; we undervalue labour, pp. 24–28. *Various Prospects*, p. 36, for More, Harrington.

49. *Various Prospects*, III.

50. *Ibid., passim.*

51. *Ibid.*, p. 4.

52. *Ibid.*, p. 26.

53. *Ibid.*, pp. 41–52; quotations, pp. 37 and 46.

54. *Ibid.*, pp. 75–76, 104–105. W. Godwin, *Political Justice, A Reprint of the Essay on Property*, ed. H. S. Salt (London, 1949), pp. 54*n*, 114–116.

55. *Various Prospects*, pp. 94–95.

56. *Ibid.*, p. 98.

57. *Ibid.*, p. 102.

58. *Ibid.*, pp. 102, 103.

59. *Ibid.*, pp. 111–125.

60. *Various Prospects*, Prospect V, quotation, p. 130.

61. *Ibid.*, p. 380.

62. *Ibid.*, p. 397.

63. *Ibid.*, p. 406.

64. Woodhouselee, *Kames*, I, 399–400; Ramsay, *Scotland*, I, on Aberdeen, 287–298, 477–502. Herbert L. Gantert, brief note on William Small, *WMQ*, 3d ser., 4, no. 4:505–511 (October 1947).

65. Ramsay, *Scotland*, I, 291–293. Lois Whitney, "Thomas Blackwell, a Disciple of Shaftesbury," in *PQ*, 5:196–211 (1926). Woodhouselee, III, appendix vii.

66. Ramsay, *Scotland*, I, 293–294. See *MR*, 7:345–348 (London, 1812), for letter by James Fordyce on the death of his brother. *Dialogues on Education* (London, 1745-1748), mentioned by Franklin in his plan for College of Philadelphia, thought wrongly attributed to Hutcheson.

67. See *Dialogues*, II, 21ff.; education for government, 221; "Studious Drudge," II, 79; education for life, Dialogue XVII; history, 297–299; training as citizens, XIII, 49–51.

68. *Ibid.*, Harrington and others, I, 33.

69. See *DNB* for life of Ogilvie (1736–1819); *An Essay on the Right of Property in Land* (1st ed., 1781; repr. 1838, 1891; and 1920 by M. Beer).

70. *Essay* (1781), *passim*, and land, pp. 11–18, 73–107, 185–232; Franklin, pp. 33, 192; Prussia, p. 65; distress of Ireland, p. 228.

71. On Millar, see Carlyle, *Autobiography*, for many references; H. Cockburn,

Memorials, I, 41; J. Mackenzie, *Memoirs,* 2d ed. (London, 1836), II, 41–42. For his effect on Marxist thought, see W. C. Lehmann, "John Millar, Historical Sociologist," in *BJS,* 3, no. 1:80 (March 1952); and R. L. Meek, as in n. 38 above, pp. 84–102. John Craig, his son-in-law, wrote a memoir, prefaced to later editions of *The Origin of the Distinction of Ranks* (Edinburgh, 1806), hereafter called *Origin,* of which six British editions, one Dutch (1778), and French (1778) and German (1772) translations appeared.

72. *Ibid.,* cv–cvi.

73. Carlyle, *Autobiography,* pp. 516–517. Millar, *An Historical View of the English Government* (1787, six British editions; ed. used here London, 1812), *passim;* III, 276f.; chaps. iv–vii. *Origin,* chap. v, Sec. 3.

74. See Craig memoir, *Origin,* xcix–cxxxiv, on his politics, *passim.*

75. David Hume, *Essays Moral and Political,* 3d ed. (London, 1748), "Politics a Science," p. 34; passive obedience, p. 312. "Treatise of Human Nature," in Hume's *Moral and Political Philosophy* (New York, 1948), p. 112.

76. See references quoted in Fagerstrom, "Scottish Opinion," as in n. 39 above. J. Boswell, *On the Grand Tour, 1765–1766,* ed. F. Brady and F. Pottle (New York, 1955), p. 165*n.*

77. J. D. Mackie, "The Professors and Their Critics," *RPSGP,* 72, Part 4 (1948), pp. 46–52; D. Murray *Memories of the Old College of Glasgow* (Glasgow, 1927), 144; and see index for many Hutcheson notes. W. Thom, *Works* (Glasgow, 1799), "Trial of a Student," pp. 374–428; "Academy for Business," pp. 302ff.; Sermon III, "The Revolt of the Ten Tribes" (1776), pp. 77–86; Sermon IV (1778), pp. 114–120; Sermon V (1779), pp. 147–148; Sermon VI (1770), pp. 157–229; on landlords, p. 166; emigration, p. 197; Indians, p. 206.

78. David Buchan, eleventh earl of Buchan, see art. *DNB* under David Stewart Erskine. Also J. Clive, "The Earl of Buchan's Kick," *HLB,* 5, no. 3: *passim* (Autumn, 1951). Buchan's most radical ideas were reflected in his introduction to *Essays on Fletcher and Thomson,* above n. 3. J. Nichols, *Literary Illustrations* (London, 1831), VI, 489–521; two letters from George Washington (1792 and 1793), pp. 520–521.

CHAPTER VII. The Contribution of Nonconformity

1. Samuel Johnson, *Lives of the Poets,* Chandos Classics (London, n.d.), p. 449.

2. Isaac Watts, *Orthodoxy and Charity United in Several Reconciling Essays,* 2d ed. (Boston, 1749), n. on p. 118, and chap. vii.

3. A. Barbauld, "On the Devotional Taste and on Sects and Establishments" (1775) in *Works,* 3 vols. (Boston, 1826), II, 146–166.

4. W. Wilson, *Dissenting Churches of London,* 4 vols. (London, 1814), IV, 343; II, 26; I, 82. *Egmont Diary,* II, 256.

5. M. A. Thomson, *A Constitutional History of England, 1642–1801* (London, 1938), Part IV, chap. x; an excellent summary of the legal position of dissent.

For Doddridge, see I. Parker, *Dissenting Academies* (Cambridge, 1914), pp. 80–81. Licenses were not required after 1779.

6. Sir John Holland, 7 June, 1661. Caroline Robbins, "Five Speeches, 1661–3, by Sir John Holland, M.P.," in *BIHR*, 28:193–196 (1955).

7. *Egmont Diary*, I, 301, 304; II, 254, 515–516.

8. *Ibid.*, on his tract, I, 302, 304.

9. Anthony Ellys, "A Plea for the Sacramental Test" (1738), in *Tracts on Liberty*, 2 vols. in one (London, 1763), I, 116–182.

10. William Hay (1695–1755), "Essay on Civil Government" (1728), in *Works*, 2 vols. (London, 1794), I, 85–88.

11. A. Barbauld, "Address to the Opposers of Test and Corporation Acts" (1790), in *Works*, II, 241–257.

12. Michaijah Towgood (1700–1792), *Dissent from the Church of England Fully Justified* (London, 1753; Boston, 1768), *passim.*

13. J. Priestley, *A Letter to the Right Honourable William Pitt*, 2d ed. (London, 1787), pp. 16–17.

14. *MR*, 13:114–122 (London, 1818), Bowring on dissent and civil rights, *passim;* also 12:163–166 (1817); 1:331 (1806); and 14:92–100 and 426–430 (1819), on Baptists. David Bogue and J. Bennett, *History of the Dissenters* (London, 1808–1812), I, preface, xxxvii–xliv; also chap. iii; also Vol. II, 119–154; and Vol. IV, 507–512. See also *Protestant Dissenters' Magazine*, 6 vols. (1794–1799), 2:238–241 (London, 1795). See also J. Toulmin, *An Historical View* (London, 1814); and the Sedden MSS. at Manchester College, Oxford.

15. *The Protestant Session*, by a Member of the Constitutional Club at Oxford, dedicated to Lord Stanhope (London, 1719).

16. *MR*, 5:627–632 (1810); Bogue and Bennett, I, 255, and III, 121–122.

17. Classic tract is Strickland Gough, *An Enquiry into the Causes of the Decay of the Dissenting Interest* (London, 1730). Bogue and Bennett, III, chap. vi, II, chap. vi; IV, chap. ix, 35–42; and for the general decline of religion, IV, chap. vi, 146–148, 311–396. *MR*, 4:323ff., and 485ff. (1809); and *PDM*, 4:99–100, 151–156 (London, 1797).

18. On statistics, see D. Coomer, *English Dissent* (London, 1946), pp. 60–62. É. Halévy, *England in 1815* (Tr. London, 1929), pp. 352–359 and 374. Bogue and Bennett, II, chap. vi, Secs. 1 and 3; *MR*, 4:323–326 (1809); *MR*, 8:341–347 (1823).

19. B. L. Manning, *Protestant Dissenting Deputies* (London, 1952). See also Joshua Toulmin, *An Historical View*, pp. 98–105; and Bogue and Bennett, II, 140–147.

20. R. Griffiths (1720–1803). See J. Nichols, *Literary Anecdotes of the Eighteenth Century*, 9 vols. (London, 1812–1815), III, 506–508, editors of the *Monthly Review*. The *Monthly Review* (1749–1803) supported the Jew Bill and favourably considered works of a distinctly "New Light" group: Abernethy, Duchal, Hutcheson, Foster, Jones. Griffiths was a friend of A. Millar and William Rose of Chiswick

(d.1787), a dissenting minister and schoolmaster from Aberdeen and compiler of textbooks.

21. Dr. Benjamin Avery (d.1764). See *DNB*. A Presbyterian, nonsubscriber at Salters Hall, who then left the ministry for medicine. He was at Edinburgh with Akenside. His daughter married Sam Wilton of the Weigh House, a zealous pro-American in the next reign. See Wilson, I, 193. Avery gave many tracts to Harvard (e.g., Tract 61), and left his library to Warrington. He is best known for his connection with the *Occasional Papers* (1716–1719) in association with S. Browne, J. Earle, N. Lardner, M. Lowman, Sam Wright, John Evans, and Ben Grosvenor in "Bagweell Papers" (from initials); and with *The Old Whig* (1735–1739) in association with George Benson, B. Grosvenor, M. Towgood, Caleb Fleming, James Foster, Sam Chandler (sometimes credited with the chief part in it) and J. Jackson. See J. Nichols, *Literary Anecdotes*, II (1812), 528*n*, for Jackson. Wilson, III, 381ff.; and *MR*, 8:443 (1813).

22. For Daniel Defoe, see Bogue and Bennett, IV, "steadfast to dissenters," 12–13. John Dunton (1659–1733), *Life and Errors* (1705; repr. by J. Nichols, London, 1818, with life). See also Nichols, *Lit. Anec.*, V, 59–83. The essay on pamphlets in *ibid.*, IV, 98–111, owed much to Dunton's collections.

23. Wilson, II, 268–269. See *DNB* for Barrington who was connected with the Abneys with whom Watts lived so long.

24. Coomer, pp. 63–79. List of voters in *MR*, 14:17, 106–107 (1819). See Stanley Pargellis and D. J. Medley, *Bibliography of British History; the Eighteenth Century, 1714–1789* (Oxford, 1951), p. 103, for good selection of tracts on Salters Hall controversy.

25. Wilson, III, 504–535; Nichols, *Lit. Anec.*, VI, 444–450 on Barrington; Bogue and Bennett, III, 245–249; chap. iv, pp. 213–263 and 489–495.

26. F. Blackburne, *Hollis Memoirs* (London, 1780), II, 582–583.

27. Best on academies, J. W. Ashley Smith, *Birth of Modern Education*. For Rowe, see Smith, chap. iii, par. 4, no. 1. Also I. Parker; H. McLachlan, *English Education Under the Test Acts* (London, 1931), valuable. Toulmin, *Hist. View*, pp. 559–592, lists of early students.

28. M. Noble, *Memoirs . . . of the Protectorate House of Cromwell* (Birmingham, 1784), II, 305–333; the story appears on 330–331. For Samuel Say, see Wilson, IV, 91–96; *PDM*, 1:297–302, 345–349 (London, 1794); Wilson, III, 91–102; *MR*, 4: Say Papers, *passim* (London, 1809).

29. Bogue and Bennett, III, 460–464; Wilson, III, 91–102.

30. Wilson, I, 113–125. Letters in Unitarian College, Manchester, no. 71 B.1.16. Wilson lists correspondents, but most cursory search of MSS. will add such persons as Fordyce, Hutcheson, and Nicholas Munckley (ca. 1759), doctor in London and friend of Hollis and others. Edward Pickard, "A Protestant Dissenter upon Formal Principles," in *Funeral Sermons* (1762).

31. D. Neal, *History of the Puritans* (New York, 1844), II, 101–105; quotation, 105.

32. For Isaac Kimber and William Harris, see *DNB* and W. C. Abbott, *Bibliography of Oliver Cromwell* (Cambridge, Mass., 1929). For Harris, also see *Hollis Memoirs*, I, 73, 273, 326, 333, 432, 445. Also *Diary of Sylas Neville, 1767–1788,* ed. B. Cozens-Hardy (London, 1950), p. 13; W. Harris, *An Historical and Critical Account of the Life of Oliver Cromwell* (London, 1762), incorporated documents, references to tracts and throughout shows much more research than Hume's works for the same period. Edmund Calamy (1671–1732), see Wilson, IV, 69–89; *DNB;* recent ed., *Calamy Revised,* by Arnold G. Mathews (Oxford, 1934); and *Historical Account of My Own Life,* 2 vols., ed. J. T. Rutt (1829). For Withers's historical works see *MR,* 4:250–275 (1809).

33. J. Manning, *Memoir of Towgood* (London, 1792), *passim,* for life. See *Dissent from Church of England Fully Justified* (1753): "On Freedom," p. 56; "On Danish Uniformity," p. 91; "On the Sacramental Test," p. 149; "On Right of People to Choose Their Own Pastors," p. 214; and *passim.*

34. For Sam Chandler (1693–1766), see Wilson, II, 360–384; Bogue and Bennett, IV, 404–409; *DNB.* Often credited with editorship of *The Old Whig;* certainly wrote for it, another Presbyterian who became virtually Victorian in later life. Avery, see above, n. 21. *MR,* 4:200–201 (1809); *MR,* 5:240 (1810).

35. *The Old Whig, or the Consistent Protestant,* 2 vols. (1739), began to appear in 1735; often referred to in *London Magazine* which reprinted last *Old Whig,* no. 103. Preface put creed well, pp. iii–viii; also no. 2 for "Whigs." For Rundle, see no. 1, p. 8; no. 4, p. 26; no. 28, p. 252; on toleration, nos. 12, 13, 28, 31, 32; for free thought and press, nos. 6, 8 and 77; natural rights, no. 9, pp. 78–79, and no. 18, p. 156; no. 55; Hay's Poor Law, no. 72; attack on Oxford University, no. 45; Quakers, no. 52; common man, no. 73; Milton, Sidney, Harrington, no. 102; office, nos. 8 and 13, p. 114; Hampden, no. 102, p. 429; law reform, no. 55; frugality and liberty, no. 22.

36. Bogue and Bennett, III, 484–486. Lowman also wrote: *A Defence of Christianity, Against the Freethinker Collins* (1733); a *Dissertation on the Civil Government of the Hebrews* (1740, and again in 1745). Dissertation, p. 9; Harrington, pp. 33, 35; militia, pp. 4of.; debts, p. 46; legislature, p. 127; Rota, pp. 58–59; agrarian, pp. 46–47; supreme court, pp. 67ff., and *passim.*

37. Wilson, II, 270–283; Johnson's praise, I, 315. Also see *DNB; MR,* 2:1–6, 57–65 (1807); *MR,* 13:167–168 (1818). Bogue and Bennett, III, 486–489. On Exeter, see Smith, *Mod. Educ.,* chap. iii, no. 5.

38. James Foster, *Discourses* (London, 1749–1752), II, 295–306.

39. Foster, *Sermons* (London, 1736); see particularly nos. 6, 12, 14, but also *passim.* See also introduction to *Discourses,* I; II, chaps. iv and v, 92–150.

40. T. Clarkson, *History of the Abolition of the Slave Trade* (Wilmington, 1816), p. 34; *Discourses,* II, chap. vii, 155; see also I, 124–125 and II, chap. viii, 172.

41. *Discourses,* II, chap. viii.

42. A. P. Davis, *Isaac Watts; His Life and Works* (London, 1948), best modern work.

43. J. Belknap, *Memoirs of Isaac Watts* (London, 1793), p. 17, quotes letter to Colman. T. Gibbons, *Memoirs of Isaac Watts* (London, 1780), ref. to prints, pp. 164, 305.

44. Isaac Watts, *Works,* 6 vols., eds. D. Jenning and P. Doddridge (London, 1753), II, 595.

45. Davis, *Watts,* p. 123. The letter is in Dr. Williams's Library, Lardner-Wiche Letters. See "Government, by an Independent" (1749); Charles died for his folly, p. 8.

46. "A New Essay on Civil Power," in *Works,* VI, 135–177.

47. Smith, *Mod. Educ.,* chap. iv, par. 1. Watts, *Works,* V. pp. 195–202, 301.

48. Watts, *Works,* V, "Improvement," p. 285.

49. *Ibid.,* pp. 191–192; chap. iv on books and reading; quotation, p. 263; chap. vi.

50. Watts, *Works,* II, 723–749 on charity schools.

51. Smith, *Mod. Educ.,* chap. iv, sec. 4, no. 5, on Bristol Academy. Wilson, II, 385–393; IV, on Amory, 311–312. Munckley was at Leyden with Wilkes; Carlyle, *Autobiography,* p. 174; *Hollis Memoirs,* pp. 353–354.

52. Henry Grove (1683/4–1738). Bogue and Bennett, III, 274–277; *MR,* 13: 89–90 (1818); life by T. Amory in *Works,* 2d ed. (London, 1741). For Taunton Academy, see Smith, *Mod. Educ.,* chap. iii, no. 5.

53. *Spectator* (1714, last year), nos. 588, 601, 626, 635.

54. Grove, *Works, Discourses, Tracts and Poems* (London, 1747), IV, 233–251.

55. *Ibid.,* Letter I, pp. 335–346; and see *Cato's Letters,* III, no. 81, 127.

56. *Tracts,* 4 vols. (London, 1740; 2d ed., London, 1741), IV, 218–223 (written in 1719).

57. Grove, *Moral Philosophy,* 2d ed., dedicated to Willoughby of Parham (1749); against slavery, II, chap. xvi, 511; on government, II, chap. xvii, 515–534; Denmark, 528. For "The Origin and Extent of Civil Power," see letters II and III in Grove, *Works,* IV, 337–369.

58. For Doddridge, see Smith, *Mod. Educ.,* chap. iv, par. 1; Job Orton, *Memoirs of Philip Doddridge* (Salop, 1766); *Doddridge,* ed. G. F. Nuttall (London, 1951); *Correspondence and Diary,* 5 vols., ed. J. E. Humphrey (London, 1829–1831), *passim.*

59. *Corres. and Diary,* III, 208, 215; ref. to riots of '37, 220–221; to elections, 125 (25 November, 1733).

60. Smith, *Mod. Educ. Also Lectures on Pneumatology and Ethics* (1763), ed. by Samuel Clark of Birmingham (1727–1769). See *MR,* 13:37 (1818), for note on editors. The third ed. was by Kippis, with help. See especially Part III, pp. 109–195. For list of pupils, see *MR,* 10:686 (1815).

61. *MR,* 19:170–174 (1824). *Orton, Memoirs, passim.*

62. See Nuttall, chap. ii.

63. Davis, on Coward and Hopkins, pp. 52–54. *GM,* 2:725 (1732). See also *DNB.* For Warrington students, see *MR,* 9:201–594 and *passim* (1814).

64. *Hollis Memoirs,* I, 14, 111–114, 200. Carlyle, *Autobiography,* p. 534. For

Thomson, see Alan Dugald McKillop, "Ethics and History in Thomson's Library," in *Pope and His Contemporaries, Essays Presented to George Sherburn,* eds. James L. Clifford and Louis A. Landa (Oxford, 1949), pp. 215–229. Thomson's use of Shaftesbury and of Molesworth's *An Account of Denmark* is noted. Johnson, *Lives of the Poets;* for Akenside, pp. 442–448; for J. Hughes (1677–1720), pp. 248–250. See also *DNB.* For Mrs. Rowe, see Davis, *Watts, passim,* and *DNB.*

65. See art. on Baron, *DNB. Hollis Memoirs,* II, 573–586 and *passim.* The MS. diary of Thomas Hollis (by kind permission of R. M. Anthony) relates many quarrels between Baron and Hollis that the compiler of the *Memoirs* left out. "Memoirs of Charles Bulkley" (1719–1797), in *PDM,* 4:281–282 (May 1797); *PDM,* 6:166–168 (London, 1799). William Blazeby, *Rotherham, the Old Meeting House and its Ministers* (Rotherham, 1906), has a great deal on Baron and the Hollises. An example of Baron's book-collecting (also described in *Hollis Memoirs*) at Harvard is MS. of Trenchard's essays which Baron acquired and gave away, annotated with his notes on "Cato"; also *The Restoration of All Things,* a reprint (London, 1721) of old tract by J. White (d.1707), Cromwell's chaplain, in which Baron notes that it was a favourite book with Mr. Hutcheson of Glasgow.

66. Much material about Baron may be found in Neville, *Diary,* pp. 13, 17, 18, 19 for quarrel with Chatham; and pp. 20, 23, 26, 30, 35, 51, 69. Baron dedicated a volume of his *Priestcraft* to J. Milner, minister and schoolmaster at Peckham, author of *Principles of Religious Liberty* (1739), and other tracts; see Wilson, IV, 370. Dr. Williams's Library, MSS. Mod. Fol. 53 (2 June, 1768), Wiche to Lardner on poverty of Baron.

67. See above, n. 65, and *Hollis Memoirs.*

68. *Hollis Memoirs,* I, 321–322.

69. Neville, *Diary,* p. 30, for Hollis's estimate of Baron.

70. Blazeby, *Rotherham; Hollis Memoirs, passim.* For Thomas III's funeral sermons (under Hollis) and MSS. and Letters in Harvard Library and Mass. Hist. Soc. Collections. *MR,* 20:55 (1825), on death of John Hollis, last of the line, aged 81 (1743–1824). In Harvard MSS., IV, 4.1, many references to family, nephew Solly, Uncle Robert Turner, Cousin Neale, good friend Watts (who lived for nine years in "my family"). Hunt married a kinswoman. One letter to Colman outlines history of family. Thomas III was a friend of Barrington, Bendish, Lowman, Avery, and others.

71. Blazeby, *Rotherham,* and personal letter from Mr. John V. Lister.

72. *Hollis Memoirs.* Also Disney, *Memoirs of Hollis,* and letters there about family feeling. See *Letters of Theophilus Lindsey* (Manchester, 1920), chap. iv, *passim,* for friends hearing American news.

73. Ward had been educated in part by the Hollis family. MS. letters of Thomas III at Harvard (January 1726–27). *Hollis Memoirs,* I, 5. Thomas Birch, *Life of John Ward* (London, 1766); *DNB;* Nichols, *Lit. Anec.,* Index; and *Hollis Memoirs* on early education of Hollis. Other biographical details, see Caroline Robbins, "The Strenuous Whig, Thomas Hollis of Lincoln's Inn," in *WMQ,* 3d ser.,

7, no. 3:406–453 (July 1950); and "Library of Liberty," *HLB*, 5, nos. 1 and 2 (Winter and Spring, 1951).

74. Robbins, "The Strenuous Whig," *WMQ*, July 1950.

75. On Chatham-Hollis relationship. MS. letter communicated by Mr. Ian Christie of Univ. Coll., London, to Stanley Porten (November 1756) about early meeting. See also B.M.Add. MSS. 26889, f. 50. Hollis to Taylor Howe (20 December, 1763) on same subject, P.R.O. London, Chatham Papers GD–8/40, Hollis Chatham Letters. Also *Chatham Correspondence*, ed. W. S. Taylor and H. H. Pringle, 4 vols. (London, 1838–40), IV, 269, 267, 273, and *passim*.

76. Difference with Priestley in MS. diary. Blackburne, compiler of the *Memoirs*, was intimate with the latter and omitted all uncomplimentary references to him.

77. Listed in Robbins, "Library of Liberty," *HLB*, 5, nos. 1 and 2, 1951.

78. William Hazlitt, *Table Talk*, Everyman ed. (London, 1908), pp. 191–192; written about 1824.

CHAPTER VIII. Staunch Whigs and Republicans of the Reign of George II

1. H.M.C., *Egmont Diary*, II, 509; for the Hampden family, see M. Noble, *House of Cromwell*, II, no. VII.

2. For John Conduitt (1688–1737), see *DNB*. Egmont frequently mentions him and Jekyll. Both contributed to the Georgia Fund in which Egmont was interested. On Jekyll (1663–1738), see *DNB*. He married one of Somers's sisters; another married James Harris of Salisbury; another Cocks, father-in-law of Philip Yorke, Lord Hardwicke. On Jekyll's politics, see H.M.C., *Egmont Diary*, I (1920), 133, 343, 361; II, 229, 507; also H.M.C., *Portland MSS.*, VII (1901), 447; also John, Lord Hervey, *Memoirs of the Reign of King George II*, ed. Romney Sedgwick, 3 vols. (London, 1931), pp. 419–420; for dissenters, pp. 121, 132, 190–192, etc. John B. Owen, *The Rise of the Pelhams* (London, 1957), a mine of information about faction and connection.

3. H.M.C., *Egmont Diary*, I, 126, 133, 153. For Sam Holden (ca.1670–1740), see *ibid.*, p. 305, and see unpublished dissertation by N. C. Hunt, "A Consideration of the Relationship between Some Religious and Economic Organizations and the Government, Especially from 1730–1742," submitted in 1951 and now deposited in the Cambridge University Library. Hervey, *Memoirs*, *passim*.

4. See art. Chatham, *DNB*. Also Basil Williams, *Life of William Pitt, Earl of Chatham*, 2 vols. (London, 1913), and Archibald P. Primrose, fifth earl of Rosebery, *Chatham, His Early Life and Connections* (London, 1910), pp. 393–394, and 495–496. For Hollis and Chatham, see above, Chap. VII, n. 75. *Letters to Thomas Pitt, Esq., Later Lord Camelford* (London, 1810), *passim*. There is not much in the published correspondence of Chatham for these years. John Gilbert Cooper, claimed by Hollis as friend to himself and to liberty, in MS. note at Harvard, in Cooper, *On Taste* (London, 1747). See *DNB*. Also *MR*, 8:223 (1813). A. Kippis,

Biographia Britannica, 2d ed., 5 vols. (London, 1778–1793). Nichols, *Lit. Anec.,*V, 602–603; I, 130–131; II, 294–297. See *On Taste,* pp. 47, 50, 51, and *Epistles to the Great* (London, 1757), pp. 10–11, 19. *The Genius of Britain* (London, 1756). Cooper was born in Nottingham and was at Trinity, Cambridge, in 1740, in the same year that Thomas Pownall was there. He married a daughter of N. Wright, Recorder of Leicester.

5. Voltaire, *Letters on the English,* repr. from Harvard Classics (New York, n.d.), p. 111.

6. C. Robbins, "Why the English Parliament Survived," no. XI, in *Studies presented to the International Commission for the History of Representative Institutions. No. XVIII at Rome, 1955* (Louvain, 1958).

7. See above, Chap. VII.

8. William King, *Political and Literary Anecdotes of His Own Times* (London, 1818). See also R. J. Robson, *The Oxfordshire Elections of 1754* (Oxford, 1949), especially bibliography.

9. César de Saussure (b.1705), *A Foreign View of England,* p. 351.

10. For Jekyll, see above, n.2. Philip Carteret Webb, Solicitor to the Treasury (1700–1770), M. P. Haslemere, 1754–1768. *DNB.* He defended the Jews' legal rights in a couple of tracts. See bibliography in C. Roth, *History of the Jews in England* (Oxford, 1941), pp. 211–221, and account of the bill there.

11. Nicholas Hardinge (1699–1758), M. P. Rye, 1748–1758. *DNB.* O. C. Williams, *The Clerical Organisation of the House of Commons, 1661–1850* (Oxford, 1954), pp. 62–69. For Hardinge's speech, see Cobbett, *Park. Hist.,* XIV (London, 1813), 1747–1753; 7 May, 1753, pp. 1395–1402. Nichols, *Lit. Anec.,* V, 338–348; VIII, 513ff.

12. Arthur Onslow (1691–1768). *DNB.* Also C. E. Vulliamy, *The Onslow Family* (London, 1953), chap. viii. *Hollis Memoirs,* pp. 85–89, 98, 542. Hollis gave T. Wilson, *Ornaments of Churches* (London, 1761) to Harvard with its beautiful picture of the Speaker in the chair at St. Margaret's Westminster. H.M.C., *Var. Coll.,* VIII, letters to and from Onslow and John Molesworth, 297, 308, 365. Nichols, *Lit. Anec.,* I, 588; II, 263, 615; VIII, 457 and *passim.* Benjamin Franklin, *History of Pennsylvania,* in *Works,* ed. Jared Sparks (Philadelphia, 1840), III, 109–110, "Dedication to the Honourable Author, Arthur Onslow." *Letters of Benjamin Franklin and Richard Jackson,* ed. Carl Van Doren, Memoirs of the American Philosophical Society, XXIV (Philadelphia, 1947), introduction, *passim,* for much about Richard Jackson (1720–1787). Jackson, an Englishman, actually wrote the *History* with material furnished by Franklin, and—after being educated at Cambridge, reading in Lincoln's Inn, practicing at the Bar—sat for Weymouth in 1762 in parliament, acted as secretary to Grenville and as agent for Pennsylvania, Massachusetts, and Connecticut. In spite of his extremely cautious character, Jackson must be termed a pro-American and an Honest Whig.

13. William Talbot (1710–1782), M. P. Glamorgan, 1734–1737. Thomas Rundle (1686–1743), *Letters . . . to Mrs. Barbara Sandys* (Gloucester, 1789), II, appen-

dix, 241–244; Talbot's letter quoted here. Henry St. John, Viscount Bolingbroke, *Miscellaneous Works*, 5 vols. (Edinburgh, 1773), III, 44.

14. George St. Armand, *An Historical Essay on the Legislative Power of England* (London, 1725), preface and p. 197. William Hay, "An Essay on Civil Government" (1728), in *Works* (London, 1794). See also *An Essay Concerning the Original of Society, Government, Religion and Laws, by a Person of Quality* (London, 1727), law reform, pp. 64–67; education, p. 55; virtue, p. 54; v. state of nature, p. 17; anticlerical, pp. 34–35.

15. Henry, Lord Paget (1719–1769), *Harmony Without Uniformity, Being a Philosophical Defence of Liberty and Charity* (London, 1740) *passim*. *Some Reflections Upon the Administration* (London, 1741), restraints, pp. 28–29; v. luxury, and proposes sumptuary laws, pp. 39–41; public education, p. 47; no powerful state lost liberty whilst virtuous, pp. 61–62.

16. *An Essay on Civil Government in Two Parts* (London, 1743), law reform, pp. 29, 264–269; rotation, pp. 19, 346; liberty, pp. 55–58; resistance, p. 167; toleration, pp. 137, 138; no large nobility, p. 349; free press, pp. 354–356; people, p. 207.

17. *Liberty and Right, or an Essay Historical and Political on the Constitution and Administration of Great Britain* (London, July, 1747), either by Dr. John Campbell (1708–1775), or by the M.P. for Pembroke (1695–1777), but the former seems most likely. The title suggests a Scot; see especially pp. 45–52 of Part II for reform suggested. Another tract of the year, 1747, was *An Essay on Liberty and Independency* (London, 1747), urging public spirit as a way of keeping even the English government, so much better than continental systems, free. Could be read as urging resistance to the ministry, pp. 25–27. John Perceval, second earl of Egmont, *Faction Detected by the Evidence of Facts* (Dublin, 1743), *passim*, but 159ff. sums up.

18. On Fielding, see F. Homes Dudden, *Henry Fielding*, 2 vols. (Oxford, 1952), I, 130, where he notes "definitely democratic cast" of Fielding's thought. See also Nicholas, *Lit. Anec.*, III, 356–385. Fielding was a friend of James Harris. *The Champion*, reprinted and bound, 2 vols. (London, 1741), I, Ubiquitarians, 103; Sidney, 59; Old Whigs, 178; a Whig program, 314–315; English government, 164–171; II, "Bridle and Saddle," 275; on Long Parliament, 88–95; Mercenary Parliament, 150–152. *Amelia* (London, 1930), chap. ii, "Observations on the Excellency of the English Constitution." *Joseph Andrews* (1742; ed. used New York, 1939), pp. 6–7. And see *Works*, 8 vols. (London, 1771), VIII, pp. 113–645, for "Essays," "*Covent Garden Journal*," "Fragment on Bolingbroke's *Essays*," and "An Enquiry," etc.

19. Squire and Newcome, Nichols, *Lit. Anec.*, II, 348–352; I, 186, 553–565. *DNB*. For a foreign reader of Squire, see V. Martinelli, *Istoria del Governo* (Pescia, 1777), p. 39.

20. Squire, *An Enquiry into the Foundation of the English Constitution* (1748), and *An Essay on the Balance of Civil Power in England* (1745), published together (Lon-

don, 1753); the dregs, p. 102; the balance and Poland, p. 390; German government contrasted with utopian schemes, pp. 84–96; the republicans, p. 359; and change necessary, pp. 383, 396.

21. *Hollis Memoirs* give much information about tracts. See also Blackburne, below, Chap. IX. For catalogue, see that of Anthony Collins (1731). On Ralph's sale, see *PMHB*, 80, no. 1:37–45 (January 1956). Other great libraries were those of John Bridges (1726), James West (1773); P. C. Webb (1770), with about 450 volumes of tracts. Nichols, *Lit. Anec.*, VI, 614–689; Henry Beaufoy (1909) and Beauclerk (1781). The Onslow Library was sold March, 1885.

22. On Birch, see *DNB;* Nichols, *Lit. Anec., passim,* and especially memoir in V, 282–290. The Birch MSS., B.M. Add. MSS. 4300–4323, reveal his wide correspondence. *Hollis Memoirs*, I, a trimmer, 364.

23. John Jortin (1698–1770). See *DNB;* Nichols, *Lit. Anec.*, II, 550–577; *Memoirs*, ed. J. Disney (London, 1792), pp. 9 and 306–307.

24. Conyers Middleton. See *DNB;* Nicholas, *Lit. Anec.*, V, 405–423, 700; also II, 35, 71; IV, 492–493. See brief memoirs prefaced to *Miscellaneous Works*, 4 vols. (London, 1752), I.

25. Coulson Fellowes (1696–1769). See Nicholas, *Lit. Anec.*, I, 589–590.

26. Leslie Stephen, *English Thought in the Eighteenth Century*, I, chap. iv, Part VI, *passim*.

27. Middleton, *History of the Life of Marcus Tullius Cicero*, 2 vols. (London, 1741), xxxv, xxxvii; and *A Treatise on the Roman Senate* (1746), in *Misc. Works*, III, Part I, 379ff., Part II, 432ff., *dernier resort*, 433. Abbé de Vertot, *The History of the Revolutions . . . of the Roman Republic*, 5th ed. of Eng. tr. (London, 1740), II, contains his answer to Stanhope. Nathaniel Hooke, *Observations on Vertot . . . Spelman . . . Middleton . . . Thomas Chapman* (London, 1758), dedicated to Onslow. Hooke was Tory, see *Hollis Memoirs*, I, 496–498. Nichols, *Lit. Anec.*, II, 615–617. His *Observations* answered by Edward Spelman, in *A Short Review of Mr. Hooke's Observations* (London, 1758). For Spelman (d.1767), see *DNB*.

28. "A Free Inquiry into the Miraculous Powers," in *Works* (1752), I; also "Letter from Rome," III, *passim,* and especially p. 59.

29. See preface to *Cicero* (1741), I, xxxv; 494–495.

30. J. Curling, *Life of Edward Wortley-Montagu* (London, 1954), chap. xiv, 146–152. Montagu was Coulson Fellowes's partner at Huntington, 1747–54, and M. P. Bossiney, 1754–1768. *Reflections on the Rise and Fall of the Antient Republicks Adapted to the Present State of Great Britain*, 2d ed. (London, 1760); lessons from history, pp. 10–11; Athens, p. 144; Carthage, pp. 176f.; Denmark, p. 367; commerce, p. 321; balance, p. 365; recent corruption, p. 377; militia, pp. 381–388. Charles Sackville (1711–1769), M.P. Old Sarum, 1734–1765, *A Treatise Concerning the Militia in Four Sections* (London, 1752); advocates milder punishments, pp. 3, 6–7, 31, 52; advocates a register, p. 63.

31. See Edward Spelman, *A Fragment out of the Sixth Book of Polybius* (London, 1743), preface, inevitability of party, pp. v–vi; annual parliaments, p. x; triennial,

pp. xii–xv; power so bewitching, p. xv; reform of parliament annual and equal representation, pp. xix–xx. See Peter Campbell, "An Early Defence of Party," in *Political Studies* (Oxford, June 1955), III, no. 2, 166–167.

32. M. Dodson, *Life of Michael Foster* (London, 1811). Foster (1689–1763), *A Report . . . on the Trial of the Rebels in . . . 1746* (Dublin, 1763) contains "Observations on Hale." *The Diary of Dudley Ryder* (1691–1756), tr. and ed. by W. Matthews (London, 1939), p. 226 and *passim*. B.M. Tracts 1972(9): tracts on game laws, among them *An Alarm* (1757). See Sidney and Beatrice Webb, *English Local Government,* Vol. I, *Parish and Country* (London, 1906), 597–599. W. Nelson, *The Laws Concerning Game,* 4th ed. (London, 1751), Introduction. For violent advocacy of law reform, see *Animadversions Upon the Present Laws of England, or an Essay to Render Them More Useful and Less Expensive to all his Majesty's Subjects* (1749), reviewed in *Mo.R* (December 1749).

33. J. Disney, *Life of A. A. Sykes* (London, 1785); on Kidman, see p. 3; on fear of popery, p. 19; a friend of Birch, pp. 128, 209; low and fat, pp. 357–358. See *Hollis Memoirs,* I, 326, 429; II, 706. Sykes not only defended Hoadly, he also defended Thomas Rundle (Disney, p. 194–202) who was of course an associate of these Latitudinarian clergy and a friend of Whiston. In general Rundle seems to have been a Whig of the same character who knew and cared more about trade and colonies than Sykes and Jackson. See *Sermon* (London, 1734) on Deut. 15:11, and *Sermon* at Christ Church (Dublin, 1735) with review of constitution, Newton's proof of God and the blessings of liberty, 12–15. Interest in lower people, p. 16; and against severity, p. 18; hopes plenty will help the poor and education will improve their religion, pp. 26–31. See memoir prefaced to *Letters* quoted above, n. 13.

34. See particularly, besides Disney's account and list of publications, Sykes's tracts: *The Test and Corporation Acts of No Importance* (London: J. Roberts, 1736); and *The Treasonableness of Applying for the Repeal* (London: J. Roberts, 1736), *passim,* Sykes and popery, pp. 278–280; Sykes and Bristow, p. 358.

35. Nicholas, *Lit. Anec.,* IX, 433–440. See Disney, *Life of Thomas Herne* (London, 1815).

36. John Jackson. See *DNB;* Nichols, *Lit. Anec.,* II, 519–531. See also Disney, *Life of Sykes,* p. 362, and *Old Whig,* nos. 33 and 39.

37. *The Grounds of Civil and Ecclesiastical Government Briefly Considered* (London, 1718), government, pp. 1–54; defense of Hoadly, pp. 55–97; *passim. Defense of Human Liberty* (1725); *Vindication* (1730), given to Harvard by Benjamin Avery, editor of *Old Whig; A Plea for Humane Reason* (London, 1730), emphasizes connection of virtue and happiness.

38. See *MR,* 8:443 (1813) on writers of *Occasional Papers.* Hopkins, *An Appeal to the Common Sense of all Christian People* (1754), table of contents and *passim; Serious and Free Thoughts* (1755), pp. 432, 446; *The Trinitarian Controversy Reviewed* (1760), *passim.*

39. John Jones. See *DNB;* Nichols, *Lit. Anec.,* I, 585–640. Many letters in Birch

MSS., including letter of 23 January, 1748–49. *Free and Candid Disquisitions* (London, 1749) begins suggested reform, pp. 22–30; ecclesiastical courts, pp. 174–178; chap. iv, survey, pp. 44–63; chap. vi, queries on creeds.

40. Edward Bentham (1707–1776), *Moral Philosophy* (Oxford, 1746). Sermon before House of Commons, 30 January, 1749–50 (Oxford, 1750), pp. 11, 13, 34, etc.

41. John Clarke (1687–1734). Nichols, *Lit. Anec.,* IX, 579; Venn, *Alumni Cantabrigienses* (Cambridge, 1922–1927); John Tickell's *Hull* (1798), pp. 825–831. Account here is a condensation of Clarke, *An Essay Upon Study* (1731), chaps. iii and iv, and *An Essay Upon the Education of Youth* (1740), on size of classes, p. 204; on teachers' pay and qualifications, p. 206.

42. Venn, *Alum. Cantab.* The two sermons are in the British Museum.

43. For Hackney, see D. Lyons, *Environs of London,* 4 vols. (London, 1842), I, 140–141. Also Somerset House wills, PCC 304 Glazier, H. Newcome of Hackney (fl.1756). Relationship, if any, of Newcome of Hackney and Grantham and John Newcome (1700–1763) of St. Johns undetermined.

44. Christopher Wordsworth, *Scholae Academicae* (Cambridge, 1877), pp. 127, 11. See also Venn, *Alum. Cantab., passim.*

45. Edmund Law. See R. S. Crane, "Anglican Apologetics and the Idea of Progress, 1699–1745," *MP,* 31, nos. 3 and 4: 273–305, 349–382 (February and May 1934). Most interesting discussion on Law and others of his connection. Memoir by Paley prefaced to 1820 ed. of *Works.* Nichols, *Lit. Anec.,* II, 65–69, gives Paley's memoir and follows it with Jones of Alconbury's memoirs. Nichols tells the story of Herring and the thesis, I, 593–594, and of his kindness to Jones, I, 630. Nichols relates that he was a relative of J. Robertson, formerly curate to A. A. Sykes and editor of Sidney's *Works* (1772) in Nichols, *Lit. Anec.,* III, 501, compare Disney's *Sykes,* p. 216. The quotations are from Paley's account of Nichols, *Lit. Anec.,* II, 68.

46. Note dedication in Law, *Considerations,* 3d ed. (London, 1755), omitted in ed. of 1820; comment on his method of education, p. iv. The advertisement to *Considerations* in *Works* (1820), xv, xvi, states idea of progress; also pp. 47 and 225–308; remarks on education, pp. 237, 249–253. See J. Harris, *Hermes* (London, 1765), pp. 364–365. All of essay III in *Considerations* (1820), "The Progress of Natural Religion and Science," deals with this topic.

47. William King, *An Essay on the Origin of Evil,* tr. by E. Law (ed. quoted, Cambridge, 1739; 1st ed., London, 1731); hereafter called *Origin.* The dedication (to Waterland) and translator's preface provide brief guides to King's work, iii–xxvi.

48. King, *Origin,* xxvii–lv, "Preliminary Dissertation." For Gay, see Venn, *Alum. Cantab.,* pp. 1, 2, 202; note reference to Hutcheson, p. 1.

49. See J. Priestley, *Hartley's Theory of the Human Mind* (London, 1775); *Essay,* II, xxiii on Gay's dissertation, and its effect on Hartley, xxiv.

50. "Progress of Natural Religion and Science," in *Considerations,* pp. 208, 211; and see dedication to *Origin.*

51. "Progress of Natural Religion and Science," in *Considerations,* pp. 225–230, 229, harm of failure to review, and n. 277.

52. For Brown, see Kippis, *Biog. Brit.,* II, 653–674. Nichols, *Lit. Anec.,* II, 293; VIII, 244, etc. Also *Hollis Memoirs,* II, 714–717.

53. *An Estimate of the Manners and Principles of the Times,* 2 vols. (London, 1758–59), Harvard shelf mark: Houghton x, 27, 20, 85.

54. *Ibid.,* I, Part I, defined ruling manners and principles and analyzed situation in England. Part II, on public effects; Part III, sources, emphasizes wealth, discusses again effects of all this, reviews the argument on Walpole, pp. 114–115. Hollis note (Harvard copy) on parliamentary reform to a statement about the origin of bribery, p. 109; on theory of history, pp. 213f. Second volume underlines some of the principles of the first, honour and virtue, p. 20, for example; discusses virtues of England, pp. 24–26; condemns universities, p. 68; reprints Molesworth's famous Chapter vii on the Revolution in Denmark in 1660, pp. 225–236.

55. Thomas Pownall, J. A. Schultz, *Thomas Pownall, British Defender of American Liberty* (Glendale, California, 1951); a long account of Pownall's American career and speeches in parliament about the colonies when he returned. See also Nichols, *Lit. Anec.,* VIII, 61–67; letter from Walpole to Pownall, IV, 709–712. C. Pownall wrote a life of the Governor trying to prove that he was Junius (London, 1908), but fails to make the point. Style alone would disqualify Pownall. His works included: *Administration of the Colonies* (Several ed.'s, 1764–1777); *The State of the Constitution of the Colonies* (1769), identified as his by Franklin's note in the Philadelphia Library Company; *A Letter to Adam Smith* (1776); *The Right Interest and Duty of the State as Concerned in the Affairs of the East Indies* (London, 1773). *His Memorials to the Sovereigns of Europe, Great Britain and North America,* coll. ed. (London, 1784) were his last publications of political interest, but he wrote antiquarian works and a tribute to Walpole as well as *Memoir of the Corn Trade,* printed with Arthur Young's *Political Arithmetic,* Part I (London, 1774).

56. *A Treatise on the Study of Antiquities* (London, 1782), *passim,* but particularly, pp. 60–90.

57. *Principles of Polity,* ed. E. Owen Warwick (London, 1752), X, 27, 21 at Harvard contains the letter pasted inside cover. The introductory note and first pages explain the scheme and the milieu of the Dialogues. An earlier draft of the *Principles* seems now to be extremely scarce; I know of only one in the B.M. Catalogue, there listed under *Treatise, A Treatise on Government Being a Review of the Doctrine of an Original Contract more Particularly as it Respects the Rights of Government and the Duty of Allegiance* (London: G. Hawkins in Paternoster Row, 1750).

58. *Principles,* pp. 14, 26.

59. Letter to Adam Smith, referring to *Principles,* p. 5. See *Principles* for the farm and mine, pp. 23–25.

60. *Principles.* Virtually all Dialogue I is on this theme; see p. 10, seeds of dissolution and anarchy; bloodshed in Europe, p. 9; servile many, p. 11.

61. *Principles,* pp. 29–30, 26.

62. *Principles;* divisions of states, p. 64, etc. See *Memorials* (the collection of 1784, bound together with a General Preface but with separate pagination for each part title, listed above n. 55), "General Preface," family compact, p. xix and in memorial to the King, for family compact, p. 13; to Europe on a congress of Europe, pp. 95, 119 and compare p. 2, and "General Preface" ix–x, xv–xvi. He not only proclaimed himself a disciple of Smith in a letter, he also endorsed his arguments in addressing Europe, pp. 113–114, 127 to the end. The grand marine dominion of English possessions both sides of the Atlantic is mentioned in *The Administration of the Colonies* (London, 1766), p. 9 and elsewhere.

63. *Memorials,* appendix in memorial to the King, fact not metaphysics, p. 51; *Administration* (ed. 1766), pp. 1–52 and appendix, Sec. 3, "Considerations on the Points lately brought into Question"; *Principles* on the Irish, pp. 20–21, 33, 141–142.

64. *Memorials,* the King, appendix throughout, but also see early editions of *Administration;* memorial to the Americans, "hardened," p. 34; memorial to Europe, in regard to Spanish American Colonies, pp. 14–27. Pownall was a friend of Miranda, see W. S. Robertson, *The Life of Miranda,* 2 vols. (Chapel Hill, N.C., 1929).

65. *Memorials,* memorial to Europe; America a poor man's country, pp. 44–46; children welcome, p. 57; safe, 69; memorial to America, game laws hated and not used in America, pp. 122–123. *Topographical Description* (London, 1766), list of flowering trees, p. 6.

66. *Letter to Adam Smith,* p. 1. *Memorials,* memorial to Europe, free port and free market, pp. 78–80; to America, p. 46; sovereignty and confederation, pp. 23, 80, 138, noting example of Interregnum, pp. 103, 137–138.

67. *Right of State* discusses throughout the limits to which even a charter like that of the East India Company could affect the political powers of the sovereign. Pownall discussed merchants with the powers and practices of princes.

68. *Memorials,* to America, slaves, p. 106f., 109–111; liberty, pp. 55–58; fuller commercial liberty, pp. 92, 95 and see n. 66 above. Harrington's politics often endorsed throughout both *Principles* and memorial to America; *Letter to Adam Smith,* pp. 6–8, the need for moderating change from one system to another.

69. Franklin and Pownall. A. H. Smythe, *The Writings of Benjamin Franklin,* 10 vols. (New York, 1905–1906), V, 197, 200, 205, 262.

70. William Coxe, *Memoirs of Sir Robert Walpole,* III, 615–620.

CHAPTER IX. Honest Whigs under George III, 1761–1789

1. L. B. Namier, "Monarchy and the Party System," in *Personalities and Powers* (London, 1955), pp. 13–38; *The Structure of Politics at the Accession of George III,* 2 vols. (London, 1929); and *England in the Age of the American Revolution* (London, 1930). H. Butterfield, *George III, Lord North and the People,* 1779–80 (London,

1949). R. Pares, *George III and the Politicians* (Oxford, 1953). John Brooke, *The Chatham Administration, 1766–1768* (London, 1956). G. S. Veitch, *The Genesis of Parliamentary Reform* (London, 1913). Lucy Sutherland, "The City of London in Eighteenth Century Politics," in *Essays Presented to Sir Lewis Namier*, eds. R. Pares and A. J. P. Taylor (London, 1956), pp. 49–74.

2. On Thomas Spence, see above, Chap. V, n. 34; and Olive Rudkin, in a life (London, 1927); and below, n. 55. This title page of *Pig's Meat.* contains the purpose quoted. Spence may have taken the idea of his penny number from such publications as *The Patriot*, 2 vols. (London, 3 April, 1792 —November 1793), "consisting of Original Pieces and Selections from writers of Merit," and quoting from Lord Molesworth on "Health and liberty," I, 397–398; Ogilvie, "Too little noticed," II, 29; and others. Henry Yorke, *These are the Times that Try Men's Souls,* in *A Letter to John Frost in Newgate Prison*, pp. 34, 50–52, 58. See also Chap. V above, n. 38.

3. Élie Halévy, *The Growth of Philosophic Radicalism, passim;* on Shelburne, Burke, and Bentham, pp. 145–148. See Ian R. Christie, "Economical Reform and 'The Influence of the Crown,' 1780," in *CHJ*, 12, no. 2: 144–154 (Cambridge, 1956). Peter J. Stanlis, *Edmund Burke and the Natural Law* (Ann Arbor, Michigan, 1958), chap. iii, pp. 29–84, attempts to show Burke's endorsement of older natural law theories.

4. Francis Blackburne. See *DNB;* W. Turner in *Monthly Magazine* (London, December 1796), p. 888; and memoir prefaced to *Works*, 7 vols. (Cambridge, 1804), I; the incident about Locke in *Works*, I, iv; "A Candid Address to the Jews" (1752), pp. 237–272. For Blackburne's description of himself in a letter to John Lee on 30 April, 1783, as an "old worn-out Whig," see Lee Papers, William L. Clements Library, Univ. of Michigan, I, 55.

5. Memoir, *Works*, I; see also *A Collection of Letters and Essays in Favour of Public Liberty, First Published in the Newspapers in the Years 1764–70 by an Amiable Band of Well Wishers to the Religious and Civil Rights of Mankind*, 3 vols. (London, 1774), II, 188; title quoted in section heading above. For this collection, see Dr. Williams's Library for identifications of authors, MS. notes; and also Priestly, *Theological and Miscellaneous Works*, 25 vols., ed. J. T. Rutt (London, 1817–1831), I (memoir) 99 n, on Blackburne's earlier anti-popery writings.

6. Dr. Williams's Library, letter to Wiche, 7 October, 1783; in a volume containing letters by Lardner, Priestly, Blackburne, MS. fol. 45, J. Toulmin and others. For J. Wiche (1718–1794), see *PDM*, 4 (London, 1797).

7. F. Blackburne, *The Confessional, or A Full and Free Inquiry into the Right of . . . Establishing Systematical Confessions* (London, 1766 and 1767, 1770). See *Hollis Memoirs*, I, 302. Blackburne, *Works*, I, Hollis's share, xxxii–xxxiii; *Works*, VII, proposals for petition. Brian Herport (d.1768), *An Essay on Truths of Importance to the Happiness of Mankind, Wherein the Doctrine of Oaths, as Relative to Religious and Civil Government, is Impartially Considered* (London, 1768).

8. Feathers Petition: W. Cobbett, *Parl. Hist.,* XVII (1813), 245–297. T. Bel-

sham, *Memoirs of Theophilus Lindsey* (London, 1812), chap. ii, pp. 56–61. Priestly, *Works*, I, 140 n. Among those who supported the Petition were the following: Sir William Meredith (1725–1790), M.P. Liverpool, 3rd Bart.; Henry Beaufoy (1751–1774), M.P. Minehead, 1783, and Great Yarmouth, 1783–1795 (Also from Warrington and a later proponent of liberty); John Sawbridge (ca.1732–1795), M.P. Hythe, 1768–1774, and London, 1774–1796 (*DNB*); Alex Wedderburn (1733–1805), 1st earl of Rosslyn, M.P. Bishop's Castle (a pupil of Leechman at Glasgow who deserted reformers later); John Dunning, later Lord Ashburton (1731–1783), M.P. Calne, 1768–1792 (*DNB*); George Saville (1726–1785), M.P. Yorks, educ. Cambridge, a Rock Whig; John Cavendish (1732–1796), M.P. York City; Fred Montagu (1733–1780), M.P. Higham Ferrars; Richard Sutton (1732–1783), M.P. St. Albans; James Townsend (1737–1787), M.P. West Looe, 1767–1774, and Calne, 1782–1787, educ. Oxford, Alderman of London; Thomas Townshend (1733–1800), M.P. Whitchurch.

9. On Lindsey, see Belsham, *Lindsey Memoirs; DNB; Letters of Lindsey*, ed. H. McLachlan (Manchester, 1920). W. Turner, *Lives of Eminent Unitarians* (London, 1843), II, 25ff. *MR*, 8:338–342 (1813). R. V. Holt, *The Unitarian Contribution* (London, 1938). Priestly, *Works*, I and II, *passim*.

10. John Lee (1733–1783). See *DNB*. Recorder of Leeds. References to him in Belsham, *Lindsey Memoirs*, pp. 70, 111–112, 176–177, 393; and in *Lindsey Letters, passim;* at the "Honest Whig," p. 15. Priestly, *Works*, XXV, 393–395; I, 86. There are three boxes of Lee Papers in the William L. Clements Library, Univ. of Michigan. These reveal the affection in which his friends held a man "unbiased by the prejudices of any sect or party," and devoted to the civil and religious rights of mankind. Lee sided with Price against Burke, *Lindsey Letters*, p. 140.

11. Priestly, *Works*, I, 226–229, 232. *Lindsey Letters*, for benefactors, pp. 28–29, Belsham, *Lindsey Memoirs*, for congregation, pp. 111–112. See also J. Adams, *Works*, 10 vols., ed. C. F. Adams (Boston, 1850–1865), III, Diary for April 1786. Some of these were persons like Francis Dashwood; Thomas Barnard (1761–1784); Samuel Shore (1738–1828), Norton Hall Derbys, a rich benefactor to both Priestly and Lindsey; Thomas Brand Hollis (1719–1804); John Calder (1733–1816); Serj. James Adair (ca.1798), Cambridge alumnus, friend of William Jones; Michael Dodson (1732–1799), nephew of M. Foster; Mrs. Elizabeth Rayner of Sunbury (1714–1800); Gilbert Wakefield (1756–1801); Augustus Fitzroy, Duke of Grafton (1735–1811); John Dunning, Lord Ashburton; Charles Lennox, Duke of Richmond (1735–1806); and others like William Taylor, Bernard Turner, E. Jennings, H. Hinkle, Lacey Primatt. On Hackney, see Smith, *Mod. Educ.*, pp. 171–178.

12. Belsham, *Lindsey Memoirs, passim;* also Lindsey Letters at Manchester Unitarian College, some of which are printed by McLachlan in *Lindsey Letters* and arranged under topics, chap. iv being political. See also ref. to Savile, p. 113; Honest Whig, pp. 15–16, 78–81. Ann Jebb in *MR*, 7:597–604 (1812). J. Rutt's notes to his ed. of Priestley's *Works* contain a mass of information about Lindsey and his friends, e.g., I, 256 and note.

13. T. Jervis, *Funeral Sermon for John Disney* (London, 1816). Jervis was Disney's son-in-law and had been a tutor in the Shelburne family. See also Turner, *Eminent Unitarians*, II, 178–213. Disney wrote for the *Monthly Repository* sketches of such men as Robert Garnham, a friend of Lindsey, and others.

14. Newcome Cappe (1733–1800), *Discourses and Memoirs* (York, 1805), *MR*, 18:1 (1823). Catharine Cappe, *Memoirs* (London, 1822); much about Turner, Priestley, Lindsey, and Blackburne families throughout; her own early life and parentage. For the Turners of Wakefield, see *MR*, 16:638 (1821), and works of William the third, who wrote *Eminent Unitarians*, II (1843), 336–381.

15. G. Wakefield, *Memoirs*, 2 vols. (London, 1804), *passim*.

16. John Hinchliffe (1731–1794). *DNB*. Nichols, *Lit. Anec.*, IX, 487–488. Indispensable is Norman Sykes, *Church and State in England in the XVIIIth Century* (Cambridge, 1934).

17. Jonathan Shipley (1714–1788). *DNB*. *Works*, 2 vols. (London, 1792), *passim;* quotation, II, 253; education, 336; happiness, 339; America, 159–197. Priestly, *Works*, I, on Shipley at "Honest Whigs," 210. R. Watson, *Anecdotes*, 2 vols. (Philadelphia, 1818), I, 136.

18. R. Watson (1737–1816). *DNB*. Watson, *Miscellaneous Collected Tracts*, 2 vols. (London, 1815). *Anecdotes*, for reflections on Cambridge contemporaries, I, 13, 30–31; Wilkes, I, 55; Burke, I, 131–132; the American struggle, I, 71; Hoadly, a republican, I, 70; Watson's philosophy, I, 140.

19. William Paley (1743–1805). *DNB*. *Memoirs* by G. W. Meadley (London, 1809). W. Glick, "Bishop Paley in America," *NEQ*, 27, no. 3:347–354 (September, 1954). *The Principles of Moral and Political Philosophy* (London, 1785), Book VI.

20. For Richard Price, see C. B. Cone, *Torchbearer of Freedom* (Lexington, Kentucky, 1952), best life so far; chap. vi on Whigs. See also J. Boswell, *In Search of a Wife* (New York, 1956), p. 300.

21. R. Price, *Observations on the Nature of Civil Liberty, the Principles of Government, and the Justice and Policy of the War with America* (London, 1776). The copy used here is the 4th ed., bound with the 2d ed. of *Additional Observations* (London, 1777); referred to hereafter as *Observations*, I and II.

22. *Observations*, I, 8–9; see also 3 to 18.

23. *Ibid.*, p. 14.

24. *Ibid.*, p. 17.

25. *Ibid.*, p. 18; and II, 6–7.

26. *Ibid.*, I, 70–71, and note.

27. *Ibid.*, II, 30; from Hutcheson, *Moral Philosophy*, II, 280.

28. *Observations*, II, 19; quotes from J. Cartwright, *Take Your Choice!* (London, 1776), II, 37; on Molyneux, I, 100; quotation from Hutcheson's *System*, II, 309, in *Observations*, II, 75–76.

29. *Observations*, I, 28–29. For a number of suggestions for giving up empire, even Gibraltar, made by such different persons as Price, Tucker, and Priestly, see Priestly, *Works*, XXV, 133–134.

30. *Observations*, I, 32.

31. "On America," in *Observations,* I, Sec. 2, 34–94; quotation, 55.

32. *Ibid.,* p. 87.

33. *Ibid.,* p. 88, 93.

34. *Ibid.,* p. 104–109.

35. *Ibid.,* II, 80–87; I, 58; II, 89. Sees MS. draft of "A Sketch of Proposal for Discharging the Public Debts, Securing Public Liberty and Preserving the State," in William L. Clements Library, Univ. of Michigan, Shelburne Papers, pp. 117, 43ff., quotation, p. 55.

36. Fitzmaurice, *Life of Shelburne, passim,* for life and many memoranda; on liberty, II, 330. The Shelburne Papers at the William L. Clements Library contain material on the relationship of Shelburne and Price.

37. The chief authority for Priestley's life and work is to be found in the monumental *Works,* ed. by J. T. Rutt. The first two volumes contain his own memoirs and many letters, with copious notes by the editor, himself a Unitarian of considerable erudition and acquaintance with the history of his sect. See also *MR,* 2:464 (1807), Wyvill's Eulogy; the Society for the Study of the Scriptures, *MR,* 8:531 (1813); *MR,* 8:229, for teaching methods and use of Bible at Warrington.

38. Priestly, *Works,* XXV, 395–398; I, 289n. Ross Hoffman, *Edmund Burke . . . Correspondence with Charles O'Hara and Others* (Philadelphia, 1956), p. 589. Watson on Burke, *Anecdotes,* I, 131–132, *Hollis Memoirs,* I, 285–288. A long discussion of different views about American independence by Rutt in Priestley, *Works,* I, notes on pp. 313–314, but it was of course written after the event. Priestley and Price do not seem to have realized how deep were the differences that separated them from Burke for some time, in spite of distrust of Mrs. Macaulay, Hollis, and others. For Burke's attack during debate on Test Corporation Act, see W. Cobbett, *Parl. Hist.,* XXVIII (1816), 432–443. According to Priestley, Sir George Savile shared his anti-imperial views, *Works,* XXV, 133.

39. Neville, *Diary,* p. 111. For remarks on Hutcheson, etc., see Priestley, *First Principles of Government,* 2d ed. (London, 1771), pp. 266, 278; hereafter referred to as *Government.* For Hartley, see Priestley, *Hartley's Theory.*

40. *The Nature of Political, Civil and Religious Liberty* (1769). *A View of the Protestant Dissenters* (1769), repr. in *Works,* XXII, 335–379. *A Letter to William Pitt,* 2d ed. (London, 1787). *A Political Dialogue on the First Principles of Government* (1791), in *Works,* XXV.

41. MS. Diary of Thomas Hollis, November, 1768, and 13 May, 1769. See Priestley, *Works,* I, 94–100, about the incident, and about Blackburne who subsequently changed his mind. Most of the paragraph here is a summary of *A View.*

42. Priestley's remarks on education were incorporated into the 2d ed. of his *Government* (1771), pp. 76–109; reference to Oxford, p. 103. Three of Priestley's most important notes on education may be found in the collected works as follows: "A Code," XXII, 40–54; "Observations," XXV, 1–80, "Liberal Education," XXIV, 7–25.

43. *Government* (1771), dedicated to David, earl of Buchan; quotation, p. viii.

44. *Ibid.*, pp. 3–5.

45. *Ibid.*, pp.32–37, and all Sec. 2 on political liberty.

46. *Ibid.*, p. 55.

47. *Ibid.*, p. 63, and Sec. 10, *passim.*

48. Priestley, *Lectures on History* (Dublin, 1788), Part I. The Lectures were dedicated to Benjamin Vaughan, old friend, pupil. Space does permit discussion of friends of like sentiments, the Vaughans, who deserve a notice of their own as Honest Whigs.

49. *Lectures,* XLI, 251; and *Government* (2d ed. quoted, 1771), Chinese land system, Beccaria, pp. 70–74.

50. *Lectures,* XLI, 253; and *Government,* game laws, pp. 65, 75, 253–268, quotation, pp. 293–294.

51. Thomas Percival, *Works* (London, 1807), in four volumes, of which the first two have memoir and political tracts. *Works* dedicated to John Haygarth; for taxation, see II, 229–285. List of Warrington students, *MR,* 9:201–594 (1814), and *passim.*

52. For Aikin, see *DNB.* Lucy Aikin, *Memoirs and Letters,* 2 vols. (London, 1823), *passim;* friends, pp. 275ff. Also *MR,* 18:52–55 (1823). Mrs. Barbauld's request for Lucy, *Works,* II, 3.

53. A. Barbauld, *Works,* II, periods of dissent, 157–160; quotation, 164. See Priestley, *Works,* I, 278–286 for letter to Mrs. B., 20 December, 1775, criticizing her *Essay.*

54. W. Carew Hazlitt, *Memoirs of William Hazlitt,* 2 vols. (London, 1867), I, *passim,* for the elder Hazlitt. Quotation from William Hazlitt, *Collected Works,* 12 vols., ed. A. R. Waller and A. Glover (London, 1902–1904), III, 263–266.

55. Edward King, *An Essay on the English Constitution and Government* (London, 1767; slightly enlarged in 1771 ed.), pp. 26–28, 79–85, quotation, p. 82. For Baron and Hollis advertisements, see *Hollis Memoirs,* I, 321–323; and Carless Davis, *The Age of Grey and Peel* (Oxford, 1929), pp. 58–70. *Political Disquisitions* (London, 1763), pp. 51–59 and *passim.*

56. The Newcastle Lecture of 1775, "The Real Rights of Man," reprinted and edited by M. Beer (New York, 1920); all would vote and the empire of "right and reason" would be maintained after the redistribution of land had been made. *The Autobiography of Benjamin Rush,* ed. George W. Corner (Princeton, 1948), pp. 41, 45–46.

57. H. Walpole, *Memoirs of the Reign of George the Third,* 4 vols. (London, 1894), III, 220. Neville, *Diary, passim.*

58. J. Sawbridge. See *DNB;* also A. Stephens, *Memoirs of John Horne Tooke,* 2 vols. (London, 1813), I, 375–418; II, 282 and *passim.* Neville, *Diary,* p. 128. For city and Wilkes, see Miss Sutherland's article, above, n. 1, *passim.*

59. L. M. Donnelly, "The Celebrated Mrs. Macaulay," in *WMQ,* 3rd Ser., 7, no. 2:173–207 (April 1949). Most of the material here is from this article.

60. Neville, *Diary;* see Index for names mentioned here. On Hanoverians and Stuarts, see p. 23; on Wilkes, pp. 61–62; on Society for Bill of Rights, p. 69; on Savile, p. 273; and Jebb, pp. 110–111, 285.

61. *Ibid.,* pp. 274–275; and also pp. 3, 50, 54, 225 (America); conversation with Timothy, p. 14; see also p. 59.

62. *An Historical Essay* (London, 1771). See note by writer in *PMHB* (July 1955); *GM*, 60, Part I:586 (1791). Unpublished thesis at Johns Hopkins University by H. Trevor Colburn, "The Saxon Heritage of Thomas Jefferson" (1952), furnished some useful material on Jefferson. See Butterfield, *George III,* pp. 267, 346, 349–350. The Society for Constitutional Information reprinted part of the Essay in a collection of their tracts (1782); also quoted in *Demophilus; the Genuine Principles of the Ancient Saxon or English Constitution* (Philadelphia, 1776).

63. *Historical Essay,* on clergy, pp. 34–37, 42–43, 77, 107; game laws, p. 131; association, p. 161; qualifications, p. 120, on taxes, pp. 179–202. See also *A Plan of Reconciliation* (London, 1776), *passim.*

64. Nichols, *Lit. Anec.,* II, 263–267; *Illustrations,* VI, 61. For Honest Whigs, see C. Van Doren, *Benjamin Franklin* (New York, 1938), pp. 401–402, 421; Cone, *Torchbearer,* chap. vi, etc. Priestley, *Works,* I, 208; XXV, 393. Among Burgh's works: *Thoughts on Education* (London, 1747); *The Dignity of Human Nature* (1754); *Art of Speaking* (1763); *Youth's Friendly Monitor* (1754); *Crito* (1766); *Britain's Remembrancer* (1746), printed five times in two years and later in Philadelphia.

65. *Disquisitions,* III, 416.

66. *Ibid.,* II, 57.

67. *Ibid.,* I, 485; and virtually all of the conclusion, III, 267–460.

68. *Ibid.,* III, 330; see also 159–172 on punishments, etc. Burgh, in Vol. I, as well as in copious footnotes which show his extensive reading in parliamentary records of all sorts, has a preface on authorities and a list of books used and quoted.

69. *Ibid.,* II, Franklin, 276–277; Davenant, 282.

70. *Ibid.,* II, 289–290, Porteous trials.

71. *Ibid.,* II, 275–340, and *passim.*

72. Art. "Earl Stanhope," *Public Characters of 1800–1801* (London, 1801), pp. 81–133, contains interesting contemporary sketch with brief laudatory remarks about his grandfather, the General. Ghita Stanhope and C. P. Gooch, *The Life of Charles, Third Earl of Stanhope* (London, 1914), *passim;* reference to Stanhope preceding Cartwright on reform, p. 38; and in F. D. Cartwright, *Life and Correspondence of Major Cartwright,* 2 vols. (London, 1826), I, 82*n.* This pamphlet has never been found, but Stanhope wrote an address to Westminster's electors in *Kent Public Advertiser,* 16 September, 1774, and a letter in the *Kentish Gazette* in the same month. For his letter, see Cartwright in Price, *Observations,* II, 37 and 68. J. Cartwright, *Take Your Choice!,* example of Denmark, applied to ministry, p. 39. Butterfield, *George III,* App. A, on Stanhope.

73. For Cartwright, see *Life and Correspondence*, II, 405–410; tribute by T. Jervis, son-in-law of Disney; also, I, 156 and 134–135.

74. The frontispiece of *Take Your Choice* contains the diagram referred to in text; see also p. 98 and *passim*. *Works of Dr. John Jebb with Memoirs of the Life of the Author*, 3 vols., ed. J. Disney (London, 1787), I, 171, Jebb on power of the unrepresented in convention. In *American Independence the Interest and Glory of Great Britain* (London, 1774), Cartwright not only advocates independence in those terms, but in a most interesting preface quotes Trenchard on Colonies and Plantations (*Cato's Letters*, no. 106), and connects the mistaken policy with regard to colonies with the corruption of the parliamentary system.

75. Jebb, *Works:* list of subscribers in I; memoir, including Lofft's funeral oration and a tribute by Brand Hollis, I, 1–247. See also Lindsey Letters and C. Wyvill, *Political Papers*, 6 vols. (York, 1794–1802), and Priestley, *Works*, I and II (memoirs), *passim*, notes and text, for many references to Jebb.

76. Jebb, *Works*, II, no. 14, 555ff.; and memoirs, I, *passim;* political papers, III, 285–423. And see Wyvill, *Pol. Papers, passim*. Compare also Wyvill to Franklin, 17 June, 1785, in *Pol. Papers*, III, 367–369.

77. Jebb, *Works*, I, memoirs, 217–223. On Jebb and Ireland, see Jebb, *Works*, II, no. 13, 517–553; and I, memoir, *passim*.

78. Capel Lofft, notes in Sidney, *Works*, ed. J. Robertson (London, 1772); in my possession. For a good summary of Lofft's politics in 1780, see *An Argument on the Nature of Party and Faction in Which is Considered the Duty of a Good and Peaceable Citizen at the Present Crisis* (London, 1780), economical reform by no means all that is necessary, p. 45; association essential to bring about the reforms so badly needed and is not to be confused with faction, p. 58.

79. [James Keir], *An Account of the Life and Writings of Thomas Day* (London, 1791), pp. 27–29; Rousseau and Dr. Small, p. 30; reform associations, p. 56; Jebb, pp. 120–123.

80. Disney, *Memoirs of Thomas Brand Hollis;* Caroline Robbins, "Thomas Brand Hollis," *PAPS*, 97, no. 3:239–247 (30 June, 1953).

81. William Jones (1746–1794). See *DNB*. *Life* by Charles John Shore, Lord Teignmouth (London, 1803); Nichols, *Lit. Anec.*, I, 463–465; VIII, 78, 136–137. Jones witnessed will of James Adair, M.P. See Fitzmaurice, *Life of Shelburne*, II, 170; III, 391. Refutation of Fielding in tract published by Society for Constitutional Information.

82. Butterfield, *George III*, chap. vii, pp. 309–333; chap. viii, pp. 337–382; and see B.M. Pol. Tracts, 1783–3 for list of forty-one published by the Society (Press mark E. 2101).

83. For Wyvill, see *DNB; Political Papers, passim*.

84. R. Price, *A Discourse on the Love of Our Country Delivered on Nov. 4, 1789* . . . (London, 1790), concluding paragraphs.

Index

The typeface used for this book is ITC New Baskerville, which was created for the International Typeface Corporation and is based on the types of the English type founder and printer John Baskerville (1706–75). Baskerville is the quintessential transitional face: it retains the bracketed and oblique serifs of old-style faces such as Caslon and Garamond, but in its increased lowercase height, lighter color, and enhanced contrast between thick and thin strokes, it presages modern faces.

The display type is set in Didot.

This book is printed on paper that is acid-free and meets the requirements of the American National Standard for Permanence of Paper for Printed Library Materials, z39.48-1992. ⊗

Book design by Richard Hendel, Chapel Hill, North Carolina
Typography by Tseng Information Systems, Inc., Durham, North Carolina
Printed and bound by Sheridan Books, Inc., Chelsea, Michigan